MINORITY POLITICS IN THE PUNJAB

MINORITY POLITICS IN THE PUNJAB

Baldev Raj Nayar

PRINCETON UNIVERSITY PRESS
PRINCETON · NEW JERSEY
1966

for Nancy and Sheila

PREFACE

THIS book is an addition to that growing body of literature which deals with the problem of what is referred to as "nation-building" in the newly independent nations of Asia and Africa. In its attention to the question of nation-building in India, the study focuses on two major aspects. First, it seeks to understand the basis and dynamics of one specific demand for the formation of a new state out of the territories of the Punjab in northwest India. Since independence in 1947, this demand of the Akali Dal has overshadowed the politics of the state of Punjab, and consequently an examination of the demand becomes, in effect, a study of the state's politics. The study examines the nature of the demand, its origins, the strategies employed by the Akali Dal to secure it, and the prospects of its achievement. It also examines the status of the Congress party in the state, and the strategies of this party to mobilize political support. This is the first full-scale study of the politics of the Punjab in the period since independence.

Second, on the basis of the examination of the politics of the Punjab, this study re-examines the statements in the current literature on Indian politics about the implications of social diversity in India for national unity and democracy. It is argued therein that the relationship between diversity and national unity, as well as between diversity and democracy, is much more complex than the simplistic and reductionist, and consequently pessimistic, statements hitherto made have implied. In doing so, it calls attention to "the uses of diversity" in the Indian political situation.

This study is the result of field work in the Punjab during 1961–62 under a fellowship from the Committee on Southern Asian Studies, University of Chicago. A fellowship from the Committee for the Comparative Study of New Nations, University of Chicago, during the academic year 1962–63 and a summer fellowship in 1963 from the Committee on Southern

Asian Studies made possible the writing of this volume. I am highly indebted to these two committees and to the Department of Political Science of the University of Chicago for their generous financial support.

For help and guidance in the execution of this study, I owe a debt of gratitude to Professors Myron Weiner, Duncan Mac-Rae and Grant McConnell. Professor Weiner has been an inspired teacher and a patient guide. Professor T. A. Bisson (Western College for Women, Oxford, Ohio) read the first draft of the manuscript and gave many valuable suggestions. I am highly grateful to the readers and staff of Princeton University Press for their helpful criticisms and suggestions which, in my estimation, have added greatly to the value of the study. However, all responsibility for errors of omission and commission as well as interpretation are solely mine. Although the study takes into account some of the more important political events in recent years in the Punjab, the analysis presented therein rests primarily on the earlier field work.

For their many kindnesses I would like to express my thanks to Mrs. Shirley Clarkson, formerly administrative assistant of the Committee on New Nations, and Mrs. Doreen Herlihy, secretary of the Department of Political Science at the University of Chicago. I am also grateful to the many political leaders in the Punjab who gave so generously of their time; if this study contributes in any measure to an understanding of the politics of the Punjab and India, it would be largely because of their help and cooperation. However, I have refrained from selecting a few leaders for special mention, for all, irrespective of party and position, have vitally contributed to this study.

Appreciative thanks are due also to the Congress party library in New Delhi for the use of its newspaper files; the office of *The Spokesman* for its generosity in loaning its back files for extended periods of time; the Congress party headquarters in Chandigarh for providing printed literature; the Akali headquarters in Amritsar for making available documents and pamphlet material; the Public Relations Department and the Development & Panchayat Department, Government of Punjab, for supplying maps of the Punjab and other government publications; the Census office and Elections office in Chandigarh for providing census and election data; the Indian School of International Studies for the use of its library at Sapru House, New Delhi; and the India office library in London. Acknowledgment is made here also for permission to quote from Penderel Moon, *Divide and Quit* (Berkeley: University of California Press, 1962). Where Hindi, Punjabi and Urdu materials have been quoted in the text, I myself have provided the translations.

I am grateful to President Fred Harcleroad and Dr. Fritz Freitag, of the California State College at Hayward, for their generous assistance in making it possible for me to present parts of the material here included before the annual meeting of the Association for Asian Studies in Washington, D. C., in 1964.

My wife, Nancy, gave willingly and abundantly of her help in the research for this study and in the typing of the manuscript.

BALDEV RAJ NAYAR

McGill University,
Montreal, Canada

CONTENTS

LIST OF TABLES

MINORITY POLITICS IN THE PUNJAB

POLITICAL DIVISIONS OF THE PUNJAB

CHAPTER I

Pressures on Nation-Building

ONE of the most impressive phenomena on the international scene since the end of World War II has been the revolution in the form of the birth of newly independent "nations" in Asia and Africa. The addition, one after another, of these nations to the international community has more than doubled the original membership of the United Nations. The achievement of nationhood by these nations marks the end of an age which began in the fifteenth century—the age of imperialism.

In their expansion across Asia and Africa, European nations had followed no predetermined plan as to where they should or should not colonize. The economic and technological position of Asia and Africa at the time allowed the European powers full play to the limit of their resources. Old boundaries were pulled down, and different ethnic, religious, and linguistic groups of people came under the tutelage of one or another foreign power. At times, a single homogeneous group was divided up among European powers, but the more common pattern was the bringing together of diverse groups of people under one political system.

Under the impact of the influences of the west itself, new social and political forces were generated in the colonies. A new set of local leaders developed now. At first, the new leadership was enamored of the alien regime, but later rose against it and appealed to the masses, in the name of self-determination, to put an end to foreign rule. Mass movements for freedom followed. In these nationalist movements, many—but not always all—groups that were different in religion, culture and ethnicity, united in their demand for the right to self-government. When power was eventually transferred to the nationalist leaders by the departing foreign powers, the political consensus at the time was, with some exceptions, basically a negative one: to be rid of foreign rule. While the foreign powers had triggered, but not necessarily intentionally, the trend toward building a "nation" out of the diverse groups in a given colony, the process of welding the inhabitants of the area into a nation had not been concluded. In some cases, the fragmented nature of society even compelled the transfer of political power to a truncated political state. At any rate, after the first flush of freedom, new strains developed in the political system as a result of political claims made now in the name, not of the nation, but of race, religion, language, caste or tribe.

Another set of leaders seemed to emerge now, or rather an existing but somewhat quiescent set now became more articulate, with its base centering around parochial loyalties, to undermine the efforts of the nationalist leadership toward the creation of a nation-state on the basis of the political system inherited from the foreign power. Either out of fear on the part of the parochial groups of being submerged in a larger nation, or out of pride in their own group, or because of the aspirations of some leaders to political power on the strength of parochial loyalties, demands were now put forth for regional autonomy and, either explicitly or implicitly, for the secession of areas where a particular religious, ethnic, or tribal group was concentrated. To meet such demands in full or in part would, in the minds of the nationalist leaders, inevitably lead to the breakdown of the political system or to its transformation, and also to the undermining of the position of the nationalist leaders themselves.

The major political problem that confronts the newly independent nation, in essence, then is: how to maintain a viable political system in the face of these divisive internal threats to its existence. While no one can dispute the priority of economic development in view of the widespread poverty existing in many of these nations and, perhaps more importantly, the aspiration to meet the other industrial powers on a basis of sovereign equality, the primary concern is still how, in some way, to hold the system together. In fact, it could be argued that the emphasis on economic development is in part an effort to reduce the significance of parochial ties by the creation of non-parochial economic loyalties. Success in this effort would depend on the relative speed with which nationalist leaders succeed in making substantial economic progress, with the resulting pride in a powerful, industrialized nation. This is not to argue that economic development may necessarily work to this end. It may in fact intensify the divisive conflicts.

THE INDIAN CASE

Social diversity resulting in divisive pressures in the new nations thus poses a serious problem for those engaged in the gigantic task of nation-building. This problem is a ubiquitous one among the new nations. In the Congo, a group of tribes located in a rich region is able, for a considerable period of time, to defy successfully a weak center. In Nigeria, a delicately balanced center struggles to satisfy regional claims and at the same time keep the political system intact. The case of India, a part of which is the subject for consideration here, illustrates vividly the nature of this problem although it has its local variations. The effort at nation-building in this case has intermittently faced serious difficulties. The very partition of India in 1947 on the basis of religion, as a concomitant of the achievement of independence, represented a setback for the ideal that the people of the Indian subcontinent, despite the great social diversity existing among them, constituted a single nation. Disheartening as the event of partition was for the Indian National Congress—the spearhead of the nationalist movement in India—this political organization remained committed to its historic goals of maintaining and furthering national unity, establishing a secular state, creating a political framework of representative democracy, and raising the standards of living of the masses through rapid economic development. As the Congress party assumed control of the government in India in 1947, it turned its attention to the achievement of these goals.

The year 1950 saw the enforcement of a new constitution, a constitution that embodied a delicate balance between the need for a strong central government and the recognition of regional diversity, between the task of building a united nation and the satisfaction of minority groups, between the increasing powers of government and the rights of the individual. Avoiding the use of the term federation, the constitution declares that India is a Union of states. In this quasi-federation, not only is the Union strong in terms of powers allotted to it, but this political arrangement itself can be transformed into a unitary one in certain types of emergencies. At the same time, in view of the vast size of India and the degree of regional diversity, the states have substantial powers during normal times. A parliamentary form of government based on universal adult suffrage prevails under the constitution both at the center and in the states.

Most importantly, the constitution establishes a secular state in India. The state is not identified with any particular religion. A bill of fundamental rights, incorporated in the constitution, guarantees the right of all persons to freedom of conscience and the freedom to profess, practise and propagate religion. Every religious denomination has the right to establish its own religious institutions and to manage its own religious affairs. Equality before law and equal protection of law are an integral part of this bill. Discrimination on the basis of religion as well as on grounds of race, caste, sex, or place of birth, is prohibited; an exception is made for the advancement of socially backward classes. Equality of opportunity is provided for in public employment.

In view of the creation of Pakistan on the basis of religion, the establishment of a secular state in India was a tribute to the loyalty of the Congress party to its past commitment to *secular nationalism*. In the opinion of some, it also represented "the maximum of generosity of a Hindu dominated territory for its non-Hindu population." [1] Though there may be an occasional lapse from the ideals set forth in the constitution, there is no other aspect of the political framework in India that commands a greater commitment on the part of the national leadership than the secular state.[2]

If national unity and the secular state have been basic commitments with the Congress party and a few other political groups, these have not gone without serious challenge by several segments of the population. In the years since independence, a variety of centrifugal political pressures have been obvious, chief among them being the growth of *regionalism* based on local linguistic and cultural ties.

Since about the middle of the nineteenth century there has occurred a renaissance among the regional languages in India and a growth of regional consciousness among the various groups in India. After independence, this regional consciousness manifested itself with great vigor in the demand for the reorganization of state boundaries on a linguistic basis. The nationalist leaders were confronted with a momentous decision, for to concede linguistic states would be to strengthen loyalties which could in the end undermine national unity. Their concern arose from the fact that

> linguistic and other group loyalties have deep roots in the soil and history of India. The culture-based regionalism, centering round the idea of linguistic homogeneity represents to the average Indian values easily intelligible to him. Indian nationalism, on the other hand, has still to develop into a positive concept. It must acquire a deeper content before it becomes ideologically adequate to withstand the gravitational

[1] Speech by Shri Lokanath Misra, in India (Dominion), Constituent Assembly, *Debates: Official Report* (Delhi: Manager of Publications, 1949), VII, No. 20 (1948), 283.

[2] For a systematic examination of this aspect of the Indian political framework, see Donald E. Smith, *India as a Secular State* (Princeton: Princeton University Press, 1963).

pull of the traditional narrower loyalties. In these circumstances, further emphasis on narrow loyalties by equating
linguistic regions with political and administrative frontiers,
must diminish the broader sense of the unity of the country.[3]

The government established several committees and commissions—the Dar Commission, the JVP Committee, and finally
the States Reorganization Commission—to inquire into the basis
for the reorganization of states. While these bodies maintained
that language alone could not be the basis for the reorganization of states, the pattern of states reorganization that eventually emerged was largely that of unilingual states.

Although the reorganization of states undertaken did not
change the power relationships between the center and the
states, it is considered to bear gravely on the future prospects
of national unity as it has revolutionized the basis of the territorial organization of the individual states. Since the political
boundaries of states correspond by and large with linguistic-
cultural boundaries, it is feared that this would surely lead to
greater regional consciousness and strengthening of regional
loyalties, thus undermining the new and seemingly fragile national unity, and must eventually result in the balkanization
of India, though perhaps a totalitarian or authoritarian system
may tenuously hold the different regional groups together.
Present evidence for these forebodings is seen in the militant
agitation for a separate homeland for the Tamil-speaking people in south India, in the armed struggle for an independent
state for the Nagas in northeast India, and in the resistance on
the part of several regional groups to the acceptance of Hindi
as the national language.

If linguistic-cultural regionalism is one type of threat to the
existing political framework in India, religion-based *commu-*

[3] India (Republic), *Report of the States Reorganization Commission*
(Delhi: Manager of Publications, 1955), p. 43.

nalism [4] is considered to constitute another, for its essence is an overriding commitment to one's religious affiliation as the basis for political loyalty, to the advancement of the interests of one's religious group even at the expense of other religious groups, to a policy of discriminatory treatment against other religious groups, to the claim perhaps of a separate homeland for the religious group, and to a program of making the value system of one's religion the determinative norm in society and politics. Religion-based communalism reached its apotheosis before Indian independence in the claims of the Muslim League on behalf of the Muslim community. Starting with rather moderate demands, the Muslim League eventually demanded and secured a separate state for the Muslim-majority areas of India. The core of the League's position, as propounded by the founder of Pakistan, M. A. Jinnah, was the "two-nation theory"; that is, Hindus and Muslims, by virtue of their belonging to different religions constituted different nations. In this manner, religious affiliation became the basis for the partition of India.

In the India of today, too, there exist several communal groups. Such, for example, are the Bharatiya Jana Sangh and the All India Hindu Mahasabha among the Hindus, and the Muslim League among the Muslims. To the extent that such communal groups are effective in politics, they create hostility between religious communities and make difficult the task of maintaining the political unity of India and of creating an Indian nationality on a nonreligious, secular basis.

Apart from the divisive factors of regionalism and communalism, there is present in India what is called *casteism*. Although caste plays an important role in the politics of India today, no territorial demands have emerged from caste divisions, perhaps because of the innumerable numbers of castes and

---

[4] Although the term "communalism" is usually employed in a pejorative sense, no value judgment is intended here.

their wide dispersal in any given region. In a pluralistic society caste politics assume more the nature of pressure group politics than political action that leads to claims for the division of the land.

Questions for Investigation

The Indian case provides a sharp illustration of the various obstacles in the path of nation-building for new nations. Such obstacles have received considerable attention from political scientists in their general concern with political stability in these nations. This interest is natural since conflict resulting from the claims of parochial groups has often manifested itself in the more spectacular forms of agitation, coercion, and violence. In fact, the frequency and intensity of political agitations raises the question of how these nations manage to survive at all. What is done to maintain the political system? What is the nature of the response to parochial claims? Few studies are available to throw light on these questions about politics in the new nations.

In any consideration of the problem of nation-building in the new nations, the question of political leadership seems an extremely important one. It is important, because the problem here, in simple terms, is one of conflict between two types of leadership with different sets of political values: one, the nationalist leadership, seeking the achievement of general societal goals regardless of ties to religion, race, or language; and, two, the parochial leadership, seeking the achievement of narrower goals *corresponding* to religious, ethnic, linguistic, or tribal groups, with little concern for general societal goals. On two important grounds a study of political leadership should contribute to an understanding of the conflict. First, the leaders themselves are embedded in the political culture on whose behalf they make various political claims. They are an important, articulate and identifiable element of that political culture. One can understand that culture, and the claims made in its behalf, most directly by a study of the leaders themselves. Second, there exists an important relationship between the group claims made and the personal goals of the leaders who articulate those claims. The satisfaction or frustration of personal goals may affect differently the future course of group claims.

It would seem then that an investigation into the nature of leadership in the context of the politics of diversity, the goals political leaders seek, the resources they have and the political strategies they employ, may supply a perspective on the prospects for stability in the new nations. For the formulation of some fruitful generalizations on the subject, one would ideally prefer several detailed case studies of political systems in different settings. This study, however, makes no claim other than to being a modest beginning in this direction. It is an exploratory study of the conflict between the two types of leadership through the investigation of a single conflict situation arising out of the demand for the carving out of a new state of *Punjabi Suba* out of the existing state of the Punjab in northwest India. In light of the preceding discussion, the following specific questions seem especially important for the study:

1. What is the social and political context in which the demand for a new state is being made in the Punjab? What is the nature of the demand made? Is it a language-based regional demand? or a religion-based communal one? Chapter II deals with these questions.

2. What is the basis and origin of this demand? What are the motivating factors behind the demand? Answers to these questions would provide us with some information about the future development of political conflict in the Punjab. Chapter III concerns itself with this aspect of the problem.

3. What are the differences and similarities in the social background of the two types of leadership in conflict over the demand? What are the changing patterns of recruitment to political leadership? What goals do the leaders seek in politics? Answers to these questions would provide some insight into the

nature of the two types of leadership, and the inter-relationships between them, as also the way in which political recruitment and the personal goals of leaders influence the course of political conflict. Chapter IV covers some of these questions.

4. What are the resources that the parochial or communal leadership commands? An evaluation of the resources of this leadership would enable us to make some judgment about the future course of political conflict in the Punjab. Chapter V is devoted to a discussion of the resources of this leadership.

5. What are the various strategies employed by the parochial or communal leadership? How does the nationalist leadership handle these strategies? An inquiry into these questions would give us some indication of the variety of methods used, and the relative effectiveness of the different methods. It would prevent us from a total preoccupation with episodic forms of political behavior, and also enable us to determine what methods may probably be adopted in the future. Chapter VI covers the subject of political strategies.

6. How does the nationalist leadership mobilize support for the political system? How successful has it been in this regard? Answers to these questions should tell us something about the various ways through which the nationalist leadership attempts, and in the future may attempt, to secure political support. Chapter VII deals with the question of support for the political system.

7. Finally, on the basis of this study of political conflict in the Punjab, what general conclusions can one draw about the prospects for national unity in India in the context of social diversity and about the role of political leadership in the achievement of national unity? Chapter VIII concludes the study with a discussion of this question.

CHAPTER II

The Punjab and Punjabi Suba

ONE of the more controversial cases in the movement for states reorganization in India has been that relating to the state of Punjab. The Punjab has continually faced political turmoil, and the frequency of agitations here has earned it the reputation of being "the land of agitations." This landlocked state is one of 16 states which constitute the Indian Union. Situated in northwest India, the Punjab is strategically an important state, bounded on the west by Pakistan and on the northeast by China. To the north of the state are Jammu & Kashmir and part of Himachal Pradesh; to the south, Rajasthan; and to the east, Uttar Pradesh. Through the Punjab lies the only land route from the rest of India to Jammu & Kashmir. Adjoining the southeast corner of the state is New Delhi, the capital of India.

The present Punjab is, in part, the result of the partition in 1947. As in the case of Bengal, the partition resulted in the division of the province of Punjab, splitting into two parts this "Land of the Five Rivers," which had often been referred to as "the shield, spear and sword-hand of India." [1] The partition constitutes a traumatic watershed in the politics of the truncated state of the Punjab which came to India's share. Since 1947, the state has been variously known as the Indian Punjab, East Punjab, and Punjab (India), but is now referred to as simply the Punjab. After the partition, the new state consisted of those districts of the parent province in which the non-Muslims were in a majority. The mass migrations following the partition made the state almost solidly non-Muslim, with only a few pockets of Muslim population. Later, in 1956, the territories of PEPSU

[1] See Reginald Coupland, *The Indian Problem: Report on the Constitutional Problem in India* (New York: Oxford University Press, 1944), Part I, p. 116.

(Patiala and East Punjab States Union), which had been formed in 1948 as an administrative unit by the merger of the former princely states located inside the boundaries of the Punjab, were incorporated in the state of Punjab, increasing both the territory and population of the state, and making it a more compact political unit.

The Punjab covers an area of 47,205 square miles (about four-fifths the size of Illinois), being about 370 miles long and 230 miles wide.[2] It is one of the smaller states in India, ranking thirteenth in area. By far the largest portion of the state lies in the Indo-Gangetic Plain. Several of the districts, however, are located in the mountainous region of the Himalayas. In 1961 the state had a population of 20.3 million, which represented an increase of more than 25 percent over the 1951 population figure of 16.1 million.[3]

Compared to many other states in India, the Punjab occupies a favorable economic position. It ranks among the top three states in per capita income. The rate of literacy in 1961 was 23.7 percent, but it has been increasing rapidly. The state has one of the best canal irrigation systems in the world, based on three major snow-fed rivers. About 43 percent of the area under cultivation in the state is covered by the irrigation system.[4]

The constitutional head of the administration in the state is a Governor appointed by the President of India. In the conduct of his administration, he is aided and advised by a Council of Ministers which is responsible, under a parliamentary form of government, to the state legislature which consists of two houses, the 154-member *Vidhan Sabha* or legislative assembly (lower house) and the 51-member *Vidhan Parishad* or legislative council (upper house). Administratively, the state is

[2] Punjab, Public Relations Department, *Fact Sheets on Punjab* (Chandigarh: Controller, Printing and Stationery, 1964), G-1, p. 1.
[3] Punjab, Public Relations Department, *Facts About Punjab* (Chandigarh: Controller, Printing and Stationery, 1964), p. 1.
[4] *Fact Sheets on Punjab*, R-2, p. 1.

divided into three divisions, each under an officer known as the commissioner. The divisions further consist of districts; the numbers and boundaries of these districts have undergone several changes since the partition, but there are now 20 districts in the state. The district, headed by the deputy commissioner, constitutes the key territorial unit for purposes of administration. The district is further divided into *tehsils;* there are 74 tehsils in the state, usually three to five for each district.[5] The capital of the state is located in the newly-built modern city of Chandigarh.

SOCIAL AND RELIGIOUS GROUPS IN THE PUNJAB

While the cultural and economic unity of the Punjab has often been remarked upon, there are several social divisions in the state which have crucial importance in the politics of the state in the period after independence. The major social division in the Punjab today is that between the two religious communities of the Hindus and the Sikhs. In 1951 the Hindus constituted about 62.3 percent of the state's population, the Sikhs 35 percent, and other religious groups 2.7 percent. In the subsequent decade a slight change has occurred in the relative proportions of these groups in the population. In 1961 the Hindus made up 63.7 percent of the population, while the Sikhs were 33.3 percent, despite the higher rate of natural increase believed to exist among the Sikhs compared to the Hindus.[6] The small decrease in the proportion of the Sikh community is explained by the "considerable migration of the Sikhs to other States of India and abroad," while "the slightly higher

[5] For a discussion of the Punjab administration and its problems, see E. N. Mangat Rai, *Civil Administration in the Punjab: An Analysis of a State Government in India* (Occasional Papers in International Affairs, Number 7; Cambridge: Center for International Affairs, Harvard University, 1963).

[6] Gurdev Singh Gosal, "Religious Composition of Punjab's Population Changes, 1951–61," *The Economic Weekly,* XVII, No. 4 (January 23, 1965), 119–20. See also Table 1-A.

than the natural rate of increase in the case of the Hindu population is obviously due to an excess of immigrants over out-migrants." [7]

Both Hindu and Sikh leaders often give the population figures as 70 percent for the Hindus and 30 percent for the Sikhs, the Hindus in order to emphasize the privileged position of the Sikhs in the state relative to their proportion in the population, and the Sikhs in order to show the overwhelming dominance of the majority community with which they live. The terms "the Panth" (the religion, the group, the community), "the Khalsa" (the pure, the elect, the chosen), or "the Khalsa Panth" are also used in referring to the Sikhs as a single organized religious community. An important cleavage in the Hindu community is that between the reformist section known as the Arya Samaj and the orthodox section called the Sanatan Dharam. Though forming a very small proportion of the Hindus in the Punjab (less than 6 percent in 1931), the Arya Samaj has played an active role in the politics of the state as well as in the educational sphere. In the past the Arya Samaj proved a major antagonist for other religious groups because of its strong posture on behalf of Hindu interests. However, the many factional splits in the Arya Samaj now have considerably reduced its effectiveness.

A political division of the state demarcates its area into what are called Hindi-speaking and Punjabi-speaking regions, but in essence representing Hindu-majority and Sikh-majority areas. The Punjab as a whole is officially considered to be bilingual, with Punjabi in Gurmukhi script and Hindi in Devnagari script as the official languages of the state. However, at the district level and below, the language of the respective regions is used for purposes of administration. The capital city of Chandigarh is treated as bilingual.[8]

---

[7] *Ibid.*, p. 119.
[8] The Hindi-speaking region consists of the districts of Ambala (except Rupar and Kharar tehsils), Gurgaon, Hissar, Kangra, Karnal, Kulu,

In 1961 the population of the Hindi-speaking region was 8.8 million (43.3 percent of the state's total population) and that of the Punjabi-speaking region 11.4 million (56.3 percent).[9] This compares with a population in 1951 of 6.7 million in the Hindi-speaking region (41.7 percent) and of 9.4 million in the Punjabi-speaking region (58.3 percent). The slight changes in the relative proportions of the two regions in the state's population reflect migration from the Punjabi-speaking region not only to other states but also to the Hindi-speaking region and also in-migration to the Hindi-speaking region from other states.

The figures from the 1951 census and those presently available from the 1961 census do not include a breakdown for the category of religion below the district level, and therefore cannot be used with precision to determine the religious composition of the two regions, since the regions include not only whole districts but also parts of some districts. Furthermore, the figures from the two censuses do not easily lend to comparison, for since 1951 the number of districts and their boundaries have been changed. However, if the divisions below the district level, which are important only in a few cases, are ignored one can get an approximate idea, but only approximate, of the relative position of Hindus and Sikhs in the two regions (see Tables 1 and 1-A). It is obvious that the Hindus are in an overwhelming majority in the Hindi-speaking region, with over 88 percent of the share in the population, while the Sikhs constitute less than 10 percent of the population. In the Punjabi-speaking region, on the other hand, the Sikhs constitute between 52 and

---

Lahaul & Spiti, Mohindergarh, Rohtak, Sangrur (only Jind and Narwana tehsils) and Simla. The Punjabi-speaking region consists of the districts of Ambala (only Rupar and Kharar tehsils but excluding Chandigarh), Amritsar, Bhatinda, Ferozepur, Gurdaspur, Hoshiarpur, Jullundur, Kapurthala, Ludhiana, Patiala, and Sangrur (except Jind and Narwana tehsils). Chandigarh city, with over 89,000 persons in 1961, is not included in either region. See *Facts About Punjab*, pp. 65–66.

[9] Figures based on *Facts About Punjab*.

TABLE 1

RELIGIOUS COMPOSITION OF HINDI-SPEAKING AND
PUNJABI-SPEAKING REGIONS IN 1951 [a]

| District | Population | Hindus | | Sikhs | | Others |
		Number	Per-cent	Number	Per-cent	Number
A. Hindi-speaking region						
1. Simla	46,150	37,287	80.8	7,417	16.1	1,446
2. Kangra	926,477	898,564	97.0	18,401	2.0	9,512
3. Hissar	1,045,645	954,714	91.3	80,394	7.7	10,537
4. Rohtak	1,122,046	1,105,046	98.5	7,907	.7	9,093
5. Gurgaon	967,664	794,019	82.0	6,310	.7	167,335
6. Karnal	1,079,379	974,959	90.3	96,458	8.9	7,962
7. Ambala [b]	943,734	681,477	72.2	232,456	24.6	29,801
8. Mohindergarh	443,074	438,347	98.9	2,615	.6	2,112
9. Kohistan [c]	147,403	130,937	88.8	13,206	9.0	3,260
Total	6,721,572	6,015,350	89.5	465,164	6.9	241,058
B. Punjabi-speaking region						
10. Hoshiarpur	1,086,224	794,688	73.2	284,320	26.2	7,216
11. Jullundur	1,008,766	429,747	42.6	569,487	56.5	9,532
12. Ludhiana	806,779	301,398	37.3	497,419	61.7	7,962
13. Ferozepur	1,308,237	505,937	38.7	780,024	59.6	22,276
14. Amritsar	1,270,320	351,710	27.7	897,309	70.6	21,301
15. Gurdaspur	761,782	346,884	45.5	354,681	46.6	60,217
16. Patiala	524,269	273,087	52.1	246,953	47.1	4,229
17. Barnala	536,728	112,635	21.0	380,811	70.9	43,282
18. Bhatinda	666,809	144,305	21.7	521,045	78.1	1,459
19. Kapurthala	295,071	104,679	35.5	187,568	63.6	2,824
20. Fatehgarh Sahib	237,397	80,141	33.7	154,714	65.2	2,542
21. Sangrur [d]	642,934	420,218	65.4	215,023	33.4	7,693
Total	9,145,316	3,865,429	42.3	5,089,354	55.6	190,533
Grand Total	15,866,888	9,880,779	62.3	5,554,518	35.0	431,591

[a] Based on statistics given in India (Republic), Census Commissioner, *Census of In[
1951*, VIII, Part II-A, 298–300.

[b] One-third of district in Punjabi-speaking region.

[c] One-fourth of district in Punjabi-speaking region.

[d] A little over half the district in Hindi-speaking region.

55 percent of the population and the Hindus between 42 and 45 percent.

Keeping in mind the reservation about the comparability of the figures for the two censuses, a comparison of the 1951 and 1961 statistics on religion shows tentatively a slight increase in the Sikh proportion in the Hindi-speaking region and in the Hindu proportion in the Punjabi-speaking region, and a corresponding small decrease in the Sikh proportion in the Punjabi-speaking region and in the Hindu proportion in the Hindi-speaking region. The small decline in the proportion of Sikhs in the Punjabi-speaking region is attributed "mostly to considerable out-migration" on their part, and also to "some amount of in-migration of Hindus." [10] However, while the Sikh proportion went down somewhat in several districts of the Punjabi-speaking region, in three districts of the region—Hoshiarpur, Ludhiana and Patiala—there was an increase in the proportion of Sikhs in the population; in fact, Patiala turned from a Hindu-majority district in 1951 to a Sikh-majority district in 1961. What these trends indicate in sum for the religious composition of the two regions in the future is difficult to tell.

The Hindi-speaking region consists of the hill districts of Kangra, Kulu, Lahaul and Spiti, and Simla, which form part of the Himalayan tract, and the largely dry plains of the southeastern districts of the Punjab known as Hariana. The term Hariana (greenland) points to a time long past when the area was a fertile plain, with the river Saraswati running through it. Although administratively a part of the Hindi-speaking region, the districts of Kangra, Kulu, and Lahaul and Spiti lie in the north of the Punjab, unconnected directly with the rest of the Hindi region (see map). The Hindi-speaking region is relatively backward economically, compared to the Punjabi-speaking region, and leaders of the region have repeatedly pressed for greater attention by the government to the development of the area. Within the Punjabi-speaking region, the areas of the

[10] Gosal, p. 121

TABLE 1–A

RELIGIOUS COMPOSITION OF HINDI-SPEAKING AND PUNJABI-SPEAKING REGIONS IN 1961 [a]

District	Population 1951	Population 1961	Hindus Number	Hindus Per-cent	Sikhs Number	Sikhs Per-cent	Others Number	Others Per-cent
A. Hindi-speaking region								
1. Hissar	1,045,645	1,540,508	1,374,258	89.2	152,719	9.9	13,531	.9
2. Rohtak	1,122,046	1,420,391	1,400,347	98.6	6,439	.4	13,605	1.0
3. Gurgaon	967,664	1,240,706	1,011,862	81.6	8,362	.7	220,482	17.7
4. Karnal	1,077,381	1,490,430	1,293,354	86.8	177,602	11.9	19,474	1.3
5. Ambala [b]	1,017,254	1,373,477	981,288	71.5	340,968	24.8	51,221	3.7
6. Simla	106,177	112,653	104,784	93.0	5,392	4.8	2,477	2.2
7. Kangra	921,278	1,062,518	1,043,387	98.2	8,854	.8	10,277	1.0
8. Lahaul & Spiti	12,728	20,453	9,575	46.8	162	.8	10,716	52.4
9. Mohindergarh	443,074	547,850	543,480	99.2	2,222	.4	2,148	.4
Total	6,713,247	8,808,986	7,762,335	88.1	702,720	8.0	343,931	3.9

former PEPSU state that were merged in the Punjab in 1956 are also somewhat more backward economically and the people of these areas, too, complain of being neglected by the government.

There is a proliferation of caste groups in the Punjab, but caste as a social phenomenon is not as strong in the Punjab, except in the Hariana area, as it is in some other parts of India. In the 1920s one government report observed:

> It would be misleading to attach too great importance to the existence of caste in the Punjab. . . . Not only is it the case that the Brahman has no practical pre-eminence among Hindus, but as between "caste" and "non-caste" Hindus the distinction is not so strongly marked as to create the political problems found elsewhere in India. . . . The problem in truth, if one exists, is rather of classes socially depressed than of "out-castes" as such; while much remains to be done for the social uplift of some of these classes, they hardly present a separate political problem.[11]

The Punjab has been pointed out as the one "notable exception" to the caste system in India.[12] As one British author has observed, "nowhere else in Hindu India does caste sit so lightly or approach so nearly to the social classes of Europe" as it does in the Punjab.[13] Whether or not caste in the Punjab parallels precisely the social classes of Europe, it undeniably has great relevance for politics, no less so than do social classes.

By caste stratification is usually understood the division of society into hereditary, hierarchically ranked, occupational groups. In the Punjab, though, tribal divisions based on com-

[11] Great Britain, Indian Statutory Commission, *Memorandum Submitted by the Government of the Punjab* (London: His Majesty's Stationery Office, 1930), x, 7–8.

[12] L. S. S. O'Malley, *Modern India and the West* (London: Oxford University Press, 1941), p. 371.

[13] James Drummond Anderson, *The Peoples of India* (Cambridge: Cambridge University Press, 1913), p. 26.

B. *Punjabi-speaking region*

10. Hoshiarpur	1,094,022	1,233,493	835,436	67.7	381,965	31.0	16,092	1.3
11. Jullundur	1,055,600	1,227,367	662,631	54.0	550,232	44.8	14,504	1.2
12. Ludhiana	807,418	1,022,519	365,429	35.7	644,266	63.0	12,824	1.3
13. Ferozepur	1,275,195	1,619,116	657,712	40.6	936,953	57.9	24,451	1.5
14. Amritsar	1,367,040	1,534,916	506,170	33.0	990,344	64.5	38,402	2.5
15. Gurdaspur	851,294	987,994	494,635	50.1	424,190	42.9	69,169	7.0
16. Kapurthala	295,071	343,778	140,828	41.0	200,117	58.2	2,833	.8
17. Bhatinda	786,889	1,055,177	285,967	27.1	762,677	72.3	6,533	.6
18. Sangrur [c]	1,111,594	1,424,688	738,816	51.9	622,227	43.6	63,645	4.5
19. Patiala	777,520	1,048,778	480,086	45.8	553,438	52.8	15,254	1.4
Total	9,421,643	11,497,826	5,167,710	44.9	6,066,409	52.8	263,707	2.3
Grand Total	16,134,890 [d]	20,306,812	12,930,045	63.7	6,769,129	33.3	607,638	3.0

[a] Based on statistics given in India (Republic), Census Commissioner, *Census of India: Paper No. 1 of 1963* (Delhi: Manager of Publications, 1963), pp. 30–35. Note that 1951 population figures here given do not agree with those in Table 1 in several places, because of changes in boundaries of districts.

[b] About one-third of district not in Hindi-speaking region.
[c] About two-sevenths of district in Hindi-speaking region.
[d] Discrepancy between 1951 and 1961 figures due to the non-availability for analysis of religious composition of some records for Jullundur district as a result of a fire.

munity of blood, as well as divisions intermediate between tribe and caste, are subsumed in the same social system. There are tribes treated as castes, and there are tribes and sub-castes within castes, as well as a great deal of differentiation within each of these divisions. In the Punjab, the underlying tribal social structure, out of which caste evolved or on which caste was imposed, has been a strong one. Ibbetson pointed out that the tribe was "far more permanent and indestructible than the caste," for "the broader distinctions of caste have become little more than a tradition or a convenient symbol for social standing, while the tribal groups are the practical units of which the community is composed." [14]

One aspect of caste in the Punjab with important political implications in both regions is the basic conflict in the rural areas between the high-caste landowning agricultural classes— whether Hindu or Sikh—and the scheduled castes along with other backward classes. The scheduled castes, also known as Harijans, are the former, so-called untouchables, who are underprivileged both economically and socially. They form, by and large, the landless agricultural and menial labor as also the sharecropper and tenant classes. In 1961 the scheduled castes constituted 20.3 percent of the state's population compared with 19 percent in 1951.[15] A rough estimate, based on 1951 statistics, would place them at about 21 percent of the population in the Punjabi-speaking region and 17 percent in the Hindi-speaking region.

Among the high-caste, landowning, agricultural classes in the Sikh community, the most predominant and prominent is the caste of the Jats. In 1931, more than 50 percent of all Sikhs in the Punjab were Jats.[16] Most of the Sikh Jats are located in the Punjabi-speaking region. In the case of the Hindu com-

---

[14] Denzil Ibbetson, *Panjab Castes* (Lahore: Superintendent, Government Printing, Punjab, 1916), p. 16.

[15] *Facts About Punjab*, p. 1.

[16] India, Census Commissioner, *Census of India, 1931* (Lahore: Civil & Military Gazette Press, 1933), XVII, Part 1, 342.

munity, the pre-eminent castes among the high-caste, landowning, agricultural classes are the Jats and Rajputs. The Hindu
Jats "form the bulk of the population of the agricultural communities in the Hariana region" and are predominant in the
districts of Rohtak, Hissar and Mohindergarh.[17] Both within
the Jats and Harijans, whether Hindu or Sikh, there is a good
deal of internal differentiation. Other caste divisions, while
they are significant in politics, do not command the same importance for the politics of the state as does the division between Jats and Harijans.

In 1961 nearly 80 percent of the state's population lived in
rural areas consisting of over 21,000 villages, while 20 percent
lived in urban areas consisting of 187 towns and cities.[18] In
1951 about 66 percent of the population was dependent on
agricultural occupations. Of this category, 61.5 percent were
cultivators of land they owned, 22.7 cultivated lands of others,
and 12.5 percent were landless agricultural laborers.[19] The Punjab peasantry is famous for its contribution to military recruitment in India. The Punjabi-speaking region is more urbanized
than the Hindi-speaking region; 22.8 percent of the former is
urban as against only 15.8 percent of the latter.[20] The rural-
urban cleavage may often reinforce a caste cleavage.

The Punjab population contains a significant number of refugees of the same general culture and language who migrated
from West Pakistan following the partition. In 1951 the refugees formed about 17 percent of the population.[21] These include the fairly prosperous Sikh Jat farmers from the canal
colonies, and Hindus and Sikhs belonging to the high-caste

[17] M. S. Randhawa and Prem Nath, *Farmers of India: Punjab, Himachal Pradesh, Jammu & Kashmir* (New Delhi: Indian Council of Agricultural Research, 1959), p. 120.
[18] *Facts About Punjab*, p. 1.
[19] Figures based on statistics in India (Republic), Census Commissioner, *Census of India 1951* (Simla: The Army Press, 1953), VIII, Part
II-B, 2–13.
[20] *Facts About Punjab*, pp. 65–66.
[21] *Census of India 1951*, VIII, Part II-A, 332.

professional and business classes. The refugees can be important as a social group in the state's politics, but the Punjab does
not display the violent and explosive pattern of refugee politics
so familiar in the case of West Bengal.

What is the significance of these various cleavages in the
population of the Punjab for the politics of the state? A precise
evaluation of their political significance would demand much
intensive and painstaking research into voting behavior, the
legislative process, the intra-party struggles in the different parties and the working of the village councils. However, a few
observations are helpful for an understanding of the politics of
the state.

Since the beginning of the twentieth century important sections of the Hindu and Sikh communities have drawn further
apart. Before and after the partition they have frequently been
on opposing sides of political claims. The conflict between these
sections is the hard fact of life about politics in the Punjab. In
the stubborn conflict prevailing intensely in the Punjabi-speaking region, caste distinctions within each community lose much
of their importance in politics. To this generalization, however,
there is one great exception and that is the stand of the Sikh
scheduled castes. The Sikh Harijans in the Punjab strongly
oppose such claims of the non-Harijan Sikh sections as would
place them completely under the domination of the powerful
Sikh Jats who, in their view, already dominate the economic
and political life of the state.

In the Hariana region, where Hindus are in an overwhelming majority, the conflict between Hindus and Sikhs, so prominent in the Punjabi-speaking region, is not perceived by the
local population in the same manner as it is in the Punjabi
region. Caste divisions play a much greater role in the politics
of this region. The fact that the Punjabi-speaking region is
more advanced, economically and socially, however, has led in
the past to the feeling that Hariana was being exploited by the
Punjabi-speaking region.

It is interesting that the Hindu leaders of the Hariana area have found it possible from time to time to cooperate and combine with political groups which the Hindus of the rest of the Punjab considered inimical to the general interest of the Hindu community. Before the partition the support of the Hindus for the Unionist party—which most Hindus considered anti-nationalist and pro-Muslim—came from the Hariana area. After independence, the Hindu leaders of this area at times directly or indirectly supported the claims of certain sections of the Sikh community, which the Hindus of the Punjabi region felt were injurious to the interests of the Hindu community. Again, within the Congress party, the change-over of governmental leadership from a Hindu Chief Minister to a Sikh one in 1956 was accomplished largely with the help of Congress leaders from Hariana. This phenomenon suggests, incidentally, that sectional loyalties can cut sharply across loyalty to a single religion. But Hariana Hindus are by no means a united group; there are several divisions among them. First, there are the Hindu refugees from West Pakistan; they are generally more sympathetic to the interests of the Hindu community in the Punjabi region. Second, there are the Harijans; they have been opposed to the Hindu Jats since before independence, when the Jats dominated the area not only economically and socially, but, through a system of weighted franchise, also politically. Apart from the refugees and the Harijans and the Jats, there prevail many factional divisions among the Hindus of the region.

Of some note is the fact that the Hindu Harijans of the Hariana area and the Sikh Harijans of the Punjabi region have found it in their interest to act in concert with the high-caste Hindus of the Punjabi region rather than with the dominant high-caste Hindus and Sikhs, respectively, of the Hariana area and Punjabi region. The Harijans have expressed their determination to oppose any arrangement which may result in unlimited power in the hands of the high-caste, landowning, agri-

cultural classes. Parenthetically, this pattern of political behavior illustrates how caste divisions cut across ties of religion,
language or dialect, and culture.

Of considerable political significance in the Punjab even now
is the division between the rural and urban areas, which in the
case of the Punjabi-speaking region largely reinforces the division between the Hindu and Sikh communities. In the pre-
partition province of Punjab, the Unionist party, a party of
notables organized around the landowning rural interests, dominated the politics of the province.[22] Since partition, instead of
hostility toward the urban classes, the government under the
Congress party has directed its attention toward a program of
rapid industrialization and urbanization. Nonetheless, the rural
bloc within the Congress party exercises considerable political
power; in fact, the replacement in 1956 of Bhim Sen Sachar by
Partap Singh Kairon as Chief Minister also represented the
"overthrow," through a coalition of rural delegates from the
two regions, of the urban-oriented leadership which had hitherto dominated the legislative wing of the Congress party. Observers in subsequent years noted the increasingly favored treatment given the rural areas by the government of Punjab.

One important political implication of social diversity in the
Punjab may be indicated here. Given a democratic framework,
only that political party or coalition which is secular and broad-
based can remain in power in the government of the state. This
hypothesis emerges from the fact that the religious and sectional
minorities in the Punjab are not small and insignificant, but
substantial minorities—whether it be Sikhs as against Hindus
in the Punjab as a whole; Hindus or Harijans as against Sikhs
in the Punjabi-speaking region; Harijans as against non-Harijan
Hindus in the Hariana area; the people of Hariana as against
the rest of the Punjab. Rule in the name of a single communal
or sectional group would be intolerable to the other groups. In

[22] On the Unionist party, see Azim Husain, *Fazl-i-Husain: A Political
Biography* (Bombay: Longmans, Green and Co., Ltd., 1946).

other words, the bias for a secular, broad-based political party, rather than a communal party, is built into the nature of social diversity in the Punjab.

The New Political Configuration

The partition made for changes not only in the social composition but also in the political configuration of the Punjab. With the migration of Muslims from the Punjab, the Muslim League ceased to be a political force in the state. The Unionist party had been disrupted before the partition, and attempts to revive it later in the Hariana area ended in failure. The Congress party now emerged as the strongest political force and assumed political power in the Punjab after the partition.

The Congress party as an all-India party occupies a unique position in the Indian political system. All three levels of the political system—government, regime, and political community —are identified with it and are, in part, its handiwork. Except for a few short periods in a couple of states, the Congress party has remained firmly in control of the government, both at the center and in the states, since independence in 1947. As a broad-based secular party, encompassing all kinds of social and political groups, the Congress party was the standard bearer of secular nationalism. During the struggle for independence, it identified and equated itself with what it considered to be the Indian nation. It claimed to be the sole representative of the entire Indian nation. When independence was finally achieved, the Congress party's claim that it was the architect of Indian freedom was generally accepted by the Indian people; the party was recognized as the creator of free India, the Indian nation or the Indian political community. Subsequent to the achievement of independence, the new constitution, with the secular state and parliamentary democracy as its cornerstones, was formulated under the leadership of the Congress party. The new constitutional system—the regime—though it borrowed heavily from earlier British enactments, was recognized as the embodiment of the aims, aspirations, and ideals of the Congress.

Apart from the Congress party, there are three other organized political parties of major significance in the politics of the Punjab: the Shiromani Akali Dal, the Bharatiya Jana Sangh (more popularly known as simply the Jan Sangh), and the Communist party. Except for the Akali Dal, the other three parties are all-India political parties although the strength of the Jan Sangh and the Communist party is concentrated only in certain regions of India. In contrast, the Akali Dal is confined to the Punjab. Moreover, it is confined only to Sikhs and, as a communal party, frankly stands for the interests of the Sikh community only. Although many Sikhs are active in other political organizations, the Akali Dal has been able to nearly monopolize the protest function in behalf of the Sikhs and to secure the political support of a significant segment of the Sikh community. The Akali Dal is opposed to all that the Congress party stands for. Ever since its inception it has been in the forefront of making extremist demands. Akali leaders openly declare that the basic ideology of their organization is the inextricable combination of religion and politics. They express dissatisfaction with a democratic system in which there are joint electorates and rule by majority. In the sphere of center-state relations, the Akali Dal wants a radical change: the center should have control over only a few subjects and grant the "fullest possible autonomy" to the states.[23] The history of the organization for a third of a century had been coeval with the political life of its supreme leader, Master Tara Singh, who bestrode "the Sikh political world like a colossus," [24] until his leadership suffered a severe setback in 1962.

The Jan Sangh, despite its protestations to the contrary, is a

[23] *The Tribune* (Ambala), January 14, 1953.
[24] Khushwant Singh, "Struggle for the Gurdwaras," *The Statesman* (Calcutta), June 18, 1959.

Hindu communal party which considers the present regime as not in harmony with Indian tradition. Its aim is suspected to be that of establishing Hindu supremacy in India. As for the Communist party, it is feared that it would inevitably establish a totalitarian regime if it ever came to power. In the case of the Punjab, the Communist party is by and large a Sikh party, both in terms of its membership and leadership.

Given the ideological positions of the major opposition parties, we can see that all of them are viewed by the Congress party as having the goal not merely of removing it from the government in the Punjab, as also eventually in the rest of India, but also of changing the very nature of the political regime, and possibly even the political community. However, the radical disparity between the Congress party and the opposition in their ideological positions should not lead the student of politics to conclude that no consensus whatever about the political process exists among the various political groups and the population in the Punjab. Consensus is more difficult to measure than cleavage, but clearly there are certain rules of the game that, even though perhaps not acceptable, are adhered to by the political groups. This adherence, in turn, points to a wider political consensus in the population.

No matter what the ultimate plans of the opposition groups may be, they all do participate in the electoral and parliamentary processes. Of course, political groups may adopt democratic methods to end democracy, but there is also the possibility that in the end they themselves may be domesticated. Participation in the electoral and parliamentary processes further serves to blunt the political effectiveness of opposition groups in securing support for any extralegal methods they may want to adopt. When these groups resort or threaten to resort to such methods, the government challenges them to test, through the electoral process, whether they have popular support for their demands. The fact that opposition groups often do, in response, participate in the electoral process indicates the acceptance of the notion that legitimacy must be established through a popular mandate.

Moreover, there are certain values to which all parties pay tribute in public, whatever their private reservations may be. They all maintain that they stand for the same noble aims— national unity, democracy, secular state, and national prosperity —though they may differ in their interpretations of these aims. They are all against communalism, and strongly object to being referred to as communal. All the parties proclaim faith in Hindu-Sikh unity and, insofar as Hindu-Sikh relations are concerned, all pose as messengers of peace and bearers of good will. The acceptance of such norms and values in public is important because it imposes restraints on political behavior that seem to be in flagrant violation of them.

It is true that the Punjab has seen many massive agitations which may have a corrosive effect on democracy, but this fact should not occasion unnecessary alarm. Not only has the Punjab managed to survive such agitations, but there are several other not so unhappy aspects which become apparent only when the situation in the Punjab is seen in the context of similar situations in other parts of India and outside, such as Belgium or Quebec. There have been massive agitations, but little organized attempt at violence. There has been no political subversion. No railroads have been uprooted, no bombs have rocked buildings and homes. No loot and arson have been committed in pursuance of political objectives. There is no inter-tribal or inter-religious warfare, nor any voices for armed rebellion. Despite communal tensions running high at times, there have been no large-scale riots. There are no pockets of territory beyond the control of the government. There is no Yenan or Telengana in the Punjab. The governmental administration and the judicial system function in a normal manner most of the time. The reluctance to pursue a policy of violence by opposition groups may stem from a realization that, given the plethora of powers at the disposal of the government, such a policy will not succeed, but also from a fear of alienating large sections of their supporters.

Important as the aforementioned rudiments of a political consensus are, obviously they are not sufficient to sustain the existing regime and political community. Massive agitations have indeed been mounted to pressure the government. Even if democratic methods are pursued, opposition groups do aim at undermining the present political system. And, commanding as they do substantial popular support, they represent powerful forces. The Congress party is conscious of this, and it has therefore to perform another role apart from governing and maintaining political stability: the role of educator and inculcator of the new values embodied in the constitution. Congress leaders incessantly preach against the evils of "communalism, casteism, regionalism, and linguism." [25] They constantly declare communal parties to be harmful for the country. At convocation ceremonies, speakers appeal to the youth to "rush out like iconoclasts to break the idols of regionalism, communalism, and linguism." [26] The primacy of national unity is emphasized; as Krishna Menon said, "no region or religion can be greater than India." [27] Others warn that "we must unite or perish." [28] Some urge "having a common religion, the religion of service of the people and of our country." [29]

The Congress party has also tried to emphasize the new values by incorporating changes in some of the important institutions of socialization and by establishing new forms of social behavior. One example is the nationalization of the school textbook industry. The new textbooks include lessons on hymns to "mother India," eulogies to martyrs of the nationalist move-

[25] See statement by Nehru in *The Hindustan Times*, September 29, 1961.
[26] M. C. Setalvad in *The Tribune*, December 24, 1961.
[27] *Ibid.*, July 19, 1962.
[28] Partap Singh Kairon, *ibid.*, July 12, 1962.
[29] Nehru, *ibid.*, January 24, 1962.

ment, biographies of important national leaders, the duties and rights of citizens, the virtues of respect and tolerance for all religions, the teachings of the great religious masters emphasizing the unity of mankind and urging peace and harmony. In 1962 the Punjab government decided to make education free up to high school, but only in public schools, in an apparent attempt to undermine the existence of communal and parochial schools.

The Punjab government has further established a policy prohibiting the recording of entries on religion and caste along with people's names in government records.[30] The government has also asked its employees not to use Hindu or Sikh forms of greetings but rather say "Jai Hind" (victory to India).[31] While the government emphasizes the importance of a secular state, which is not identified with any particular religion, it is not so much secularism but respect for all religions that it stresses in practice. The Punjab government even sets aside funds for the celebration of important holidays of the various religions.[32]

The various measures adopted by the government to inculcate the new values of secular nationalism and parliamentary democracy are of long-term significance, but the threat to the existing regime is here and now. To some extent, all the major opposition groups in the Punjab endeavor to change the present regime, but the most serious challenge in this regard comes from the Shiromani Akali Dal over its demand for Punjabi Suba. This demand has been at the center of politics in the Punjab since independence, and has been the basis of an extraordinary, long-range political combat between the Congress leadership with its commitment to secular nationalism, on one hand, and the Akali leadership speaking in the name of the Sikh community, on the other.

[30] *Ibid.,* December 25, 1961.   [31] *Ibid.,* December 23, 1961.
[32] *Ibid.,* February 5, 1962.

Punjabi Suba: The Akali Demand

Although the demand for Punjabi Suba, or a Punjabi-speaking state, has been in the forefront of politics in the Punjab since the partition, its first systematic presentation was made before the States Reorganization Commission appointed by the Government of India in 1953. In a memorandum to the Commission [33] the Akali Dal urged the formation of Punjabi Suba by putting together the so-called Punjabi-speaking areas of Punjab, PEPSU, and Rajasthan.[34] It suggested that those areas in Punjab and PEPSU, where, according to it, Punjabi was not

[33] Shiromani Akali Dal, *Punjabi Suba* (Urdu, ed., Amritsar: Panthic Tract Society, n.d.); see also Hukam Singh, *A Plea for Punjabi-Speaking State* (Amritsar: Shiromani Akali Dal, n.d.). For other published documents presenting the viewpoint of the Akali Dal and its sympathizers on the subject of Punjabi Suba, see Amar Singh Ambalvi, "Presidential Address," *The Sikh Students' Bulletin*, v, Nos. 10–11 (January–February 1958), 7–10; Hukam Singh, *The Tenth All India Akali Conference: Inaugural Address* (Amritsar: Reception Committee, 10th All India Akali Conference, 1956); Hukam Singh, *40th Sikh Educational Conference: Presidential Address* (Delhi: General Printing Company, 1957); Hukam Singh, *The Punjab Problem: An Elucidation* (Amritsar: Shiromani Akali Dal, n.d.); Hukam Singh, *The States Reorganization in the North* (Delhi: East Punjab Printing Works, 1955); Gurnam Singh, *A Unilingual Punjabi State and the Sikh Unrest* (New Delhi: Super Press, 1960); Jaswant Singh, *Facts Without Rhetoric: The Demand for Punjabi Suba* (New Delhi: Super Press, 1960); Jaswant Singh, *A Plea for a Punjabi State* (Amritsar: Shiromani Akali Dal, 1960); Lal Singh, *Punjabi Suba Convention of Sikh Intelligentsia: Presidential Address* (Delhi: Gurdwara Parbandhak Committee, 1961); and the Sikh Youth Federation, *The Demand for the Punjabi Suba: A Most Crucial Challenge to Indian Secularism* (Calcutta: The Sikh Youth Federation, n.d.).

[34] Although the desired boundaries of Punjabi Suba have undergone several changes, the Akali Dal demanded the following areas in its memorandum to the Commission: (1) *Punjab:* Districts of Gurdaspur, Amritsar, Ferozepur, Ludhiana, Jullundur, Hoshiarpur, Ambala, Karnal (except Panipat tehsil), and Hissar (only Sirsa and Fatehabad tehsils and Tohana sub-tehsil); (2) *PEPSU:* Districts of Patiala, Barnala, Bhatinda, Kapurthala, Fatehgarh Sahib, and Sangrur (except Jind and Narwana tehsils); (3) *Rajasthan:* District of Ganganagar. These areas would give the Punjabi Suba a territory of 35,185 square miles. While providing evidence before the Commission, the General Secretary of the Akali Dal waived claim to any area in Karnal district and Ganganagar district (except Hanumangarh and Ganganagar tehsils).

spoken should be detached from these states and merged in Himachal Pradesh in the north and added to Delhi in the southeast.[35] The Akali Dal argued that the demand for Punjabi Suba was in line with demands in other parts of India for the linguistic reorganization of states. In its opinion unilingual states were necessary in order to provide for the conduct of education and administration in the language of the area. Furthermore, any language of an area corresponds to a special culture, and this cultural manifestation should have opportunity for growth through a linguistic state of its own.[36] The Akali Dal maintained that the Punjabis have a distinctive common culture [37] and a common mother tongue, and they should therefore have their own state.[38]

The Akali Dal said that Punjabi is a distinct language, and has been so recognized in the Indian constitution. It is an ancient language with roots in the distant past, and a dynamic one that has made phenomenal progress. It is also endowed with a special script known as Gurmukhi, which is not derived from the Devnagari script of Hindi, but from Brahmi. The Devnagari script is not a fit medium for the writing of Punjabi, the Akali Dal maintained.[39]

The Akali Dal characterized as unjust any allegation that the Sikhs had asked for Punjabi Suba out of sinister communal motives. The Sikhs have been the greatest of patriots, and they are Indians first and last, the Akali Dal asserted. Moreover, Punjabi Suba was not going to be an independent country, but

[35] The areas that the Akali Dal wanted excluded at the time were: *Punjab:* Districts of Kangra, Rohtak, Gurgaon, Karnal (only Panipat tehsil) and Hissar (except Sirsa and Fatehabad tehsils and Tohana sub-tehsil); and *PEPSU:* Districts of Mohindergarh, Sangrur (only Jind and Narwana tehsils), Kandaghat and Kohistan.

[36] Akali Dal, p. 5.

[37] *Ibid.*, p. 12. Hukam Singh also stated: "The citizens of Punjabi-Speaking areas . . . come from a common stock, have common peculiarities of culture, dress and way of life. They have common traditions and history, and intermarriages are common. There are common achievements and failures." Hukam Singh, *A Plea*, p. 12.

[38] Akali Dal, p. 12.   [39] *Ibid*, pp. 7–10.

would be subject to central control. Hindus will continue to
have a majority of 55 percent in the population, according to
the Akali Dal. To argue that a 70 percent majority of Hindus
is required for the security of India, said the Akali Dal, is to
betray a lack of faith in the Sikhs.[40] It is criminal, maintained
the Akali Dal, to suggest that Hindus will be eventually evicted
and the Punjabi Suba converted into a Sikh state.[41]

In conclusion, the Akali Dal said that the formation of Punjabi Suba would lead to the following beneficial results, among
others: (1) the creation of a geographically compact, economically sound, and financially viable state; (2) the eradication of
the causes of the present unrest in the Punjab and the restora-
tion of communal harmony which is essential in a border state;
(3) the elimination of the language controversy, and the provision of education through the mother tongue in a single language state, thus assuring further progress in the state; and (4)
the securing of a contented Sikh community for the country.[42]

The demand of the Akali Dal for Punjabi Suba received in-
cidental support from some Hindu leaders and organizations in
the Hariana area, an area that the Akali Dal desired to be excluded from the Punjab. These leaders and organizations maintained that their area had been neglected in economic development, and also that culturally they were different from the rest
of the Punjab. They demanded therefore the separation of
Hariana area from the Punjab, and asked for the establishment
of a separate Hariana state, which would also include several
western districts of neighboring Uttar Pradesh. Opponents of
the Punjabi Suba criticized the demand for Hariana state as
having been inspired by the Akali Dal, for if Hariana state
were conceded the cause of Punjabi Suba would be helped
tremendously. Whether in fact the demand for Hariana state
owed its inspiration to the Akali Dal is questionable, but some
financial help seems to have been given by Akali leaders for

40 *Ibid.*, pp. 26–27.   41 *Ibid.*, p. 27.
42 *Ibid.*, pp. 31–32.

the organization of the movement for the demand.[43] Later, for some years, several Hariana leaders opposed Punjabi Suba and were not enthusiastic about a Hariana state. The reason seemed to be the firm opposition on the part of the Congress leadership to any proposal which would lead to the dismemberment of the existing state of Uttar Pradesh. The realization that since Hariana by itself is too small an area to constitute a viable state and that if Punjabi Suba were established, the various districts of Hariana may be split up and merged with the states of Uttar Pradesh, Rajasthan and Greater Delhi, made for—though temporarily—a lack of enthusiasm for Punjabi Suba. As one leader explained, "if Hariana is divided up our condition will be worse for then there will be no Hariana region." [44] Even when the movement for Hariana state has been quite strong, it has met with opposition from Harijans and refugees from West Pakistan in the region.

Linguistic versus Communal Basis

Although the Akali argument before the States Reorganization Commission, and on other occasions, has been that language is the basis for the demand of Punjabi Suba, this is not a complete description of the Akali position. Many Akali leaders have left no doubt as to the basic political objectives in the demand for Punjabi Suba. These objectives range from the attainment for the Sikhs as a community the dominant position in the political affairs of the Punjab to the establishment of an independent and sovereign Sikh state. Akali pronouncements on the subject are numerous.

A former Akali leader recalls a speech given by Master Tara Singh at Patiala during the 1951–52 elections.[45] Tara Singh started out by saying that it was wrong to allege that he wanted

[43] From an interview with a member of the executive committee of the Akali Dal during 1955 and 1956.

[44] From an interview with an MLA from Hariana.

[45] "Punjab ki Sikh Siyaasat: No. 2" [Sikh Politics of the Punjab], by a Sikh politician, in *Pratap* (New Delhi), March 10, 1962.

a Sikh state; he desired only a state based on the Punjabi language. He then went on to make fun of political manifestoes published by other parties and said that the disease of manifesto-making had spread even to the Akali Dal, as it had produced one too. However, he did not feel the need to read it, he said, for he had only one manifesto and that was "the Panth, the Panth, the Panth." When this statement was greeted with enthusiastic slogans, he announced that he frankly wanted Sikh rule. He added that some Akali leaders had told him not to mention the word Sikh rule but to talk only of a linguistic state, but he wanted to declare that Sikh rule was at hand.

In an interesting article [46] discussing the objectives of the demand for Punjabi Suba, Master Tara Singh acknowledged that the Akali Dal had decided that such a state was the best method to maintain the independent existence of the Sikhs. What he wanted, he said, was a state where the Sikhs would be in a majority so that they could escape from Hindu dominance in the legislature. He reiterated that the aim was to free the Sikhs on a provincial basis. He further mentioned that he would like to secure for Punjabi Suba internal autonomy of the kind granted to Kashmir since states had now become merely big district boards.

Tara Singh declared that the Hindus were fanatic communalists, and that the Sikhs could not be saved under Hindu dominance.[47] Therefore, he said, "for the sake of religion, for the sake of culture, for the sake of the Panth, and to keep high the flag of the Guru [spiritual teacher], the Sikhs have girded their loins to achieve independence." [48] He pointed out that he did not care for any particular method but that he wanted to free the Sikhs from Hindu dominance.[49] He emphasized the desire for an area in India where, on the birthdays of the Gurus, armies march in the streets, the Sikh flag flies alongside

[46] Master Tara Singh, "Punjabi Suba," reprinted as chapter x in Gurcharan Singh, *Sikh Kya Chahtey Hain?* [What Do the Sikhs Want?] (Delhi: New India Publications, [1950]), p. 122.
[47] *Ibid.,* p. 124.   [48] *Loc. cit.*   [49] *Ibid.,* p. 127.

the national flag on government buildings, and the Sikhs have a free environment where they can decide their own fate according to their thinking and their traditions.[50]

Another instance which is frequently quoted as revealing the real intentions of the Akali Dal is an interview between Master Tara Singh and the then Chief Minister Bhim Sen Sachar on January 21, 1955.[51] During the interview, "Master Tara Singh stated that he did not believe in a linguistic Punjabi State. What he had in mind was a Sikh State wherein the Sikhs would be in a numerical majority." The Chief Minister then asked, "So you want a land wherein the Sikhs should dominate," to which Tara Singh answered, "This is exactly what I have in mind," and continued: "This cover of a Punjabi-speaking State slogan serves my purpose well since it does not offend against nationalism. The Government should accept our demand under the slogan of a Punjabi-speaking State without a probe. What we want is *Azadi* [independence]. The Sikhs have no Azadi. We will fight for our Azadi with full power even if we have to revolt for our Azadi. We will revolt to win our Azadi." On other occasions, too, Master Tara Singh has expressed similar sentiments. At a press conference on January 11, 1961, he declared that "we have adopted the linguistic principle because it suits. We know that a unilingual Punjabi-speaking State will be such that the Sikh religion will be more safe in it."[52] In his view the main problem is protection of Sikh religion, and Punjabi Suba is being demanded only because it would improve the position of the Sikhs.[53] On the question of making Punjabi the official language for the whole of the Punjab, he has commented, "You might declare it to be the language of the whole of India. How could that help the Sikhs?"[54]

[50] *Loc. cit.*

[51] The interview is quoted in several places, including Virendra, "Punjabi Suba or A Sikh State," *The Spokesman* (New Delhi), xi, No. 27 (July 17, 1961), 10.

[52] *Indian Affairs Record*, vii, No. 1 (January 1961), 18.

[53] *The Spokesman*, xi, No. 2 (January 16, 1961), 2.

[54] *Loc. cit.*

Earlier, in 1955, he declared that "I feel we cannot save our religion without attainment of political power in the Punjabi-speaking region." [55]

Another important Akali leader, Pritam Singh Gojran, has gone so far as to say that the Sikhs should not play around with a secular demand like that of a Punjabi-speaking state, but openly demand a Sikh state. He said that as long as the objective was the protection of the Sikh Panth, the Sikhs should be unambiguous about their demand. He added that the executive committee of the Akali Dal, led by Master Tara Singh, had demanded an independent Sikh state in a resolution passed on March 22, 1946, and that it had in 1950 demanded a Sikh state with internal autonomy, but that later the demand had been changed to Punjabi Suba without internal autonomy. [56]

A senior vice-president of the Akali Dal, Harcharan Singh Hudiara, warned in 1961 that the government better concede Punjabi Suba now, because later "the new leadership among Sikhs might give a call for an independent Punjabi State instead of a Punjabi Suba." [57] *The Spokesman*, which before 1956 voiced the Akali viewpoint, had from time to time indicated what the real objective of the demand has been. In 1956 it declared that "the Sikhs have no vain craze for the mere name of Punjabi Suba. They seek the substance of it, which would make them equals and ensure the preservation of Punjabi and Punjabi culture." [58] A few months earlier it had referred to this language and culture as those of the Sikhs when it said that "the demarcation of what is called a Punjabi Suba seems to be the only way to preserve the language, culture, and religion of the Sikhs." [59]

---

[55] *The Tribune*, September 12, 1955; *The Times of India*, September 12, 1955; and *The Spokesman*, v, No. 36 (September 21, 1955), 9.

[56] *The Tribune*, October 27, 1958 and December 30, 1958; also *The Hindusthan Standard*, June 13, 1958.

[57] *The Spokesman*, xi, No. 26 (July 10, 1961), 1.

[58] *The Spokesman*, vi, No. 7 (February 20, 1956), 3.

[59] *Ibid.*, v, No. 34 (September 7, 1955), 3.

Even when the Akali Dal has attempted to make the demand for Punjabi Suba in linguistic terms, it has been unable to dissociate the demand from specific Akali claims and alleged grievances of the Sikhs. From the record it would seem evident that the primary consideration is the satisfaction of Akali claims, but that the linguistic principle is employed as an additional argument. A resolution passed by the Akali Dal in 1950 states:

> The callous and unsympathetic treatment of the government has made respectable life impossible for them [Sikhs], they, therefore, strongly feel the utter necessity of the speedy creation of a Punjabi-Speaking Province for the protection and preservation of their culture, language and self-respect; particularly when this solution is universally recognized as democratic, and to which even the Indian National Congress stands pledged.[60]

The demand is made here in consideration of Sikh grievances, though here again Punjabi is a language of the Sikhs; but the Akali Dal has shown extreme reluctance in ever specifying these grievances. The manifesto published by the Akali Dal for the 1951–52 elections also provides an indication of the relative importance Akali leaders attach to the linguistic principle and their own political claims in behalf of the Sikh community. The manifesto said, in part:

> 4(a) To bring home this sense of freedom to the Sikhs, it is vital that a Punjabi speaking Province should be carved out from the different states of the country on the basis of Punjabi language and culture.

> 4(b) The Shiromani Akali Dal is in favour of formation of provinces on linguistic and cultural basis throughout India, but holds it as a question of life and death for the Sikhs for a new Punjab to be created immediately.

[60] *Ibid.,* XI, No. 10 (March 13, 1961), 1.

4(c) The Shiromani Akali Dal has reasons to believe that a Punjabi speaking Province may give Sikhs the needful security. It believes in a Punjabi speaking Province as an autonomous unit of India.[61]

It is interesting to note that before 1956 the Akali constitution included a clause stating that the "Shiromani Akali Dal stands for the creation of an environment in which the Sikh national expression finds its full satisfaction," [62] an aim more explicitly stated in the Punjabi version by the use of the expressive term *desh-kaal*, whose literal meaning is "country and era." This clause had in the past been made a basis for the demand of an independent Sikh state, and was eliminated in 1956 as part of a political settlement with the Congress party. But there was pointed criticism for giving up the "demand of a separate Sikh state" through the elimination of this clause, "in spite of the fact that the Panth daily resolve and say 'Raj Karega Khalsa' [the Khalsa shall rule]." [63] Interestingly enough, this same clause, which led to the demand for a separate Sikh state, also formed the basis for the demand of Punjabi Suba. In 1956 a prominent Akali leader, who had also served as president of the Akali Dal, stated: "The constitution provided that the objective of the Akali Dal would be to create environments (area and atmosphere) wherein the Sikh religion, culture and traditions could survive and grow unhampered. The Akali Dal believed that the formation of a Punjabi speaking State in North India could bring such an atmosphere and the desired environments. It was in pursuance of these aims in the constitution that the demand for a Punjabi Suba was made and sacrifices offered to achieve this." [64]

[61] *Ibid.*, I, No. 2 (August 29, 1951), 9.

[62] Ambalvi, p. 9. Ambalvi was General Secretary of the Akali Dal for several terms before and after the partition, and has held other important positions in the organization.

[63] *Loc. cit.*

[64] Hukam Singh, "Constitution of Shiromani Akali Dal Amended," *The Spokesman*, VI, No. 48 (December 3, 1956), 1–2.

Finally, one may note that in early July, 1965, at a conference in Ludhiana, Akali spokesmen openly demanded political power specifically for the Sikh community, as allegedly "the lot of the Sikhs could not improve unless they had political power in their hand." In a resolution, moved by Gurnam Singh, the leader of the Akali group in the Punjab legislature, and seconded by Giani Bhupinder Singh, a protégé of Master Tara Singh, Akali supporters pressed for a *"self-determined political status for the Sikhs* within the Indian Union," with the particular autonomous state having the right to frame its own constitution. (My italics.) (More on this may be found in *The Tribune* for July 5, 14, 1965; *The Hindustan Times,* July 16, 1965; and *The Spokesman,* July 19, 1965.)

It is difficult to probe into the motives and intentions of Akali leaders (and, for that matter, of any political leader or human being). One cannot help but note, however, the impressive refrain in the speeches, interviews, and published material of Akali leaders and sympathizers that the Sikhs as a religious community, on the basis of being a religious community, should hold political power in a definite territorial area. It is precisely the juxtaposition of the two arguments about Punjabi Suba— the principle of the linguistic demarcation of states, and a Sikh-majority area being a question of life and death for the Sikhs— that has given the demand a completely communal orientation. Of some interest is the fact that *The Spokesman,* after about a decade of advocacy of the Punjabi Suba demand, commented in 1960 that "all admit, however, that there is great room for improvement in the presentation of the Punjabi Suba demand. Its previous communal and religious hue must be replaced by a purely political complexion." [65] The same weekly had previously charged time and again that labeling the demand as a communal one was a sinister attempt on the part of its opponents to give the dog a bad name and then condemn it.

[65] *Ibid.,* x, No. 22 (June 6, 1960), 3.

Opposition to Punjabi Suba

Given the Akali position, there has been vigorous opposition to the demand of Punjabi Suba from the Hindu community, the Sikh Harijans, and the nationalist leadership. In several memoranda to the States Reorganization Commission, various Hindu political organizations, including the Jan Sangh,[66] the Hindu Maha Sabha,[67] and the All-Parties Maha Punjab Front Samiti,[68] not only opposed the demand of Punjabi Suba but pressed their own demand for Maha Punjab (Greater Punjab) which would include the territories of Punjab and PEPSU but also of Himachal Pradesh, Delhi, and some districts of Uttar Pradesh. They considered these territories to be a single region geographically and economically, culturally, and ethnically.

The main thrust of the arguments advanced by the Hindu organizations was that the demand for Punjabi Suba on the supposedly innocent basis of language was merely a camouflage for the attainment of Sikh hegemony and the establishment of a base for an eventual sovereign Sikh state.[69] They described the demarcation of the boundaries of Punjabi Suba by the Akali Dal as a shrewd attempt to convert the 30 percent Sikh minority into a 53 percent majority and "an ingenious endeavour to congregate 96 percent of the total Sikh population of Punjab and Pepsu in the compass of a small area." [70]

Turning to the question of language as a basis for the formation of states, the various Hindu organizations argued that the people covered by the proposed Greater Punjab spoke some variant of the same generic language, and that all the dialects in this area are derived from the same language.[71] There are no

[66] Punjab Jan Sangh, *Why Maha Punjab?: Memorandum Submitted by Punjab Jan Sangh* (Ambala Cantt: The Utthan Publications, 1954).

[67] Gokul Chand Narang, *Transformation of Sikhism* (5th ed.; New Delhi: New Book Society of India, 1960), pp. 208–09.

[68] Alakh Dhari, *States Re-organization Commission: Maha Punjab: Memorandum Stressing the Need for Re-integration of Punjab, Pepsu and Himachal Pradesh into One Administrative Unit* (n.p., n.d.).

[69] *Ibid.*, p. 12.   [70] *Ibid.*, pp. 12–13.   [71] *Ibid.*, p. 18.

greater differences between the dialects of Punjabi Suba and those of the areas designed to be excluded from the Suba, they claimed, than there are among the dialects within the proposed Suba. More specifically, it was pointed out, there is no difference between the people of Gurdaspur district which has been included in the proposed Punjabi Suba, on one hand, and those of the adjacent Kangra district which has been excluded, on the other, except that the latter includes a Hindu majority of 98 percent.[72] Especially after the migration of five million refugees with their various Punjabi dialects from West Pakistan, these organizations argued, the entire area of the Greater Punjab had become "now conventionally and literally a continuous zone of Punjabi speaking population."[73] The Akali Dal, they charged, had excluded from the proposed Punjabi Suba many areas whose dialects "are every whit as true and natural Punjabi as the dialects of the areas included in the Punjabi Suba."[74] The only reason for their exclusion, they emphasized, was that they contained an overwhelming majority of Hindus. Incidentally, it should be noted that while some organizations called the generic language of Greater Punjab territory as Punjabi, others called it Western Hindi.

These Hindu organizations were quick to point out that the demand for Punjabi Suba was the demand of a communal minority anxious to achieve political supremacy, and that 70 percent of the people of the Punjab were opposed to it.[75] They further alleged that the Communist party was the only party that was supporting the Akali demand, because it was eager to weaken India's defense and to seize power.[76] They further blamed the Akali Dal for creating, through its many agitations, an atmosphere reminiscent of the days when the Muslim League agitated for Pakistan, and warned that the formation of Punjabi Suba would result in the same kind of grave con-

[72] *Ibid.*, p. 14. [73] *Ibid.*, p. 16.
[74] *Ibid.*, p. 17. [75] *Ibid.*, p. 19.
[76] Punjab Jan Sangh, *Maha Punjab Kyoon?* [Why Maha Punjab?] (Ambala Cantt: The Utthan Publications, 1954), p. 20.

sequences as followed the creation of Pakistan.[77] In the opinion
of these organizations, the solution to the linguistic, communal,
and political problems of the state lay in the formation of
Greater Punjab.

Punjabi and Hindi

The Hindu opposition to the demand for Punjabi Suba went
beyond the mere expression of objection to the formation of
such a state. To the Akali emphasis on Punjabi language as
the basis for the formation of Punjabi Suba, the Hindus in the
Punjab reacted by disowning the Punjabi language itself. They
declared that Hindi—which is also the national language of
India—not Punjabi, is their language. A Hindu-dominated mu-
nicipal committee in Jullundur passed a resolution soon after
independence, favoring Hindi as the medium of instruction in
schools within its jurisdiction.[78] Some Akali leaders have maintained that this action in Jullundur more than anything else
convinced the Sikhs of the communal motives of Hindus in the
Punjab and that from then on the Sikhs became determined to
achieve Punjabi Suba which would not only have Punjabi as
its official language but would also reduce the power of the
Hindus in relation to the Sikhs.

On the other hand, the Hindus argue that their attachment
to Hindi is of no recent origin and that, while they speak a
Punjabi "dialect" in their homes, they have never used it in
correspondence or for commercial, educational or religious purposes. They consider the imposition of Punjabi as an attempt
to establish Sikh supremacy over them, since never before in
the state's history—not even during Sikh rule—has Punjabi been
used as an official language.[79] The Hindus emphasize the fact
that long before the Sikhs developed any concern for Punjabi
in their schools, Hindi was being promoted in Hindu schools

[77] *Ibid.*

[78] Ganda Singh (ed.), *Bhai Jodh Singh Abhinandan Granth: Punjab*
(Patiala: Khalsa College, 1962), p. 403.

[79] Punjab Jan Sangh, *Maha Punjab Kyoon?*, p. 14.

in the Punjab. Before independence even the Akali Dal seems to have given recognition to this fact, as the Sikander–Baldev Singh Pact provided for the same treatment for Hindi as for Gurmukhi.[80] In fact, in 1945, one Sikh scholar chided the Sikh community that "what our Arya Samajist friends are doing for Hindi in their schools and colleges should be done by us in ours for Gurmukhi." [81] Thus long before the present conflict the Hindus seem to have shown a marked preference for Hindi. Similarly, the Muslims in the pre-partition Punjab preferred Urdu and would have nothing to do with Punjabi. On the other hand, Punjabi in Gurmukhi script came to be patronized solely by the Sikhs. This divergence between Hindus and Sikhs in their choice of language was obvious as far back as the 1920s from the preference shown by them in university examinations in Hindi and Punjabi.[82] This divergence in university examinations continues today. In 1955 the States Reorganization Commission stated that in the Jullundur division (all of which the Akali Dal wants included in Punjabi Suba), for the language examinations of the Punjab university in the five years prior to the Commission's report, 62.2 percent of the candidates took Hindi and 37.8 percent took Punjabi. Further, in the history and geography examinations for the matriculation diploma of the Punjab university, out of 103,758 candidates in the four years preceding the report of the Commission, 73.5 percent of the candidates chose to answer through the medium of Hindi and 26.5 percent in Punjabi.[83]

Some Hindus maintain that Punjabi is not even a language,

[80] Bhagat Singh Tangh, *Azad Punjab ke Mutalaq Pothohari Nukta-nigah* [Pothohari Viewpoint Concerning Azad Punjab] (Amritsar: Dyal Singh, Assistant Secretary, Shiromani Akali Dal, 1943), p. 42.

[81] Kartar Singh, *Rekindling of the Sikh Heart* (Lahore: Lahore Book Shop, 1945), p. 169.

[82] As one example, in 1922 there were 71 Hindus but only 1 Sikh taking the examinations for proficiency, high proficiency, or honors in Hindi. In the same year, for the examinations for proficiency, high proficiency, or honors in Punjabi, there were only 7 Hindus but 122 Sikhs. See *Punjab Legislative Council Debates,* IV, No. 11 (1923), 1147.

[83] *Report of the States Reorganization Commission,* p. 144.

which understandably irks the Sikhs. For such Hindus, Punjabi is merely a dialect of Hindi like other dialects in north India. Just as people in Uttar Pradesh, while speaking different dialects, consider Hindi as their language, so too do some people in the Punjab. Moreover, some feel that if people in other parts of India—for example, in Rajasthan and in Himachal Pradesh—can make Hindi their official language even though their mother tongue may not be exactly Hindi,[84] so too can people in the Punjab. They say that the Sikhs may by all means use Punjabi for their purposes, but have no right to impose it on the unwilling, especially when Punjabi in Gurmukhi script is exclusively the religious language of the Sikhs.

Other Hindus, who would recognize Punjabi as a separate language, emphasize that there should be freedom to use the Devnagari script (employed in writing Hindi). The Gurmukhi script, they maintain, is an artificial invention of the founders of the Sikh religion and that, before the invention of Gurmukhi, the Devnagari script had been used in the writing of Punjabi, and several Sikh scriptures were written in that script.[85] Many of the Gurmukhi characters, they argue, are imitations of Devnagari[86] and that, from a scientific point of view, Devnagari is a more appropriate script for the writing of Punjabi.[87] Before independence, they say, Punjabi was written not only in the Gurmukhi script but also in the Persian and Devnagari scripts.[88] They consequently object to the enforcement of Gurmukhi as the sole script for the writing of Punjabi.

---

[84] Grierson tells us that "the Rajasthani dialects form a group among themselves, differentiated from Western Hindi on the one hand and from Gujarati on the other hand. They are entitled to the dignity of being classed as together forming a separate, independent language. They differ much more widely from Western Hindi than does for instance, Panjabi." G. A. Grierson, *Linguistic Survey of India* (Calcutta: Superintendent Government Printing, India, 1908), IX, Part II, 15. Curiously, however, Rajasthani does not find a place among the fourteen languages recognized by the Indian constitution.

[85] Alakh Dhari, p. 20.   [86] *Loc. cit.*

[87] Punjab Jan Sangh, *Maha Punjab Kyoon?*, p. 15.

[88] *Ibid.*, p. 14.

As one Hindu leader has said, "there could be a mother tongue, but not a mother script." [89]

The Sikhs interpret the move to have Devnagari as an additional script in the writing of Punjabi as an attempt to kill Punjabi, and insist on Gurmukhi as the only script appropriate for Punjabi. The communal conflict between the Hindus and the Sikhs thus finds its expression in the controversy over language, and is in turn reinforced by it. With the Hindus "the spread of Punjabi has come to be associated with communal dominance based on separatism." [90] For the Sikhs, the denial by Hindus of the Punjabi language is perceived as an attempt to destroy their culture. Whereas the Hindus want to be relieved of any requirement to study Punjabi and do not want any further extension in the use of Punjabi for official business of the state, the Sikhs, as one Akali leader put it, want to end any regional role in the Punjab for Hindi.

One of the factors contributing to the language controversy is the close relationship between Hindi and Punjabi. Punjabi, Rajasthani, and Gujarati, along with Western Hindi, belong to what Grierson calls the central group of Indo-Aryan languages. Of this group, Western Hindi alone is a pure member while the rest are mixed languages. Grierson explains the development of north Indian languages by distinguishing historically between the language of the "inner circle" and several languages surrounding it belonging to the "outer circle." Over the centuries the language of the "inner circle" spread out and overlaid the languages of the "outer circle." At the present day, *Lahnda*—belonging to the "outer circle"—is the language of west Punjab (Pakistan) whereas Punjabi is predominantly the language of east Punjab (India). At some time in the past, the Lahnda language was prevalent all over the Punjab, east and west, but an old form of Hindi—belonging to the "inner circle"

[89] Sher Singh, *The Case of Haryana and Hindi Region of the Punjab* (Rohtak: Haryana Lok Smiti, 1962), p. 28.

[90] Letter of Rala Ram, *The Tribune,* July 22, 1955.

—"gradually spread over the whole of the eastern Panjab, superseding, or overlying, the old Lahnda language." [91] The result of this expansion of Hindi is that Punjabi "is a composite language," its substratum "is a language of the Outer Circle akin to modern Lahnda, while its superstructure is a dialect of Western Hindi. The superstructure is so important, and has so concealed the foundation, that Panjabi is rightly classed, at the present day, as a language of the Central Group." [92]

Even in 1914, Grierson was aware of the controversy over whether Punjabi is a dialect of Hindi or a language by itself. He himself did not consider it as a mere dialect. At the same time, he mentioned that "Panjabi has a very scanty literature. The oldest work which is usually said to be written in the language is the *Adi Granth,* the sacred Scriptures of the Sikhs; but, although the manuscripts of the book are universally written in the Gurmukhi character, a very small portion of its contents is really in the Panjabi language. It is a collection of hymns by various poets, most of whom wrote in some form of Western Hindi. . . ." [93]

It is this closeness of the two languages, such that the same manuscript is a work of Punjabi and of Hindi, that has made it possible for the Hindus to adopt Hindi. At the same time, this very closeness has made imperative an effort—including the imposition of Punjabi on those unwilling to accept it—on the part of the Sikhs to prevent the submergence of Punjabi in Hindi not only for its own sake, but also as symbolic of the separateness of the Sikh community.

Because the Devnagari script facilitates an effective liaison with Hindi, the Hindus insist it should be recognized as one of the scripts for the writing of Punjabi. They believe that the Gurmukhi script is a creation of the Sikh religion. On this point, Grierson writes that at the time of the second Sikh Guru,

[91] Punjab, Language Department, *Grierson on Panjabi* (Patiala: Language Department, Punjab, 1961), p. 8.
[92] *Ibid.,* p. 9.   [93] *Ibid.,* p. 12.

the alphabet used in writing the local language in the Punjab was *Landa,* but that "Angad found that Sikh hymns written in Landa were liable to be misread, and he accordingly improved it by borrowing signs from the Deva-nagari alphabet (then only used for Sanskrit manuscripts), and by polishing up the forms of the letters, so as to make them fit for recording the scriptures of the Sikh religion. Having been invented by him this character became known as the *Gur-mukhi,* or the alphabet proceeding from the mouth of the Guru. Ever since, this alphabet has been employed for writing the Sikh Scriptures, and its use has widely spread, mainly among members of that sect." [94] However, in illustrating Punjabi writing, Grierson himself uses the three scripts of Gurmukhi, Persian and Devnagari. [95] Even the Akali Dal before independence, while demanding that Punjabi should be the official language of the Punjab, allowed the option to use either Persian or Gurmukhi scripts. [96]

In light of the history of the development of the two languages and the different sentiments about them among the Hindus and the Sikhs, the Hindus during the 1951 census operations simply declared Hindi, and not Punjabi, as their mother tongue. By such a declaration, the Hindus attempted to undercut the very basis of the formation of a Punjabi-speaking state by trying to show that about half the population proposed to be included in the Punjabi Suba did not speak the language on the basis of which a linguistic state was being demanded by the Akali Dal and, as a consequence, there was no

[94] *Ibid.,* p. 18. A group of Sikh theologians and scholars state in a publication that "Guru Angad was the founder of Gurmukhi Script in which the Adi Granth is written." UNESCO, *Selections from the Sacred Writings of the Sikhs* (London: George Allen & Unwin, Ltd., 1960), p. 120. The translators of the selections are: Dr. Trilochan Singh, Bhai Jodh Singh, Kapur Singh, Bawa Harkishen Singh and Khushwant Singh.

[95] *Grierson on Panjabi,* pp. 40–41, 59–60, 84, 91.

[96] Non-Party Political Conference, Non-Party Conciliation Committee, *Constitutional Proposals of the Sapru Committee* (Bombay: Padma Publications Ltd., 1945), p. lviii.

reason for the formation of such a state. Further, they tried to demonstrate that in the Punjab as a whole over 60 percent of the population spoke Hindi and therefore the formation of Punjabi Suba would be contrary to the wishes of the majority of the population of the state.

On the other hand, the Akali Dal asserted that there exists a Punjabi-speaking area whose inhabitants speak the Punjabi language, and demanded that Punjabi Suba should be formed regardless of the "betrayal" of the mother tongue by some of the area's inhabitants. However, in the actual demarcation of the Punjabi-speaking state, the Akali Dal tended to exclude—accidentally or otherwise—areas where Punjabi dialects are spoken according to Grierson, but where the Hindus are in an overwhelming majority.

Opposition by the Harijans

Whatever the ethics of the Hindu denial of Punjabi as a mother tongue, it is intelligible in the light of their patronage of Hindi long before independence and in light of the contemporary conflict between important segments of the Hindu and Sikh communities in the Punjab. However, what was more surprising at the time of the 1951 census operations was the declaration by the largely illiterate Harijans, even when they belonged to the Sikh religion, that Hindi and not Punjabi was their mother tongue. Their opposition stemmed from the nature of village society in the Punjab. While Sikhism emphasizes equality, village society in the Sikh-majority areas, in successfully defying its prescriptions, has been, by and large, physically and socially divided into two worlds—Harijan and Jat Sikh—where caste and economic divisions reinforce each other. The Harijans fear that in case Punjabi Suba, whose most enthusiastic supporters are the more numerous Jat Sikhs, is established, they will be further "crushed" since effective political power would then pass even more completely into the hands of Jat Sikhs. Therefore, the Harijans, too, in order to undermine the very basis on which the demand for Punjabi Suba was being made, declared Hindi as their language. A speech given by a Harijan member in the Punjab legislature is revealing in this respect: "We intentionally asked for Hindi. We got this done with vengeance. It was done only on the threats of the population living in the villages of these areas. They threatened us on the platform and through the press. The protagonists of Punjabi threatened boycott of those who would enter Hindi in the census. They told us that they will not allow us to use the fields for satisfying natural calls. They will make our life miserable. They will kill us. But the Harijans of Jullundur refused to be cowed down by their threats. They did not want to be suppressed in this manner. They took the lead and a bold step. They told the protagonists of Punjabi that in the democratic set up of the country no one can dominate over others in the matters of religion and language. Everyone has a right to have his own say. We wanted to take off the yoke of domination of one community over the other. This was how we got entered Hindi as our mother tongue." [97]

The attitude of the Hindus and the Harijans toward the question of language demonstrates once again that, where the vital issue of political domination as between different intra-regional groups comes to the forefront, there can be no enduring loyalty on the part of some groups to a linguistic region and, on the part of others, to a common religion.

---

[97] Speech by Master Gurbanta Singh, in *Punjab Vidhan Sabha Debates,* I, No. 18 (March 23, 1956), 21. The resentment on the part of Harijans against being intimidated into declaring Punjabi as their language in 1951 has an interesting background. At the time of the 1931 census, several of the Harijan castes, such as Chuhras and Chamars, wanted to declare their religion as "Ad-Dharmi" in order to consolidate their political position. However, writes the author of the census report, "a tug-of-war started in some districts, and Ad-Dharmis were required by Sikhs and Hindus not to return themselves as Ad-Dharmis. Particularly in Ambala, Ludhiana, Ferozepore, and Lyallpur the Sikh land-owners employed all sorts of measures, not infrequently bordering on terrorism, to secure the return of religion of Chuhras and Chamars as Sikh." *Census of India, 1931,* XVII, Part I, iii–iv.

THE NATIONALIST OBJECTION

The nationalist objection to the demand for Punjabi Suba has been that it is a communal demand and is directly opposed to the conception of the secular state. In 1961, speaking before the Indian parliament, Nehru declared that the demand for Punjabi Suba is "a communal demand, even though it is given a linguistic base." [98] He said that the Punjab constituted "a definite social and linguistic unit" and that "another partition now would cause it deep injury." [99] He pointed out that "the whole of Punjab, whether it is in regard to language, whether it is in regard to the ways of living, whether it is the food you eat and so many other things, it is a unity—whether it is Hindu or Sikh or, I may add Muslim—now there are not many Muslims there. There are not those differences due to religion or due to language which you find elsewhere in India." [100] He was convinced that to form Punjabi Suba was "inviting disaster, and disaster to the poor Punjabi State or the Suba that might be formed, absolute disaster to it," for consequences similar to the earlier partition would follow "because the way it has grown up—there is no doubt about it that it has grown up not as a linguistic issue but as a communal issue; I have no doubt about it—because it has grown up as a communal issue, other communities take objection. And they oppose it, and they will go on opposing it, for, Punjabis have many virtues, but yet they are very quarrelsome people." [101] There is, in addition, the unstated fear that such a state may later become the base of a secessionist movement, especially when it borders on a hostile neighbor, and thus become a serious blow to India's national unity. Enthusiastic receptions given to visiting Akali leaders in Pakistan have only served to intensify such a fear. At times,

[98] India (Republic) *Lok Sabha Debates,* LVII, No. 16 (August 28, 1961), 5193.
[99] *Ibid.,* p. 5194.
[100] *Ibid.,* No. 17 (August 29, 1961), pp. 5681–82.
[101] *Ibid.,* pp. 5687–88.

some Congress leaders have even openly alleged collusion between Akali leaders and Pakistan.

The States Reorganization Commission, which may be considered to represent the nationalist viewpoint, dealt with the Akali demand at great length. In fact, the section on the Punjab occupies more space than any other section in the whole report of the Commission.[102] This Commission rejected the demand of Punjabi Suba on grounds of lack of popular support and the impossibility of demarcation of linguistic boundaries in the Punjab. It found that the Punjab problem was unique since, unlike other linguistic demands, the demand for Punjabi Suba was opposed by large sections of the population who supposedly spoke the same language.[103] The Commission thought the formation of Punjabi Suba might in fact amount to imposing the will of a substantial minority on the majority.[104] Turning to the question of language, the Commission expressed the opinion that the objective of creating linguistic states was to facilitate communication among the people and between the people and the government. In applying this criterion to the Punjab case, however, the Commission found that

> there is no real language problem in the State of the Punjab as at present constituted. This is so because the Punjabi and Hindi languages as spoken in the Punjab are akin to each other and are both well-understood by all sections of the people of the State. Nobody has seriously argued before us that the present set-up presents any difficulty so far as the communicational needs of the people are concerned.[105]

In the Commission's view, the distinction between the two languages as spoken in the Punjab was "more theoretical than real," [106] and that the settlement of large numbers of Punjabi-speaking refugees from West Pakistan all over the state had

[102] *Report of the States Reorganization Commission*, pp. 140–56.
[103] *Ibid.*, p. 141.   [104] *Ibid.*, p. 146.
[105] *Ibid.*, p. 141.   [106] *Ibid.*, p. 142.

blurred the distinction even more. With such an intermingling of people speaking the two languages, the Commission thought "it would be impossible to create a compact unilingual state." [107] In mentioning that the Akali Dal had revised its earlier version of the boundaries of Punjabi Suba, the Commission seemed to imply that the Dal itself was not sure where the line of demarcation should be. [108]

The Commission further observed that the establishment of Punjabi Suba would not solve the problem of internal tension in the state since such "tension follows communal and not territorial lines." [109] In view of the communal controversy over language, the Commission felt that large sections of the Hindu community would continue to demand Hindi as their medium of instruction in any Punjabi Suba. Without going into the merits of the practice of Hindus in the Punjab to declare Hindi as their mother tongue, the Commission realized that "there is no method by which a person can be compelled to adopt a mother tongue other than that for which he himself shows his preference." [110] Under these circumstances, the entire area of any Punjabi Suba would have to continue to be bilingual in that both Punjabi and Hindi would have to be used in education and official business. [111] The Commission noted further that the present sentiment among the Hindus in the Punjab for Hindi could not be said to have been prompted by recent communal tension. In support of this argument, the Commission quoted statistics from university examinations showing the great preference for Hindi over Punjabi, and observed that "motives cannot well be attributed to examinees at university examinations who must have exercised their option on the basis of their own literary needs and family traditions." [112] Summing up its case against Punjabi Suba, the Commission said:

---

[107] *Ibid.*, p. 145. [108] *Ibid.*, pp. 141, 145.
[109] *Ibid.*, p. 146. [110] *Ibid.*, p. 144.
[111] *Loc. cit.* [112] *Loc. cit.*

The case for a Punjabi-speaking State falls, firstly, because it lacks the general support of the people inhabiting the area, and secondly, because it will not eliminate any of the causes of friction from which the demand for a separate Punjabi-speaking State emanates. The proposed State will solve neither the language problem nor the communal problem and, far from removing internal tension, which exists between communal and not linguistic and regional groups, it might further exacerbate the existing feelings.[113]

The Commission's answer to the problem was the creation of a United Punjab through a merger of PEPSU and Himachal Pradesh with the Punjab, and the advice that the communities should learn to live amicably. In making the recommendation for the merger, the Commission was impressed, apart from other considerations, with the natural and economic unity of the area, which it felt had been further strengthened by a common irrigation system.[114] Eventually, in 1956, PEPSU—but not Himachal Pradesh—was merged into the Punjab.

SUMMARY AND CONCLUSIONS

The demand for Punjabi Suba, or a Punjabi-speaking state within the Indian Union, has been made in line with the movement for the linguistic demarcation of states in India. The support for the demand has come largely from the Akali Dal, an organization that claims to be the sole and exclusive representative of the Sikh community. The Hindu community and the Harijans have opposed the demand as they consider it to be an attempt on the part of the Akali Dal to establish Sikh political hegemony, especially in view of many explicit Akali pronouncements to that effect. The nationalist leadership has opposed the demand, perceiving it to be a threat both to the secular state and to national unity in India. At the same time, the opposition to Punjabi Suba on the part of Hindus and

[113] *Ibid.,* p. 146. [114] *Ibid.,* p. 154.

Harijans powerfully suggests that sub-regional loyalties, such as those of religion and caste, can decidedly weaken regional loyalties and, as a result, moderate region-based centrifugal pressures on the center.

Despite the rejection of Punjabi Suba by the States Reorganization Commission and the Indian government, and the opposition to it by the Hindus and Harijans of the Punjab, there has been no let-up in the pursuit of the demand by the Akali Dal. Agitations in support of the demand have kept the state in political turmoil since independence. The intensity with which the Akali Dal has pursued the demand, and the vigorous support it has received from a substantial segment of the Sikh population, raises the question as to what are the basic factors motivating the demand. Why is it so essential for the Akali Dal to acquire a territorial unit in which the Sikhs as a community should wield political power? What, in short, is the background of the Akali demand for Punjabi Suba?

CHAPTER III

Background of Punjabi Suba

THERE seem to be four major factors that provide the basic impulse for the aspiration to political power by the Akali Dal on behalf of the Sikh community through the medium of a Punjabi Suba. These factors are: the nature of the Sikh community as interpreted by leaders, intellectuals and sympathizers of the Akali Dal; the momentum of separatist claims before the partition of India; the fear about the possible disintegration of the Sikh community resulting from religious unorthodoxy; and a sense of grievance about alleged discrimination against the Sikh community.

THE NATURE OF THE SIKH COMMUNITY

Sikhism as a religion has its origins in the religious ferment in the Hinduism of fifteenth-century India. Under the impact of Islam, new schools of thought developed among the Hindus both through the assimilation of certain Islamic ideas, such as the belief in a single God and recognition of the equality of man, and through the resurrection of older ideas with the object of reforming Hinduism to enable it to more effectively meet the Islamic challenge. One new school of thought was the Sikh religion started by Guru Nanak (A.D. 1465–1539), the first Guru of the Sikhs. He was succeeded by nine more Gurus over a period of about two centuries. All ten Gurus came from the Kshatriya caste of the Hindus. Nearly all the followers of the Sikh Gurus came from among the Hindus, especially large numbers from the Jat peasantry in the central Punjab. Though then considered of a caste lower than the Brahmans and Kshatriyas, the Jat Sikhs later acquired political power and became the ruling class and eclipsed in social status the so-called higher castes. The followers of Sikhism are today concentrated in the Punjab where the religion itself had its origins.

Authorities differ as to the influences that worked to create the Sikh religion. Some hold that Sikhism represents a mixture of Hinduism and Islam.[1] Others say that while Sikhism was a a synthesis of Hinduism and Islam, "in its general system of belief it was closer to Islam than Hinduism." [2] Another authority dismisses the idea that Sikhism is a mixture of Hinduism and Islam, and asserts that "although precipitated by Islam, Sikhism owes nothing to that religion. It is, on the other hand, a phase of Hindu religious revival and has in consequence, retained all essential features of real Hinduism." [3] Still another authority, the burden of whose work is the insistence that Sikhism is a new "way of life," distinct from Hinduism and Islam but "aiming at the final synthesis and convergence of both these religious and cultural streams into itself," [4] nonetheless admits that Sikhism accepts Hinduism's "basic philosophic concepts though these concepts are, in some respects, interpreted differently and evaluated otherwise, than in the various cults of Hinduism. Viewed thus, Sikhism is essentially and basically a Hindu religion." [5]

In Sikhism there is belief in the unity of God,[6] though some authors say that the God of Guru Nanak's conception is pantheistic rather than monotheistic.[7] God is equated with truth, and is endowed with the attributes of "omnipresence, omniscience, formlessness, timelessness, and the power to destroy (evil)." [8] The Sikhs believe in the ten Gurus, but there is no belief in divine incarnation. There is no idol worship, but extreme respect is given the *Adi Granth*, the book of the Sikhs. There is great emphasis on the potency of prayer. The equality

---

[1] Charles Eliot, *Hinduism and Buddhism: An Historical Sketch* (London: Routledge and Kegan Paul Ltd., 1921), II, 262–73.

[2] Khushwant Singh, *The Sikhs* (London: George Allen and Unwin Ltd., 1953), p. 45.

[3] Narang, pp. 254–55.

[4] Kapur Singh, *Parasharprasna* (Jullundur: Hind Publishers Ltd., 1959), pp. 8, 31.

[5] *Ibid.*, p. 19.   [6] Khushwant Singh, *The Sikhs,* p. 34.

[7] Narang, p. 258.   [8] Khushwant Singh, *The Sikhs,* p. 35.

of man is emphasized; the caste system is attacked though Sikhism has been unable to get rid of it. Asceticism is rejected, spiritual progress is recommended to be made in a social context, and worldly ambition is held compatible with spiritual success.

The more important aspect of Sikhism is not so much its religious ideas as its social makeup. Initially, the Sikhs were a quiet, pietistic group that later became extremely militant in reaction to the repressive policies pursued by several of the successors of the tolerant Moghul Emperor Akbar. The Moghul rulers publicly executed the ninth Guru (1621–1675). The Sikh crusade against the Muslims was epitomized in the last of the ten Gurus, Guru Gobind Singh (1666–1708), who gave the Sikhs a thoroughgoing military organization, transformed a religious group into a military society to challenge the might of the Moghul Empire, sanctified the use of the sword, and convinced the Sikhs that victory was on their side in this crusade because "the Sikh Khalsa shall rule and its enemies will be scattered."

Guru Gobind Singh laid down a baptismal ceremony for all Sikhs, and required them all to wear on their persons the five distinguishing "K's" as the mark of every true Sikh: (1) the *Kesh,* or unshorn hair; (2) the *Kacchha* (short drawers); (3) the *Kara* (iron bangle); (4) the *Kirpan* (steel dagger); and (5) the *Kanga* (comb). Those who went through the baptism and wore the five K's became members of the order of the Khalsa and recognized Guru Gobind Singh and his wife as their parents. All male members of this order assumed the last name of Singh. Through these actions the tenth Guru tried to create a group distinct from other groups. Finally, Guru Gobind Singh proclaimed that the line of the Gurus shall end with him, and that henceforward the visible body of the Guru shall be present in their book, the Adi Granth, and in the Panth or the organized Sikh community.

The new militancy in the Sikh community, along with the

elaboration of its outward forms and symbols, made for a certain differentiation within the Sikh community. At first, there were the followers of the tolerant and pacifist doctrines propounded by Guru Nanak. These followers considered themselves Sikhs and were faithful to the tenets of the first Guru. Except for their beliefs in the doctrines of Guru Nanak, however, they could not be distinguished physically and socially from the Hindus, with whom they often intermarried and had close social relationships. Many of these Sikhs became members of the order of the Khalsa, established by the tenth Guru, and started wearing the five distinguishing K's; they were now not only Sikhs but Singhs. These Sikhs are known as *Keshadhari* Sikhs, who consider themselves to be the more genuine Sikhs and the term Sikh in practice seems to apply exclusively to them.[9] Members of the other group, who do not wear the five symbols, are known as *Sahajdhari* Sikhs (the slow adopters). The distinction between these two types of Sikhs continues even today.

Apart from constructing a unique military organization out of his followers, the tenth Guru left behind a tradition of undying hostility toward the Muslim rulers. A long struggle between the Sikhs and the Muslims ensued, in which the Sikhs made tremendous sacrifices. Finally, in the mid-eighteenth century the Sikhs became a sovereign power, with several Sikh chiefs ruling over different parts of the Punjab. At the beginning of the nineteenth century, Maharaja Ranjit Singh, who is known as "the Lion of the Punjab" and is often compared with Napoleon, subdued several other Sikh chiefs and brought the northwest of India under his monarchical rule. After his death in 1839, however, the Sikh kingdom became unstable and was finally annexed by the British in 1849 and made part of the British empire. But Sikh rule in the Punjab for about a

[9] The surname of Singh is not confined to the Sikh community; therefore, while all male Keshadhari Sikhs are Singhs, all Singhs are not Sikhs.

century is the basis of strong historical memories among the Sikhs.

An important but unresolved issue in relation to the Sikh religion is its relationship to Hinduism. Among many Hindus there is the common assumption that the Sikhs are merely a part of the Hindu community, just like the Jains, the Arya Samajists and several other sects. Many Hindus maintain that all the ten Sikh Gurus were Hindus who followed Hindu customs and rites in their actual lives. They emphasize that Guru Nanak had no intention of starting a new religion.[10] They even challenge the Sikhs to produce any statement of the Gurus themselves—not the works of historians or observers— that asserts the contrary. According to them, the Gurus made no radical departure from Hinduism but only reformed it in certain respects. They say that the creation of the Khalsa Panth by Guru Gobind Singh was merely the development of an armed wing for the protection of Hinduism and not the creation of a separate religion. The fact that the major part of the hymns in the Adi Granth are by Hindu saints is advanced as proof that the Gurus did not intend any departure from Hinduism; in this manner the Gurus are held to be in the general line of Hindu saints.

Sikh leaders and writers who contest the claim that the Sikhs are a part of the Hindu community, however, are agreed upon the point that, at the time of the arrival of the British in the

[10] See Tara Chand, *Billa Shuba Naveen Sikh Hindu Nahin* [Undoubtedly the New Sikhs Are Not Hindus] (Kotarkhana: Sat Sangh Kutiya, n.d.); Tara Chand, *Sikh Mat Ke Dharam Pustak* [The Religious Scriptures of Sikhism] (Delhi: Punjab National Press, n.d.); and Alakh Dhari, *Case for United Punjab* (Ambala Cantt: Abha Printing Press, 1956), pp. 60–65. See also Eliot, ii, 267–68, who says that Guru Nanak "did not at first claim to teach a new religion" and that "there is no indication that at this time the Sikhs differed from many other religious bodies who reprobated caste and idolatry"; and Khushwant Singh, *The Sikhs*, p. 183, who says: "There is little evidence to support the belief that Guru Nanak planned the founding of a new community synthesizing Hinduism and Islam. He simply planned to reform Hinduism."

Punjab, the Hindu and Sikh communities were very close to each other and were considered as kith and kin. They inter-married, and often in the same family there were members of both faiths. The close relationship between the two communi-ties is attributed to a number of historical causes, but this much is accepted: that the differences between the Hindus and Sikhs did not amount to very much. As one Sikh writer points out, "they worshipped the same old gods and indulged in the same old superstitious practices from which their Gurus had so heroi-cally worked to extricate them. Their baptism and five symbols became a mere anomaly." [11] Whether any different state of affairs, in fact, ever existed earlier remains a matter of contro-versy.

The Singh Sabha Movement

However, after the British conquest, several reform move-ments arose in Sikhism. One of the more important of these was the Singh Sabha movement in the last quarter of the nine-teenth century. The purpose of this movement was "to study the original sources of Sikhism, and to restore it to its pristine purity." [12] The process of reform took the shape of "de-Hindu-ising" the Sikhs, since "the only trouble with Sikhism at that time was that its doctrines and institutions had been completely Hinduised." [13] The movement aimed "to rediscover the pure doctrine and then to preach it to the ignorant masses." [14] As-sociations known as Singh Sabhas were opened in various parts of the Punjab to further the objectives of the movement. The main business of these associations was the holding of weekly meetings where "lectures were delivered against Hindus and their institutions, or debates were held to controvert the attacks of the Arya Samajists." [15] A new literature was developed em-

[11] Teja Singh, *Sikhism: Its Ideals and Institutions* (Lahore: Lahore Book Shop, 1938), p. 97.
[12] Teja Singh, *Essays in Sikhism* (Lahore: Sikh University Press, 1944), p. 119.
[13] *Ibid.*, p.130.   [14] *Loc. cit.*   [15] *Ibid.*, p. 141.

phasizing the distinctive character of Sikhism, including the work known as *Ham Hindu Nahin* (We Are Not Hindus) by Bhai Kahan Singh, which "did more to dehinduise the Sikhs than anything else." [16]

As part of the reform movement, new rites and ceremonies, different from previous Hindu ones, were instituted for the Sikhs. The reformers also opened Sikh schools which provided not only education but "also served as strongholds of Sikhism wherever they were established." [17] The spread of education brought political consciousness among the Sikhs and, together with the particular doctrines disseminated by the Singh Sabha movement, made for demands in the political sphere for the recognition of the Sikhs as a separate community in politics and in law and the grant of rights and privileges to them on that basis.

The Role of the British

Various authorities are in dispute as to the role of the British in the birth of the Singh Sabha movement and its anti-Hindu orientation. Some leaders believe that the British encouraged separatist tendencies among the Sikhs for their own imperial interests.[18] It was natural that the British should look favorably upon any Sikh attempt to assert their separate entity, since the Sikhs had helped the British quell the Indian mutiny in 1857 and thus saved the British empire in India. The growing nationalism in India in the latter part of the nineteenth century also made it a political necessity for the British "that as many elements as possible should be segregated from the general body of Hindus who were responsible for the agitation for political reform in India." [19] Significantly, the rules of the Singh Sabha associations required that no discussion of an anti-government nature should take place at Sabha meetings.[20] Some hold that

[16] *Ibid.*, p. 136.   [17] *Ibid.*, p. 142.
[18] Mangal Singh, "Hindus and Sikhs Are One," *The Tribune,* April 1, 1951.
[19] Teja Singh, *Essays,* p. 129.   [20] *Ibid.*, p. 132.

the Singh Sabha movement would have developed an anti-Hindu character in any case, because any reform of Sikhism could take place only through eliminating Hindu influences.[21] Others believe that the movement itself and its anti-Hindu form took place as a result of the anti-Sikh propaganda by certain sections of the Hindu community, notably the Arya Samaj.[22]

At any rate, the British themselves before long began to draw a distinction between Hindus and Sikhs for official purposes. As one British observer stated in connection with census operations, "at former enumerations village Sikhs in their ignorance generally recorded themselves as Hindus, as indeed they virtually were. With the experience gained by time, a sharp line of demarcation has now been drawn between Sikhs and Hindus."[23] Evidently, then, the British authorities took upon themselves the task of determining what a person's religious classification should be. They, however, went further and provided preferential treatment for members of the Sikh community. In listing the reasons influential in strengthening the power of the Sikh community and preventing its disruption, the Punjab census report of 1891 mentioned, among other things, "the marked preference shown for Sikhs in many branches of government service."[24] This preference for Sikhs in government service was especially noticeable in military recruitment. Although they were less than 2 percent of the Indian population, their proportion in the army at times went up to as high as 33 percent. The premium on recruitment of Sikhs to the army helped in the conversion of many Hindus to Sikhism. One British historian noted: "My experience during 1917

[21] *Ibid.,* p. 130.

[22] Khushwant Singh, *The Sikhs,* p. 98; and Hukam Singh, "Sikh Character and the SGPC Election," *The Spokesman,* ix, No. 30 (Annual Number, 1959), 27.

[23] M. Macauliffe, *A Lecture on the Sikh Religion and Its Advantages to the State* (Simla: Government Central Printing Office [1903]), pp. 27–28.

[24] Quoted in *Census of India,* 1931, xvii, Part 1, 305.

and 1918 in Ludhiana and the adjacent territories was that there was a large number of families of the Hindu zamindar class of which those members who had enlisted in the Army had, as a matter of course, become Sikhs. . . . This developed into any ordinary Hindu of the zamindar class being taken by Sikh Recruiting Officers on condition of his becoming a Sikh. . . . it was almost a daily occurrence for—say—Ram Chand to enter our office and leave it as Ram Singh—Sikh recruit." [25]

In the case of the Sikhs, the British government even made an exception to its traditional policy of religious neutrality. It made the baptismal ceremony a condition for enlistment of Sikhs to the army, because the separate Sikh regiments into which they were organized would then be able "to serve as important agencies for the encouragement and promotion of Sikhism." [26] Sikh soldiers were further required to keep the five external symbols of Sikhism. Because of these various measures implemented by the British, it was noted that "there has been considerable revival of Sikhism." [27] The British believed that "the orthodoxy of a Sikh means loyalty to his sovereign" and that the British government would benefit from "a rigid belief in Sikhism and faith in their Gurus" by the members of the Sikh community.[28] Even outside the military sphere, the British government tried to preserve Sikh traditions. Positions in legislative bodies and in government offices reserved for the Sikh community were allocated to those who adhered to Sikh symbols.[29]

All these measures and privileges were greatly appreciated

[25] H. L. O. Garrett, quoted in India, Census Commissioner, *Census of India 1921* (Lahore: Civil and Military Gazette Press, 1923), xv, Part I, 179.

[26] Remarks by Lieutenant Governor, in M. Macauliffe, *A Lecture,* pp. 28–29.

[27] *Loc. cit.*

[28] M. A. Macauliffe, *The Sikh Religion: A Lecture Delivered Before the Quest Society, at Kensington Town Hall, May 12, 1910* (n.p. [1910]), p. 26.

[29] Khushwant Singh, *The Statesman,* June 18, 1959.

by the Sikhs. "This friendship," comments a Sikh scholar, "put some heart again into Sikhs, and they began to enlist themselves in the British army, where they could keep their baptismal forms intact." [30] But as friendship developed between the British government and the Sikh community, so did friction between the Hindus and Sikhs; at any rate, "the Hindu-Sikh schism in its active form dates from the British annexation of the Punjab." [31] On the intellectual plane, the gulf between the two communities widened, some Hindu leaders allege, as a result of the biased works on Sikh religion and history by Britishers like Macauliffe.

The Akali Movement

Whatever the role of the British during the Singh Sabha movement, the next event which further strained relations between Hindus and Sikhs brought the Sikh community into conflict with the British government. Known as the Gurdwara Reform movement or the Akali movement, it superseded the Singh Sabha movement, especially in the political sphere. The leadership of the Singh Sabha movement had come from the Sikh aristocracy which was sympathetic to the British government. This movement's influence had been confined only to the white-collar Sikhs in the towns, and had not spread to the rural areas.

At the end of World War I, certain sections of the Sikh community felt that radical changes in Sikh rites and ceremonies could be brought about only through a change in the management of Sikh shrines which were at the time, and had been for generations, by and large under the control of Sahajdhari, and not Keshadhari, priests. Furthermore, there was the economic attraction, since these shrines controlled huge properties and vast lands. The leaders of the Akali movement attempted to oust these priests and bring the management of the

[30] Teja Singh, *Sikhism*, p. 97.
[31] Khushwant Singh, *The Sikhs*, p. 184.

gurdwaras (Sikh shrines or temples) under the popular control of the Sikh community. This move created resentment among the Hindus, since it meant not only the removal of priests who served as a bridge between the two communities but also the breaking of Hindu idols and elimination of Hindu elements in worship at Sikh shrines.[32] In the attempt to forcibly evict the priests, the Sikhs ran into conflict with the British government which felt that it was its duty to protect the right of property and to maintain law and order.

The struggle of the Sikh community against the priests and the British government lasted for about five years and developed into a mass movement which spread into the rural areas. Thousands of Sikhs came forward as volunteers to oppose the government and occupy the gurdwaras; "a semi-military organization called the 'Akali dal' (the Akali army) was formed."[33] The formation of the Akali Dal marked the transfer of political leadership from the landed aristocracy to the Sikh middle classes.[34] The Akali Dal superseded the Chief Khalsa Diwan, the organizational expression of the Singh Sabha movement, which until now had attempted to be the sole political organization of the Sikhs.

The Akali movement served to widen the gulf between the Sikhs and Hindus of the Punjab. The Hindu feeling was that shrines, which had hitherto been sacred to and used by both Hindus and Sikhs, were being expropriated by extremist sections of the Sikh community who were anxious to drive a wedge between the two communities. The Sikhs, on the other hand, were equally insistent in separating themselves and their religious institutions from the Hindus. Referring to the question of whether Sikhs were Hindus in the debate over the gurdwaras at the time, Mehtab Singh remarked that "even if it were true, the Sikhs have obtained the rights of separate com-

[32] Vasdev Verma, "Hindu Sikh Ekta" (Hindu Sikh Unity), *Pratap* (Jullundur), December 31, 1961.
[33] Khushwant Singh, *The Sikhs,* p. 109.
[34] *Ibid.,* p. 141.

munal representation," and that "if the Sikhs do not wish to remain in the fold of Hinduism, why should the Hindus seek to force them to do so." He then added that "we wish to manage our own affairs and look after our own gurdwaras and are determined to do so." [35] Eventually, the Punjab legislature passed a law giving the right of management of the Sikh historic gurdwaras to the Sikh community.

Religion, Politics and Nation

The doctrine which is held to be the basic motive force behind the various reform movements in Sikhism and is presented as having a strong hold on the Sikh mind today—at least of those belonging to or sympathizing with the Akali Dal—is that the Sikhs are a separate political entity. According to this doctrine, Sikhism is not a religion like other religions. By religion others understand a relationship between the individual and God, whereas the Sikh religion concerns itself with the whole activity of man in the context of this world.[36] Religion and politics are said to be combined in Sikhism. The sixth Guru wore the two swords of *miri* (worldly power) and *piri* (religious authority). The Akal Takht (the throne of the Timeless One) in the city of Amritsar is the highest seat of both religious and political authority for the Sikhs.[37] Guru Gobind Singh made the Panth supreme in matters both religious and political.[38] According to Master Tara Singh, the Panth is a political organization which has been founded upon religion.[39]

It is further maintained that participation in politics, with the Sikh community acting as a single political group and as a single group alone, is imperative for the existence of the Sikh

[35] *Punjab Legislative Council Debates*, 1 (1921), 545, 584.

[36] Teja Singh, "Religion and Politics," *The Spokesman*, VI, No. 25 (June 25, 1956), 11–12.

[37] Harbans Singh, "Future of Sikhs' Central Political Organization," *The Statesman*, April 4, 1948.

[38] *Loc. cit.*

[39] Master Tara Singh, *Charhdi Kala: Present Sikh Politics No. 2* (Amritsar: Panthic Tract Society, n.d.), p. 46.

religion. Without political organization and participation in politics, the Sikh religion cannot survive. It was precisely for this reason, it is said, that Guru Gobind Singh established the Panth; other than organizing the Sikhs into a political community, he made no change in the Sikh religion as started by Guru Nanak. If the Sikhs were to give up political activity as a community and, as a result, their political organization, the entire Sikh community would be scattered.[40]

Not only is political activity and organization considered essential for the protection of Sikh religion and the prevention of its disintegration, but some hold that participation in politics by the Sikhs as a community is built into Sikh religious ideology. The Panth was created, it is indicated, "for the avowed purpose of facilitating the emergence of the global Fraternity."[41] Being dedicated to this cause, political activity is inherent in the Panth, "and it is in this context that the litany which is repeated in every Sikh congregation, throughout the World, every morning and evening, to the effect that, 'The Khalsa shall rule and none shall defy them' is to be understood and appreciated. The Order of the Khalsa, as divorced from political activity, and not dedicated to the achievement of political ends, aiming at the eventual establishment of universal equalitarian global Fraternity, has no intelligible connotation."[42] Further, it is argued that the Sikh religion requires the Sikh to combine in himself both wisdom and power, in equal measure; hence, the compulsion to obtain "control of the commercial and industrial machine which is the State today, and control of the organized military power, which was the State always."[43] Expressing the same thought in a different way,

[40] *Ibid.*, pp. 3–46. In a foreword to a book by Sarup Singh, *The Forgotten Panth* (Amritsar: The Sikh Religious Book Society, 1945), Master Tara Singh says, "there is not the least doubt that the Sikh religion can live only as long as the Panth exists as an organized entity."

[41] Kapur Singh, p. 40. A former member of the ICS, Kapur Singh has been an adviser of the Akali Dal; in 1962 he was elected a member of parliament on the Akali ticket.

[42] *Ibid.*, p. 41.   [43] *Ibid.*, p. 42.

Master Tara Singh has said that the "Khalsa Panth will either be a ruler or a rebel. It has no third role to play." [44]

Loyalty to the political organization of the Panth has furthermore to be a complete one on the part of Sikhs. A Sikh individual cannot owe loyalty to any other political organization "without violating his loyalty to the first—the Khalsa Panth—of which he is a member as soon as he is born." [45] Master Tara Singh has said, "I am a Sikh first and last" and that nationalism "has a place but in a corner." [46] The Panth, as a whole, may conceivably enter into coalitions with other political organizations "for some common purpose on the basis of honour and equality." However, "a member of the Panth cannot become, over its head, a member of some other body, e.g., the Indian National Congress, without violating his loyalty to the Panth, for their spheres clash—the Panth itself being a religious-cum-political organization of the Sikhs." [47]

From the Panth as an exclusive political organization, with its membership coeval with and confined to the Sikh religious community, the analysis is carried one step further to convert the Panth into a nation. It is proclaimed that "the Khalsa Panth was, based as it was on the common ideology of the Sikh religion, a nation." [48] It is emphasized that the ideology of the Khalsa Panth brings a transformation in its converts, welds them together in "a kinship which transcends distance, territory, caste, social barriers and even race," [49] and through this process of conversion the Sikhs have become a nation.

It is in the context of this interpretation of Sikhism that the Akali Dal seeks some territory in which the Sikhs as a community exercise political power. And it is this same interpretation

[44] *Hindusthan Standard,* July 4, 1958. See also Master Tara Singh, "The Sikh Will Be Either Ruler or Rebel," *Prabhat,* March 14, 1963.

[45] Sarup Singh, p. 20. Sarup Singh was an active and prominent Akali leader until 1961 when he was expelled from the Akali Dal because of differences with Tara Singh. He also served as vice-president of the Akali Dal.

[46] *Hindusthan Standard,* March 30, 1959.

[47] Sarup Singh, p. 20.   [48] *Ibid.,* p. 10.   [49] *Loc. cit.*

that explains the Akali hostility to the secular state and to the idea that Sikhs should be members of other political organizations.

Hindu-Sikh Relations

The assertion that the Sikhs are a separate political entity was and is aimed primarily at distinguishing them from the Hindus. While the Hindus continue to emphasize, outwardly at least, that the Sikhs are a part of the Hindus, the sentiment is but rarely reciprocated. On the contrary, "nothing provokes the Sikhs so much as this description of the Sikhs as merely Hindus." [50] The Sikh considers not only that "to call him a Hindu is to insult him," but also finds that "the expression of such affection is nauseating." [51] The Hindus, for their part, make fun of the Sikhs, especially their external forms and symbols. A century of political developments, whether the work of Hindu or Sikh reformist movements, has thus brought about the result that the Hindu and Sikh communities, which in the middle of the nineteenth century were so closely linked, socially and culturally, have drifted widely apart.

At the same time, however insistent the emphasis on the part of some that the Sikhs are a separate political entity, with nothing in common with the Hindus, there is a certain dilemma present in the situation. It may or may not be true that Guru Nanak intended to create a new religion. Yet, even those who have argued that Sikhism is a new way of life have recognized that the basic philosophical postulates of Sikhism are those of Hinduism,[52] and the Adi Granth contains the works of many Hindu saints. So the dilemma between the urge to mark out a distinctive path, on one hand, and the earlier development of Sikhism, on the other, frequently manifests itself

[50] Gurbachan Singh and Lal Singh Gyani, *The Idea of the Sikh State* (Lahore: Lahore Book Shop, 1946), pp. 27–28.
[51] Sadhu Swarup Singh, *The Sikhs Demand Their Homeland* (Lahore: Lahore Book Shop, 1946), pp. 19–20.
[52] Kapur Singh, pp. 8, 31.

on a personal level when one's judgment of the works of the Gurus contradicts the contemporary doctrine that the Sikhs are separate from the Hindus,[53] and in intermittent public statements by Sikh leaders that Sikhs are Hindus. When tension between the two communities builds up, appeals are issued for Hindu-Sikh unity by references to their belonging to the same religion, tradition, and culture. In 1956, for example, an appeal, signed among others by Baldev Singh, stated that "the Sikh Panth was brought into being by the Gurus as a branch of Hindu Dharma for the defence and protection of the Hindu culture. In fact Hindus and Sikhs are at the root one and are like twin brothers. They interdine, intermarry, have all social relations with each other, have common culture and customs, have common shrines and temples." [54] In another statement, the Maharaja of Patiala declared that Hindus and Sikhs were "inextricably intermingled." [55] On one occasion, when stressing the need for Hindu-Sikh unity, even Master Tara Singh said, "the Sikhs are Hindus and I feel they are so. But I do not say so, as in that case the Hindus would absorb the Sikhs." [56] At election time, Akali candidates tell Hindu audiences that there is no difference between Hindus and Sikhs except that the Sikhs wear unshorn hair.

On the other hand, the movement to separate the Sikhs from the Hindus has developed a momentum of its own and resolves the dilemma by a complete repudiation of any connection between the two communities. Some Sikh leaders suggest that every Sikh should take "a vow not to say hereafter that the Sikh and the Hindu cultures are the same," for "he who still persists in saying so is either a case of incomplete conversion from, or a case of backsliding and reconversion to, Hinduism." [57]

[53] See Diwan Singh Maftoon, *Naqable Framosh* [Unforgettable] (Delhi: Diwan Singh Maftoon, 1957), pp. 611–14.

[54] *The Tribune*, July 27, 1956.

[55] *Ibid.*, July 29, 1956.   [56] *Ibid.*, July 31, 1956.

[57] Ambalvi, *Sikh Students' Bulletin*, v, Nos. 10–11, 9.

Despite the inherent dilemma, and regardless of the way in which it is resolved, the twentieth century has seen the two communities pull further apart. The result of the Sikh reform movements was to put the social relations between Hindus and Sikhs on a one-sided basis. Hindus went to Sikh shrines, not Sikhs to Hindu temples; Hindus hung pictures of Sikh Gurus in their homes, not Sikhs of Rama and Krishna; Hindus became converts to the Sikh religion, those who left Sikhism were declared "apostates"; Sikhs married Hindu girls, rarely were Sikh girls married to Hindus; Hindu families brought up some of their children as Sikhs, not the other way round. However, under the impact of more recent Sikh and Hindu agitations, even this one-sided relationship has, by and large, come to an end. Hindus, even Sahajdhari Sikhs, now refrain from going to Sikh shrines because of their highly politicized condition.[58] No more Hindus, including Harijans, become converts to Sikhism; the process of conversion to Sikhism from among Hindus in the Punjab has come to a halt. No more do Hindu families raise some of their children as Sikhs. Even Keshadhari Sikhs and Hindus in the same family have drawn further apart.

Recognizing the serious consequences that have resulted for Hindu-Sikh relations, and more especially for government-Sikh relations, from the pursuit of the ideal of the Panth as a separate political entity, some Sikh leaders have in recent years criticized this concept. They have no objection to the Sikh community having a single organization dealing solely with religious affairs, but they feel that in the political sphere its presence will lead to dangerous consequences. The submission of Sikhs to one political ideology, they say, will mean not only the isolation and estrangement of the Sikh community from other communities, but will also work "havoc" within the Sikh community itself by stopping all independent thinking.[59] Some

[58] Hukam Singh, *The Spokesman*, ix, No. 30 (1959), 27.
[59] Lal Singh, "Separation of Religion from Politics," *The Hindustan Times*, August 20, 1956. See also the several statements by Gian Singh

of these leaders point out that the combination of religion and politics in Sikhism was a relevant solution in the specific times in which it was evolved, but in the changed times of today, with a secular state, it is no longer necessary to keep religion and politics together.[60] This was recognized by some even before the partition, when Principal Teja Singh, realizing that if the Sikh Panth really acted in political affairs it would immediately come into clash with the secular political authority, advocated the idea that the Panth should pass a resolution confining its activities to the religious sphere only.[61] In 1956, in fact, the Akali Dal did pass a resolution declaring that it would no longer participate in political activities, but soon after repudiated its decision in practice.

Implications for Punjabi Suba

The basic doctrine of the Akali Dal has thus been that religion and politics are inextricably combined in Sikhism and that the Sikhs are a separate political entity. The exposition of this doctrine at times goes hand in hand with the demand for Punjabi Suba on a linguistic basis. This is evidenced, among other things, in one of the pamphlets [62] widely distributed at Akali conferences supporting the demand for the establishment of Punjabi Suba, prepared in 1960 by the legal adviser to the Akali Dal. In the second chapter, on "The Theopolitical Status of the Golden Temple," the author tries to establish firmly that (1) "there is no ultimate dichotomy in the true Sikh doctrine between this world and the next, the secular and the religious, the political and the spiritual," and (2) the metalegal constitu-

---

Rarewala in 1956, including those in *The Statesman,* June 14, 1956, and *The Tribune,* June 15, 1956.

[60] Hukam Singh, *The Spokesman,* IX, No. 30 (1959), 27.

[61] Teja Singh, *Sikhism,* pp. 58–60. Sarup Singh draws the opposite conclusion: that in order to avoid the clash the Sikhs should have a sovereign state. Sarup Singh, p. 19.

[62] Gurnam Singh, pp. 11, 12–13, 17. Gurnam Singh was elected in 1962 to the Punjab Vidhan Sabha on the Akali ticket and then became leader of the Akali party in the legislature.

tion of the Sikhs prescribes that "they must be approached and dealt with at state level as a collective group and entity" and "not by atomising them into individual citizens."

However, this ideological position of the Akali leaders not unexpectedly raises a doubt in the minds of the Hindus who would be included in the Punjabi Suba as to the nature of the state the Akali Dal aspires for. The advocates of Punjabi Suba hold that it will be a political unit not unlike any other state organized on a linguistic basis in India, and charge that the Hindus display a narrow communal mentality in opposing a demand which is in accord with nationally recognized principles. But the advocates of the Punjabi Suba are also the ones that maintain that the Panth must act as a united group in politics. As a consequence, the Hindus feel that in a state where one religious community acts as a united group and does not even allow its members the freedom, as individuals, to join other political groups, there could be only one result if such a religious community were politically powerful—the imposition of its rule, as a religious-cum-political community, over other religious communities. Whether such a state is in accordance with the letter and spirit of the constitution or not may be debatable. But perhaps the doctrinal basis of the Akali Dal provides a clue to the determined opposition of the Hindus in the Punjab—granting for the moment that the demand is tenable on a linguistic basis—to the formation of Punjabi Suba. Further, the Hindus do not put much faith in a probable abdication of the political role of the Panth by the Akali Dal, pointing out that in the past it has only been a momentary commitment, a maneuver made only to drive a hard bargain.

The Pre-Independence Legacy of the Akali Dal

If the particular doctrine of the separate political entity of the Sikhs is intimately connected with the contemporary demand of the Akali Dal for Punjabi Suba, the demand itself has not emerged suddenly full-blown on the political scene in the post-independence period in India. In fact, the demand for Punjabi Suba flows out of the pre-independence pattern of political claims made by the Akali Dal in behalf of the Sikh community. Again, the persistence and the vigor with which the demand has been pursued is related to the hopes raised and the passions aroused among the Sikhs through separatist claims before independence, as also to the disappointment resulting from the rejection of such claims. On the other hand, if the demand for Punjabi Suba is connected with separatist claims before 1947, the opposition to Punjabi Suba, too, is explained by the memory of those claims in the past.

Prelude to Azad Punjab

Even though the Akali movement in the 1920s meant increasing friction between the Hindu and Sikh communities in the Punjab, yet, insofar as it became an anti-government movement, it received the sympathies and support of the nationalist leadership and the Congress party. When the Congress party launched its own non-cooperation movement against the British government in the 1920s, the Akali movement began to be considered a part of it although the specific purpose of the Akali movement was to bring the shrines under the control of the Sikh community. A reciprocal relationship thus developed between the two movements: the Akali movement became a part of the nationalist movement and, in return, received the blessings of the Congress leadership in its objectives.

As a result of this association in the early 1920s, the Akali Dal—which emerged as a para-military political organization during the Akali movement—although careful to maintain its separate organization, continued to lend support to the Congress party in the freedom movement against the British empire. At the same time, the Akali Dal functioned as a pressure group for the Sikh community in relation to the Congress party; for instance, it opposed the report of the Nehru Committee because it considered it not particularly advantageous for the Sikhs. For its part, the Congress party, while receiving support from the Akali Dal, aggregated and channeled Sikh demands as part of the nationalist demands. Thus, in 1929, at its session in Lahore, the Congress party acceded to the demand that it should not agree to a constitution which was not acceptable to the Sikh community. While cooperating with the Congress party, the Akali Dal engaged independently in political activity to secure political privileges specifically for the Sikh community. Here it felt that the Muslim community in the pre-partition Punjab was the main block to its program of greater representation for the Sikh community in the Punjab legislature.

Earlier, following the turn of the century, as increasing emphasis was being placed on the separate political entity of the Sikhs, demands were made for separate and weighted representation for the Sikh community in the services as well as in the representative bodies. Under the Montagu–Chelmsford Reforms of 1919, the Sikhs were given separate electorates and representation in the Punjab legislature to the extent of 18½ percent of the total number of seats even though they were only 13 percent of the total population of undivided Punjab.[63] The Muslims, who were in a slight majority of 55 percent in the population, received reserved representation of 50 percent in the legislature. The Hindus, who were a little over 30 percent of the population, received about the same share in the legislature as they had in the population.

This allocation of seats, however, did not satisfy the Sikh community. Sikh organizations and Sikh representatives at various conferences and in representations to various commissions continued to urge for an even greater representation for the Sikh community. More specifically, they wanted an allocation of seats in the Punjab legislature which would give the

[63] Great Britain, Indian Statutory Commission, *Memorandum Submitted by the Government of the Punjab* (London: His Majesty's Stationery Office, 1930), x, 18.

Sikhs 30 percent of the seats, the Hindus 30 percent, and the Muslims 40 percent.[64] Above all, they were interested in preventing the Muslims from having a majority in the legislature. At the same time, they assured the Muslims that the latter had nothing to fear from a combination against them of other groups in the legislature for "the Sikhs have hitherto thrown in their lot more often with Mahomedans than with Hindus, especially as their interests, as a rural and agricultural community, have coincided with those of the Mahomedans." [65] The Muslims, however, were strongly opposed to any such proposition. They insisted that a majority community in the population should not be made a statutory minority in the legislature. Further, they maintained "that the distinction which of late has been drawn for political purposes between Hindus and Sikhs is non-existent" and "artificial," that the Hindus and Sikhs belonged to the same community, and that together they constituted such a large minority of about 45 percent in the population that they did not merit special safeguards.[66]

Finally, in 1932, when the British government made another decision on the allocation of seats through the Communal Award, the result was the establishment of a statutory majority for the Muslims in the Punjab legislature. The Sikhs received representation to the extent of 19 percent of the seats in the legislature.[67] However, the Akali Dal, which by this time had become the major force in Sikh politics, was dissatisfied with this arrangement, and it now agitated for a solution that would

[64] Great Britain, Indian Statutory Commission, *Selections from Memoranda and Oral Evidence by Non-Officials,* xvi, Part i, 135–47. The oral evidence was presented by several important Sikh leaders, including Sir Sunder Singh Majithia, Teja Singh, and Jodh Singh.

[65] *Ibid.,* p. 137.

[66] Oral evidence by the deputation of the All India Muslim League, *ibid.,* p. 125.

[67] Maurice Gwyer and A. Appadorai, *Speeches and Documents on the Indian Constitution, 1921–47* (Bombay: Oxford University Press, 1957), I, 261–65.

give the Sikhs an even larger representation and at the same time rescind the Muslim majority in the legislature.

During the 1930s the Akali Dal strongly opposed not only the Muslim League, which frankly stood for Muslim interests, but also the Unionist party which the Akali Dal considered to be promoting primarily Muslim interests under the cover of a secular economic program oriented toward the rural areas. It was bitterly critical of any Sikhs who associated with the Unionist party. In 1937, when another Sikh political organization joined with the Unionist party to form a ministry in the Punjab, the Akali Dal immediately characterized its leaders as "traitors" and "enemies" of the Sikh Panth.[68] Afterwards, the Akali Dal continued its determined opposition to the Unionist government and mounted a vigorous agitation against it.

After the elections of 1937, which the Akali Dal contested as a separate political group, the Dal aligned itself more closely with the Congress party and even asked its members to join the Congress. Many of its functionaries came to occupy important positions in the Congress organization. It is alleged by some that the Akali Dal joined the Congress at this time in order to use the Congress party machinery for its own purposes.[69] Be that as it may, the Akali Dal's policy first of cooperation and then of collaboration with the Congress party continued until 1939, when differences began to develop and the Dal moved away from the Congress.

As World War II started in 1939, political events in India and in the Punjab began to move at a rapid pace. When India was declared a belligerent country by the British government, the Indian nationalist leaders were indignant at the declaration being made without any consultation with them, and the provincial ministries headed by the Congress party resigned from

[68] Hira Singh Dard, *Panth: Dharam te Rajniti* [Panth: Religion and Politics] (Jullundur: Phulwari Office, 1949), p. 43.

[69] From an interview with a prominent political leader who was active both in the Akali Dal and the Congress party in the 1930s.

office in protest. Since the nationalist leaders and the British government could not reach any agreement whereby the Indian leaders could play an honorable part in the war effort, the Congress party decided to pursue a policy of non-cooperation with the British government.

At this time, Master Tara Singh was a member of the working committee of the Punjab Congress party and of the All India Congress Committee. Despite the official policy of the Congress not to extend any cooperation to the war effort, Master Tara Singh met with the British Viceroy of India in October 1939,[70] then resigned from the Congress party and actively engaged in the recruitment of Sikhs to the British army in India through the Khalsa Defense of India League. His rationale was that if Sikh recruitment to the army suffered at this time, the future political influence of the Sikh community would decrease.[71] One biographer of his says that if "in the intoxication of nationalism," Tara Singh had boycotted Sikh recruitment to the army then "the Sikh position today would have been nil." [72] Master Tara Singh has never regretted his role during the war,[73] but the nationalists considered that role as "anti-nationalist."

Although Tara Singh himself resigned from the Congress party he did not ask other Akali leaders to resign nor did he press the Akali Dal organization to change its policy toward the Congress.[74] When the Congress started its civil disobedience movement in 1940, many Akali workers are stated to have taken part in it. But, steadily, Tara Singh and his organization

[70] Giani Raghubans Singh Chopra, *Punjabi Sube Ka Masla* [The Problem of Punjabi Suba] (Amritsar: Risala "Panch Bhoomi," n.d.), p. 15.

[71] Giani Gurcharan Singh, *Ankhi Soorma: Jiwan Master Tara Singh Ji* [Life of Master Tara Singh] (Delhi: Sikh Literature Distributors, 1950), pp. 126–31; see also Master Tara Singh, *Meri Yaad* [My Memory] (Amritsar: Sikh Religion Book Society, 1945), pp. 129–49.

[72] Giani Gurcharan Singh, p. 129.

[73] See the interview by Master Tara Singh on the occasion of his 78th birthday, in *Prabhat,* June 24, 1962.

[74] Giani Gurcharan Singh, p. 127.

moved further away from the nationalist organization. Not only did he and several of his other lieutenants in the Akali Dal support the British government in the war effort, they also joined hands with those whom they had considered as their "enemies" a few years earlier. They now arrived at a settlement —known as the Sikander–Baldev Singh Pact—with the Unionist party, and one of the Akali leaders, Baldev Singh, was included as a minister in the Unionist government.

When the Congress party launched the Quit India movement in 1942, there were two opposing factions in the Akali Dal: one, headed by Giani Kartar Singh, favored a policy of active cooperation with the British government; the other, under the leadership of Udham Singh Nagoke, wanted to extend support to the nationalist movement and the Congress party.[75] Master Tara Singh is stated to have been in a dilemma as to which group he should support, but finally decided to prohibit the Akali Dal from participation in the Quit India movement on a party basis, although allowing followers of the Nagoke group to take part in the movement if they so desired.[76] Later, the Akali Dal entered into an agreement with the Muslim League, whom it had so determinedly opposed in the past.[77] One of the members of the Akali Dal, Ajit Singh Sarhadi, became a minister in the Muslim League ministry in the North-Western Frontier Province. These activities of the Akali Dal caused deep bitterness in nationalist ranks, and one veteran Congress leader was moved to write: "There is one party in the Punjab who always gained advantages through their connection with the Congress party but who betrayed it during 1942–45. I mean the Akali Party. This Party and some of their

[75] *Ibid.*, p. 137. One writer, who had been active in the Akali movement and had continued his contacts within the Akali Dal organization, alleges that these groups were a deliberate creation on the part of the Akali Dal in order to secure political advantages for the organization from both the British government and the Congress party. See Dard, pp. 43–44.

[76] Giani Gurcharan Singh, p. 134.

[77] *Ibid.*, p. 137.

notable leaders preached hatred against Mahatma Gandhi and
the Congress and gained paltry advantages at the cost of honour
and patriotism, at the hands of the Government and the Authorities that were out to crush the Congress." [78]

Meanwhile, as the estrangement deepened between the Akali
Dal and the Congress party, the Muslim League stridently
pushed forward its separatist claims on behalf of the Muslim
community. In 1940, at its session in Lahore, the Muslim
League passed what came to be known as the "Pakistan Resolution" in which it demanded a separate sovereign state for the
Muslims in India. The Punjab formed the linchpin of this
scheme of Pakistan. Though the Muslims were only a little
more than half the population of the Punjab, and were largely
concentrated in its western districts, the Muslim League demanded the inclusion of the whole province in Pakistan.

With the growing popularity of the demand for Pakistan
among Indian Muslims, the Akalis, too, began to look for some
political arrangement that would secure a favorable political
position for the Sikhs. This became especially necessary in
view of its estrangement from the Congress party.

Azad Punjab

In 1942 Sir Stafford Cripps came to India for negotiations
with Indian political leaders on the Indian constitutional problem. But the Cripps Mission ended in failure because of the
deadlock among the chief parties concerned—the British government, the Congress party, and the Muslim League. Nevertheless, the proposals of the Cripps Mission constituted the
first official acceptance on the part of the British government
of the principle of Pakistan insofar as they gave the provinces
in India the right of non-accession to an Indian federation
which was proposed to be established at the end of World War

[78] Duni Chand, *Congress Service Series: Events of 1937 to 1946* (Indore: Bhargava Fine Art Printing Works, 1946), p. 3.

II.[79] At the same time, the Congress party also seemed to have conceded the principle involved in the demand for Pakistan, since its working committee had resolved that it "cannot think in terms of compelling the people of any territorial unit to remain in an Indian Union against their declared and established will." [80]

These developments greatly perturbed the Akali leaders, who now formulated what is known as the "Azad Punjab" (Free Punjab) scheme in order to secure greater political leverage for the Sikh community. In its conception, the scheme was not new since similar proposals had, in the early 1930s, been presented before the Round Table Conference in London and in deputations to the Viceroy and to Mahatma Gandhi.[81] However, the designation of Azad Punjab was new and so was the strident agitation in support of it. In essence, the Azad Punjab scheme involved a redemarcation of the boundaries of the Punjab so as to detach the Muslim majority districts from the Punjab and to create a new province Azad Punjab, in which the maximum of Sikh population would be included and no single religious community would have a majority. It should be noted that in the pre-partition Punjab, the western districts of the province were overwhelmingly Muslim, while the eastern districts were overwhelmingly Hindu. The Sikhs were concentrated in the central districts but nowhere in these districts did they command a majority; the population of these districts was about equally divided among the three religious groups.

In June 1943, the Akali Dal, meeting under the presidentship of Master Tara Singh, elaborated on the Azad Punjab scheme. It issued a statement which said, in part:

[79] Coupland, Part II, pp. 262–86.   [80] *Ibid.*, p. 279.
[81] Tangh, pp. 6–7, and Gurbachan Singh and Lal Singh Gyani, *The Idea of the Sikh State,* p. 6. Ujjal Singh presented the proposal before the second session of the Round Table Conference; the deputation to Gandhi included Master Tara Singh and Principal Jodh Singh; and the deputation to the Viceroy was led by Sir Sunder Singh Majithia.

In this connection, the Shromani Akali Dal hereby declares
that in the Azad Punjab the boundaries shall be fixed after
taking into consideration the population, property, land revenue and historical traditions of each of the communities . . .
if the new demarcations are effected on the above-mentioned
principles then the Azad Punjab shall comprise of Ambala,
Jullundur, Lahore Divisions and out of the Multan Division
Lyallpur District, some portion of Montgomery and Multan
Districts. The Shromani Akali Dal shall make its demand of
these demarcations and shall fight for the same.[82]

The Akali Dal published in 1943 a short pamphlet [83] in
which the demand for Azad Punjab was explained in greater
detail. The author of this pamphlet said that the primary purpose in the formation of Azad Punjab was "to break" the Muslim majority in the Punjab and to create a province where the
Sikhs should hold the "balance of power." He believed that in
such a province—formed after the exclusion of Muslim-majority
districts—the Muslims would be only 40 percent of the population and the Hindus another 40 percent, while the Sikhs—of
whom the maximum number was to be included—with a population of 20 percent, were to serve as the balancer between
the other two communities. The Sikhs would have the alternative of combining either with the Hindus or the Muslims
and thus be able to maximize their political advantages. He
further mentioned that in course of time the Sikh princely
states would be merged in the Punjab, and this would raise
the Sikh percentage in the population of Azad Punjab to 24
percent. Again, he noted that the Sikh population had been
increasing quite rapidly, and so shortly the Sikh proportion in
the population might reach as high as 30 percent, which would
be even more beneficial for the Sikh community.[84]

82 *The Indian Annual Register, 1943*, I, 298.
83 Tangh, pp. 16–21.
84 *Ibid.*, p. 22.

The demand of the Akali Dal for Azad Punjab was opposed by the "nationalist" Sikhs, as also by the leaders of the Hindu community and the Hindu daily press. At several conferences in 1943, Baba Kharak Singh, the veteran Sikh leader, criticized the demand for Azad Punjab and asked the Sikh community to support the Congress. He felt there was no distinction between Pakistan and Azad Punjab and that both schemes involved the vivisection of India, and destruction of Indian unity and integrity.[85] He also charged that Jinnah and Master Tara Singh were both sailing in the same boat as agents of British imperialism, and that Azad Punjab would be suicidal for the country, the Panth, and the Punjab.[86] For their part, Akali leaders bitterly criticized all those who opposed the Azad Punjab scheme. In 1943 the Akali Dal passed a resolution condemning the Hindu press of the Punjab, while one Akali member "delivered a tirade against the Hindus in general and the Arya Samajists in particular." [87] However, militant as Akali support for Azad Punjab was, this particular scheme was soon overtaken by the march of events and even more extreme Akali demands.

Prelude to Demand for a Sikh State

As a result of the Quit India movement, most of the top important leaders of the Congress party had been thrown into jail. Meanwhile, the Muslim League became a mass movement among the Muslims as a result of its adoption of the demand for Pakistan. It now became a political force to reckon with. Some form of compromise on the basis of the demand for Pakistan seemed necessary if any progress was to be made toward the goal of Indian independence.

Working on this assumption, one Congress leader, C. Rajagopalachari, devised a formula under which the Muslim League would support the demand of the Congress for independence for India at the end of World War II, and the Con-

[85] *The Indian Annual Register, 1943*, I, 295.
[86] *Ibid.*, II, 300.   [87] *Loc. cit.*

gress for its part would agree to the establishment of a commission to demarcate contiguous Muslim-majority districts—not Muslim-majority provinces which formed the basis of the demand for Pakistan—in northwest and northeast India as a solution of the demand of the Muslim League for Pakistan. Rajagopalachari obtained Gandhi's approval of this formula and then entered into discussions and correspondence with Jinnah, who finally rejected the formula since it gave him only "a shadow and a husk, a maimed, mutilated and moth-eaten Pakistan." [88]

The Rajagopalachari formula nonetheless immediately created apprehensions among the Hindus and Sikhs in the Punjab province, which would be divided into two parts, one consisting of Muslim-majority districts and the other of Hindu-majority districts, but each with considerable minorities. The Sikhs were now confronted with a proposal that would split their community into almost two equal parts, one in Pakistan and the other in India. The Akali Dal therefore strongly opposed the acceptance of such a formula involving the partition of the Punjab, and at the same time condemned and criticized Gandhi as well as the Congress party for being associated with the formula. The breach between the Akali Dal and the Congress party widened further.

An All-Parties Sikh Conference, dominated largely by pro-Akali elements, held in Amritsar in August 1944, asked Master Tara Singh to appoint a committee to go into the question of an independent Sikh state.[89] In a speech at this conference Tara Singh declared that the Sikhs were a nation and if there was going to be a division of the country then they should not be made slaves of Pakistan or Hindustan.[90] At the same conference, Giani Kartar Singh also asked for an independent state for the Sikhs, and said that no appeals should now be made to

[88] V. P. Menon, *The Transfer of Power in India* (Princeton: Princeton University Press, 1957), p. 163.

[89] *The Indian Annual Register*, 1944, II, 212.

[90] *Ibid.*, p. 213.

the Sikhs in the name of India as there would be no such thing after the partition of the country.[91]

One of the important landmarks in the relations between the Shiromani Akali Dal and the Congress party during this period is the fifth session of the All India Akali Conference held at Lahore in October 1944. Speaking at the conference, Master Tara Singh declared that there were two dangers to the Sikh community, one from the Communists and the other from Gandhi and Jinnah. He warned his community to beware of both the dangers which were "strong storms blowing against us." [92] He said that, while the Sikhs were opposed to the British who had deprived them of their freedom, they were also opposed to "tyrants" like Gandhi and Jinnah who wanted to impose Hindu and Muslim dominance over the Sikhs by splitting up India.[93] He, however, expressed willingness to return to the Congress, provided Gandhi was deprived of all his positions in the party.[94]

At the same conference, Giani Kartar Singh gave a speech, which one newspaper characterized as an "impeachment" of Gandhi, in which he used the strongest epithets in criticizing Gandhi for the "great sin" he had committed in "going back from his word given to the Sikhs" and treating them with "such disrespect and discourtesy" as they had not experienced in the last century.[95] He is stated to have excelled even Jinnah in the manner he poured ridicule on Gandhi and other Congress leaders for their "injustice" to the Sikhs.[96] The president of the Akali Dal at the time, Jathedar Pritam Singh, announced that Gandhi would sell the Sikhs to Jinnah,[97] and demanded an independent state for the Sikhs.

[91] *Ibid.*, p. 214.
[92] *Ibid.*, p. 218.
[93] *Loc. cit.*
[94] *Ibid.*, p. 221.
[95] *Ibid.*, p. 218.
[96] *Loc. cit.*
[97] *Ibid.*, p. 219.

The Demand for a Sikh State (Sikhistan)

Meanwhile, World War II came to an end, and the British government sought again to reach some solution to the Indian problem. The Viceroy of India called a conference at Simla in 1945 to which were invited most of the important Indian political leaders, including the Congress leaders who had now been released from jail. Master Tara Singh attended the conference on behalf of the Akali Dal. At the discussions of the Simla conference, Tara Singh is stated to have said that the Sikhs did not "identify themselves with the Congress though insofar as the Congress favored India's freedom they were in sympathy with it." [98] He believed Pakistan to be a greater danger for the Sikhs than for the other communities, but was "quite prepared to agree to Pakistan if Jinnah on his part would agree to a separate state for the Sikhs." [99] However, the Simla conference also ended in failure, as the Muslim League and the Congress could not come to any agreement.

As it became more and more clear that a settlement between the British government, the Congress party, and the Muslim League would have to be reached on the basis of some form of Pakistan, the Akali leaders began to press more and more for a sovereign Sikh state, variously called "Sikhistan" and "Khalistan." In a memorandum submitted by 29 Sikh leaders [100] to the non-official Sapru Committee, the Sikh leaders stated that they favored a united India under several conditions being met in the Punjab. However, despite their opposition to Pakistan, these leaders insisted "on the creation of a separate Sikh State," in case Pakistan was conceded. [101] This goal was later officially adopted by the Akali Dal on March 22, 1946 through a resolution of its executive committee, which stated:

[98] Menon, p. 197.   [99] *Ibid.*, p. 212.
[100] Among the signatories were Master Tara Singh, Principal Jodh Singh, Giani Kartar Singh, Swaran Singh, Ujjal Singh, and Isher Singh Majhail. See *Constitutional Proposals of the Sapru Committee.*
[101] *Ibid.*, p. lx.

Whereas the Sikhs being attached to the Punjab by intimate bonds of holy shrines, property, language, traditions, and history claim it as their homeland and holy land which the British took as a "trust" from the last Sikh ruler during his minority and whereas the entity of the Sikhs is being threatened on account of the persistent demand of Pakistan by the Muslims on the one hand and of danger of absorption by the Hindus on the other, the executive committee of the Shiromani Akali Dal demands for the preservation and protection of the religious, cultural, and economic and political rights of the Sikh nation, the creation of a Sikh state which would include a substantial majority of the Sikh population and their sacred shrines and historical gurdwaras with provision for the transfer and exchange of population and property.

In the same year, in a memorandum [102] to the Cabinet Mission, which had been sent to India by the British government, the Akali Dal preferred a united India, because any partition of India would either bring the Sikh community under Muslim rule or split it into two halves. It demanded, however, that the statutory majority given to the Muslims in the Punjab legislature should be removed and that the Sikhs should be given increased representation in the legislature. Alternatively, if this were not acceptable, the Akali Dal asked, re-echoing the Azad Punjab scheme, for the creation of a new province out of the territories of the Punjab. But in case Pakistan was formed, then the Sikhs must have an independent state of their own.

Although the Cabinet Mission recognized that the Sikhs were the third important community in India, its proposals really aimed at a settlement between the Muslim League and the Congress party. The Cabinet Mission rejected any proposal

[102] Memorandum submitted by Master Tara Singh to the Cabinet Mission, in Gwyer and Appadorai, ii, 624–26.

for the division of India, but suggested instead a confederation type of constitutional system consisting of three tiers—provinces, "groups of provinces," and a very weak center. Three groups of provinces were involved, of which two were Muslim-majority groups, one on the northwest and the other on the northeast of India. The whole of the Punjab was included in the northwest Muslim-majority group, no special weightage was given to the minorities, and representation was granted on the basis of the relative numerical strength of the communities. As part of the long-term arrangements, a Constituent Assembly was to be established for the drafting of a constitution for India. As for the short-term arrangements, an interim government was to be formed consisting of representatives of the major political parties.

These proposals placed the Hindus and Sikhs of the Punjab, without what they considered sufficient safeguards, in the Muslim-majority province of Punjab and in the Muslim-majority northwest group of provinces. As a consequence, the two communities were opposed to the proposals. Master Tara Singh felt that under such a constitutional arrangement the future of the Sikhs was doomed.[103] However, it was not so much that the Cabinet Mission had not wanted to evolve an arrangement whereby the Sikhs would get the kind of treatment given to the Muslims, as that the demographic compulsions of the situation made it difficult for the Mission to evolve any special proposal for the Sikhs. Sir Stafford Cripps, a member of the Cabinet Mission, explained the issue thus to the parliament in July 1946: "The difficulty arises, not from anyone's under-estimate of the importance of the Sikh community, but from the inescapable geographical facts of the situation . . . it will be seen that what they demand is some special treatment analogous to that given to the Muslims. The Sikhs, however, are a much smaller community, 5½ as against 90 millions, and, moreover, are not geographically situated so that any area as yet

103 Menon, p. 272.

devised—I do not put it out of possibility that one may be devised in the future—can be carved out in which they would find themselves in a majority." [104]

Meanwhile, to voice their protest against the proposals of the Cabinet Mission, about 800 representatives of the Sikh community in north India met in Amritsar in June 1946 in a highly belligerent mood. Appealing to the Sikhs "to stand united in this grave hour for the Sikh Panth," Master Tara Singh asked them "to prepare to die in the struggle ahead." [105] The conference condemned the Cabinet Mission proposals and appointed a "council of action" so as "to give a tough fight to the British government." [106] Tara Singh announced that the Akali Dal would enter into negotiations with the other political parties before launching any struggle, and added that "the Congress and the Muslim League are the two parties concerned." [107]

It seems, however, that negotiations between the leaders of the Akali Dal and the Muslim League had in fact started long before this announcement was made. Lord Birdwood writes: "The understanding was that if the Muslim League succeeded in establishing its demand for Pakistan the Sikhs would retaliate with a counterclaim for 'Azad Punjab.' Quite obviously some hard bargaining had taken place between the Akali Sikhs and the Muslim League. Concessions to Sikhs covering their representation within a Pakistan Government were to be balanced by Sikh support of the League case for their Muslim State. This much was clear from a conversation I recall with Giani Kartar Singh, the recognized brain of the Akali party, after his talks with Mr. Jinnah in November 1943." [108] Obviously, such negotiations were a source of irritation to the Congress leaders and in April 1946 Nehru accused Master Tara Singh of "sitting at one and the same time on about fifteen

[104] Gwyer and Appadorai, ii, 638–39.
[105] *The Indian Annual Register, 1946,* i, 202.
[106] *Ibid.,* p. 203.   [107] *Ibid.,* p. 205.
[108] Lord Birdwood, "India and the Sikh Community," in *The Hindustan Times,* December 26, 1954.

stools." To this, Tara Singh retorted that he did not need a permit from Nehru to see Jinnah or anybody else and that he intended to secure an independent position for the Sikhs.[109] Apparently, however, more than negotiations between the Muslim League and the Akali Dal was involved. On the initiative of some of the Akali leaders, reportedly, joint processions of Sikh and Muslim students were organized, raising slogans for Pakistan and Khalistan, but "Death to the Congress"; speeches were delivered in Sikh shrines vilifying Gandhi, Nehru, the Congress party, and Nehru's sister Vijayalakshmi Pandit; and platforms from which Nehru was to speak were set on fire.[110]

The negotiations between Akali and League leaders appear to have been mediated through several British officers in the government of India. In his book on the communal disturbances in the Punjab in 1947, Moon writes in some detail of his own role as a 'go-between' as also the role of Major Billy Short who had been included in the staff of the Cabinet Mission as "a small but graceful gesture to the Sikhs." [111] Major Short had been instrumental in winning over the Akalis to a policy of encouraging Sikh recruitment to the army and had played an active part in bringing together the Akalis and the Unionists during the period of World War II. These and other British officers [112] suggested to the Akali leaders that they should throw in their lot with the Muslims, and support the League's demand for the inclusion of the entire Punjab in Pakistan. They told the Akali leaders that in this fashion the Sikh community would not be divided and that, since the Muslims had only a very small majority in the Punjab, the Sikhs would hold the balance of power.[113]

---

109 *The Times of India,* April 8, 1946.

110 Durlab Singh, *Sikh Leadership* (Delhi: Sikh Literature Distributors, 1950), pp. 107–08. This book is critical of Akali leadership not so much for its activities, as such, but for its failure to secure a special position for the Sikhs.

111 Penderel Moon, *Divide and Quit* (Berkeley: University of California Press, 1962), p. 43; see also Durlab Singh, p. 18.

112 *Ibid.*   113 Moon, p. 49.

Meanwhile, the Congress party accepted the Cabinet Mission plan with some reservations. On its appeal to the Sikh community, the Akali Dal too accepted the plan although reiterating that the plan was unjust to the Sikhs. Under Nehru's leadership, an interim government was formed. The Akali Dal was represented in the interim government by Baldev Singh. The Muslim League first decided to stay out but some time later also joined the government. However, the arrangement of an interim government proved unworkable. The nationalist leaders became convinced that no government which included the Muslim League could function and thought that the partition of India alone would be the solution. Outside the government, with the Hindu and Muslim communities poised against each other, the country stood on the verge of civil war.

Finding that the Cabinet Mission plan had proved unworkable, Prime Minister Atlee sent Lord Louis Mountbatten as Viceroy to India in early 1947 to attempt a solution of the Indian crisis. After negotiations over a period of a few months, the leaders of the Congress party, the Muslim League, and the Akali Dal agreed, through an announcement in the first week of June 1947, to the Mountbatten Plan for the partition of the country and the formation on August 15, 1947 of two dominions—India and Pakistan—with the Hindu-majority districts of the Punjab and Bengal included in India. Apparently, the Akali Dal had been unsuccessful in getting a separate dominion for the Sikhs. On the other hand, the alternative of partitioning the Punjab, though it involved a division of the Sikh community, evidently seemed a lesser evil to the Akali Dal than Muslim domination of the whole community within Pakistan.

After the announcement of the Mountbatten Plan, Moon got in contact with the Akali leaders again, suggesting that the Sikhs should join with the Muslims in the Punjab and become a part of Pakistan.[114] At first, the Akali leaders were unresponsive to his suggestion because they were afraid that the

[114] *Ibid.*, p. 84.

Muslims would not abide by any agreement which they might now reach with the Sikhs. Later, however, they became "more favorably disposed." [115] Moon was unable to guess at the time the reason for this change, but he subsequently "surmised that this change of attitude was occasioned by the failure of the Sikhs to get all they wanted from the Congress. They were really hankering after a quasi-autonomous east Punjab, shorn of the four Hindu districts in the southeast so that it would have more of a Sikh complexion. Congress was not agreeable to this; hence an inclination to try to get it from the Muslims." [116]

About the end of June 1947, Moon wrote to Lord Ismay, who was on the staff of Lord Mountbatten and is considered by some as another 'go-between' for the Akali Dal and the Muslim League, to see if there was any possibility that a settlement could be reached between the Akali Dal and the League whereby the whole of the Punjab would be included in Pakistan, with certain special safeguards provided for the Sikhs. Lord Ismay wrote back that "Baldev Singh had recently seen the Viceroy and told him that there was no sign of the major parties making any concession to the Sikhs." [117] No agreement could be reached between the Akali Dal and the Muslim League, for "if the Sikhs were lukewarm about a settlement; the Muslims were icy cold." [118] It seems that the Akali Dal wanted the Sikhs to be considered not only a sub-nation, but also to be given the right of secession.[119] Moon found, however, that Jinnah was unwilling to make any concessions to the Sikhs.[120]

Having been unable to secure a special position for the Sikh

[115] *Ibid.*, p. 85.   [116] *Loc. cit.*
[117] *Ibid.*, p. 86.   [118] *Loc. cit.*
[119] Speech of Master Tara Singh, in *The Tribune*, July 23, 1959.
[120] Moon, p. 97. See also Harbans Singh, *Sikh Political Parties* (New Delhi: Sikh Publishing House Ltd., n.d.), p. 11, who comments that "an important part of Mr. M. A. Jinnah's political strategy was a deliberate and studious disregard of the Sikhs. By his masterly manoeuvering, he had converted the Indian problem to a Hindu-Muslim question."

community, the Akali Dal reconciled itself to the partition of the Punjab, but it desired now that in the actual demarcation of the boundaries between India and Pakistan, an effort should be made to include as large a part of the community in India as possible. At the same time, Akali leaders kept reiterating intermittently, even after their agreement to the Mountbatten Plan, the demand for a separate Sikh state. The final demarcation of the boundaries, however, split the Sikh community into two halves, one in India and the other in Pakistan.

The partition on August 15, 1947, was followed by mass rioting and murder. The result was the migration of about 12 million people. The entire Hindu community and Sikh community moved out of West Pakistan and India accepted and welcomed them both. Similarly, almost the entire Muslim population from east Punjab (India) moved to Pakistan. The Muslim and non-Muslim communities have blamed each other for the killing and the migration. According to some explanations, the Muslims in west Punjab (Pakistan) fell upon the Hindus and Sikhs who then fled to India and, in turn, acted to evict the Muslims in east Punjab in order to make room for themselves. One author believes that the "instinctive migration of Hindus and Sikhs" in the Punjab, unlike the Hindus in East Bengal, is intelligible only in the light of the history of the region with its "tradition of republican independence," and mass movements of tribes, going back to the time of Alexander the Great.[121] However, Moon argues that, in the case of the Sikhs, a more rational objective was behind the mass migration: "This factor was none other than the determination of the Akali leaders to ensure the survival of the Sikhs as a compact, coherent, undivided community. In the situation which had developed by 1947 this basic objective of Sikh policy could only be realized by the forcible expulsion of Muslims from East Punjab; for only so could accommodation be found on the Indian side for the two million Sikhs who would otherwise be

[121] Kapur Singh, p. 342.

left in Pakistan. So in falling upon the Muslims in East Punjab *vi et armis* in August 1947 the Sikhs were not only gratifying their desire for revenge but also helping to secure a more rational objective—the integral survival of the Sikh community. The migratory movements that were thus set going became, no doubt, largely spontaneous and instinctive, the natural product of fear and danger, but there lay behind, as the original source of the initial impulse, this rational motivation. To grasp this is to grasp an important clue to the understanding of these events. The determination of the Sikhs to preserve their cohesion was the root cause of the violent exchange of population which took place. . . ."[122] To substantiate his point, Moon cites instances in which Sikhs migrated en masse to India from areas where there had been no attacks on them. He attributes this mass migration to earlier Akali propaganda, though some say that the Akali Dal had merely tried to condition the Sikhs for a possible exchange of population on a peaceful basis.[123] Moon adds: "For the Sikhs, on the other hand, the preservation of their cohesion was a natural, intelligible objective. It had long been uppermost in the minds of influential Akali leaders. Even as far back as 1942 they had been thinking in terms of concentrating all Sikhs on the Indian side of the border, if the Muslims insisted on Partition. When, therefore, Pakistan became inescapable and the Mountbatten Plan for dividing the

[122] Moon, pp. 279–80; see also Alan Campbell-Johnson, *Mission with Mountbatten* (London: Robert Hale Ltd., 1951), pp. 66, 149, 174–75, 188, 191, 204, and 357. Criticizing Akali leadership for its inability to secure a state under the political influence of the Sikhs, one Sikh author regretfully notes that the Sikh leaders did not heed the warning of some people that they should not force the eviction of the Muslim population in Ambala division—parts of which Akali leaders now want to be excluded in the formation of Punjabi Suba—because in so doing they would replace Muslim domination over the Sikhs by Hindu domination. The implication is that the presence of a large Muslim population in east Punjab would have given the Sikhs substantial bargaining power in Punjab politics. See Durlab Singh, p. 109.

[123] From an interview with a former president of the All India Sikh Students Federation.

Punjab—and so the Sikhs—was announced, they accepted it, but, in order to meet it, privily perfected their own plans for Sikh concentration." [124]

Whatever the causes, the Sikh population, as a result of the mass migration, became heavily concentrated in the northwestern districts of the Punjab and PEPSU in independent India. Most of these districts now became Sikh-majority districts, whereas the southeastern districts and the northern hill districts continued to be Hindu-majority. Some Hindu leaders allege that this concentration of the Sikhs in the northwestern districts was a deliberate design on the part of Akali leaders. They point out that at the time of resettlement of the refugees the two most important portfolios in the Punjab ministry—Home Affairs and Rehabilitation—were headed by Sikh leaders who had been prominent in Akali politics before the partition.[125] Part of the reason for this concentration is perhaps the official policy of the Punjab government to resettle refugees, insofar as possible, in their ancestral districts from where they had originally migrated to west Punjab (Pakistan). A large section of the Sikh refugees consisted of settlers in the canal colonies who had originally gone there from some of these districts. In any case, the concentration of the Sikhs in these districts eliminated the major block to the earlier territorial demands of the Akali Dal, especially that of a sovereign Sikh state—the absence of a geographically compact Sikh-majority area. On the other hand, the departure of the British meant that a leadership wedded to secular nationalism had come to power in India, which would not countenance any religion-based communal demands, especially after the experience with Pakistan.

[124] Moon, pp. 280–81. It should be noted that Moon writes that "I am not myself conscious of any bias for or any against any of the three communities except perhaps a sneaking sympathy for the Sikhs." *Ibid.,* p. 9.

[125] From an interview with a Hindu leader in Jullundur.

Sikh Province and Punjabi Suba

As it turned out, the Punjab had hardly recovered from the shock of murder and mass migration when the demand for a Sikh-majority province began to be made. In February 1948, Master Tara Singh announced that "we want to have a province where we can safeguard our culture and our tradition." [126] He also said that "we have a culture different from the Hindus. Our culture is Gurumukhi culture, and our literature is also in Gurumukhi script." [127] On the point of whether this was a communal demand, he stated that "I want the right of self-determination for the Panth in matters religious, social, and political. If to ask for the existence of the Panth is communalism, then I am a communalist." [128] He made it clear, however, that what he was asking for was not a sovereign Sikh state, but rather a province within the Indian federation. He recognized that Hindus and Sikhs had close cultural and social relations, but he did not foreclose the possibility of an exchange of population if the relations worsened.[129]

It was clear, however, that so soon after the partition of the country, with the grave consequences that followed in its wake, no strictly communal demand would be acceptable to the nationalist leadership. Equally clear was the fact that any plan to create a Sikh-majority province or state would be met with determined opposition from those Hindus who were likely to be included in such a province. Either because of these considerations or because of a newly found genuine commitment

[126] *The Tribune,* February 26, 1948, quoted in Satya Mehta, "Partition of the Punjab," (Ph.D. dissertation, University of Delhi, 1959), pp. 476–77. The demand seems to have been made even earlier, as Mountbatten's press attaché notes on September 23, 1947, that "already the solution which has been mooted of creating a new Indian province of Sikhistan fails to measure up to Sikh demands." Campbell-Johnson, p. 205.

[127] *The Tribune,* February 26, 1948, quoted in Mehta, pp. 476–77.

[128] *The Statesman,* February 29, 1948.

[129] *The Tribune,* August 1, 1948, quoted in Mehta, p. 477.

to the principle of linguistic demarcation of provincial boundaries—a principle which by then was becoming highly important
in Indian politics—the Akali Dal, along with several other Sikh
leaders, began to demand at this time a Punjabi Suba covering
the so-called Punjabi-speaking areas, but which inadvertently
or otherwise was an area that would mean a Sikh majority in
the legislature. The advocates of this demand were not able,
however, to divest it of its communal association and implications. Rather, the demand for Punjabi Suba itself began to be
made as an alternative to a cluster of other more explicit political concessions for the Sikh community as such. It was given
out that Akali leaders would give up the demand for a language-based Punjabi Suba if certain other demands made on
behalf of the Sikh community were accepted. In the latter half
of 1948, all the Sikh members of the East Punjab Legislative
Assembly except Partap Singh Kairon were reported to have
presented a list of thirteen demands for the consideration of
the Constituent Assembly of India, then framing an Indian
constitution. The more important of these demands were:

1. The Sikhs should be provided with 50 percent representation in the legislature and cabinet of the Punjab.

2. The positions of Governor and Chief Minister in the
Punjab should be alternately held by a Hindu and a Sikh.

3. Representation in the services of the Punjab should be
40 percent for the Sikhs and 60 percent for the Hindus.

4. Sikhs should be provided with 5 percent representation in
the central legislature. In other provincial legislatures of India,
Sikhs should receive representation either by nomination or by
reservation.

5. There should be one minister and one deputy minister
belonging to the Sikh community in the central government.

The significant point in the memorandum, however, was
that in case the demands outlined therein were not acceptable,
then the Sikhs should be allowed to form a separate province

consisting of seven districts.[130] One student of Punjab politics
has noted the "parallel" between the demands presented in this
memorandum and the Fourteen Point Formula of Jinnah,
wherein the Muslim League had demanded parity between
Hindus and Muslims in the cabinet as well as reservations in
the services and legislatures for the Muslim community. That
student further noted that "it is ironical that while the Muslim
League ultimately led the Muslims towards Pakistan, in their
8th point, the Sikhs also submitted that in case their demands
were rejected they should be allowed to form a new province
of seven districts including Ambala where they would be in a
numerical majority. The only difference appears to be that
while the Muslim League demanded an independent sovereign
state for the Muslims, the Sikh communal leadership continued
to swear their loyalty to the Indian Union. But the parallel between the two patterns was so unmistakably clear that the
growth of apprehensions in the minds of the rest of the population was not completely unjustified." [131] However, neither
the Constituent Assembly nor the Congress party—with their
commitment to the secular state and their determination to
avoid the communal politics which had dominated pre-inde-
pendent India—could bring themselves around to accepting
such demands.

With the increasing national commitment to a secular state
and the emergence of demands in other parts of India for the
reorganization of states on linguistic lines, Akali leaders began
to emphasize more and more the linguistic basis for their demand of Punjabi Suba. Despite this shift, Akali leaders could
not overcome the communal context in which the demand itself
had emerged, and the communal color that was lent to the demand by the pronouncements of Akali leaders themselves.

[130] See *The Statesman,* November 9, 1948, and *Hindusthan Standard,* November 15, 1948.
[131] Mehta, p. 479.

Implications for Punjabi Suba

An overview of Akali activities before independence demonstrates the amazing continuity of Punjabi Suba with earlier Akali demands asking for the redemarcation of the boundaries of the Punjab. Akali pronouncements now about the real objectives of Punjabi Suba strangely echo the same arguments as were used for Azad Punjab. The demarcations of Punjabi Suba itself correspond closely to those that Moon suggests the Akali Dal wanted specifically for meeting Sikh claims from the Congress party on the eve of the partition. The purpose now, as then, seems to be to create a province or state where the maximum number of Sikhs would be concentrated and as a community would be the effective wielders of political power. For this purpose, it is power in the legislature that is initially important and not any proportion in the population.

The demand for Sikhistan made prior to the partition also has great relevance to an understanding of politics in the Punjab today. The importance of Sikhistan lay not so much in the demand itself, but in the particular doctrines that were advanced for its establishment, more especially that the Sikhs constitute a separate political entity, that they must act as a single group in politics, that they can only be rulers or rebels, and that religion and politics are inseparable. And when the same leaders who had with such forceful logic been pressing for a sovereign Sikh state into the first half of 1947, began agitating in the first half of 1948, or even before then, first for a Sikh province and then for Punjabi Suba; equally understandable is the reaction on the part of the Hindus who would be included in this Suba as perhaps also the apprehensions in the minds of the nationalist leadership about the potential threat to the political unity of India inherent in the doctrines and the pre-partition activities of the Akali Dal.

On the other hand, the intensity of passion with which Akali leaders have pursued the demand for Punjabi Suba is also

understandable in light of the events before independence.
First, Akali leaders and part of the Sikh community had committed themselves so intensely to the idea of a sovereign Sikh
state that they felt compelled later in independent India to
search for a substitute arrangement giving the Sikhs political
power in some region and the pursuit, in turn, of the substitute
of Punjabi Suba committed some even further. Such demands
became tied with the individual lives and fortunes of political
leaders. For example, Master Tara Singh has stated in relation
to Punjabi Suba: "Now my own life, at least my public life is
tied up with this demand. If I give up this demand or agree
to lessen it, I cannot live physically, not at least in the political
field." [132] Finally, the Akali leaders assumed before 1947 that
a politically autonomous, Sikh-controlled territorial unit was
within the realm of possibility, for had not the Cabinet Mission
recognized them as the third major community? So when the
disappointment came it was bitterly felt. As Master Tara Singh
has put it, "the Hindus got Hindustan, the Muslims got Pakistan, what did the Sikhs get?" [133] As a consequence, the Akali
Dal has persisted in its objectives through the medium of the
demand of Punjabi Suba.

THE THREAT OF RELIGIOUS UNORTHODOXY

The third main factor which "forms the main motive, but
not the argument for the demand of Punjabi Suba" is the
growth of religious unorthodoxy among the Sikhs today.[134]
The impact of the scientific age and the industrial revolution
upon religious and spiritual values, in general, has often been
commented upon. Sikh authors, too, have attempted to evaluate
the impact of these factors on Sikhism specifically. They have

[132] Quoted in statement by Darbara Singh, *The Tribune,* October 4,
1958.
[133] See Virendra, *The Spokesman,* XI, No. 27 (1961), 10.
[134] From an interview with an influential intellectual of the Akali Dal.
See also Khushwant Singh, *The Statesman,* June 18, 1959; and Khushwant Singh, *The Sikhs,* pp. 184–85.

noted that, as a result of the contact with Western science and thought, there is a questioning among the Sikh youth about the values of Sikh religion. As one writer has pointed out: "The educated youth feels no emotional concern for Sikhism because it embodies no values that he recognizes. His values are different. You appeal to him in the name of the *Gurus*, the *Gurus* of his ancestors; you take him to *Gurdwara*; you quote *Gurbani* to impress him, but everything leaves him cold. Nothing carries force with him. You fail to enlist his emotions because you fail to illumine his valuational sense." [135]

Along with this element of doubt about religious values, there is noted the decline in the observance of Sikh rites and ceremonies. At home, the regular reading of scriptures no longer takes place.[136] The gap between the principles professed and the actual life lived by the exponents of Sikhism causes pervasive dissatisfaction. So does the gap in political life where Sikh leaders preach harmony and brotherhood to other Indians, but "fall to denouncing Sikh leaders belonging to a rival group and to declaring them unworthy of a place in the community." Sikh shrines for some are "no longer the radiating centers of the Sikh faith." Hymns in the shrines are set to the music of movie songs, with the result that when "the sacred hymns are being sung in such tunes, our minds are running on the songs heard in the pictures, and we cannot give thought to the theme of the hymns." [137] In general, the coming of the radio and the movies has distorted all spiritual values. Instead of attending to prayers as required by Sikhism, people spend their time at the movies and before the radio.[138]

It would seem that the impact of the modern scientific industrial age on Sikhism is no different than on other religious systems. The question then arises as to why Akali leaders feel

[135] Ratan Singh, *The Revolt of the Sikh Youth* (Lahore: Modern Publications [1943]), pp. 132–33.
[136] Kartar Singh, pp. 29–30.
[137] *Ibid.*, p. 183.
[138] *Ibid.*, p. 30.

so concerned about religious unorthodoxy and seek a political solution for it. The answer is that the impact, insofar as Sikhism is concerned, becomes dramatically visible because if unorthodoxy proceeds far enough it involves the cutting or complete removal of hair from head and face, contrary to the strict injunction of the tenth Guru. Akali leaders further feel that once the process of unorthodoxy sets in for individuals it culminates in their absorption in the Hindu community, and they fear that eventually it must mean the assimilation of Sikhs into Hinduism. Such a prospect must, indeed, seem dreadful to a set of leaders who over the years have advocated the separation of Sikhs from the Hindu community.

The basis for this assimilation is alleged by some to be the close social and cultural relations between Hindus and Sikhs,[139] and by others that, apart from the outer forms and symbols, there is nothing to distinguish Sikhism from the reformed sections of Hinduism.[140] Consequently, if one gives up the forms and symbols, the sole defense against absorption into Hinduism is eliminated.[141] Khushwant Singh traces the process of absorption into Hinduism as a gradual development from one generation to another. The trimming of facial hair in one generation is followed by shaving and cutting of hair on the head in the next generation, and so on. He sums up the process of assimilation in four successive stages: (1) orthodox Sikh; (2) unorthodox Sikh; (3) Sahajdhari Sikh; and (4) Hindu.[142]

Khushwant Singh assumes that the process of unorthodoxy

[139] In one interview, Master Tara Singh has said that the need for an independent political organization for the Sikhs was "very great because they have so close social and cultural relations with the Hindus that the Sikhs can be easily absorbed." *The Tribune*, July 6, 1956.

[140] The remarks of one author concerning Sahajdhari Sikhs are significant in this regard; he says that "there is no such thing as a Sahajdhari Sikh. For all practical purposes he is a Hindu believing in Sikhism." Khushwant Singh, "Future of the Sikhs," *The Spokesman*, II, No. 1 (January 3, 1952), 4.

[141] "The dividing line between Sikhs and Hindus is the external appearance of the Sikh." Khushwant Singh, *The Sikhs*, p. 180.

[142] *Loc. cit.*

starts with the trimming of the beard and mustache. However, the process seems to have its antecedents in the use of hair-fixers, nets, and other equipment for the decoration of facial hair. Kapur Singh says that the injunction against shaving of hair seeks, among other things, to curb vanity in man, for the custom to shave has grown out of the vain desire for perpetual youthfulness.[143] Having grown out of "gross vanity," the custom "is sustained by unthinking ignorance." [144] It is imperative, therefore, for the Sikh to keep uncut hair "in the cultivation of a mature and integrated personality, which deliberately outgrows personal vanity and boyishness, and accepts the principle of growth and aging as fundamental to religious discipline." [145] If the purpose of the injunction is, among other things, to curb vanity, then the attempt to appear more handsome through using of hair-fixers and decorating the beard and mustache in other ways undermines the basis of the injunction, without literally violating it but subtly laying the groundwork for further unorthodoxy. Once the values behind the injunction are undermined, the rest of the process easily sets in. Understood in this sense, trimming is not an isolated development but the continuation of a more profound process which is hardly recognized and even less appreciated. While criticism of trimming and shaving is universal among the more orthodox Sikhs, it is surprising that Akali newspapers throughout the year carry advertisements of hair-fixers, with pictures of the 'before and after' look, and the organization allows the sale of such products at its periodical conferences and in the neighborhood of Sikh shrines. At any rate, the shaving of the beard immediately renders a Sikh an "apostate" though the trimming of hair is in general overlooked.

According to some authorities, the process of unorthodoxy among Sikhs seems to be well advanced.[146] One author says

[143] Kapur Singh, p. 105.
[144] *Loc. cit.*
[145] *Ibid.*, pp. 106–107.
[146] Khushwant Singh, *The Sikhs,* pp. 179–80.

that if a random sample were taken of 500 Sikh students in Punjab colleges, it would be found that only about 1 percent of them adhere to the tradition of keeping the five external symbols. He predicts that in the not very distant future Sikh youths will discard their beards and turbans in the fashion of the majority of Sikh students who go abroad to England and America.[147] Some Sikh leaders question such statements about the rapid decline in the observance of Sikh forms and symbols, alleging that they are based on life in a metropolitan city like Delhi. However, one cannot help but notice this type of un-orthodoxy in the towns and villages of the Punjab. Even at village gurdwaras one may run into Sikhs who seem merely to have not shaved for a couple of weeks but who, surprisingly enough, have recently returned from serving a jail sentence for their participation in some Akali agitation. Also, some of the cutting of hair seems necessary for certain kinds of farm work.

Although the presence of unorthodoxy among the Sikhs can be easily verified by observation, there is no empirical evidence as to whether it represents (1) a relapse from an earlier state of orthodoxy in the observance of Sikh forms and symbols, or (2) a continuing phenomenon of which Akali leaders have re-cently become more acutely aware, or (3) a combination of both. If it is the second point, then the present concern over unorthodoxy may essentially represent unfinished business from earlier reform movements, aiming at separating the Sikhs from the Hindu community. At any rate, one of the most impressive demographic aspects of the Punjab until recently has been, far from any absorption of Sikhs in any other community, the tremendous growth in Sikh population. From 1.9 million in 1881, the Sikh population grew to 6.2 million in 1951; its per-centage in the Indian population grew from 0.7 to 1.7 over the

[147] Harbans Singh, "The Future of the Sikh Community," *The Spokesman*, x, Nos. 41–42 (Guru Nanak Number, 1960), 59–60.

same period.[148] The rate of population growth of the Sikh community has been far higher than any of the other communities in the Punjab. This is attributed not only to a higher fertility among the Sikhs,[149] but also to the massive conversions to Sikhism from the Hindu community.[150] The Hindu community has in the past served as the great reservoir from which Sikhism has drawn its converts. This process of conversion can be graphically observed in the social history of many castes which have moved from the "Hindu" to the "Sikh" column from one decennial census to another.

Nonetheless, whatever unorthodoxy exists is galling to the Akali leadership, but a solution to the problem is sought through the establishment of Punjabi Suba. Among the many statements of Master Tara Singh on the subject is an interview in May 1961 he gave the editor of a New Delhi newspaper, in which the relationship between unorthodoxy and Punjabi Suba is elaborated:

> During a long talk we had last Saturday, Master Tara Singh made no secret of his motives in asking for a Punjabi Suba. The Sikhs as a distinctive community, he emphasized, must be preserved, and they could be preserved only in a "homeland" of their own. Left in their present position, he asserted,

[148] Figures from Kingsley Davis, *The Population of India and Pakistan* (Princeton: Princeton University Press, 1951), p. 182, and United Nations, *Demographic Yearbook 1956* (New York: United Nations, 1956), p. 275.

[149] Davis, p. 182. Apparently the Akali leadership is aware of this. In an interview with the correspondent of an American newsmagazine, Master Tara Singh is reported to have said: "We multiply faster than Hindus and are more virile." Evidently in reference to Punjabi Suba, he continued: "In ten years we will be in an absolute majority, leaving the soft-fleshed Hindus to trail behind." *The Hindustan Times,* July 3, 1955. However, the considerable out-migration of Sikhs from the Punjabi-speaking region since 1951 may run counter to such expectations.

[150] In some quarters it is alleged that Akali leaders plan to convert forcibly, or at least nominally register as Sikhs, the remaining Harijan population when a Punjabi Suba is formed, if the Sikhs do not command an absolute majority in such a state.

the Sikhs would be gradually "absorbed" by the majority community—this he must avoid, at least in his own lifetime. His clear thesis is: The Sikhs with their exterior symbols of distinction can last as a separate community only if they enjoy power and can extend patronage for the continuance of the symbols.[151]

In 1955 Tara Singh said, "I feel we cannot save our religion without attainment of political power in the Punjabi speaking region and if somebody tells me a way without it I shall be prepared to accept that way." [152] And again: "We must achieve Punjabi Suba at all costs without which the Sikh Panth will certainly perish." [153] In the same year, the important Sikh weekly, *The Spokesman,* wrote:

> The Sikhs felt like orphans everywhere and hence the apostasies. This is why too many Sikhs fear their extinction. This is why the Sikhs seek to be equals of the Hindus in political power. They can think of no other way to escape from extinction, except the demarcation of a Punjabi Suba, wherein the Sikhs would be about 45%.[154]

Apart from their chief objection to the establishment of any state on a communal basis, the Hindus in the Punjab question how unorthodoxy among the Sikhs means absorption into Hinduism unless—they remark with a feeling of self-satisfaction—the two are the same to begin with. If the latter is true, the Hindus feel, then it knocks out the case for an independent political entity of the Sikhs so carefully built and sustained over the past century. How fragile the claim of the Sikhs to nationhood is in reality, they point out. However, they absolve themselves of any responsibility for unorthodoxy in Sikhism; they

[151] Prem Bhatia, "Prospect and Retrospect: Alternatives Before Akalis," *The Times of India,* May 16, 1961.

[152] *The Tribune,* September 12, 1955; *The Times of India,* September 12, 1955; *The Spokesman,* v, No. 36 (September 21, 1955), 9.

[153] *The Tribune,* September 26, 1955.

[154] Vol. v, No. 38 (1955), 4.

challenge the Sikhs to point out any activities of the Hindus to encourage Sikh absorption into Hinduism, though they feel such activities would be justified in view of the Sikh community's own record of proselytization. Nonetheless, they believe that the Sikh symbols, like the Hindu symbols of the sacred thread and tuft of hair on head, will have to go because there is no scientific reason for their retention.[155]

The answer of the Sikhs is that through ridiculing the forms and symbols of Sikhism, life is made uncomfortable for Sikhs, who then tend to drift away from their religion. They further charge that encouraging unorthodoxy on the part of Hindus assumes a subtle form where preference is allegedly shown to clean-shaven Sikhs in promotion in government services, including the army.[156] It is also suggested that unorthodoxy among Sikhs is encouraged not so much through open acts in public but through subtle attempts at their demoralization by denying them their rightful position in the country. The refrain in such statements is that Punjabi Suba is essential to stem the unorthodoxy. However, there is no clue as to any specific way in which the proposed Suba would deal with the problem of unorthodoxy.

Would laws be passed in the Punjabi Suba to prohibit the trimming and shaving of beards?[157] How would this be consistent with the secular nature of the Indian constitution? In fact, the matter was taken several times to Prime Minister Nehru who expressed his willingness to investigate any complaint and take immediate remedial action about any encouragement on the part of the government to unorthodoxy among

[155] An effort to support the wearing of unshorn hair on a scientific basis is the work of Chanda Singh, *The Hair and Health* (Kot Kapura: Human Hair Research Institute, 1956).

[156] *The Spokesman*, III, No. 5 (February 4, 1953), 2.

[157] One author comments that "in the Sikh state the Sikhs would not only be free of Hindus and Hindu influences, but the Sikh youth would also be persuaded (if necessary compelled) to continue observing the forms and symbols of the faith." Khushwant Singh, *The Sikhs*, pp. 184–85.

Sikhs, but clearly stated his inability, under a secular state, to implement the teachings of any religion.[158] Indeed, the reason why Master Tara Singh declares both Hinduism and secular nationalism as equally dangerous for Sikhism [159] is explained by the requirements of a secular state to stand above the enforcement of doctrines of any religion. In actual fact, what the Sikh leadership is up against is not the presence of any anti-Sikhism but the decline in traditional religious values as such among various religious groups.

If laws prohibiting unorthodoxy are impossible to enact under the constitution, would Sikhism be made attractive in the Punjabi Suba through preferences in government patronage, as Master Tara Singh seems to suggest? Would this be any more consistent with the constitution which prohibits discrimination between citizens on the basis of religion? If these measures are not feasible under the constitution, is it logical then to assume that pressure would be exerted later to change the very basis of the constitutional framework? Can the Punjabi Suba then really be potentially a state like any other state in India, as Akali leaders maintain? If unorthodoxy cannot be stopped in the Punjabi Suba, would a sovereign state for the Sikhs be then demanded? Under such conditions, how is the Hindu community and the nationalist leadership going to be persuaded to agree to the formation of such a Suba? In fact, it is precisely such questions—of which the Hindus seem to be acutely aware—that are inherent in the logic of the basis for the demand that makes for such a vigorous denunciation by Hindus in the Punjab of any concessions toward the formation of Punjabi Suba.[160]

The answer of some Sikh leaders is that the establishment of Punjabi Suba would stop unorthodoxy among Sikhs, not so

---

[158] From an interview with a Sikh member of parliament.
[159] *The Tribune*, September 11, 1961.
[160] Virendra, *The Spokesman*, xi, No. 29 (1961), 11.

much through the enactment of laws prohibiting unorthodoxy or through preferential treatment in government patronage, but through the sense of political power which it will give the Sikhs because of their influential position in a given region of India. In the Punjabi Suba, the Sikhs will no longer be the "impotent minority" they allegedly are now. An equi-balanced position between the Hindu and Sikh populations, it is stated, would put the communities on an equal footing, and assure the Sikhs that they are not treated as an inferior community. Others, however, maintain that the former Sikh princely states in the Punjab had far greater power than any Indian state today possesses; except for foreign affairs, defense, and communications, the princely states were completely autonomous. Yet the phenomenon of unorthodoxy was not only present in these states but was perhaps worse than in other parts of the Punjab and had even affected the royal families.[161] It is also pointed out that the exercise of complete sovereign political power by the Sikhs under Maharaja Ranjit Singh coincided with a decline in Sikhism. Some other Sikh leaders say that the Sikh religion should stand on its own virtues and merits, and go so far as to remark that it may as well not exist if it has to rely on government patronage. They suggest a radical reform instead in the preaching of Sikh religion which, they maintain, is presently controlled by vested political interests.[162]

Whatever the solution, the issue of unorthodoxy and Punjabi Suba points to an interesting case of how a social phenomenon makes for demands on the political system. It poses at the same time a challenge for the Sikh community in its confrontation with a secular state and the era of science, industry and urbanization.

[161] From an interview with a former prominent Akali leader now in the Congress party.

[162] For some thoughtful comments on the state of preaching in the Sikh religion today, see Hukam Singh, *The Spokesman,* IX, No. 30 (1959), 27.

SENSE OF GRIEVANCE ABOUT DISCRIMINATION

The fourth main factor which seems to form the basis of the demand for a separate Punjabi-speaking state or Punjabi Suba is the sense of grievance among the leaders and the rank and file of the Akali Dal that there is discrimination against the Sikh community.[163] It is felt that only if there is a state in which the Sikhs are in an influential political position can an end be put to this discrimination, and justice assured for the Sikh community.

Initially the charge of discrimination repeatedly made concerned public employment: recruitment, promotion, and treatment of Sikhs in the services. The Indian government's response was that "it is no good making vague and general charges" and that if the Akali Dal had any specific grievances to present on behalf of the Sikh community the government would be willing to consider them.[164] Apart from the general allegation of discrimination, however, the Akali leaders have preferred not to make any specific charges against the government. At one press conference, when asked to give concrete instances of discrimination, Master Tara Singh answered that "it may not be possible at a moment's notice to give many instances. I am, however, convinced that there is a sustained and calculated effort to discriminate against the Sikhs of free India." [165] One journal, which has consistently supported the demand for Punjabi Suba, observed that on the specific instances of discrimination, "his advisers shot forth a document which was not only unconvincing but also betrayed little appreciation of the change in times." [166]

In 1961, to clear the air, the Indian government set up a

---

[163] "It is only the Akalis who protest against discriminations (largely imaginary) practised against Sikhs in the Services and interference in their religious affairs." Khushwant Singh, *The Statesman,* June 18, 1959.

[164] Statement by Nehru, *The Spokesman,* xi, No. 27 (July 17, 1961), 1.

[165] *Loc. cit.*   [166] *Ibid.,* No. 28 (July 24, 1961), p. 3.

commission—known as the Das commission, after the name of its chairman—to go into charges of any discrimination against the Sikh community. The Akali Dal, for reasons of its own, refused to provide any evidence of discrimination before the commission. However, a group of nationalist Sikhs did present a memorandum which, far from showing any discrimination against the Sikh community, established the fact that the Sikhs had received generous treatment from the Congress government in patronage and political representation. This group further said in its memorandum:

> We feel that in public services as in political representation, in social legislation or in the grant of state patronage in business and industry, the Government of the day has been not only just but generous with us.[167]

The Sikhs have held in the Punjab legislature and the Indian Parliament political representation commensurate with their historical, and social importance. Though they are only 34% in Punjab's population, their representation on the Punjab Cabinet ever since independence has been 40 to 50%. Punjab's representatives on the Central Cabinet have also been Sikhs ever since 1947. There is a Sikh Chief Minister of Punjab—and a powerful one at that—a Sikh Governor of a province, several Sikh Ambassadors and holders of other important political positions. The Sikhs in and outside the Punjab are an honoured part of the Indian society.[168]

There are 9 Sikh heads of departments out of 17 in the Punjab Secretariat, 8 heads of districts out of 18, 10 S.P.s in districts out of 18, and over 60% in the police services. In other important services too, like engineering, medical, veterinary, revenue, cooperation, judicial and administrative

[167] "The Sikh Case: Presented by Nationalist Sikhs to the Das Commission" (mimeographed, 1962), p. 9. To Dr. Gopal Singh Dardi, member of parliament, the author's grateful thanks for supplying a copy of the memorandum.

[168] *Ibid.,* pp. 12–13.

services their number is in no way less than their due. They are, we believe, maintaining their historic position in the Indian army, both in the officers' and in men's ranks.[169]

The Sikh Chief Minister mentioned in this memorandum resigned in 1964, but soon after another Sikh was named as India's first Foreign Minister. Though this memorandum did not go into representation in the services at the national level, it is believed that though the Sikhs are less than 2 percent in the Indian population, they constitute about 20 percent of the Indian army, and have double their proportionate share in the Indian administrative services. In 1961 the then Deputy Defense Minister stated that "the number of Sikhs in the Indian Army today is much higher than it was during the British regime." [170]

In another memorandum [171] to the same commission, the Punjab government stated that the Sikhs "are, by no means, underrepresented," and that "they have had a fair share and, in some services, even a preponderant share in the public services." Maintaining that there was no discrimination against the Sikhs in the political sphere either, the Punjab government pointed out that of 154 members of the state legislative assembly (1957–62), 41 percent were Sikhs; of 22 members of parliament (1957–62) from the Punjab, over 45 percent were Sikhs; in the Punjab cabinet the share of the Sikhs had ranged from 44 to 55 percent; and that "the Sikhs have had more than their share in all the Houses and in the Government of the day throughout after the partition." Eventually, after examining the oral and written evidence presented by 83 individuals either on their own behalf or on behalf of organizations, the commission concluded that there was no case of discrimination against Sikhs in the Punjab.[172] It noted that the memorandum

[169] *Ibid.*, p. 13.
[170] *The Hindustan Times,* October 31, 1961.
[171] *Ibid.*, May 6, 1962.
[172] *The Tribune,* February 10, 1962.

by the nationalist Sikhs had categorically and emphatically stated that the Sikhs as a community had no grievance arising out of discrimination on any of the four grounds: (1) constitutional and legal, (2) political and social, (3) public services and (4) government patronage to business and industry.[173]

Though the commission did not refer to the position of the Sikhs in the Congress party organization, here, too, the privileged Sikh position is quite obvious. Since the partition, for over 15 years one Sikh leader or another remained president of the Congress party in the Punjab until 1963 when a Hindu protégé of Chief Minister Kairon was installed as president. Representation for the Punjab in the central working committee of the Congress party, as in the central cabinet, has since independence been a privilege exercised by leaders belonging to the Sikh community alone. It is in this total context that in 1961 one Sikh leader, Surjit Singh Majithia, stated, amidst public complaints that there was discrimination against Sikhs, that "we have no such grievance and the only grievance can be that the Sikhs are over-represented." [174] In fact, the demand has been mounting on behalf of the Hindu community in the Punjab that a commission should investigate discrimination against the Hindus in the state.

The Akali Dal has also made charges about government interference in the religious affairs of the Sikhs, but has not presented any concrete evidence on the subject. Some years back, the allegation of discrimination was made in respect to Sikh Harijans, but this was taken care of by the government extending to Sikh Harijans the same privileges that had been given Hindu Harijans even though Sikhism recognizes no caste.

The Akali Dal has also charged discrimination against Punjabi language, and therefore demanded Punjabi Suba where such a language would flourish. But, as Nehru maintained,

[173] *Loc. cit.*
[174] *The Hindustan Times*, October 31, 1961.

"Punjabi has made more progress in the last eight or ten years than in the last hundred years," and was anxious to know "where any obstruction has come in the promotion of the Punjabi language" in the absence of a Punjabi Suba.[175] The States Reorganization Commission, too, pointed out that the Akali Dal's own statistics, designed to show the rapid progress made by Punjabi, demonstrated that there was no hindrance to the development of this language.[176] That Commission further failed to see how the formation of Punjabi Suba would help in the growth of the Punjabi language. On the contrary, its creation would serve only to restrict the area of its dissemination, since the Punjabi language is at present a subject of compulsory study throughout the Punjab.[177] It should be noted here that the Punjab government itself allocates funds for the progress of Punjabi and it has also established a Punjabi university.

Another alleged grievance against the Congress party and the government is that certain pledges were made to the Sikh community before independence, which the Congress party subsequently failed to honor. Consequently, it is said that the Sikhs cannot put any trust in paper promises of the Congress and would like an area in which their own political influence would count. In elaborating this point, there is no camouflage of the linguistic argument. For example, in 1955 the Akali viewpoint was presented thus:

> The demarcation of what is called a Punjabi Suba seems to be the only way to preserve the language, culture, and religion of the Sikhs. . . . After all, it is for the Punjab Assembly to enact and abrogate these formulas [such as the Sacha formula]. What the present Assembly may concede today, could be unmade tomorrow.[178]

175 *Lok Sabha Debates*, LVII, No. 16 (August 29, 1961), 5693.
176 *Report of the States Reorganization Commission*, p. 142.
177 *Ibid.*, p. 145.
178 *The Spokesman*, v, No. 34 (September 7, 1955), 3.

And again in 1956:

> No arrangement that reduces the Sikhs to an impotent minority could be acceptable to the Sikhs. No paper safeguards could protect an ineffective minority. Either the Sikhs must live as equals or accept virtual extinction.[179]

Congress leaders maintain that there are no outstanding commitments to the Sikh community. In regard to the pledge given in 1929 that the Congress would not agree to a constitution which was not acceptable to the Sikhs, the Congress leaders say that the partition settlement was made with the full concurrence of the Sikh leaders. Furthermore, the present constitution was passed with the support of the elected Sikh representatives. As for any promises alleged to have been made in 1946, Congress leaders have denied any commitments. In a speech on the subject in the Constituent Assembly in 1949, Sardar Patel said: "If I can have any concrete expression of a promise given by Congress leaders, I might, and if so I do not think there is any one Congressman who will go against that promise. I have not however understood the psychology of the Sikh leaders—some of them—who often charge everybody with breach of faith, and always complain of minorities being ill-treated." [180]

Allegations of discrimination, however, still continue to be made against the government, although the content of such allegations has undergone a change over the years. Now it is held that the denial of Punjabi Suba itself is a discrimination against the Sikhs as a community. Akali leaders maintain that the opposition of the Hindu community and the refusal of the Indian government to establish a Punjabi Suba is indicative of bad faith toward the Sikh community and a lack of trust in it, for if the Hindus had been in a majority in the Punjabi Suba it

[179] *Ibid.*, VI, No. 6 (February 6, 1956), 3.
[180] India (Dominion), Constituent Assembly, *Debates: Official Report,* X, No. 7 (1949), 247.

would have been established forthwith. Since in their mind the question of the prestige and honor of the Panth has thus been involved, Punjabi Suba must be established whatever the cost in the struggle. As Master Tara Singh explained on one occasion, "Punjabi Suba is not the target, the target is Sikh honor. There was a battle of Panipat, but it was not to win Panipat. The fight is for the honor and prestige of the Sikh Panth, and not for Punjabi Suba as such."[181]

SUMMARY AND CONCLUSIONS

The emotional intensity with which the Akali Dal has pursued the demand for Punjabi Suba is understandable in the background of the efforts on the part of important segments of the Sikh community, over a period of more than three quarters of a century, to separate the Sikhs, religiously and politically, from the Hindu community. In the historical perspective, the demand for Punjabi Suba is but another stage in the furtherance of the aim of earlier reform movements and political claims toward the creation of a separate political entity of the Sikhs apart from the Hindus. The demand for Punjabi Suba, however, acquires a special urgency from the alleged contemporary threat to the accomplishments of the reform movements, insofar as religious unorthodoxy among the Sikhs today would mean reversion to Hinduism. The fear of reversion to Hinduism stems from a realization of the common basic philosophical postulates of the two religions as well as the close social and cultural relations between the two religious communities.

In one respect, the demand for Punjabi Suba represents the political aspirations of a religious group to nationhood, especially in view of the historical memories of having been the sovereign rulers of the Punjab about a hundred years ago. In another respect, it represents the channeling into the political

[181] Remarks made in a departure from the text of speech delivered at the thirteenth All-India Shiromani Akali Conference at Gurdwara Rakabganj in New Delhi on December 13, 1961.

system of a social problem, that of religious unorthodoxy, that the religious community feels unable to handle by itself without political power in the hands of this community as such.

The nationalist leadership opposes the demand of Punjabi Suba, for it views it as a potential threat to the present secular regime and to Indian national unity. Besides, it perceives the demand as increasing hostility and bitterness among the different communities in the Punjab. In the state of Punjab, there is, among the leaders who profess belief in secular nationalism, a large body of representatives from the Sikh community who vigorously oppose the demand for Punjabi Suba and some of the politico-religious concepts underlying it. The conflict over the demand for Punjabi Suba is not merely between the Hindu and Sikh communities, or some parts thereof, but more importantly between two groups of leaders among the Sikhs themselves: Akali leaders, who make communal demands in the name of the Sikh community; and Congress leaders who believe in secular nationalism. For an understanding of the conflict, it becomes essential then to explore the nature of these two types of leadership in the Punjab—their social background, their goals in politics, and the patterns of their recruitment to politics.

CHAPTER IV
Political Leaders:
Akali and Congress

THE case of the Punjab provides an interesting illustration of the influence of political ideology and political conditions on patterns of recruitment to political leadership and, in turn, the influence of particular patterns of political recruitment on political ideology. Since independence in 1947, the political and ideological conflict between the Akali leadership, which makes religion-based communal demands, and the Congress leadership, which proclaims belief in secular nationalism, has dominated the politics of the state of Punjab. Many newly independent nations and some of the states in India are also faced with similar conflicts. In the Punjab, religious loyalties serve as the basis of the challenge to secular nationalism, while in other places ethnic differences and tribal loyalties may form the basis of such a challenge. Since secular nationalism makes its appeals on a broader basis than what are considered to be the narrow loyalties of religion, race, or tribe, it is generally assumed in discussions on the subject that those who make nationalist appeals are more educated and "modern," and that those who make communal appeals are less educated and more "traditional." How far is this assumption correct? Are there significant differences between political leaders who profess belief in secular nationalism and those who support communal demands?

In order to provide some answers for these questions, a statistical analysis was made of the social background of members who were elected to the Punjab Vidhan Sabha (legislative assembly) in 1957.[1] In addition, this analysis was supplemented

[1] For more details and statistics, see Baldev Raj Nayar, "Contemporary Political Leadership in the Punjab" (Ph.D. dissertation, University of Chicago, 1963), pp. 227–41. The statistics in the succeeding sections

by a more intensive study through personal interviews of Akali and Congress candidates who ran for the Punjab legislative assembly in 1962 from Ludhiana district, one of 20 districts in the Punjab and a stronghold of the Akali Dal. Of the total of 154 members elected in 1957 to the Punjab legislative assembly, 62 members were Sikhs, not including a few members who may have Sikh names but declare their religion as Ad-Dharmi. All of these 62 Sikh leaders were elected from the Punjabi-speaking, Sikh-majority area. For the 1957 elections, under a political settlement, candidates recommended by the Akali Dal ran on the Congress ticket along with other Congress candidates. Of the 62 Sikhs that were elected to the Punjab assembly in 1957, 26 belonged to the Congress party and 28 to the Akali Dal (including the Rarewala group), and these two sets of leaders provide the basis for a comparison between secular nationalist leadership and communal leadership, respectively. There are, to be sure, another 66 non-Sikh MLAs (members of legislative assembly) who were elected on the Congress ticket, but a sharper comparison between two groups of leaders belonging to the same religious community but professing belief in the two contending political ideologies seems more desirable.

SOCIAL BACKGROUND OF SIKH POLITICAL LEADERS

What emerges from a comparison of the social background of Congress Sikh MLAs and Akali MLAs is the striking similarity between the two groups. Apart from the question of age, there are no important differences between the two groups with respect to caste, marital status, education, and occupation.

Among both Congress Sikh MLAs and Akali MLAs, the men far outnumber the women (over 90 percent). Both form an overwhelmingly married group (about 90 percent). Both Congress Sikhs and Akalis are overwhelmingly of rural origin (over 75 percent), though Congress Sikhs are more so. Only

---

should be read more for their suggestive value than their precision, for often there is no information available for some of the MLAs.

a small number were born in a town or city. Furthermore, they almost entirely represent rural constituencies (over 90 percent). In terms of age, the Congress Sikhs represent a slightly older group than the Akalis. The average year of birth for the Congress Sikh MLAs is 1911; for the Akali MLAs, 1915.

As far as caste composition is concerned, both groups show the predominance of the same caste groups. Among both Congress Sikhs and Akalis, the Jats are the predominant caste group (over 50 percent) though more so for the Congress Sikhs (70 percent) than for the Akalis (54 percent). The second largest caste bloc among both Congress Sikh MLAs and Akali MLAs is that of the representatives of the Harijans, though larger in the case of Akalis than in the case of the Congress Sikhs. The larger proportion of Harijan MLAs in the Akali group is more a function of non-Harijan Sikh support than of Harijan support for the Akali Dal. The Jats and the Harijans together nearly monopolize the legislative representation among both Congress Sikhs and Akalis (over 90 percent).

Contrary to popular belief, the Congress Sikhs are not more educated than the Akalis. If anything, the Akali group has a higher level of education than the Congress Sikhs, especially in view of the fact that the Akali group includes a larger proportion of Harijans who usually have not had the opportunity for better education. A breakdown of the Sikh MLAs by Harijans and non-Harijans shows that no Harijan MLA has gone beyond high school in his education. A comparison of only non-Harijans shows that the Akali group has a higher proportion of people with high school and college education. Among the non-Harijans in the Akali group, 28 percent passed high school, 22 percent received intermediate college education, 33 percent secured the B.A. degree, 11 percent the M.A. degree and 33 percent the law degree; [2] the corresponding figures for the non-Harijan Congress Sikh MLAs are 14, 14, 28, 5, and 19 percent, respectively. Both Congress Sikh and Akali non-Harijan MLAs

[2] Figures for the law degree are also included under B.A. or M.A.

have about the same proportion (6 percent or less) of people with no education. While some 24 percent of the non-Harijan Congress Sikh MLAs had some education below high school, all non-Harijan Akali MLAs who received education went beyond high school into college or professional studies. The reason for the higher educational level of the Akali leaders seems to lie in their being a younger group, for the younger generation not only has had greater access to the developing opportunities for education but also did not have to leave its studies unfinished, as many older leaders did, in response to the call of some nationalist leader during the independence movement. Another reason seems to be that the All India Sikh Students Federation is very active among college students and encourages the recruitment of educated leadership to the Akali Dal.

By and large, both Congress Sikh and Akali MLAs have had their education in the Punjab (over 90 percent) rather than in other parts of India or abroad. Over 50 percent of them had studied at either Lahore or Amritsar. Now in Pakistan, Lahore was until the partition the cultural center of the Punjab, especially for the Hindus. Amritsar, near the border with Pakistan, is the religious capital of the Sikhs. A significant proportion of both Akalis (18 percent) and Congress Sikhs (21 percent) had some part of their education at Khalsa College in Amritsar. This pioneer Sikh institution for higher learning has been the main source of educated political leadership among the Sikhs.

In terms of occupation, both Akalis and Congress Sikhs display a common trend. Agriculturists form the major occupational category in both groups, though there is a higher proportion of them among the Akalis (60 percent) than among the Congress Sikhs (42 percent). The term "agriculturist" does not indicate that the person necessarily tills the soil himself; rather agriculture is the source of income and the person himself may be a full-time politician. The second largest occupational category is that of professional workers, that is those for whom politics is a full-time business, and both Akalis and Congress

Sikhs have about the same proportion (32 percent). The third largest occupational category for both groups is that of lawyers, though the Akalis have a slightly higher proportion (20 percent) than the Congress (16 percent).

The striking similarity in the background of the Akali and Congress Sikhs that emerges from an analysis of the members of the Punjab legislative assembly is further confirmed by a comparison of the background of Akali and Congress Sikh leaders who ran for election in the 1962 general elections from Ludhiana district, although the number of leaders involved here is rather small. By and large, Akali and Congress Sikh leaders here, too, have a similar social background.

What these two studies demonstrate then is that, in the Punjab at least, the commonplace assumption is not valid that those who make "parochial," "primordial," or "particularistic" appeals are in any way less advanced than those who make "secular," "rational," and "nationalist" appeals.

THE POLITICAL MOBILITY OF AKALI LEADERS

The more interesting fact derived from an observation of trends in political recruitment in the Punjab is that any dichotomy between nationalist and communal leaders is misleading over a period of time because the leaders change their party affiliations. Although there are nationalist and communal appeals, there are, apart from a few but extremely important exceptions, no enduring communal and nationalist leaders over a significant period of time. At any given moment, it is possible, of course, to identify leaders who belong to a communal organization like the Akali Dal and those who belong to a secular nationalist organization like the Congress party, and to assume that political leaders belonging to these parties profess belief in the diametrically opposed ideologies of the respective parties. Over a period of time, however, it is difficult to classify any political leader as communal or nationalist. Certainly in politics, individual political leaders may undergo changes—gradual or sudden—in their ideas and therefore may switch from one party to another. But what has been occurring in Punjab politics is the phenomenon of a periodical but large-scale, and at times wholesale, influx of Akali leaders into the Congress party, with or without a political settlement.

For instance, the 28 Akali MLAs who served as the Akali group for purposes of comparison with the Congress Sikh group, were in 1956 members of the Akali Dal; most of them had taken part in the Akali agitation of 1955 and, as a consequence, had even served time in jail. Subsequently, under a political settlement between the Akali Dal and the Congress party, they were elected on the Congress ticket to the Punjab legislative assembly in 1957. When the Akali Dal once again decided to take part in politics as an independent political party, it asked these members to return to the Akali Dal. Only seven of them returned; the others all stayed in the Congress party. They not only remained in the Congress party, but many of them openly criticized their parent organization and its leader, Master Tara Singh.[3] These large-scale "conversions" to secular nationalism therefore preclude any rigorous classification of political leaders over a period of time as nationalist and communal. Political leaders who would have been characterized as staunch Akalis, and who were vigorous proponents of the concept of the Panth as an independent political entity, are found five years later in the camp of secular nationalism and, when necessary, opposed to the Akali Dal.

Among the candidates who ran for the Punjab legislative assembly from Ludhiana district in 1962, there were five Sikh leaders who were on the Congress ticket. Of these, three leaders —Ajmer Singh, Ramdayal Singh, and Gopal Singh Khalsa— had been elected to the Punjab legislature in 1952 on Akali tickets against Congress candidates. Khalsa served as the leader of the Akali party in the legislative assembly from 1952 to

[3] See the proceedings of the Punjab legislative assembly, *The Tribune,* September 23, 1961.

1956. The other two had at one time been on the executive committee of the Akali Dal. At that time, one of them was highly critical of Sikhs in the Congress party, characterizing them as mere "showboys" and "hirelings" who "can always be bought by the party in power." [4] All three leaders had before 1956 bitterly criticized the Congress party, yet there was no doubt of their vigorous opposition to the Akali Dal in 1962. Only one of them was successful in the 1962 elections and was immediately made a minister in the Congress government in the Punjab.

Lest it be understood that the large-scale "conversion" of Akali leaders to the Congress party in 1956 is an isolated event, it needs to be pointed out that it has been until the present a recurring feature of Punjab politics. Except for Master Tara Singh, who has tried to maintain his leadership outside the Congress party, and a handful of other Akali leaders who have been unable to find a place in the Congress party, almost all of the important Akali leaders in the last twenty-five years have gone over not only as individuals, but in groups, to the Congress party.

In 1937, the Akali Dal fought the elections as an independent political organization, at many places opposing the Congress party, but the elected members joined the Congress party as a body after the elections. Among the important Akali leaders in this group who did not later return to the Akali Dal were Partap Singh Kairon (later general secretary and president of the Punjab Congress party, a minister, and finally Chief Minister of the Congress government in the Punjab) and Gurmukh Singh Musafir (later president of the Punjab Congress party and a member of parliament). In 1942 a biography of Master Tara Singh listed, along with short character sketches, 19

[4] Ajmer Singh, "Shiromani Akali Dal Enjoys Confidence of Overwhelming Majority of the Sikhs," *The Spokesman*, iii, No. 26 (July 1, 1953), 12.

prominent colleagues of his in the top echelon Akali leader-ship.[5] A cursory glance at these names now would show that most of them subsequently joined the Congress party, with some becoming presidents of that party and ministers in Con-gress governments.[6] This trend toward joining the Congress party gathered even more strength after independence as there was greater political power to be shared with the Congress party being in control of the government. Insofar as the Akali Dal chooses to restrict itself to one community, it reduces its representation in the legislature to the position of a permanent political minority. Unless Akali leaders devote their lives to participation in agitations, they must seek other channels of political power and activity. Therefore, considerable numbers of Akali leaders are ready to switch over, after they have at-tained a position of political prominence in the Akali Dal, to the Congress party not merely for personal goals but also per-haps with a desire to maximize political power for the Sikh community.

Thus, immediately after independence, one of the two fac-tions of the Akali Dal joined the Congress party, including such important leaders as Udham Singh Nagoke, Isher Singh Majhail, and Swaran Singh (later to become Foreign Minis-ter). This group was joined in 1948 by the other faction of the Akali Dal, including important leaders like Giani Kartar Singh

[5] Durlab Singh, *The Valiant Fighter: A Biographical Study of Master Tara Singh* (Lahore: Hero Publications, 1942), pp. 140–49.

[6] (1) Those who later joined the Congress party include: Jathedar Udham Singh Nagoke, Jathedar Teja Singh Akarpuri, Jathedar Bhai Mohan Singh, Giani Kartar Singh, Isher Singh Majhail, Sohan Singh Jalalusman, Giani Gurmukh Singh Musafir, Gopal Singh Qaumi, Partap Singh Kairon, Darshan Singh Pheruman, Sampuran Singh, Baldev Singh, and Master Ajit Singh Ambalvi; (2) those who left the Akali Dal: Jathedar Chanan Singh Urara and Giani Dhanwant Singh; and (3) those who continued with the Akali Dal: Harnam Singh Advocate, Prin-cipal Ganga Singh, Babu Labh Singh, and Harcharan Singh Hudiara. This classification is based on information from newspaper sources and through conversations with Bhai Harbans Lal, a former president of the All India Sikh Students Federation.

(who served as minister in the Punjab government and then returned to the Akali Dal) and Baldev Singh (who was Defense Minister in the Indian government). Again, those who joined the Congress party in 1956 and did not return to the Akali Dal included the political leaders Hukam Singh (later speaker of the Lok Sabha), Giani Kartar Singh and Gian Singh Rarewala (who became ministers in the Punjab government in 1957), and Ajmer Singh (who became a minister in 1962).

The result of the periodic shifts of Akali leaders to the Congress party makes for a high rate of turnover of political leadership in the Akali Dal. As leaders with years of experience move to the Congress party, younger leaders move in to take over their positions in the Akali Dal. Akali representatives in the Punjab legislative assembly are therefore not only somewhat younger, but they also do not have the same length of party membership as do Congress representatives. Sixty percent of the Akali MLAs elected in 1957 had less than 10 years of membership in the Akali Dal, although the corresponding figure for membership of Congress Sikh MLAs is only 19 percent. Whereas 32 percent of the Congress Sikh MLAs had been in the Congress between 26 and 45 years, the corresponding figure for membership of Akali leaders in the Akali Dal is 15 percent. The rate of turnover in Akali representation in the Punjab legislative assembly has been so high that not one of the 19 Akali representatives elected to the assembly in 1962 was a member of the assembly through the 1957 general elections. On the other hand, most of the Congress Sikh leaders have had a record of active membership in the Akali Dal. In fact, it would be no exaggeration to say that almost every important Sikh leader in the Congress party has served a period of active membership in the Akali Dal. Some of the Congress Sikh leaders are reluctant to admit their past association with the Akali Dal; others rationalize it by saying that the Akali Dal was before independence a nationalist organization which worked in cooperation with the Congress party, and that therefore they have always been nationalist Sikhs.

Ideological Change

In view of the periodic influx of Akali leaders into the Congress party, an important question arises as to the nature of ideological change that takes place, if any, among the new entrants who a few years earlier had professed belief in a philosophy opposed to that of the Congress party. The crucial difference between the Congress party and the Akali Dal is over the role of religion in politics. In the presence of the diametrically opposed viewpoints of the two parties on this matter, what is the nature of ideological change involved in the transfer of political leaders from a communal party to a secular nationalist party? A complementary question, which is not considered here, would be: How is the ideology of the secular nationalist party affected by the influx of leaders from a communal party?

Most Akali leaders, especially the very few who left the Congress party to return to the Akali Dal, allege that there is no ideological change among former Akalis who are now in the Congress party. They further allege that these Akali-Congressmen think just as they did before about Akali claims and say so to them in private and even confide that they are working for Akali goals from within the Congress party, but that for opportunistic reasons they have now cast their lot with the Congress party. No other word is more repeatedly used in this connection, or in politics in general in the Punjab, than the word "opportunism."

On the other hand, former Akali leaders who choose to continue in the Congress party maintain that their ideas on the role of religion in politics do undergo change. They assert that they honestly and firmly believe in the Congress ideology that religion and politics should not be mixed together, and some even go to the extent of saying that they were misguided in their earlier political career in doing the contrary. While the truth may lie somewhere between the two extreme viewpoints, some ideological change is built into the new situation in which former Akalis find themselves in the Congress party.

The Congress party requires its members to refrain from participation in any communal activity. Members can be subjected to disciplinary action for overtly or covertly violating the secular policies of the party, and some have even been quietly retired from office and others forced out of the party.

Ideological change may also result from a redefinition of the external world for Akali leaders who enter the Congress party. These leaders find that the old slogans which they had repeated innumerable times about discrimination against Sikhs do not hold after all. On the contrary, they find, and they so argue with their constituents, that the Sikhs have more than their share of political power. Moreover, in contrast to their earlier experience, these leaders find themselves for the first time working in a cooperative endeavor within the Congress party with leaders from other religious communities. This is an important consideration, for contacts between Akali leaders and leaders from other communities are not very frequent.

Another significant factor in ideological change is perhaps the very nature of political recruitment to the Akali Dal. Recruitment takes place in periodic waves when some alleged grievance of the Sikh community furnishes the cause for a general denunciation of Hindus, the Congress party, and the government, and for the launching of an agitation. Some of the younger elements mobilized at this time will come up later in the Akali ranks through the Sikh Students Federation, while others will immediately rise to positions of leadership in the Akali Dal. Some persons of prestige, not involved in politics, will yield to the pressure and persuasion of Master Tara Singh or his personal emissaries and enter the Akali Dal; they feel honored by the attention given them though they are not politically oriented. Thus, many persons are drawn into the Akali Dal who may be persuaded as to the rightness of the allegations made by the party at the time of the agitation but do not believe at all in the total philosophical position of the Akali Dal in regard to religion and politics.

The result is that there may be at any one moment some groups and individuals who find themselves at odds with the policies of the top leadership and are on the lookout for an honorable way to make a transition to another party with a more secular and less communal outlook. For example, in the Akali Dal in PEPSU, there was a left wing group, known as the Raman group, that felt itself to be in disagreement with the allegedly reactionary policies pursued by the Akali Dal under the leadership of Master Tara Singh. Again, during the period of the general elections in 1962, young Jagdev Singh Jassowal, who had joined the Akali Dal during an agitation in 1960, was offered the position of general secretary of the Akali Dal. He not only declined the offer but actually left the organization, for he had found it "pregnant with conservative and reactionary elements which are eclipsing and retarding the pace of peace and progress in the country." [7] Similarly, there are other persons and groups in the Akali Dal whose intellectual horizon extends beyond the Sikh community; though they are pulled into the Akali Dal by a sudden agitation or by the attraction of Akali election tickets, they cannot adjust to a party whose politics is confined to a single community. Such people, when they move to the Congress party, remark in retrospect that they "felt suffocated in the narrow political atmosphere of the Akali Dal"; they heave a sigh of relief and say that whereas hitherto they were "confined to a well" they "now scan the seas." [8]

On the other hand, some observers allege that politicians in the Punjab are not committed to any ideology, communalism or secular nationalism. They charge that the sole aim of these politicians is the acquisition of political office and political power, which only a party that is in control of the government,

[7] *The Tribune,* January 26, 1962.   [8] From several interviews.

such as the Congress party, can provide. It may take a lifetime, however, to achieve political power and patronage through the regular channels of the Congress party, for other people in the party may have better claims. Consequently, many ambitious people join the Akali Dal, rise to a position of political eminence in the organization on the basis of the communal appeal of the Akali Dal, and then transfer to an equivalent position in the Congress party, with all the advantages which membership in a party in power may bring, plus the added prospects of ministerships and other appointments. One former civil servant remarked concerning the frequent changes in party affiliation among political leaders in the Punjab: "They are neither communal nor nationalist, they are opportunists. If they want to leave the Akali Dal they say it is communal. If they want to leave the Congress they say it is corrupt. What is true is that they themselves are communal and corrupt." [9]

To the charge that they are opportunists who forsook the ideology of the Akali Dal for political power and office in the Congress party, many of the Akali-Congressmen reply that even though they may feel some concern for Akali aims, they cannot go on agitating all their lives, that their mission in politics is not simply arousing agitations continuously, but also to do some good for the Sikh community and this can be done only in association with members of other communities. If a canal has to be built, it has to be for members of all communities, not just for the Sikhs. Therefore, they confess, they have belatedly realized that they should work in cooperation with other communities, and that the Congress party is the best medium for this. They now hold, after their experience in the Congress party, that communal parties are moribund in Indian politics since they have no program for constructive work.

Nonetheless, the process of ideological change among the new entrants in the Congress party from the Akali Dal is not an easy one. It is difficult for the new entrants to change overnight

[9] From an interview.

from one ideology to an opposing ideology. It requires time, patience, and sympathy on the part of the old-timers to assimilate the new members. Even self-respect dictates that the change in publicly expressed ideas should be gradual and clothed in rationalizations. As one former Akali leader, now in the Congress party, remarked: "It took five years for me to change from the blue turban of the Akalis to this present turban of a lightish green hue. It would perhaps take another five years to change to the white turban of the Congress Sikhs." [10] The same slow and gradual process perhaps works in the realm of ideological change as it does in the external insignia. One Akali-Congressman, after describing how he believed in secular nationalism and the joint endeavor of all communities to build an Indian nation, an hour later wistfully remarked, "the Sikhs are trying to become a nation, but the Hindus won't let us." Some Akali-Congressmen even use their position in the Congress party to help the Akali Dal indirectly by pressing for Akali demands from within. Then there is the hard core of former Akalis who staunchly stick to the Akali ideology, form themselves into a separate faction within the Congress party and act as an outpost for the Akali Dal. Some of these Akali-Congressmen return to the Akali Dal when asked to do so. One factor that hampers ideological change here is that the old social relations with other Akali members continue. Sometimes one will hear Akali-Congressmen remark that they have more Akali than Congress friends, and one can observe important Akali leaders visiting former Akali leaders in the Congress party at the cafeteria attached to the legislative lobbies in Chandigarh.

It should not be assumed that all those who refuse to return to the Akali Dal in response to the call of Master Tara Singh do so merely because of change in ideological convictions. Some of them cannot afford to return because their political base in the Akali Dal has been eroded in the meantime; other individ-

[10] From an interview with a former MLA.

uals have risen to positions of leadership within the Akali Dal, holding responsible offices which they previously held. On the other hand, they have achieved important offices in the government or in the Congress party organization as a result of their association with the Congress party. At times it may seem highly idealistic and brave to leave the Congress party in a grand gesture for the Panth, but it may not be practical in terms of their own political careers. Here, as elsewhere, politics is the art of the possible.

It is difficult to determine what ideas former Akali members in the Congress party may secretly hold. However, the process of ideological change can be perceived, in a tentative fashion, in the statements and actions of a few political leaders themselves over the years after they have joined the Congress party. The cases of these different political leaders can be analyzed under three categories:

1. In the first category are those who not only have repeatedly professed belief in secular nationalism in the period since independence but who also, when there has been an opportunity, have demonstrated their opposition to the Akali Dal, its demand for Punjabi Suba, and its other communal demands. The prime example in this case is that of Chief Minister Partap Singh Kairon. At one time a lieutenant of Master Tara Singh, he came to be considered by the latter as his chief antagonist and the main stumbling block to all his plans. Another political leader who deserves mention here is Gurdial Singh Dhillon, who served as speaker of the Punjab legislative assembly from 1954 to 1961.

2. In the second category are those leaders who, while they may express sympathy with the demands of the Akali Dal, do so on a noncommunal basis. Moreover, they do not favor the methods they once themselves employed in the achievement of those demands, and now urge consideration of the wider political implications of Akali methods rather than the single-minded pursuit of Sikh interests. Again, there is open question-

ing on their part of some of the postulates concerning the role of religion in politics which were hitherto considered as outside discussion. Hukam Singh, the speaker of the Lok Sabha, provides an interesting example in this connection.

Born in 1895 in Montgomery in west Punjab, Hukam Singh received his B.A. at Khalsa College in Amritsar and the law degree in Lahore. He became active in the Singh Sabha movement, then took part in the Gurdwara Reform movement and served two years in jail from 1924 to 1926. In 1946 he was elected on the Akali ticket to the Constituent Assembly, where he vigorously pressed for special rights for the Sikh community. He had been a member of the Akali party since 1921, but became especially prominent in Akali politics after independence. In 1950 he was elected president of the Akali Dal and served in that office for three years.

When in the Akali Dal, his opinion was that the Congress party was an organization of opportunists,[11] and that Sikhs in the Congress party could not serve the interests of their community because they "adjust to whatever Nehru says. They have no ideals of their own but cling to whatever he says so they can remain in power."[12] He felt that the Sikhs in the Congress party were mere "sycophants and showboys."[13] On the other hand, the Akali Dal, according to him, was the "only representative body" of the Sikh community and Master Tara Singh "the undisputed leader."[14]

At this time, Hukam Singh's weekly journal, *The Spokesman,* also attacked the Congress party in sensational headlines, such as "Democracy Reduced to a Mockery: Congress Secularism Cloak for Communalism,"[15] and in general poured invective on Congress leaders. Several times *The Spokesman* carried articles vilifying Gandhi and Nehru. In one piece entitled "Political Dishonesty," it declared:

11 *The Spokesman,* IV, No. 32 (September 1, 1954), 1–2.
12 *Loc. cit.*   13 *Ibid.,* No. 35 (September 22, 1954), 1–2.
14 *Ibid.,* VI, No. 8 (February 27, 1956), 1–2.
15 *Ibid.,* II, No. 27 (July 9, 1952), 9.

Pt. Nehru is, to say the least, the spear head of militant Hindu chauvinism, who glibly talks about nationalism, a tyrant who eulogises democracy and a Goblian liar—in short, a political cheat, deceiver and a double dealer in the service of Indian reaction.[16]

The journal was even more critical of nationalist Sikhs. In one issue, it commented:

> . . . there is always an element in every society which is immature, egocentric, paranoic and destructive. . . . They suffer from a serious mental disease underneath. Some of them . . . grow up as dacoits, sexual perverts, maniacs, political traitors and war saboteurs. . . . These political perverts are so egocentric, selfish and morally debased that they would sell their country to the highest bidder. . . . The Nationalist Sikhs amongst us, is the latest version of this unscrupulous, immoral and shamefaced gang which is out to sell, undermine, and malign their own community for personal gains or out of sheer malice for their own brothers.[17]

To Hukam Singh, at this time, the demand for Punjabi Suba was an urgent necessity for the Sikhs and could not be postponed: "The formation of the Punjabi Speaking Province is the most fundamental demand of the Sikhs. To give it up would have been nothing short of signing our own death warrants, and to postpone it the worst form of opportunism and a clear violation of the Sacred Sikh traditions of open fight and chaste politics." [18]

For the achievement of Punjabi Suba, Hukam Singh was actively involved in the agitation of 1955, and was arrested for his activities.[19] After the agitation, when one Akali leader—

[16] *Ibid.*, No. 3 (January 16, 1952), 3.
[17] *Ibid.*, III, No. 7 (February 18, 1953), 3–4.
[18] *Ibid.*, II, No. 9 (March 5, 1952), 1.
[19] Karam Singh Jakhmi, *64 Roza Akali Morche Da Ithas* [History of the 64-Day Akali Morcha] (Amritsar: Panthic Tract Society, 1955), pp. 118–19.

Gian Singh Rarewala—decided to join the Congress party and recommended that the Akali Dal should cease mixing religion and politics, Hukam Singh vehemently criticized him not only personally as "an adventurer who would run after power," [20] but also for his stand on the relationship of religion and politics and the political role of the Akali Dal.[21] However, when the Akali Dal subsequently did precisely what Rarewala had suggested, Hukam Singh became a member of the Congress party in 1956. Meanwhile, sponsored by Nehru and the Congress party, he had been made deputy speaker of the Lok Sabha in 1956, and in 1962 he was elevated to the position of speaker.

When in 1960 Master Tara Singh asked former Akalis to leave the Congress and come back to the Akali Dal, Hukam Singh refused to return. On the contrary, in several statements he criticized Tara Singh. *The Spokesman* also became critical of Tara Singh for his mixing of religion and politics and thus being himself responsible for the failure to achieve Punjabi Suba.

That Hukam Singh had begun to do some rethinking on the role of religion in politics since his estrangement from Tara Singh was apparent in an article [22] he wrote on the subject. He observed in the article that the slogan "Panth is in danger" was being exploited for political purposes by interested parties, and that the "fusion of religion and politics inside the shrines has resulted in the defeat of religion" and in making the gurdwaras "the arena of battles between rival political belligerents." He agreed that in the past, religion and politics had been combined in Sikhism and that he himself had supported the view for many years, but he advocated a reappraisal of the situation as things were radically different now, especially with an elected government based on popular suffrage and subject to public opinion. He observed that "there cannot be a government of

---

[20] Hukam Singh, "Sardar Rarewala Runs After Power," *The Spokesman*, vi, No. 30 (July 30, 1956), 1.

[21] *The Tribune*, June 17, 1956.

[22] Hukam Singh, *The Spokesman*, ix, No. 30 (1959), 27.

one community alone." He now urged the separation of religion from politics, at least in the Sikh shrines "if we desire to restore the sanctity of these holy reservoirs."

Such views would have been utterly unthinkable—or at least would not have been openly expressed—while within the Akali Dal. On the other hand, Hukam Singh has consistently supported the demand for Punjabi Suba, but even here a change is discernible. Coercive methods are no longer approved, and emphasis is laid on carrying along the other communities that are opposed to Punjabi Suba. At the height of one agitation for Punjabi Suba, he expressed himself in favor of the demand, but deprecated "the clumsy way in which it is presented and the indiscreet arguments advanced to support it." [23] He realized that "Punjabi Suba would incidentally improve the position of the Sikhs," but pointed out that "this benefit can only be derived if Punjabi Suba is achieved by goodwill and mutual accommodation." [24] This viewpoint was in direct contrast to his views when he was in the Akali Dal. Rather than plunge into the agitation as he had done in 1955, regardless of the consequences in terms of Hindu-Sikh harmony, he now counseled that if the Akali Dal persisted in its methods the relations between the Hindu and Sikh communities and between the Sikhs and the government would be so strained that "ultimately Punjabi Suba would be of no avail to the Sikhs." [25]

3. In the third category is that group of leaders who find membership in the Congress party a suitable instrument for the pursuit of either personal or community goals but are ready to forsake that party the moment such goals are frustrated and return to the Akali Dal. An interesting example here is that of Giani Kartar Singh.

Born in 1901 in a Jat Sikh family in a village in Amritsar district, Kartar Singh was brought up in the new canal colonies in Lyallpur district. He studied at Khalsa College in Amritsar,

[23] *Ibid.*, XI-A, No. 1 (Tenth Anniversary Number, 1961), 71–72.
[24] *Loc. cit.*   [25] *Loc. cit.*

but did not complete his college education. He joined the Akali Dal in 1923, participated in the Gurdwara Reform movement and the civil disobedience movement in 1930, and also served time in jail. In 1937 and again in 1946, he was elected to the Punjab legislative assembly on the Akali ticket. He served for two years as president of the Akali Dal, and remained general secretary of the Akali Dal for several terms. His reputation in Punjab politics derives from his skills as a political manipulator. One author characterizes him as "the brain behind the Akali Party," "the most cunning intriguer," a "most constructive thinker," with "none of the fiery confusion of thought so prevalent amongst Sikh politicians." [26] Before independence, he led the group that wanted to reach an accommodation with the Muslim League. Kartar Singh is known to be the author of most of the political formulas that have come out of the Akali Dal—the Azad Punjab scheme, Sikhistan, Sachar formula, and the regional formula.

In 1948, along with other Akali members, Kartar Singh joined the Congress party and became a minister in the Punjab cabinet. As president of the Akali Dal at the time, he called a meeting of his executive committee and had a resolution passed stating that henceforth the Akali Dal would not engage in political activity. While in the Congress party, he was able to extract major concessions. In 1950, when asked, he refused to return to the Akali Dal and continued to serve as a minister in the government. Unable to get a Congress ticket for the general elections in 1951–52, he bolted the Congress party and went back to the Akali Dal. With Akali support he was elected to the Punjab legislative council (upper house). He took part in the Punjabi Suba agitation in 1955, and again went to jail.[27] As part of an Akali-Congress compromise, he joined the Congress party in 1956 along with other Akalis. In 1957 he was elected on the Congress ticket and became a minister in the

26 Khushwant Singh, *The Sikhs*, p. 143.
27 Jakhmi, p. 32.

state government. He fought the 1962 elections, again on the Congress ticket, and continued as a minister until the end of 1962.

During his term as minister in the state government, differences developed between him and Master Tara Singh to such an extent that he declared that there was no question of reconciliation between the two. He was dubbed "traitor" to the Panth, while he said that Tara Singh merely used the Punjabi Suba and "Panth is in danger" slogans in order to maintain his political leadership. He also thought at this time, in contrast to the period when he was in the Akali Dal, that a common platform of all communities in the Punjabi-speaking area was a prerequisite to the formation of Punjabi Suba.[28] When former Akalis in the Congress party were asked to return to the Akali Dal, he refused. In 1961, however, when the Akali Dal was at the height of its most serious confrontation with the government, Kartar Singh began thinking of leaving the Congress party again for the Akali Dal in a dramatic gesture of solidarity behind the Panth in what may have seemed its hour of crisis. He gave up the idea when two of his lieutenants—Ramdayal Singh and Rajinder Singh—refused to go along because of their commitment to the ideology of the Congress party.[29]

The same kind of tortuous loyalty to the Congress party and its ideology is obvious in the case of Sarup Singh. Sarup Singh was born in 1917 in a Ramgarhia family, studied at Amritsar and Lahore, then started practice as a lawyer. He joined the Akali Dal in 1942, and became the co-founder of the All India Sikh Students Federation. In 1945, before independence, he wrote a book, with a foreword by Master Tara Singh, in which he argued that the Sikhs were a nation and should therefore strive for a separate sovereign Sikh state.[30] He maintained that

[28] *The Tribune,* January 19, 1959.
[29] *Ibid.,* September 1, 1961.
[30] Sarup Singh, *The Forgotten Panth.*

Sikhs as individuals could not become members of other political parties without violating their loyalty to the Panth.[31]

After independence, Sarup Singh continued to be active in Akali politics, with his political base well entrenched in the Sikh Students Federation which came to be considered his private preserve. He later became vice-president of the Akali Dal. During the period he was with the Akali Dal he went to jail three times for his participation in Akali movements. In 1952 he was elected to the Punjab legislative assembly on the Akali ticket. In 1957, after the Akalis joined the Congress party, he was elected again to the assembly, but this time on the Congress ticket. When asked to return to the Akali Dal, he came back and was made leader of the Akali party in the legislature. In 1961 differences arose between him and Master Tara Singh, which resulted in his expulsion from the Akali party.[32] In 1962, without formally joining the Congress party again, he made desperate attempts to obtain the Congress ticket for election to the Punjab legislative assembly in the third general elections. At one time he was hopeful, but was eventually unable to get the Congress endorsement.

At a lower rung of political leadership, it may be noted that two Congress leaders, Shamsher Singh (Ludhiana) and Mihan Singh Gill (Patiala), who had come to the Congress party from the Akali Dal in 1956, applied for a Congress nomination for election to the Punjab legislative assembly in 1961. On their failure to obtain the Congress nomination, however, they promptly applied to the Akali Dal and ran on its ticket. Watching the spectacle of political leaders switching their political loyalties in order to get elected to legislatures, the common man in the Punjab ruefully comments that even the most ardent nationalist Sikh would leave the Congress party were he denied a ticket to the assembly. Such is the evaluation by the public of the personal goals of political leaders in the Punjab.

31 *Ibid.*, p. 20.
32 *The Hindustan Times*, June 1, 1961.

The Akali Appeal and the Extra-Parliamentary Leader

Whatever the significance of ideological change among Akali members who enter the Congress party, the periodic influx of Akali leaders into that party does not eliminate the political challenge of the Akali Dal. There may be a question about the sincerity or consistency of belief in the Akali ideology on the part of Akali leaders, past and present, but there is no doubt about the effectiveness of the Akali appeal among a substantial part of the Sikh community. Political leaders who have displayed belief at the moment in the Akali ideology or rather, until recently, have paid deference to the supreme Akali leader, Master Tara Singh, have received support from large sections of the Sikh community, untrammeled by any consideration about their future political behavior. As a consequence, the ranks of Akali leadership have been quickly replenished when an earlier set of political leaders moved to the Congress party. After receiving training in the Akali Dal for some time, the newer leadership also manages to find its way into the Congress party. Little wonder then that Master Tara Singh has been known as the trainer of political leaders in the Punjab.

Although most of the important Akali leaders have, after a period of apprenticeship and prominence in the Akali Dal, left the organization for the Congress party, Master Tara Singh has not only remained with the Akali Dal but for nearly a third of a century exercised almost continuous control over it. In 1962 his leadership was seriously challenged after he had made some grave political mistakes. His own personal character was tarnished in the process. New rivals emerged and eroded his political base. Now past eighty, it is entirely doubtful, especially after his group's defeat in the SGPC elections of 1965, that he can ever recover the prestige and support that he has lost. But it is remarkable how any one man could control an organization like the Akali Dal for more than thirty years and, through control of the organization, repeatedly marshal large numbers from among the Sikh masses against the government.

Before 1962 his unique position among the Sikh masses was due to the kind of image of himself that he was able to project as the only consistent and long-suffering upholder of the doctrine of the Panth as a separate political entity, as the one Sikh political leader who relentlessly pursued the goal of political power territorially organized for the Sikh community, and as a selfless and dedicated leader without personal ambition. At school and college he was called "pathar" (stone) for his fearless participation in soccer and hockey, where he did not care whether he hurt others or was hurt.[33] The same kind of persistence and ruthlessness has characterized his political life. He spent many years in jail for the sake of the Sikh community. After independence, when other leaders left the Akali Dal to join the Congress party, Tara Singh stuck with his organization, continued the struggle against the government for what he considered the just political claims of the Sikhs, and served jail sentences, sued for compromise when beaten, but never wavered in his goal to achieve a territorial area under Sikh political control. He never held any legislative office or ministerial position. His opponents charge that he does not have to aspire to government office since no ministership could give him the power he commands through the control of gurdwara funds running into millions of rupees, but the Sikh masses felt that his staying away from government office spoke of his self-abnegation, and many have been the stories of how he could not be "purchased." His personal character was considered by the Sikh masses to be above reproach—an element that weighs strongly with the Indian people. His honesty was often remarked upon, and was the reason why the Sikh masses and big businessmen were willing to trust him with liberal contributions. Whatever other criticisms were made of him, no man in the street doubted his personal incorruptibility.

[33] Tara Singh, *Meri Yaad*, p. 35.

Over and above all this was his mass appeal to the Sikh community, for he knew how to reach the core of the Sikh heart—the sentiment for the Sikh religion—and induce great religious-cum-political fervor. He could arouse the Sikh masses to a high pitch by an imagery depicting the Panth in danger, beset by hostile forces from all sides, but urging in the name of the Gurus that all unite and crush the enemies, in which mission success is certain, he would assure, for the Gurus are on their side. In a style reminiscent of Mossadegh of Iran, he could bring tears to his own eyes as well as to the eyes of his audience by poignantly declaring that his goal was that he may die so that the Panth may flourish. On a purely religious plane, there was no doubt of his appeal to the Sikh masses and, by the same token, the antagonism he aroused among Hindus, Muslims, and nationalist Sikhs. Where the electorate was solely Sikh, he was unbeatable. All this has changed to a great extent since 1962, but his appeal before to the Sikh masses was all the more surprising in that he was not born a Sikh.

He was born in a Hindu family in 1885 in a small village near Rawalpindi, and was named Nanak Chand. His father was a village official and later a money-lender, and belonged to the Malhotra sub-caste of the Kshatriyas or Khatris as they are known in the Punjab, the caste from which had come all the ten Sikh Gurus. It is significant of the time that though his family was Hindu it revered the Sikh Gurus.[34] Nanak Chand's interest in Sikhism was stimulated in his school days. The Singh Sabha movement was extremely active at the time, and he regularly attended the Sabha meetings. While a student in the ninth grade, he converted to Sikhism and was baptized Tara Singh.[35] In 1903 he passed high school, but could not get admitted to medical school because of his short stature. So he went to study at Khalsa College in Amritsar, where he developed an interest in politics. His father's influence and the Singh Sabha movement had made him pro-British, but his at-

[34] *Ibid.*, p. 18.   [35] *Ibid.*, p. 28.

titude changed following the partition of Bengal in 1905, the agitation by the Sikh peasantry in Lyallpur under Arya Samaj leadership, and government attempts at greater control over the Khalsa College.[36]

Tara Singh graduated from college in 1907, and decided to devote his life to the service of the Panth. He joined a teachers training college at Lahore, and then offered his services for a nominal salary of Rs. 15 (about $3.00) a month if the Sikh community would establish a Khalsa high school in Lyallpur. He had been irked by the fact that the Arya Samaj had provided the leadership for the agitation by Sikh peasants and that it was now planning to open a high school in that town. His offer was accepted and at 23 he became the headmaster of the school, and thus the honorific "Master." After the outbreak of World War I he tried his hand at business but did not succeed, and went back to teaching. He continued to take an interest in political matters and became an important figure on the Sikh political scene at the time of the Gurdwara Reform movement in the early 1920s.

During the movement he courted arrest several times. After the government approved the organization of the Shiromani Gurdwara Parbandhak Committee (SGPC) as a central body to manage Sikh shrines, Tara Singh was elected vice-president of the SGPC. Although he was now an important political figure, his rise to the foremost position among Sikh political leaders came during the controversy in the Sikh community over the constitutional proposals of the Nehru Committee. One group of Sikh leaders, led by Mangal Singh, favored acceptance of the proposals for the sake of nationalism, even though they did not adequately meet the claims of the Sikhs. Another group, led by Baba Kharak Singh, so thoroughly disagreed with the proposals that it turned against the Congress party. As an astute leader, Tara Singh took a middle position; he voiced support for the Congress party, since the Sikhs were a minority and

[36] *Ibid.,* pp. 35–38.

"there was no wisdom in standing aloof from the greatest and the only country-wide political organization," [37] but at the same time he condemned the proposals and demanded their withdrawal. As one biographer comments, "he was a staunch supporter of the Congress no doubt, but only up to the limit that it did not interfere with the legitimate rights of the Sikhs." [38] Later, when the Congress party withdrew the Nehru Committee proposals, Tara Singh emerged as a leader who had fought for the demands of the Sikh community and also had the support of the nationalist organization. His stand thus "ensured his leadership in the community for the coming years." [39]

When the Congress party launched the civil disobedience movement in 1930, Tara Singh supported it and went to jail while Baba Kharak Singh opposed it; it seems "this event marked the fall of Babaji and rise of Masterji in Sikh politics." [40] While still in jail, Tara Singh was elected president of the SGPC and "thus Masterji came at the helm and since then, i.e., 1930 up to the present day, he is the leader of the community and his leadership is undisputed and unprecedented." [41]

Later, Master Tara Singh led several militant agitations in support of Akali claims, first against the British government, then the Unionist government in the pre-independence period, and finally against the Congress government after independence. His break with the nationalist organization came during World War II when he supported the British in the war effort. This event underlined the fact that the interests of the Panth, as he conceived them, took precedence over any talk of nationalism. As he has said on another occasion, "I am ready to leave the country for the sake of the Panth, but for the sake of the country I cannot leave the Panth." [42] Before independence, he raised the demands of Azad Punjab and Sikhistan. He was

[37] Durlab Singh, *The Valiant Fighter,* p. 104.
[38] *Ibid.,* pp. 90–91.   [39] *Ibid.,* p. 104.   [40] *Ibid.,* p. 108.
[41] *Ibid.,* p. 115. When Durlab Singh wrote the book he was an admirer of Master Tara Singh, but later became a vehement critic of him.
[42] *The Statesman,* February 29, 1948.

critical of Sikhs who were deceived by "nation worship" and who ignored the possibility that behind nationalism there may be some trick or the "communal worship" of some other group.[43] As for himself, he said, "I am not such a fool that I should not understand that there is no desirability of Sikh rule." [44] In general, his relations with other groups and leaders have been characterized by a suspicion of conspiracy to undermine the Sikh community and, more particularly, his personal leadership.

In his political thinking, the concept of the Panth as an independent political entity has been foremost. People who disagree with him on this point are declared traitors. Since the Congress party endeavors to maintain a secular state, Tara Singh has felt that the struggle must go on for the separate political entity of the Sikhs, and toward this end he has launched numerous agitations. Of his own dedication in this struggle, he once wrote: "My life and death are with the Panth. It cannot be that the Panth should die and I should keep living. Those who worry more about their own lives than the life of the Panth, they may decide what they want to do. But for me the path is obvious." [45] Such words were thrown back at him in 1961 when he did not go the whole way for the sake of the Panth. But from 1930 to 1961, the most striking feature of Akali politics was the "perpetual leadership" of Tara Singh.

Through skillful control of the treasury and party press, and through the employment of political workers, he was able to retain the supreme leadership of the Akali Dal. He effectively kept the purse strings of the Akali Dal in his own hands. The party newspapers—*Prabhat* (in Urdu) and *Jathedar* (in Gurmukhi)—were managed under his personal control, not the party organization's. Incidentally, the newspaper *Prabhat* has regularly carried over its masthead the statement, "the only

[43] Tara Singh, *Meri Yaad*, p. 149.   [44] *Ibid.*, p. 145.
[45] Tara Singh, *Charhdi Kala*, pp. 41–42.

spokesman of the Panth, published under the auspices of Master Tara Singh." Suggestions that the papers be brought under the control of the party were stoutly resisted. Tara Singh himself is a journalist of some repute and regularly contributes signed articles to these papers. In addition, in every important town and district of the Punjab he has had political workers in his personal employ to look after his interests. These workers have been a source of political intelligence, and a political instrument to check those in the party organization attempting to threaten his position. Furthermore, the weighty advantage of over forty years of experience in politics served him well and, until recently, often made other contenders seem like political amateurs. Many of his former colleagues allege that even the periodic dispatch of Akali leaders to the Congress party has been a well thought out strategy on his part to maintain his leadership and control of the Akali Dal. One of his former leading associates, now in the Congress party, explained: "As soon as he feels that there are certain persons who are just having some following among the Sikhs, there are apprehensions raised in his mind that one or more of them might become a challenge to his leadership. Then certainly he would try either to demolish them by character assassination, and if that cannot be done then he probably would just see that they are sent out to the Congress." [46] Another of his trusted lieutenants, now no longer with the Akali Dal, speaking in bitterness about how he had been treated by Tara Singh, said: "He has decided once for all to be the grand leader of the opposition in India. What does he do? Every five years, he patches up with the Congress party and all the seasoned workers and leaders who start measuring up to him are sent to the Congress under some blooming pact, and then that pact is disowned after a year and then all those people are called traitors who are sticking to their legislative memberships, to their ministerships, and this old man is there, selfless and so on and so forth." [47]

[46] From an interview.   [47] From an interview.

Whatever the motivations behind the sending of Akali leaders to the Congress party, one result of these movements, or perhaps the reason for them, was the added importance of relatives of Tara Singh in the Akali party organization. Since other leaders seemed, or were, migratory, close relatives, as the only ones constant in their loyalty, came to be relied upon in party work. Or perhaps the important party positions with real political power were so inaccessible to persons outside the family that other Akali leaders thought it best not to take out a life membership in the Akali Dal. At any rate, the father-in-law of one of the sons of Tara Singh wielded a great deal of political power in the party organization. Again, in 1962, one nephew was not only a private secretary to Tara Singh, but also the propaganda secretary of the Akali Dal, while one of Tara Singh's sons managed the party press. The tight control over the party organization, added to his great mass appeal in the past among the Sikh masses, enabled Tara Singh to constantly hurl political challenges at the Congress party and government.

His recent political setbacks and his advancing age preclude the possibility that Tara Singh can ever give the Akalis the vigorous and determined leadership he provided in the past. However, his political career does suggest the sort of image that Akali leadership in the future may seek to project and the relationship it may seek to establish with the Sikh masses in order to secure popular support if it decides to persist in the present policy of challenging the forces of secular nationalism.

THE NATIONALIST RESPONSE: STRONGER SIKH LEADERSHIP

The condition of "perpetual crisis" that has prevailed in the Punjab as a result of the Akali challenge has had important implications for the nature of recruitment to political leadership in the Congress party. Before independence, when there were separate electorates, Congress representatives in the Punjab legislature had, by and large, come from the Hindu community. The Congress representation in the legislature had more of an urban orientation, for the Hindu representatives from the rural areas of southeast Punjab were, in the main, supporters of the Unionist party. Some Sikh leaders in the legislature were elected on the Congress ticket, but their number was not very large and they formed a small part of the total strength of the Congress party in the pre-independence Punjab legislature. In short, the top leadership of the Congress party in the legislature was in the hands of urban Hindu leaders. When the Congress party assumed political power in the Punjab after independence, it seemed natural then that the government should be headed by a Hindu leader with an urban background. An additional reason was the fact that the Hindus now constituted over 60 percent of the population of the Punjab.

Although the legislative representatives of the Congress party in the Punjab had mostly come from the Hindu community, the party organization did not reflect this position. On the contrary, many of the important positions in the party organization were held by non-Hindus. While the appeal of secular nationalism made by the Congress party was not successful in the pre-independence period among the separate electorates of Muslims and Sikhs in enabling it to get representatives from these communities elected in any large numbers to the legislature on its ticket, the party was anxious to prove its bona fides as a secular party by offering important positions in the party organization to non-Hindus. Also, the presence of factions among Hindu Congressmen in the party made it easier for well-knit, non-Hindu groups to bargain for important offices. Thus, after 1937, Akali representatives secured important positions in the Congress party organization. In this manner, many important positions in the Congress party came to be occupied by Muslims and Sikhs before independence. As one veteran leader of the Congress party writes: "Indisputably it is the Hindu community in the Punjab which has contributed most to the Congress. It was they who flocked to the Congress from the earliest days and joined its ranks. Money, sacrifice and service all have come mostly from the Hindus to make the Congress a success. The proportion of non-Hindus in the Congress Organisation is comparatively very small. But the Hindu majority has given a lion's share to the non-Hindu minority in the Congress Organisation. In all districts of the Punjab non-Hindu Congressmen have been given places of importance in spite of their number being small and sometimes insignificant." [48]

In terms of religious affiliation, there was then a disjunction between the top leadership in the legislative wing and the organizational wing of the Congress party. After independence the position of Chief Minister of the Punjab was occupied by two Hindus in succession until the end of 1955. The Congress party organization, on the other hand, was under the control of Sikh leaders. Partap Singh Kairon was recognized as one of the top leaders in the Punjab Congress party after independence. He had been made general secretary of the party in 1941, and he continued in that strategic position until 1950, when he became president of the party. In fact, the presidency of the Congress party in the Punjab until the end of 1962 remained under the control of one or another Sikh leader: Gurmukh Singh Musafir, Partap Singh Kairon, again Musafir, and then Darbara Singh.

Any Chief Minister of the state of Punjab had, however, to reckon with the communal demands of the Akali Dal and the militant agitations in support of them. He could either reach an accommodation with the Akali Dal at the state level and buy a temporary truce, or resist its demands and meet it head-on in the maintenance of law and order. The former method was tried only to raise an uproar about appeasement of communal forces, not only from Hindus but also from nationalist Sikhs. Among other reasons, dissatisfaction with the alleged policy of appeasement weighed in the revolt among Congress legislators against Chief Minister Gopi Chand Bhargava, and resulted finally in his ouster from office. Another Hindu Chief Minister,

[48] Duni Chand, p. 20.

Bhim Sen Sachar, after conciliating the Akalis in one term, tried to meet the challenge of their agitations, the result of which encounter was interpreted as a "victory" by the Akalis and eventually involved further concessions to the Akali Dal.

Part of the reason for the lack of success of those two Chief Ministers in meeting the Akali challenge may perhaps have been due to the personality and ability of the leaders. However, any Hindu Chief Minister, confronted with the threat of Akali agitations mounted on behalf of the Sikh community, suffered from an obvious handicap. For him to instigate stern police measures to control an Akali agitation would only serve to heighten the intensity of the agitation. The Akali Dal could then effectively proclaim that the Sikhs were being really repressed by the Hindu community as represented through the Chief Minister. Thus any state government headed by a Hindu suffered from the inherent weakness—in its confrontation with Akali agitations—that it would open itself to charges of repression of a minority community, and was consequently subject to intimidation. Furthermore, there was evidently the handicap springing from the social background of these leaders. Being urban-based, they were not politically skillful in controlling agitations in which a large part of the Sikh peasantry was mobilized. Again there was disharmony—resulting either from a different religious background or from political ambition—between the leadership in the Congress government and the leadership of the Congress party organization, which adversely affected the ability to counteract agitations on a party basis.

All this rendered the Hindu leadership of the Congress government vulnerable to charges of weakness from within the Congress party. It is in the context of this situation that a strong Sikh leader, Partap Singh Kairon, rose to the position of Chief Minister.[49] In the period from 1956, when Kairon became

[49] It is interesting that only Sikh leaders were reportedly considered as possible replacements for Bhim Sen Sachar. Kairon is said to have emerged as the choice through a process of elimination: Swaran Singh

Chief Minister, to 1964, when he resigned, he was able to bring about the failure of every single agitation launched against the government. Being a Sikh himself, he suffered from none of the hesitations that evidently beset his predecessors. A peculiar blend of organization man and mass leader, a knowledge of the inner working of the Akali Dal and the tactics of its leaders, and a secure base in the party organization and the blessings of the Congress leadership at the center—all reflected in his background—enabled him to handle successfully threats to the maintenance of law and order in the Punjab.

Partap Singh Kairon took his name Kairon after the village in Amritsar district where he was born in 1901 into a Jat Sikh family. His father had been an influential leader in the Singh Sabha movement, and later had close and friendly relations with Master Tara Singh. After studying at Khalsa College in Amritsar, Kairon went to the United States for higher studies. He received his M.A. in economics and political science at the University of Michigan. During his nine-year stay in the United States, he worked on an assembly line at the Ford Motor Company, and was also associated with the activities of the Indian revolutionaries in America. His stay in the United States later led his opponents to label as "the American technique" the various tactics he employed to achieve his political objectives.

After his return to India in 1929, Kairon joined the Akali Dal under the influence of Master Tara Singh. He edited a newspaper called *New Era,* took part in the civil disobedience movement in 1931, and was sentenced to imprisonment for several years. In 1934 he became the general secretary of the Akali Dal, and served his political apprenticeship under Master Tara Singh. He soon gave proof of his organizational ability

---

did not have any political following in the legislative wing of the Congress party, and Baldev Singh was unwilling to take on the responsibility. Interestingly enough, all three had been prominent leaders of the Akali Dal. See *The Tribune,* January 17, 1956.

in the contest with the veteran nationalist leader Baba Gurdit Singh in the 1937 elections. Kairon, then running on the Akali ticket and using the Panthic appeal, won. In 1937, when the Akalis joined the Congress party, Kairon became a member of the Congress party. In 1941 he became the general secretary of the Congress party in the Punjab. For some time he kept up his contacts with the Akali Dal, but then differences arose between him and Tara Singh over collaboration with the British in the war effort. He finally broke away from the Akali Dal in 1942 when it entered into an alliance with the Unionist government.

After the war, Nehru made him a member of the working committee of the All India Congress Committee, thus giving him a place in the highest councils of the Congress party. This position he held until 1959, even after he became Chief Minister. After independence he served as a minister in the Punjab cabinet from 1947 to 1949, and again from 1952 to 1955. Since he was the general secretary of the Congress party in the Punjab before and after independence, it fell to him to reorganize the party after the chaos resulting from the partition and also to widen the base of the party in the rural areas, for the party hitherto had an urban orientation. From this vantage point in the organization, subsequently enhanced by his assumption of the office of president of the Punjab Congress from 1950 to 1952, he was able to control the party organization and build a loyal base both in the organizational wing and, through control over the distribution of election tickets, in the legislative wing, thus assuring for himself the top position of Chief Minister. After the 1952 general elections Kairon's group had a majority in the Congress legislature party, but the Congress leadership at the center preferred Sachar for the position of Chief Minister. The struggle between the various factions within the party continued and finally came to a head in 1955. Confronted again with a choice between Sachar and Kairon, the central leadership chose to side with Kairon. With Kairon's installation as Chief Minister, both party organization and government came under the same leader, serving to strengthen the position of the Chief Minister.

During his tenure as Chief Minister, Kairon was eminently successful in "crushing" agitations through what seemed to some as strong-arm methods. The Who's Who for the Punjab legislative assembly describes him to be "well-known as an administrator of dash, drive and decision" who "has handled successfully a number of agitations and stirs in Punjab." [50] He built for himself an image of being a second Ranjit Singh—not only in his ability to control threats to the peace and stability of the state, but also in restoring "the rule of the Jats" in the Punjab. It would seem that his ability to control agitations derived from the years of experience in party organization and managing people, apart from the personal support of Nehru. Though he spent some nine years in the United States, Kairon chose to keep close to the soil, and before independence took part in peasant agitations. He was extremely accessible to the villagers of Punjab and was considered to be a ruralite at heart and genuinely concerned with the welfare of the Punjab peasantry. Described as a "political psychologist" in his ability to divine the next move of his opponents, Kairon was said to delight in handling emergencies and political crises. A measure of his self-confidence was the declaration, on the eve of one of the toughest agitations against the government, that "I shall not let a single leaf stir in the Punjab." An index of his ability was that he fulfilled the declaration. In dealing with agitations he proved a master strategist, which gave rise to the myth of his indispensability. Allegations were made in some quarters that, in order to stay in power, Kairon himself created situations which forced opposition parties to launch agitations.

Though Kairon was in the Akali Dal for nearly ten years, his apologists have argued that the organization was then "an anti-

[50] Punjab Vidhan Sabha, *Who's Who 1960* (Chandigarh: Controller, Printing and Stationery, 1960), p. 93.

imperialist, progressive, non-communal and militant force." [51]
It is in light of this evaluation that Kairon himself remarked
that he left, not the Akali Dal, but Master Tara Singh who
cooperated with the British. At any rate, during his term as
Chief Minister he set himself firmly against the Akali Dal and
its leader, and at times the struggle assumed the form of a
combat between master and disciple-turned-opponent. His success in crushing Akali agitations made him enemy number one
with Master Tara Singh, whose principal aim then became the
ouster of Kairon from the office of Chief Minister. For his part,
Kairon saw the struggle as between good and evil: "I am playing for high stakes. On one side is the integrity, unity and
prosperity of my dear country and on the other communal and
disruptive forces coming in various forms and changing slogans
which wish to pull my country down. I am up against these
forces. I fight against them because I love my country and my
people. If in the fight I have to face death, I would welcome
it because that would be a glorious death. What is my life after
all when millions of other lives are at stake?" [52] With the opponents fighting in the name of diametrically opposed ideologies, the struggle was bitter, with no quarter given and none
asked.

Kairon was not only able to meet successfully the challenge
from the Akali Dal, but also managed to retain against great
odds his leadership within the Congress party. How was he
able to maintain control over the administration and the party
organization? His methods in this regard are popularly known
in the Punjab as "the American technique"; two excerpts from
interviews will illustrate their nature. One cabinet minister remarked: "His technique is manipulating and setting one leader
against the other. That is what I found. Just to illustrate it. I
am elected from a particular constituency. I will not get all

[51] S. S., "Kairon—The Man and the Crusader," *The Indian Express*
(Punjab Industries Supplement), February 27, 1962.
[52] *Loc. cit.*

the help I need, but the person who opposed me, and who can be considered my rival in that constituency, he will get all support from him. He undermines everybody in that manner. He is particular to see that a person does not go beyond certain limits. Everyone should be kept within limits, that has been his policy. Hs is a shrewd politician. He has those inclinations of a fascist or dictator." One of his protégés, once an important Akali leader but afterwards an admirer of Kairon, stated: "His major technique is to solve personal problems—personal economic problems—immediately. He will give you a job, a permit, a job to your wife, a membership in some board, some contract. He must deal with it immediately and he is a great leader who makes decisions. He believes in nobody, he makes decisions himself. He is a dictator, a king."

A former colleague of Kairon's, but later a vigorous opponent, said, "this is his biggest technique—to corrupt politically. Everyone can be purchased, this is his thesis." While these methods and techniques helped him retain control over the government for more than eight years, they also led to his downfall in ignominious circumstances. Both opposition and Congress leaders, increasingly embittered with him, led a persistent clamor for investigation into charges of corruption and nepotism against him. Kairon resigned in June 1964 after a commission established by the Indian government found that he had used his "influence and power for his own benefit in some cases and also abused powers through his colleagues and subordinates to help his sons and relatives." [53] His political career thus abruptly finished, Kairon was subjected to great public humiliation and harassment in the following eight months. In February 1965, he was shot and killed by a four-man band outside Delhi.[54]

After Kairon's resignation from the Chief Ministership, there were several claimants for the office, but the final contest came to center around two Sikh leaders, Darbara Singh and Giani

[53] *The Hindu Weekly Review,* June 29, 1964.
[54] *New York Times,* February 7, 1965.

Zail Singh. The group followings of these two leaders were so strongly opposed to each other, however, that finally the Congress high command chose the 51-year-old Congress veteran Ram Kishan, a Hindu, for he was without any strong enemies. He had joined the nationalist movement in 1929 during his student days. Whether Ram Kishan may be only "the Sachar" before "the Kairon" will depend on what the Akali Dal does and the extent to which the center intervenes on his behalf, plus the sincere support of his colleagues. Perhaps the Kairon legacy of handling Akali challenges, including the precedents Kairon established, and factional divisions in the Akali leadership, will work in his favor.

New Trends in Leadership Recruitment

Kairon's tenure as Chief Minister saw several changes in the patterns of political recruitment, some of them to sustain his own supremacy within the Congress party. His elevation to the position of Chief Minister had come as a result of the intervention of the Congress party at the center. Certainly he had a sizable bloc of supporters in the legislative wing of the Congress party in the Punjab, but by no means all the members were with him. In fact, there were many party members who were highly antagonistic toward him. While the search for security in political office may be universal, it acquired a special importance in the Punjab. Any Chief Minister having to contend with the political problems of the Punjab, had to give them his complete attention, untrammeled by any fears of being thrown out of office. The successful handling of the political problems was in itself a prerequisite to continuance in office, but in turn, security of office was necessary to attend adequately to the problems. The Chief Minister had to have his position of leadership safeguarded in order to handle effectively the problems that faced the state.

When Kairon assumed the office of Chief Minister there were a large number of leaders in the legislative wing who were the products of the nationalist movement. They had participated in the various movements launched by the Congress party, and as a result had undergone considerable hardship in the form of police beatings; long hours of interrogation; having their properties attached by the government, with their regular sources of income dried up; and additionally spending years in jail. These members had been drawn into politics by their urge to see the country independent. Many had left schools and colleges in response to the appeals of Congress leaders. They had not come into politics expecting to share in the spoils of office, but when the Congress party started participation in parliamentary activity, many of them were elected to central and state legislatures. Beginning with the 1946 general elections, people without any record of participation in the nationalist movement began to receive the Congress endorsement,[55] but by and large it was the veterans of the nationalist movement who were elected to legislatures.

Such people in the Punjab legislature, who had a record of service and sacrifice during the nationalist movement, were not ready to be blind followers of any leader who was until recently one of their colleagues. As one important Congress leader put it: "Now many members had a feeling that Partap Singh Kairon was a newcomer, he had joined Congress ten years after I had. So he could not expect me to dance attendance. Most of my colleagues were old Congressmen. They could accept him as first among equals, but not as a demigod." [56]

Moreover, even if party interest might induce contingent loyalty to the leader of the party, such leaders could not always be relied on, for those who had rebelled against the might of the British empire could certainly rebel against the Chief Minister. Their political background had turned them into hardened individualists. They could not give unquestioning loyalty to the leader. On the contrary, many of them were contenders for that office themselves. On the other hand, the Chief Minis-

[55] Duni Chand, pp. 23–24.   [56] From an interview.

ter wanted in his party a group of followers who could be loyal
to him through thick and thin, so that he was not constantly
required to attend to the task of assuring his continuance in
office. To be sure, the party organization had been under his
control, but hitherto he did not have to contend with the problem in the legislative wing and some of these old-timers were
even his allies in the rise to power. Now efforts were directed
to the control of both the party organization and the legislative
wing. What are the changes in political recruitment that can
be discerned in the search for security by the party's top leader?
The following trends seem obvious in the changing patterns of
political leadership of the Congress party in the last decade or
so.

The first thing to be noted is the decline, in terms of numbers and political power, of the veterans of the nationalist movement. Many of the old stalwarts who may have constituted a
threat to the Chief Minister were gradually squeezed out of
the party. Many of them were denied any share in political
power so as to prevent the emergence of centers of potential
revolt against the Chief Minister. If they were given seats on
the cabinet, it was politely or otherwise indicated to them that
the real decision-making powers must remain with the Chief
Minister. Some stayed on the sufferance of the Chief Minister,
but many felt their position uncomfortable enough to quit.
Others were forced out by invoking questions of party discipline. Still others left the party when attempts were made to
undermine their political position by denying, through control
of the party organization, election tickets to their followers in
the legislature. Reasons were found to deny tickets to some of
the old leaders themselves. But more effectively, some of them
were humored through the award of tickets only to have their
election torpedoed by the party organization at the local level
and thus killed politically. The casualties resulting from these
tactics have been many: Udham Singh Nagoke, Ishar Singh
Majhail, Ch. Devi Lal, Sri Ram Sharma, Professor Sher Singh,

Ch. Lehri Singh, Lala Jagat Narain, Kedar Nath Sehgal and many others. "It's all a big purge," remarked one Congress leader. Another veteran, no longer active in politics, wrote: "I did not look upon the regime of either Dr. Gopichand Bhargava or Mr. Bhimsen Sachar as free from serious shortcomings and like many other public men, criticized them severely. But there is one marked difference between their regimes and the regime of S. Partap Singh Kairon. While the first two did not studiedly prevent such honest Congress elements as did not see eye to eye with them from sharing responsibility for the working of the new democratic set up in Punjab, the present regime appears to have tried hard to eliminate these elements from all those positions in the State Congress or in the State government wherefrom they can serve the people." [57]

The main consideration in the elimination of the "old guard" was the prevention of any threat to the security of office of the Chief Minister, but the axe seemed to fall more heavily on the Hindu leaders since they were the ones with a greater record of service in the Congress party. This is not to suggest that the old leadership completely vanished from the Congress party in the Punjab. Those that remained, however, did not constitute a threat to the Chief Minister, though they did have, as a supporter of Kairon remarked, "nuisance value." Some of them could not tear themselves away from a party in which they had spent all their adult life. Others extended support to the Chief Minister, because the party with which they had been identified for so long was faced with political challenges that threatened its very existence. One of these was finally to replace Kairon as Chief Minister in 1964.

With the departure of the old guard leaders, the most important criterion in the recruitment to legislative leadership of the Congress party became personal loyalty to the Chief Minister. At times, new leaders with no record of membership in the

[57] Letter of Duni Chand, "Democracy in Punjab," *The Tribune,* September 29, 1959.

party suddenly emerged as deserving of the party's ticket to the legislature. The attempt was clearly to recruit people who owed their political position solely to the favor of the Chief Minister. The consideration most of the time was not the qualities that should be the necessary equipment of a legislator, but fidelity to the leader. The less the new leaders were capable of thinking for themselves, the better for their role as "yes-men." The result of the attempt to have strong leadership at the top was to have weak leadership at the lower levels—a strong head over a weak body. The recruitment of new political leaders, without any record of service or political contribution, was a source of great resentment to the old-timers, who bitterly remarked about the replacement of the spirit of sacrifice by what they called "political opportunism" as the motive in joining politics by the new leaders whom they derisively characterized as "political dummies."

The emphasis on political loyalty received its most complete manifestation in the recruitment of relatives to legislatures. During the 1962 elections the following relatives of Partap Singh Kairon were given tickets by the Congress party for election to legislative office: Hardip Singh, Amritsar; Mangal Singh, Ludhiana; Harcharan Singh, Ferozepur; and Inder Mohan Singh Grewal, Ludhiana. Thus, in the search for security, ascriptive criteria became important in the recruitment to political leadership. The appointment of Sikh leaders to important positions in the government and party organization may also be explained by the need for a loyal following. One is apt to have more loyal friends in one's own religious community than outside. Moreover, a larger number of political offices for Sikhs seems necessary for their morale in the struggle against communalism.

While loyalty thus became the prime factor in the selection to leadership, the change in the nature of politics since independence has also affected the type of people who are recruited.

Before the achievement of independence, while politics was a full-time business with the small segment of organizational leadership, most of the leaders had a marginal though intense connection with politics; they did not live off politics though they were very much in it. They were mostly doctors, lawyers, journalists, small businessmen, or teachers and agriculturists who made their living in these occupations but participated in the political field because of their concern for the country's freedom. Political work at the time consisted of agitating against the government rather than, except for a brief period, running it.

With the achievement of independence, a change occurred in the purpose of the Congress party. Former agitators assumed positions as administrators in the governance of the country. The leaders now had to serve as administrators or supporters of the administration rather than agitate against the government in intermittent movements. There was a change in the relationship of the leader to his constituency: the leader was now supposed to nurse the constituency and channel its demands to the administration and serve as its mouthpiece, rather than merely mobilize it for agitation as before. On the other hand, his accountability to the electorate through periodic elections implied that he must satisfy his constituents if he were to continue his leadership. The top leadership of the Congress party also required political leaders and workers who were available to mend the fences in the districts on a regular basis. Politics was no longer a part-time business, but demanded the full-time attention of Congress leaders and workers. The trend toward the professionalization of political leadership had started. A class of workers or leaders who made their living from politics emerged as a by-product of the change in the nature of politics since independence. People with good education and family background are unwilling to take on the responsibilities of politics as a full-time profession, and people

with lesser education have filled the role. However, they are
generally looked down upon as those who are in politics because they are incapable of finding a job "in the market."

Such political workers, once they attain some political office,
are able to establish independent sources of livelihood through
obtaining government contracts for coal depots or brick kilns,
and do not remain entirely dependent on politics. If elected to
the legislative assembly they are assured for five years a salary
of Rs. 300 ($63.00) a month plus allowances when the assem-
bly is in session. When it was mentioned to one political leader
of the old guard that the professional political worker fills a
necessary role and that economic benefit may be just one of
many motives in recruitment to politics, he sharply retorted:
"Economic gain is not *one* of the motives, but the *only* motive
in recruitment to politics today [my italics]. These people could
not find a job for Rs. 60 in the open market and here they
amass huge sums. They make money in salaries, and through
quotas and permits. When election time comes, they save on
campaign funds which the party and friends have given them.
Whether they lose or win the election, they emerge richer." [58]

Another class of people that has assumed importance in the
new pattern of political recruitment are those with money. In
the period before independence, the nationalist appeal was considered sufficient to ensure election to the legislature. There
was some element of truth in the remark that people would
elect a lamp-post if the Congress cared to nominate one. Since
then, election to legislatures has become an expensive business.
It is not within the means of most to bear the expenses involved
in election to the legislative assembly. Provided loyalty to the
leader is assured, some of the tickets go to people who are able
to fend for their own elections and do not constitute a drain
on the party's war chest.

On the other hand, for people with money, election to the
legislature has its complementary economic attractions. The

[58] From an interview.

fees of the lawyer who gets elected go up, for the people believe that court cases handled by an MLA will receive more
favorable consideration. Businessmen who have been elected
can get better attention for their applications for quotas and
permits. Not only does wealth enable them initially to achieve
legislative and political office, but the latter in turn enables
them to enhance their monetary position. When one business-
man-turned-politician was asked by his assistant why he wanted
to waste so much money in the election, he answered, "You
don't know. When you are not an MLA you can't even get
inside the secretariat. You have to plead with another MLA
to take you there, and then you have to remain beholden to
him."

One should not, however, overemphasize the economic factor. There is, in addition, the vague yearning for prestige which
mere money cannot bring. As one person remarked: "When a
minister comes to town, you are just one of five hundred businessmen invited to a party whereas there are just a few MLAs.
When the Republic Day celebrations are held, they give the
front seat to the MLA, the others are seated behind. A busi-
nessman does not gain much respect unless he enters politics."
Then there is the influence the MLA wields over the district
administration and the allocation of development funds in the
constituency. In addition, there is the feeling of importance
that comes from being the representative of more than a hundred thousand citizens. And finally there is the feeling of satisfaction in that one is needed politically; as one aspirant remarked, "My leader wants me." There is further the feeling
that if people with money, who incidentally are educated, do
not enter politics, then "the wrong kind of people"—meaning
the professional political workers—will dominate politics.[59]

[59] This discussion of the new trends in political recruitment in the
Congress party is supported by an examination of the social background
of the candidates running for the Punjab legislative assembly from
Ludhiana district in the 1962 general elections. Nearly all the Congress
candidates joined the Congress party after the achievement of independ-

SUMMARY AND CONCLUSIONS

The following conclusions would seem to emerge from a study of political leadership in the Punjab in the period from 1947 to 1964: Any political group, while having a potent political appeal, is likely to find it difficult—unless it can provide alternative sources of political power—to count on the continued loyalty of its members if it chooses to remain a permanent political minority in a regime where opportunities exist to share in political power in association with other groups. The appeal of the group would perhaps serve as a useful instrument in political recruitment, but it may not be adequate in ensuring a sustained commitment to the group. In due course, the appeal itself may be looked upon as merely an effective political weapon for recruitment to leadership, not as an object of ideological commitment.

In the specific case of the Akali Dal, it would seem that political leaders have been able to mobilize political support on the basis of the appeal of the Sikh Panth as a separate political entity, but their political behavior, in public at least—barring a few exceptions—does not indicate an enduring commitment to the concept underlying the appeal. Despite the radical disparity between the Akali ideology and the Congress ideology, there have been several large migrations of Akali leaders to the Congress party in the period since independence.

ence. Only one person (Harbhagwan Maudgil) claimed to have entered the party in 1936, but this claim was hotly contested by political workers of the district, who maintained he had entered the party after 1947. At any rate, he had not gone to jail in any of the Congress movements. Two candidates in these elections had joined the Congress party before independence (Babu Bachan Singh in the 1920s and Jagdish Chander in 1930), but both ran on independent tickets against Congress candidates. Most of the candidates were either full-time political workers or people with adequate wealth, whether as landlords, businessmen, industrialists, or lawyers. Two of the businessmen (Inder Mohan Singh Grewal and Dina Nath Aggarwal) joined the Congress party not long before their endorsement for the election by the party. One of the candidates (Inder Mohan Singh) was a close relative of Partap Singh Kairon. Three of the Congress candidates were leaders of the Akali Dal before 1956.

This is not to suggest that the pursuit of personal goals is the sole motive in the subsequent adoption of a secular stance by Akali leaders and in the transfer of such leaders to the Congress party. On the contrary, there may well be in addition a vital interest on the part of Akali leaders to maximize political power for the Akali Dal or the Sikh community, which can be done only through joining a party that is in control of the government. Both personal and group goals may thus be pursued at the same time. But the continued political struggle between the Akali Dal and the Congress party eventually results in some conflict between such personal and group goals, for the nature of the struggle requires former Akali leaders in the Congress party to take a public stand on the issues involved. Repudiating the Akali ideology, most such leaders have remained in the Congress party. Whatever their motivations, their public stand demonstrates that the preference for personal goals or the new loyalty to secular nationalism supersedes their former public commitment to the Akali ideology. In the end, such frequent shifts may mean that future Akali leaders may really not be committed to the Akali ideology even though they may repeatedly proclaim belief in it in public. Ambitious persons may merely utilize the communal appeal of the Akali Dal to acquire conveniently positions of leadership in the Akali Dal in the expectation that there may be opportunities later for transfer to a party with real political power and patronage.

As for the Congress party, involved in an intense political conflict with a militant political group, but obligated to seek political support from a common base within a democratic framework, it tended to develop certain patterns of political recruitment similar to the group to which it was opposed. The Akali Dal has been a group confined to the Sikh community and militantly engaged in making communal demands under the leadership of a strong Sikh leader. In its attempt to cope with the Akali Dal in the political field, the Congress party in the Punjab produced an equally strong leader, also a Sikh, and additionally provided Sikh leaders in the party a share in political power disproportionate to the numerical strength of the Sikh community and the ability of these leaders to mobilize political support from the community for the party.

Furthermore, a hard and drawn-out struggle between the two political groups tended to consolidate power in the hands of the strong leader in both groups, and the necessity of preserving that power tended to result in the replacement of a commitment to ideology, by personal loyalty to the leader, in political recruitment to the two groups. In their attempt to maintain control of the party organization, these strong leaders managed to deprive all possible rivals of important positions, and even membership, in their respective parties. Their heavy-handed methods were eventually to provoke a revolt among their colleagues and to lead to their own downfall. However, in the meantime, the result was not only a certain continuous flux among political leaders in the party, but also the emergence of weaker leadership at levels below the strong leader. The struggle between the Akali Dal and the Congress party, under the circumstances, almost assumed the form of a personal contest between the two top leaders of the two parties, while the course of the conflict was powerfully influenced by the resources each leader and his party could command.

CHAPTER V

Resources of the Akali Dal

IN THE period since independence, the Akali Dal has been the prime mover on the political scene in the Punjab; the Congress party has merely reacted and responded. In its conflict with the Congress party, the Akali Dal has continuously held the initiative. The ability to recruit new leaders, to mobilize mass support and to engage in a continuous struggle against the government, is a measure not only of the effectiveness of the Akali appeal but more significantly of the resources of the Akali Dal. The first and foremost source of its strength lies in the nature of the Akali Dal organization itself.

SHIROMANI AKALI DAL

The objective of the Akali Dal is "the protection of the Panth," [1] or more specifically, "the protection of Sikh rights and ensuring the Sikhs' continued existence as an independent entity." [2] Indeed, the very existence of the Akali Dal is related to the concept of the separate political entity of the Sikhs. This concept implies, in the opinion of Akali leaders, that there must be unity of the Panth, and that "unity means one path to be followed" and the "formation or organization of a fully representative body of the Sikhs" to chalk out "this path" and "to control and direct the politics of the Sikhs." [3] As a political party, the Akali Dal consists of only those who care to enroll as its members, but in the actual political world the Akali Dal has pre-empted exclusively for itself the role of the representative body or agent of the Panth. Master Tara Singh has con-

[1] See the statement of Master Tara Singh in *Prabhat,* quoted in *The Tribune,* August 2, 1958.

[2] *Loc. cit.* See also clause 1 of *Shiromani Akali Dal Di Bantar De Niyam* [Constitution of the Shiromani Akali Dal] (Amritsar: Secretary, Shiromani Akali Dal, 1961), p. 3.

[3] Tara Singh, *Charhdi Kala,* pp. 43–44.

tended that the "Shiromani Akali Dal exists as a political body and the only representative organization of the Sikhs, unlimited in its scope and activities." [4] The attempt on the part of any other political group to acquire the role of being the representative of the Panth is immediately denounced and its efforts effectively scotched.

Not only does the Akali Dal proclaim itself as the only representative body of the Panth, but it goes further and equates itself with the Panth; it considers itself to be the Panth. In his presidential address to the All India Akali Conference held at Gujranwala before independence, Babu Labh Singh declared: ". . . there is only one Khalsa Panth which was founded by Guru Gobind Singh. And there is only one definition of the Panth—one that is devoid of selfish interest, is beloved of the country and seeks the shelter of no one except the Guru. Such a Panth alone can be called the Panth of Guru Gobind Singh and that is the existing Shiromani Akali Dal. None other can call itself the Panth." [5] As a consequence of this position, one finds that the candidates of the Akali Dal for elections are presented as Panthic candidates, and the Akali group in the legislature is called the Panthic party. For the Akali Dal, the presence of Sikhs in any area must automatically mean their representation by the Akali Dal, no matter what the political views of the Sikhs in the area may be. Thus in 1948, when the state of PEPSU was formed and no elections were contemplated for some time, the Akali Dal demanded that, since "the Sikhs constitute an effective majority in the Patiala and East Punjab States Union," the Akali Dal should be "called to form the Ministry with the cooperation of the minority parties" as it "alone represents the Union Sikhs." [6]

It is in the context of this equation of the Akali Dal with the Panth that it becomes intelligible why all those who oppose

[4] *The Tribune*, June 17, 1956.

[5] Quoted in Tara Singh, *Charhdi Kala*, pp. 8–9.

[6] Resolution of the executive committee of the Akali Dal, *The Tribune*, July 29, 1948.

the Akali Dal are not only considered anti-Akali but are also characterized as anti-Panth and immediately labeled as "traitors" to the Panth. Outside of the Communist parties, there is perhaps no other political party in the world that employs with greater frequency the term "traitor" than does the Akali Dal, especially its leader, Master Tara Singh. However, it is individuals who must act for organizations, and in the end the identification of the Akali Dal with the Panth has in the past meant the identification of the Panth with the personal leadership of Master Tara Singh himself. Any Akali leader who has questioned his leadership in the Akali Dal or in the Shiromani Gurdwara Parbandhak Committee has been immediately suspended or expelled from the Akali Dal on the charge of either engaging in anti-Panthic activity or being an agent of the government.[7] As one political leader has said, "the thing is that with Master Tara Singh, the Panth is Master and the Master is Panth." [8]

However, the identification of the Akali Dal with the Panth is of the utmost political significance, for it makes the Akali Dal heir to a tradition of political organization par excellence —heir to the organization of the Khalsa by Guru Gobind Singh. Some compare the creation of the Khalsa by the tenth Guru to the founding of the Communist party by Lenin. For example, Toynbee writes: "Lenin succeeded because he set himself to create something which would meet the situation. His All-Union Communist Party was not, indeed, a thing entirely without precedent. In Iranic Muslim history it had been anticipated in the slave-household of the Ottoman Padishah, in the Qyzylbash fraternity of devotees of the Safawis, and in the Sikh Khalsa that had been called into being by a decision to fight the Mughal ascendancy with its own weapons. In these

[7] For a recent example note the suspension and later the expulsion of several members of the Akali executive committee in 1961–62.

[8] Harkishen Singh Surjeet, *Master Tara Singh Di Siyaasat Te Akali Party Di Sankat* [The Politics of Master Tara Singh and the Misfortune of the Akali Party] (Jullundur: Punjabi Suba Committee, 1958), p. 5.

Islamic and Hindu fraternities the ethos of the Russian Communist Party is already unmistakably discernible." [9]

In discussing Toynbee's statement, one Sikh scholar, who was elected on an Akali ticket to the parliament in 1962, argued that it is the Khalsa alone that bears comparison with the Communist party, for what distinguishes it, compared to the enlightened self-interest and local patriotism involved in the Islamic groups, is "the deathless pledge and loyalty of the Khalsa to a universal Idea and Ideal, for the upholding and propagation of which the Khalsa is sworn to a dedicated life on this earth. It is something of this ethos which has inspired the Russian Communist Party of Lenin, and the Order of the Khalsa is, therefore, the latter's true prototype." [10]

The successors of Guru Nanak had very early in the history of Sikhism sought to give greater organization to his followers through a network of gurdwaras and local associations. However, it was the tenth Guru, Gobind Singh, who placed the final capstone on the political and military organization of the Sikhs in 1699. He transformed the Sikhs into the elite corps of the Khalsa or the Panth. The tenth Guru himself emphasized the importance of the Panth when he declared that after his death succession to the office of Guru would cease and that in the future the visible personality of the Guru would be the Panth. The significance of this last point hardly needs emphasis. As Panikkar has pointed out: "The philosophical conception of the community as a body in which the will of God manifests and through which the purpose of human life can be fulfilled gives the Sikhs a conception of the State and the Church which has made them a compact and united nation." [11] Panikkar further stated that the Hegelian "subordination of individual will to the collective will . . . is most complete in Sikh-

---

[9] Arnold J. Toynbee, *A Study of History* (New York: Oxford University Press, 1957), Abridgement of Vols. VII–X, p. 187.

[10] Kapur Singh, pp. 11–12.

[11] K. M. Panikkar, *The Ideals of Sikhism* (Amritsar: Sikh Tract Society, 1924), p. 20.

ism" and that the general will here "exists as a real will and not merely as a metaphysical fiction for the Sikhs as a result of the belief that the Guru is present in the Khalsa and the opinion of the community is the will of the Guru. It is this feeling that has given the Sikhs their political and social unity and their loyalty to the *Panth*. It gives them an ideal for which no sacrifice is deemed too much." [12]

In addition to vesting the Panth with the personality of the Guru, the Tenth Guru also ordered that whenever there was executive work to be done the Panth should appoint five members known as "the Five Beloved Ones" to conduct such business.[13] However, he did not provide for any continuing central authority to take the place of the personal leadership of the Guru.[14] The need for such a central authority to act for the Panth was not felt at the time as the number of Sikhs was small and they usually met annually or semi-annually as "the *Sarbat Khalsa* [the whole people] at the Akal Takht" in Amritsar.[15] Decisions were taken through resolutions known as *gurmattas,* obedience to which was obligatory on all members of the community. In the first half of the eighteenth century, however, meetings of the Panth at the Akal Takht became "impossible," since the Sikhs were involved in military conflict.[16]

When the Sikhs assumed sovereign power in the Punjab in the second half of the eighteenth century, their numbers had increased but they were not organized into a single sovereign state. On the contrary, they were divided into twelve independent principalities, or *misls,* governed by Sikh chiefs who were military leaders. Even though their collective territories were small, significantly they aspired to eventually controlling "the whole of Punjab, from Jamuna to Indus." [17] While many of them held office through hereditary succession,[18] "these chiefs exercised their sway with the goodwill of their followers, who

[12] *Ibid.,* pp. 16–17.   [13] Teja Singh, *Sikhism,* pp. 44–45.
[14] Teja Singh, *Essays,* p. 217.   [15] *Loc. cit.*   [16] *Loc. cit.*
[17] Kapur Singh, p. 353.   [18] Narang, pp. 145–66.

always went through the ceremony of electing their chiefs." [19]
Insofar as the interests of the whole Panth were concerned, the
Sikh chiefs would meet at the Akal Takht to make decisions
for the entire Panth.[20] In actual practice, these meetings were
a rare phenomenon for they were held only in case of extreme
danger to the Sikh religion.[21] When Maharaja Ranjit Singh
succeeded in establishing a centralized monarchy in the Punjab,
he abolished the infrequently used custom of meetings at the
Akal Takht on behalf of the Panth to make political decisions.[22] In the governance of his kingdom, Ranjit Singh chose
to be guided by his own advisers, who were drawn from the
various religious communities. He let the custom of Panthic
meetings continue for religious affairs, but such meetings became rarer and gradually the custom degenerated "out of all
recognition." [23] After the British annexation of the Punjab in
1849, the British government made political decisions affecting
the Sikhs as well as other religious groups, and even brought
some of the important Sikh gurdwaras under its own supervision.[24] In the subsequent almost three quarters of a century,
several associations of educated Sikhs grew up, but with no
central organization capable of speaking in the name of the
entire Sikh community.

After the advent of the Gurdwara Reform or Akali movement in the 1920s, representatives of the Sikh community met
in Amritsar and established the Shiromani Gurdwara Parbandhak Committee (SGPC) to manage those gurdwaras from
which the unorthodox priests had been or would be evicted.[25]
Meanwhile, the Akali Dal emerged as a para-military political
organization out of the thousands of blue-turbanned, sword-

[19] *Ibid.*, p. 169.   [20] *Loc. cit.*
[21] Teja Singh, *Sikhism*, p. 48.
[22] *Ibid.*, p. 49.   [23] *Ibid.*, p. 51.
[24] Khushwant Singh, *The Sikhs*, p. 103, and Teja Singh, *Essays*, p. 179.
[25] *Ibid.*, p. 170.

wielding volunteers that came forward to oppose the government and occupy the gurdwaras. Both the SGPC and the Akali Dal were soon declared illegal bodies but the struggle continued until 1925 when the government put the SGPC on a statutory basis for the management of Sikh shrines.

Since the days of the Gurdwara Reform movement, the Akali Dal has sought to fill the gap of a central body for the Sikh community, holding itself to be the sole representative of the Panth. Although the SGPC is more representative of the Sikh community since it is elected by the Sikh masses, its functions are circumscribed technically merely to the management of Sikh historic gurdwaras. The Akali Dal has therefore assumed the task of directing and controlling Sikh politics, not only in view of its solid achievement in bringing the gurdwaras under the popular control of the Sikhs, but also because of the sacrifices that its volunteers and supporters made at the time of the Gurdwara Reform movement. During the movement's six years, some 400 Sikhs were killed, about 2,000 wounded, and over 30,000 Sikh men and women courted imprisonment.[26] It is the association of the Akali Dal with this revolutionary period in Sikh history, a period of much sacrifice and suffering, combined with the subsequent invariable adoption by it of an extreme position on behalf of Sikh claims in politics, that has enabled it to draw on the loyalties of a significantly large segment of the Sikh population and, in turn, to feel reinforced in its conviction that it is the sole representative of the Sikh community.

The headquarters of the Akali Dal are located within the precincts of the Golden Temple at Amritsar, the "Mecca of the Sikhs." [27] It is characteristic of the Akali Dal that its headquarters, as also its branches and local offices, are always located inside gurdwaras. This is due not only to the Akali doctrine of

[26] Khushwant Singh, *The Sikhs,* p. 116.
[27] Gurnam Singh, p. 9.

the inseparability of religion and politics, but also because normally places of worship are "privileged sanctuaries" against the police in India. Membership in the Akali Dal is open only to Sikhs over eighteen years who are not apostates and do not belong to any other organization considered anti-Panthic by the Akali Dal.[28] The total enrollment of the Akali Dal is placed at 300,000, but there is considerable bogus recruitment. The areas of heaviest membership concentration are the districts of Gurdaspur, Amritsar, Ferozepur, Ludhiana, and Jullundur; membership is relatively low in the areas of the formerly Sikh princely states. In terms of active workers, the Amritsar district is "the backbone" of the organization. The basic unit of the Akali Dal is the village or city branch, known as Akali Jatha, with a minimum of ten members.

At the head of the Akali Dal is a president, formally elected by a General Body consisting of about 400 delegates from the district branches. Since 1930 the president has been either Master Tara Singh himself, some protégé or some party leader loyal to him. The president nominates an executive committee of 22 members, chosen on the basis of their loyalty to the president and of group and sectional representation. The president is authorized to suspend any member of the executive committee on a charge of anti-Panthic activities or on any other complaint.[29] The president can also nominate five advisers to the executive committee; usually they are men of legal acumen or theoreticians.

Funds for the party come from Sikh big businessmen in Delhi, Bombay, Calcutta and Kanpur. However, the single most important resource of the Akali Dal is the SGPC, which not only represents the Akali Dal's great achievement of the 1920s in bringing the gurdwaras under the Sikh community's centralized control but, in turn, with its large funds and vast patronage, contributes to the basic strength of the Akali Dal.

[28] *Shiromani Akali Dal Di Bantar De Niyam,* pp. 3–4.
[29] *Ibid.,* p. 19.

Shiromani Gurdwara Parbandhak Committee

A creation of the Sikh Gurdwaras Act of 1925,[30] the SGPC is considered as virtually "a state within a state," and, in view of its large resources, it is often remarked that "whoever controls the SGPC, controls Sikh politics." The SGPC does possess a sort of legislature, executive, judiciary, and centralized bureaucracy. The Sikh Gurdwaras Act of 1925 has, since it was first enacted, undergone 28 amendments, but the basic institutions it established continue to be the same, now with a history of operating for 40 years.

The SGPC is "a body corporate"[31] and consists of 160 members, of whom 140 are elected and the other twenty are either nominated or are members ex officio. Only Sikhs over 25, literate in Gurmukhi, and not apostates, can become members.[32] The 140 elected members come through a direct election, held normally once every five years, from electoral constituencies established by the Punjab government in consultation with the SGPC.[33] In the group elected in 1960 there was only one woman and it seems no Sahajdhari Sikh.[34] About 80 percent of the group lived in rural areas. The electorate in the SGPC elections consists solely of Sikhs over 21 who are not apostates.

The members of the SGPC annually elect an executive committee of 9 to 15 members, including a president, with such salaries or remuneration as the SGPC may decide. A central bureaucracy of about 100 employees, with the offices located within the Golden Temple at Amritsar, assists the executive committee in the performance of its duties. There is a judicial commission consisting of three Sikh members, who are ap-

[30] Punjab, *The Sikh Gurdwaras Act, 1925* (Chandigarh: Controller, Printing and Stationery, 1959).

[31] *Ibid.*, Sec. 42(3).

[32] *Ibid.*, Secs. 45, 46.

[33] *Ibid.*, Sec. 44.

[34] Information from a printed list with names and addresses of SGPC members, furnished by the SGPC office in October 1961.

pointed by the Punjab government from a panel of names recommended by the SGPC.[35]

The SGPC has jurisdiction over all "historic" Sikh gurdwaras
in the Punjab included in the original legislation or later noti-
fied as connected with Sikh history and tradition, and over such
other Sikh gurdwaras as may wish such jurisdiction. There are
some 350 scheduled gurdwaras (listed in a schedule to the
enactment) and several hundred nonscheduled gurdwaras,
spread all over the Punjab, under SGPC jurisdiction; in addition, there exist hundreds of other gurdwaras which are not
under SGPC jurisdiction. Except for the ten more important
Sikh gurdwaras (known as Section 85 gurdwaras), for which
the SGPC itself acts as the committee of management, there is
a committee of management for one or more gurdwaras. Each
gurdwara derives its income mainly from daily donations and
from agricultural lands attached to the gurdwaras.

The SGPC has powers of "control, direction and general
superintendence over all committees," [36] and is further competent "to hold and administer trust funds for purposes of a
religious, charitable, educational, or industrial nature." [37] An
index of its large financial resources is the annual budget of
about 6 million rupees. The SGPC income comes from (1)
regular contributions from gurdwara committees through a
well organized system of revenue collection, and (2) the ten
more important historic gurdwaras under direct SGPC management, which contribute more than 50 percent of the annual
budget. An important item in SGPC expenses is the special
fund for propagation of the Sikh religion, which is administered
by a committee consisting of the SGPC president and seven
other members.

Since its inception the SGPC has been under the control of
the Akali Dal, which has won in all the gurdwara elections. In

[35] *The Sikh Gurdwaras Act, 1925*, Secs. 70, 71.
[36] *Ibid.*, Sec. 125.
[37] *Ibid.*, Sec. 127.

the annual elections of the SGPC president between the gurdwara elections, control of the SGPC has at times passed into
the hands of groups opposed to the Akali Dal because of de-
fections from the Akali ranks, but this has usually been a
passing phase. At the next gurdwara elections, the Akali Dal
succeeds in assuming power in the SGPC again.

To have the resources of the SGPC at the disposal of a political party is obviously a great advantage, but to command
them over a period of forty years, as the Akali Dal has done, is
to wield an instrument of tremendous power. The control of
the SGPC gives vast powers of patronage, directly in the ten
more important historic gurdwaras and in gurdwaras with an
annual income of less than Rs. 3000, and indirectly in other
gurdwaras. In addition to the appointment of a staff in a wide
network of gurdwaras spread all over the Punjab—a staff whose
purpose is not merely the proper management of gurdwaras
but the furtherance of the interests of its employer, the Akali
Dal—the authority to spend funds for almost any nonpolitical
purpose adds up to a powerful leverage in securing political
support from strategic groups in the Sikh community. Schools
and colleges, including an engineering college, have been
started, and gurdwaras have been established for members of
the backward classes. The fund for the propagation of Sikh
religion serves additionally as an especially useful means for
political work, and that is perhaps one reason it is under a
committee headed by the SGPC president. Missionary workers
and folk musicians who are recruited for the purpose of propagating the Sikh religion can be directly used for party work.
One general secretary of the Akali Dal explained the rationale
behind such use of religious preachers: "We consider religion
and politics to be combined. So it does not make any difference
if the preachers engage in political work. The Akali Dal and
the preachers say the same thing. So what the Akali Dal says,
they say. All of them have been in the Akali Dal. All those who
are chosen have been through the Akali Dal. We have given

them employment. This is all that they can do. There is no misuse of money!" [38]

In view of the large resources that go with control over the SGPC, the Akali Dal values greatly its hold on the SGPC. Therefore, in addition to the five-yearly gurdwara elections, the annual elections of the president and executive committee assume great importance. All kinds of inducements are given members to preclude change of loyalties. Supporters, including toughs, are brought in and stationed in front of the SGPC offices to create an atmosphere of certain victory for one party or another.

Important as the resources of the SGPC are, the political significance of the SGPC lies in another realm: the quinquennial gurdwara elections to the SGPC serve as *a source of group legitimacy* insofar as the Sikh community is concerned. The gurdwara elections, conducted under government auspices and supervision, are unique in India in that they provide evidence, authenticated by the government, concerning the position of different political parties among the followers of a single religion, that is, Sikhism. No other social or religious group in India exercises a similar privilege. The outcome of these elections would not be important were the gurdwara elections to be fought on issues centering around the original purpose of the SGPC—the management of Sikh gurdwaras—but every single gurdwara election has been fought on some momentous political issue—the communal award, Sikhistan, independent political entity of the Sikhs, the combination of religion and politics, and Punjabi Suba.

Since independence, the conflict between secular nationalism and communalism manifests itself not only in the general elections but also in the gurdwara elections. The radical difference, however, between the electorate in the general elections, where members of all communities participate, and the electorate in the gurdwara elections, where only Sikhs are entitled to vote,

[38] From an interview.

makes for a radical disparity in the popular mandate given by the respective electorates. In the general elections under a system of joint electorates, Sikh candidates running on the Congress party ticket can win a larger number of seats than the Akali Dal, for they can then count on the votes not only of some segments of the non-Harijan Sikhs but also of Harijan Sikhs and Hindus who, when confronted with a choice between a Congress Sikh and an Akali Sikh, tend generally to vote for the Congress Sikh candidate. On the other hand, in the case of the gurdwara elections with a completely Sikh electorate, Congress Sikh candidates are not able to win any significant number of seats. They do poll a large number of votes, especially from the Harijan Sikhs, but everywhere it is a minority vote. For the Congress party, overwhelming defeat is the inevitable result in the gurdwara elections, whereas for the Akali Dal it is usually a tremendous victory. In 1960, for instance, the Akali Dal won 136 out of 140 seats, leaving a bare four seats to other parties.

The Akali Dal's tremendous success in the gurdwara elections enables Master Tara Singh and other Akali leaders to assert that the Akali Dal is the only representative body of the Sikh community and to charge that the Sikhs in the Congress party are "show-boys" and "political dummies" since they lack support from their own community. To be sure, Congress Sikh leaders do maintain that the results of the gurdwara elections have no bearing on the political issues of the Punjab as they concern only the management of Sikh gurdwaras. Yet the participation of Congress Sikhs in the gurdwara elections, in order to seek control of the resources of the SGPC and also to prevent the use of gurdwaras against the government, has seemed to imply that unwittingly they too subscribed to the notion that Congress Sikhs must have support not only from a joint electorate but also from a separate electorate confined to the Sikhs. The experience gained from the two gurdwara elections in 1954 and 1960 would suggest that Congress Sikhs may well

try to repudiate any such notion and, by desisting from participation in future gurdwara elections, seek to deflate their importance and immunize the general politics of the Punjab from
SGPC politics. In so doing, Congress Sikh leaders may further
deprive the Akali Dal of the opportunity to rally the Sikh
masses in opposition to the Congress party. As it is, every time
the Akali Dal has emerged triumphant from gurdwara elections,
Master Tara Singh, proclaiming a mandate from the Sikh community, has asked that Akali demands be conceded forthwith
and, in the event they are not met, has felt justified in launching agitations against the government.[39]

It would seem, however, that while the number of seats won
by the Akali Dal in the gurdwara elections points to the powerful support that the Akali Dal commands in the Sikh community, statistics on the actual votes polled do not uphold the
claim of the Akali Dal to be the sole representative of the total
Sikh community. In the gurdwara elections of 1960, although
winning 136 of 140 seats the Akali Dal polled a little over two-
thirds of the total vote cast, which in turn represented only a
third of the potential electorate.[40] Master Tara Singh had made
these elections a plebiscite over the question of Punjabi Suba,

[39] In 1964, the Congress party, indeed, decided to refrain from any
participation in the gurdwara elections of 1965, leaving the field to two
major groups, each claiming to be the genuine Akali Dal. In these elections, the group led by Sant Fateh Singh emerged victorious with 95
seats out of 140; the group led by Master Tara Singh secured only 36
seats; some seven seats went to independents. The Communist party had
thrown its support behind the Sant group. See *The Spokesman,* xiv,
No. 22 (January 25, 1965), 19.
[40] There were four main groups that contested the 1960 gurdwara elections: (1) Akali Dal; (2) Sadh Sangat Board (Congress); (3) Desh
Bhagat party (Communist); and (4) independents. They received 68,
22, 6 and 4 percent, respectively, of the total vote polled—1,155,011. The
number of voters who registered for the elections was 2,094,045. The
Sikh population in the Punjab in 1951 was 5.5 million. See *Ibid.,* x,
No. 4 (February 1, 1960), 1–2. In the 1965 SGPC elections, the number of registered electors was about 2.2 million, from among a total Sikh
population of about 6.8 million. The total vote polled in the elections
constituted only 40 percent of even the registered vote. *Ibid.,* xiv, No. 22
(1965), 3.

but what the election results demonstrated was, as *The Spokes-man* pointed out, that there was only minority support for the demand since one-third of the Sikhs plus all the Hindus, who would be about 45 percent of the Suba's population, were opposed to it.[41]

Despite these considerations, the fact still remains that the Akali Dal makes a tremendous impression in the gurdwara elections. What then are the causes of the strength of the Akali Dal in these elections? First and foremost is the strong sentiment in the Sikh community against any possible government influence over the gurdwaras. Since the gurdwara elections concern the management of gurdwaras, even though political issues are invariably raised, Akali leaders seem able to make a convincing case to the Sikh public that, if the Congress party wins in the gurdwara elections, then the gurdwaras would come under the control of the government and thus the great achievement of the Gurdwara Reform movement would be undone. Significantly, the Akalis refer to the Congress party as the "sarkaria" party (the government party) and Congress candidates as "sarkarias" (government men). Many Congress Sikh ministers often campaign for Congress candidates in these elections, and Sikh voters seem to really believe that, if the Congress party ever won, the government would assume control of the gurdwaras. Often Sikh voters refuse to listen to such ministers during these elections, but assure them that they would vote for the Congress party in the general elections. As against this, the Akali Dal is the political group which in the 1920s brought the gurdwaras under the control of the Sikh community.

Moreover, while Congress candidates can only raise issues concerning the proper management of the gurdwaras and the removal of politics from these shrines, they are inhibited from making communal appeals since they belong to a secular nationalist organization. The Akali Dal, on the other hand, is

[41] *Ibid.*, X, No. 4 (1960), 1–2.

able to make an appeal in the name of the Panth to the members of the Panth; it further reduces the choice before members of the Panth from that between the Congress Sikhs and the Akali Dal to that between Gandhi and Guru Gobind Singh.[42]

Aside from the effective appeal that the Akali Dal is able to make, there are certain organizational factors that work in its favor. Because of its position on the relationship of religion and politics, the concern for gurdwaras on the part of the Akali Dal is a full-time business and participation in gurdwara elections is an important element in its political program. The Congress party, in contrast, being a secular party, discourages the formation of groups inside the party organization on the basis of religion. Consequently, Congress Sikhs do not possess any organization with a continuing interest in gurdwara affairs. Until independence, Congress Sikhs showed no interest in the gurdwaras and even afterwards this interest has expressed itself only at five-year intervals through participation in the gurdwara elections by forming a patched-up organization each time with a new name. No doubt large funds are poured into the election campaign in a crash program but the lack of an organization with a sustained interest in the gurdwaras represents a serious handicap.

Moreover, the Congress is left to fight from nonreligious platforms in what are essentially religious elections, because the gurdwaras are and have been under Akali control since the inception of the SGPC. The Akali Dal was the first to come into power in the SGPC and it consolidated its initial control "as thousands of posts—of priests, missionaries, managers and servants—were filled with judicious care, and influential men were given a stake in the future of the group which employed them." [43] The Akali Dal can thus use the gurdwaras as platforms against the Congress to reach large Sikh congregations. Since it regards religion and politics as inseparable, the Akali

---

[42] From an interview with a Sikh member of parliament.
[43] Khushwant Singh, *The Sikhs*, p. 141.

Dal suffers from no inhibitions in making use of gurdwaras for political purposes at election time or in agitations.

The weakness of Congress Sikhs, because of the lack of a sustained organization, is compounded by the nature of voter registration for gurdwara elections. The advantage in these elections lies with the party that can get the maximum number of its supporters registered as voters. In contrast to the general elections where government officials register voters through visits to their place of residence, any Sikh who wishes to register as a voter for the gurdwara elections must make a specific application stating his name, father's name, age, caste, occupation and residence, and must also submit a signed declaration that he neither trims nor shaves his beard or head hair, and that he neither smokes nor takes alcoholic drinks.[44] Bands of Akali workers go from village to village and get Akali supporters registered, whereas the Congress Sikhs have no comparable organization to encourage registration. Support for the Congress party in the gurdwara elections comes from the socially depressed and economically underprivileged Harijan Sikhs, but the Congress loses many of their votes since they are unable to register without help because most of them are illiterate. It is also likely that those who do not have a religious bent of mind, or those who are against communal politics, may tend to refrain from participation in gurdwara elections and from voter registration for these elections. To these initial handicaps must be added the fact that the Congress is the party in power in the government in any case, and has only a passing, even if intense, interest in the gurdwara elections, whereas for the Akali Dal, control of the SGPC is crucial to its strength.

Apart from the quinquennial gurdwara elections, other operations of the SGPC, especially the annual elections of the SGPC, have important repercussions in Punjab politics. It is understandable that if Master Tara Singh wins in the gurdwara

[44] Punjab, Home Department, *General (Gurdwaras) Notification No. 1207*, dated July 16, 1959.

elections or in the annual SGPC presidential elections, he interprets his victory as a mandate from the Sikh community to issue an ultimatum to the government to accept Akali demands or reckon with an agitation. If he loses in the annual election, however, he charges his defeat to machinations on the part of the government to bring about his downfall, and once again he has a cause to launch an agitation, since the gurdwaras have now come "under the control of the enemies of the Panth." [45] As his defeat in the annual elections is a result of change in the loyalties of the duly elected SGPC members, apparently his conviction is that control of the SGPC by the Akali Dal alone, and more specifically by him personally, is in accordance with the will of the Sikh community.[46]

The SGPC furthermore provides the occasion for a continuous stream of charges against the government for interference in gurdwara affairs. The fact of the matter is that the Sikh Gurdwaras Act, under which the SGPC was established, provides for continuing government responsibility at almost every level of SGPC operations. There is hardly a section of the Gurdwaras Act in which the government does not have some sort of responsibility—the establishment of judicial tribunals, the registration of voters, the delimitation of electoral constituencies, the management of the elections, the investigation of corrupt election practices and election disputes, the appointment and removal of members of the judicial commission, the formation of committees of management, the audit of SGPC accounts. Besides, the SGPC and other committees of management are formally constituted only after the government issues a notification to that effect. Although the concept of the separation of "church" and "state" historically refers to the absence of church control over the state and not state control and regulation of the church, some observers are of the opinion that the Gurdwaras Act, a legacy from the British regime, is *ultra vires*

[45] Surjeet, p. 5.
[46] *Loc. cit.*

in terms of the present secular constitution.[47] However, the Congress party has apparently reconciled itself to the Act, since to rescind it would be to create another explosive political situation in the Punjab.

As for the Akali Dal, the establishment and continuance of the SGPC under a statute enacted by a secular government is a refutation of its stand on removing the Sikh religion from outside influence. Withdrawal of the SGPC from government supervision, however, would also mean elimination of elections under government supervision, and is therefore unacceptable to the Akali Dal since the authenticity of election results would be diminished under other than government auspices. Suggestions made from time to time to constitute a trust, removed from elections, for managing the Sikh gurdwaras have been rejected by the Akali Dal.

Meanwhile, the intermeshing between the government and the SGPC frequently enables the Akali Dal to make a political issue of alleged government interference in gurdwaras though it has been unable to present any conclusive proof of the charge. In 1959 a committee of government and Akali representatives was established to inquire into any charges made by the Akali Dal, but Akali leaders did not press any charges. To some, it seems that what the Akali Dal calls government interference in gurdwaras is the attempt on the part of other political groups to break "the Akali monopoly over gurdwaras" and to assume power in the SGPC.[48] Others feel that Master Tara Singh himself forces the Congress party to intervene insofar as participation in gurdwara elections is concerned. Hukam Singh writes on the subject: "It is our misfortune that Master Tara Singh provokes others to meddle in the Gurdwara affairs and then complains that there is interference. He uses the Gurdwara platforms as bases for attacks on his political opponents and then cries if they are compelled to fight to capture

[47] *The Tribune,* August 11, 1957.
[48] Surjeet, pp. 4–5.

those bases. Master Tara Singh digs his trenches inside the shrines and bombards others from inside, but makes a grouse that the others are unfair, if they run forward to oust him from these trenches. He raises issues which can only be fought among the political parties, and then desires that no party to these issues should draw near the arena." [49]

In short, apart from being a source of great power and an instrument of group legitimacy, the SGPC provides the Akali Dal with an opportunity for the manufacture of grievances against the government and a network of platforms from which to voice such grievances and to launch agitations. Furthermore, the five-yearly gurdwara elections and the annual SGPC presidential elections, in addition to the general elections, prevent politics in the Punjab from ever "settling down."

The main purpose in the establishment of the SGPC was to remove the unorthodox elements from the gurdwaras and to provide a management more in accordance with the precepts of the Sikh religion as understood by the reformist sections of the Sikhs at the time of the Gurdwara Reform movement. The importation of politics into shrines in subsequent years has, however, met with serious criticism by Sikh leaders on the ground that it has led "to a rot" in the Sikh religion.[50] The gurdwara committees seem to have become a mere "stepping-stone to politics" for ambitious young men.[51] Some Sikh leaders point to the spectacle of the many cases before the courts on disputes between rival factions over control of gurdwaras. Some of the disputes over control have even resulted in serious violence. Several Sikh leaders have therefore raised the issue of whether the SGPC is really the best instrument for the man-

[49] *The Spokesman,* IX, No. 34 (September 21, 1959), 1–2.

[50] Letter of Ajmer Singh, *The Tribune,* October 5, 1958.

[51] *Loc. cit.* See also Hukam Singh, *The Spokesman,* IX, No. 30 (1959), 27–28; Bhagat Singh, "Gurdwaras and Politics," *ibid.,* No. 28 (August 3, 1959), p. 7; Prem Singh Prem, "Sanctity of Gurdwaras," *The Tribune,* July 22, 1955; and statement of Pritam Singh Gojran on "Danger to Sikhism from Within," *ibid.,* December 1, 1961.

agement of gurdwaras. For those who are concerned for the future of the Sikh religion, the SGPC under Akali control seems to have failed precisely in the area which needs the greatest attention—making Sikhism meaningful to the educated youth, especially in regard to the Sikh injunctions prohibiting the trimming or shaving of bodily hair and smoking. It is charged that the Akali Dal has been recruiting, for the propagation of the Sikh religion, unsophisticated workers without much education who, though probably quite useful for political work, are ineffective in making any impression on the Sikh intelligentsia and the large body of Sikh students.

All India Sikh Students Federation

While the SGPC under the Akali Dal may seem to have been delinquent in its efforts to make Sikhism intelligible to educated youth, the All India Sikh Students Federation (AISSF) has stepped in to perform the role of propagating the Sikh religion and, more importantly, of spreading the Akali ideology among the Sikh student body. The AISSF was established in 1943 by a group of Akali leaders who felt the need for an organization of Sikh students that would be acceptable and sympathetic to the Akali Dal. They had found that while the educated Sikhs looked upon Akali leaders as "uneducated or semi-educated, highly irrational and unreasonable, with no program except having good meals at the gurdwaras," the Akali leaders ridiculed the educated Sikhs as "primarily opportunists, cowards and highly selfish men." [52] They organized the AISSF therefore to bring the Sikh intelligentsia closer to the Akali Dal. Another aim in the establishment of the AISSF was to promote interest in Sikhism among Sikh students, for it was feared that "modern" influences were carrying them away from the religion. Figures on membership of the AISSF are not available but they range between 10 and 15 thousand. Until the mid-1950s the AISSF was under the control of a few Akali

[52] From an interview with one of the founders of the AISSF.

leaders, but in recent years it has shown more organizational independence.

The basic philosophy and aims of the AISSF are the same as those of the Akali Dal, but pursued in the past with more consistency. Through study circles in schools and colleges, conferences and training camps for Sikh students, sponsoring baptismal ceremonies, and publishing a bulletin for Sikh students, the AISSF seeks to indoctrinate Sikh students in the separate political entity of the Sikhs and in the necessity of "the creation of 'desh-kaal' in which our national expression can find its full satisfaction." [53] The AISSF has been an ardent supporter of the Akali demand for Punjabi Suba and wants "an autonomous constitutional set-up of the proposed state, on the lines of Kashmir." [54] When pressing for this demand at AISSF conferences, student leaders and Akali leaders also make criticism of so-called Hindi imperialism,[55] the cultural offensive of the Hindus,[56] and of bearded stooges in the Congress party.[57] Though it asks for Punjabi Suba on linguistic grounds, the AISSF leaves no doubt as to the real nature of the demand as is evident from one news item from the AISSF's journal:

S. Jaswant Singh President of A.I.S.S.F. made it plain that the creation of a Unilingual Punjabi-Speaking State is not an end in itself. Our ultimate aim is the realisation of such an order of society where the national aspirations of the Sikhs would find their fullest satisfaction. He said that the Punjabi-Speaking State is the minimum which should be created to safeguard the Sikh rights, "we shall try it and see whether it can protect us adequately. It is a means to an end. If we are

[53] Bhan Singh, *All India Sikh Students Federation Da Aaeen* [Constitution of the All India Sikh Students Federation] (Amritsar: General Secretary, AISSF, 1950).

[54] "The AISSF Executive Committee Demands Punjabi State Soon," *The Spokesman*, III, No. 3 (January 21, 1953), 9.

[55] *The Sikh Students' Bulletin*, v, Nos. 10–11 (January–February 1958), 8.

[56] *Ibid.*, vi, No. 8 (November 1958), 4.

[57] *Ibid.*, v, Nos. 10–11 (1958), 8.

persecuted even in the Punjabi-Suba, we shall extend our struggle to get rid of such a kind of vicious cycle of religious persecution." [58]

The AISSF has been a source of tremendous strength to the Akali Dal not only in being a recruiting ground for educated leadership for the party, but also in providing active assistance at times of elections and agitations, and further in being an effective instrument for the political indoctrination of Sikh youth in the ideology of the Akali Dal—the independent political entity of the Sikhs. However, more recently a drastic and almost revolutionary change has occurred in the AISSF in regard to politics. Disgusted with the factional disputes in Akali politics, the AISSF reportedly decided in 1963 to remove itself from politics.[59] This would seem to be a repudiation of its traditional stand of the inseparability of religion and politics and the independent political entity of the Sikhs.

AKALI DAL AND THE INDEPENDENT POLITICAL ENTITY OF THE SIKHS

Although the Akali Dal declares that the ideal aim of the Sikh community to act as a single political group in the political arena, which forms the *raison d'être* for the existence of this organization, is rooted in the basic philosophy of Sikhism, yet the evidence that history provides is of divisions in the Sikh community since the death of Guru Gobind Singh, if not even earlier.

The Khalsa Panth acted as a united group under the leadership of Banda for some time after the death of Guru Gobind Singh, but soon split up into two groups, the followers of Banda and his opponents, the remaining Khalsa.[60] At this time, the

[58] *Ibid.*, vi, No. 8 (1958), 16.
[59] From an interview with a former AISSF president. See also the report of the meeting of former AISSF presidents, *The Tribune*, February 19, 1964.
[60] Narang, p. 113, and Harbans Singh, *Sikh Political Parties*, p. 1.

Khalsa gave assurances to the Moghul emperor that it would not help Banda, and would even assist the emperor in case of foreign invasion.[61] The relations between the two groups were so strained that there was the possibility of civil war over the possession of the Golden Temple in Amritsar.[62]

In the second half of the eighteenth century, when the Sikhs assumed sovereign power, they were divided into twelve different principalities governed by Sikh chiefs. These chiefs occasionally acted together, but their relations were governed more by mutual hostility, conflict and war, which "nearly disrupted the Khalsa." [63] Then Ranjit Singh set out to establish a centralized Sikh monarchy by subduing many of his co-religionist Sikh chiefs through war and diplomacy. Rather than be overwhelmed by a powerful monarch of their own faith, however, the Sikh chiefs below the Sutlej river sought the protection of the British against the expanding kingdom of Maharaja Ranjit Singh.[64] On the other hand, Ranjit Singh demolished the basis for the exclusive political unity of the followers of the Sikh religion by depriving the Akal Takht at Amritsar of all political authority,[65] and attempted to establish a Punjabi nationality through a secular state.

With the annexation of the Punjab by the British, the Sikh community was deprived of all political authority, and with it vanished any semblance of political unity among the Sikhs. Under the impact of the west, local associations developed among the educated Sikhs during the period of the Singh Sabha movement, but their mutual relations were marked by rivalry,[66] and "no one association was able to take the central place among them." [67] The Gurdwara Reform movement found

[61] Narang, p. 113.   [62] *Ibid.*, p. 115n.

[63] Harbans Singh, *Sikh Political Parties,* p. 2. See also Hari Ram Gupta, *History of the Sikhs* (Lahore: The Minerva Book Shop, 1944) Vols. II and III.

[64] Teja Singh, *Essays,* p. 93, and Ganda Singh, *The British Occupation of the Punjab* (Patiala: Sikh History Society, 1955), pp. 13–14.

[65] Teja Singh, *Essays,* p. 94.

[66] *Ibid.*, pp. 123–44.   [67] *Ibid.*, p. 218.

the new militant group of the Akalis in opposition to the more moderate and aristocratic Chief Khalsa Diwan, but the latter considered "itself as competent to decide the Panthic affairs as the S.G.P.C.," which was under the control of the Akali Dal.[68] These two political groups became especially bitter toward each other after the 1937 elections when the Chief Khalsa Diwan formed an alliance with the Unionist party. The Akalis at times also vigorously opposed some of the Sikh princes. After independence, the importance of the Chief Khalsa Diwan as a political body declined, but Sikhs have been prominent in the Congress party and the Communist party.

The Akalis themselves have been torn by dissensions since the days of the Gurdwara Reform movement. The emergence of two opposing groups among the Akalis followed the enactment of the Sikh Gurdwaras Act in 1925. As one writer has remarked, "the Panth emerged from the struggle victorious, but divided against itself." [69] The two groups later crystallized into two different organizations—the Shiromani Akali Dal and the Central Akali Dal—which remained bitterly opposed to each other until independence, when the Central Akali Dal faded from the political scene. At one time, however, the Central Akali Dal was popular enough to be in control of many gurdwara committees, including the important ones of the Golden Temple in Amritsar, Nankana Sahib, and Muktsar, even though the Shiromani Akali Dal was in power in the SGPC.[70] Then there was the bitter struggle between Master Tara Singh and Gyani Sher Singh, the leaders "who had become the symbols of this 'Civil War.'" [71]

In the mid-1930s the Shiromani Akali Dal was divided into two major groups—the Giani group and the Nagoke group—while Master Tara Singh with his own following remained neutral between the two groups. The Nagoke group, led by Udham Singh Nagoke, favored closer cooperation with the

[68] *Ibid.,* p. 146.   [69] Harbans Singh, *Sikh Political Parties,* p. 3.
[70] *Ibid.,* p. 4.   [71] *Ibid.,* p. 5.

Congress party, while the Giani group led by Giani Kartar Singh "stood for an independent and powerful Panthic entity" [72] and later cooperated with the British. The struggle between the two groups continued until after independence when prominent leaders of the Nagoke group were finally expelled from the Akali Dal on grounds of collaboration with the Congress party. After independence the Maharaja of Patiala also sponsored a rival Sikh organization, the Panthic Darbar, though the organization soon disintegrated.

In the early 1950s the Akali Dal in PEPSU was divided into two groups—the so-called Raman group, which considered itself to be leftist, and the Master Tara Singh group. The conflict between the two groups became so intense that they fought the 1954 elections in PEPSU on separate tickets, and by so splitting the Akali vote, made it possible for the Congress party to assume power in the state.

Subsequent to the entrance into the Congress party in 1956 of most of the Akali stalwarts, Master Tara Singh brought to the forefront in the Akali organization a Sikh saint, Sant Fateh Singh. It was given out that this saint-turned-politician of fifty years or so was being groomed to answer the question, "After Master Tara Singh who?" However, Sant Fateh Singh established his own political base within the Akali Dal and achieved enough popularity to be regarded as a threat to Tara Singh's leadership. In 1962, when Tara Singh attempted to undermine the position of Sant Fateh Singh through the expulsion of some of his rival's lieutenants from the Akali executive committee, Fateh Singh set up his own Shiromani Akali Dal and characterized the Akali Dal under Tara Singh's leadership as a bogus organization. Meanwhile, the Panthic party in the Punjab legislature split into two hostile and almost equal parts, each speaking in the name of the Panth. In the following SGPC presidential election in 1962, Tara Singh's group was defeated and a nominee of Fateh Singh was installed as president. In

[72] *Ibid.*, p. 9.

the ensuing months of bitterness between the groups, observers found it difficult to tell which was the more genuine Akali Dal.

It would thus seem that the Panth in Sikh history, and the Akali Dal since its inception in the 1920s, have not been the monolithic political entities that would conform to the public claims made by Akali leaders and theoreticians from Sikh religion and philosophy for a single and exclusive political entity of the followers of the Sikh religion. Leaving the general elections aside, even in the elections concerning the religious shrines of the Sikhs, the Akali Dal does not command the total support of the Sikh population. In the 1960 gurdwara elections, one-third of the Sikhs who exercised their franchise voted for parties other than the Akali Dal. Indeed, no one is more aware of the divisions among the Sikhs than the leader who wants them to act as a single political group, Tara Singh. In his autobiography, he states: "I don't say that other nations don't have such anti-nation people, but among the Sikhs there are more of them than in others. This has always been the great weakness of the Panth and will remain so." [73] Political divisions among other religious groups in India are as deep as in the Sikh community, if not more so, but it seems that the divisions in the Sikh community are felt more acutely by Akali leaders in view of their determined goal of a single political group for the Sikhs.

One prominent Sikh leader, in giving an explanation for the divisions among the Sikhs, stated that "it cannot be the Sikh religion but some tribal heritage which the community has not been able to overcome in the past as well as in the present." [74] A British officer with long experience with the Akali Dal and the Sikhs, attributed the divisions in the Sikh community to the Sikh religion. In his opinion, the strength and weakness of Sikh politics lay in the Guru's teaching that "where five of you

[73] Tara Singh, *Meri Yaad,* p. 68.
[74] See the foreword by Jogendra Singh, in Gupta, *History of the Sikhs,* II, viii.

are gathered together, there am I." [75] Thus, as long as matters gravely affecting the Panth, for which decrees may be issued from the Akal Takht, are not concerned, several groups may claim to speak in the name of the Panth. Moreover, even though the ethos of the Khalsa Panth may be similar to that of Lenin's Communist party, as Kapur Singh maintains,[76] the Panth is not strictly comparable to the Communist party. There is nothing of the membership requirements in the Panth which renders the Communist party such an elitist group. Membership in the Panth is today largely a concomitant of birth though there is a formal baptismal ceremony. None of the complex and authoritarian Communist party structure appears in the case of the Panth. However, even Communist parties that are not backed by state power, and operate in an environment of individual freedom, have to reckon with divisions.[77] Furthermore, even if the Khalsa were the prototype of the Communist party,[78] one would have to concede that there is no one Communist party, but many Communist parties in the world to implement "the deathless pledge and loyalty . . . to a universal Idea and Ideal." [79] Apart from differences over interpretation of doctrine, the Communist apparatus, like any other party based on a single ideology, must contend with territorial, economic, and social divisions.

The major social division in the Sikh community is that between the Harijan and non-Harijan Sikhs; and it has proved an insurmountable obstacle in the Akali Dal's effort to make itself the sole representative of the Panth. Caste and class reinforce each other here, and in addition, there is the past legacy of bad treatment meted out to the Harijans, especially their

[75] Major Billy Short, quoted in Campbell-Johnson, p. 204.

[76] Kapur Singh, p. 11.

[77] It may well be that the Akali Dal leaders aspire for precisely the situation in which state power would be at the disposal of the Akali Dal so that their goal of the independent political entity of the Sikhs could be attained through coercion, and all Sikhs thus cast in a single mold as far as political thought is concerned.

[78] Kapur Singh, p. 11.   [79] *Loc. cit.*

womenfolk, by the non-Harijan Sikhs. Therefore, the more the non-Harijan Sikhs support the Akali Dal, the more the Harijans oppose that organization. There are some sections of Harijans who may demonstratively support the Akali Dal in order to rise higher in the social hierarchy of the Sikh community by moving closer to the political stand of the non-Harijan Sikhs, but Harijan Sikhs have by and large remained the Achilles heel of the Akali Dal.

A further social division within the Sikh community is that among the non-Harijan Sikhs as between Jats and non-Jats. The Jats provided the great mass of the early converts to Sikhism and later became the political rulers for nearly a century in the Punjab before the British conquest. As a rural-based population, the Jats did not have much opportunity for education. During Sikh rule in the Punjab and the early period of British rule, large numbers of non-Jats—that is, the Khatris and their associate caste, the Aroras—converted to Sikhism. They were the trading, banking, and money-lending classes, and were ahead of the Jats in education and financial resources. As a result, in the early part of British rule "the Sikh personnel of all the higher services, civil or military, had become predominantly non-Jat." [80]

At the turn of the century, when the British government started taking an interest in the condition of the agriculturist classes, "the scales were reversed. A Sikh got a job reserved for a Sikh not because he was a Sikh but because he was a Jat Sikh," and the Jats "benefited enormously." [81] The earlier schism based on caste, occupational and rural-urban differences widened as a result of the application of caste criteria in recruitment. Voices were raised by non-Jat Sikhs against the distinction between Jats and non-Jats, but the Jat Sikhs were not willing to forego the protection given them. Even the Akali Dal tacitly accepted the division. The Jat even began "to appropri-

[80] Khushwant Singh, *The Sikhs,* p. 181.
[81] *Ibid.,* pp. 181–82.

ate the title Sikh exclusively for himself and accept all the privileges attaching to it." [82]

Since independence, distinctions on the basis of caste—except for the Harijans and the scheduled tribes—have been abolished in recruitment to public services. However, the Jats constitute the largest single caste group in the Sikh community and perhaps a majority of the Sikh population, and are predominant among the Sikhs in the Congress party and in the Akali Dal. The acquisition of political power through control of the Congress party—for instance, in 1962 both the Chief Minister and the president of the Punjab Congress were Jat Sikhs—has added further to their social and economic importance in the Sikh community.

The leadership of Master Tara Singh, who belongs to the Khatri caste, was at times questioned on the basis that he represented the "bhapas," the non-Jat traders and businessmen, primarily refugees from west Punjab. Giani Kartar Singh raised the question of Jats and non-Jats openly again in 1959, and though he was criticized by some Sikh leaders for doing so,[83] the critics were largely non-Jat Sikhs. Within the Akali Dal the question is not brought out in the open, but the feeling of Jat and non-Jat has operated below the surface. Jat leaders in the past felt that they had for too long been deprived of the top leadership in the Akali Dal by Master Tara Singh's monopoly of the organization for over thirty years. The non-Jats in the ranks of the Akali Dal, on the other hand, did not feel secure in the prospect of positions of responsibility and power in the Akali Dal after Tara Singh. Many of them have therefore preferred to continue in the Congress party even after the Akali Dal has asked them to return to the Dal.

When Sant Fateh Singh and his supporters established a rival Akali Dal in 1962, this was interpreted as a move on the

[82] *Ibid.,* p. 182.
[83] Teja Singh, "Solution in Hands of Sikh Intelligentsia," *The Tribune,* February 22, 1959.

part of the Jat Sikhs in the rural areas of the Punjab to over-throw the leadership of Master Tara Singh, allegedly representing non-Jat Sikhs of the urban areas. Analysts of the results of the SGPC elections of 1965 pointed out that the support for Tara Singh's group came from the urban areas, whereas that for the Sant Fateh Singh group came from the rural areas.[84]

In addition to caste divisions within the Sikh community, there are economic divisions between the wealthy business class on one hand, and a growing labor class on the other. Further, there is the regional division between the Sikhs of the Majha area, the so-called Prussia of Sikhism, and the Malwa area.[85] To some extent, this regional division was the basis of the Nagoke and Giani groups in the Akali Dal in the 1930s and 1940s. While the distinction is not as important today, there is still the feeling on the part of the Malwa Sikhs that they have been neglected by the Akali Dal, and they tend to establish rival organizations to further the interests of the Malwa area.[86] Also there are the divisions between refugee Sikhs from west Punjab and the local Sikh population. Then there are doctrinal differences which emerge in the Sikh sects, such as the Namdhari sect.[87]

Summary and Conclusions

The Shiromani Akali Dal presents a formidable challenge to the Congress party in view of its ability to mobilize the support of a significantly large part of the Sikh masses—because of its past role in the Gurdwara Reform movement and its monopoly of the protest function in behalf of the Sikh community

[84] See *The Spokesman*, xiv, No. 21 (1965), 3.
[85] Majha refers to the southern part of the area between the rivers Ravi and Beas—that is, the districts of Amritsar and Gurdaspur and, before the partition, also Lahore. Malwa refers to the Sikh-majority districts below the river Sutlej.
[86] See the statement of Gopal Singh Khalsa, *The Tribune*, January 11, 1958.
[87] On sects in Sikhism, see Teja Singh, *Sikhism*, pp. 62–83; Teja Singh, *Essays*, pp. 120–28; and Narang, pp. 188–90.

—and in view of its ability to utilize the large monetary and manpower resources of the SGPC. On the other hand, to the extent that a substantial segment of the Sikh population withholds its support from the Akali Dal, it adversely affects the Akali position—not so much in depriving the Akali Dal of more supporters as in undermining the crucial Akali claim to be the sole representative of the Panth. The Akali Dal's failure to substantiate in practice its claim to be the sole agent of the Panth renders ineffective, in turn, its attempt to demoralize Sikh leaders in the Congress party through characterizing them as renegades from the Panth. Despite this weakness in the moral position of the Akali Dal, the resources at its disposal make it a strong political force. What is more significant is that the Akali resources cannot be dispossessed by the Congress party, since any attempt to do so would be considered an assault not only on the Akali Dal but on the Sikh community. The Congress party will therefore have to reconcile itself to the "irritant" of a continuous conflict in different forms until such time as it can weaken the Akali Dal by attracting further political support from the Sikh community. The various ways in which the Akali Dal may meanwhile utilize its resources in the conflict can be discerned in the different strategies it has hitherto employed.

CHAPTER VI

Political Strategies of the Akali Dal

IN ITS struggle for the achievement of Punjabi Suba, the Akali Dal is able to rely on large financial and manpower resources and on the support of an extensive segment of the Sikh population. How then does it utilize these important resources in the pursuit of its goal? What are the various methods and techniques that the Akali Dal employs toward the achievement of Punjabi Suba? To some extent the methods and techniques employed by the Akali Dal are influenced by the nature of political institutions prevailing in India. The methods which transcend the institutional framework have been the ones, by virtue of their dramatic impact, to receive the most publicity, but in fact the goal of Punjabi Suba has been pursued at many levels of political activity. The existing political institutions do not necessarily always set limits to the methods employed by the Akali Dal but provide some of the channels through which the Akali Dal has additionally tried to achieve its aims. The more important political institutions in this case are those of liberal democracy with guaranteed freedoms, a parliamentary form of government, an independent judiciary, and periodic elections based on "joint electorates" including members of all religious communities rather than "separate electorates."

In the context of these political institutions and its own considerable financial and organizational resources, the Akali Dal has employed a variety of political strategies which can be discussed under three major headings: (1) constitutional, (2) infiltrational, and (3) agitational. In the discussion that follows, one will note that many of the techniques and tactics

used by the Akali Dal are similar to those of the Communist
party.

Constitutional Strategy

The constitutional strategy involves the use of methods that
are within the framework of the existing constitutionally guaranteed rights, that do not violate properly enacted laws, and
that are employed in the open view of the public. Though carried out in the Punjab, the constitutional strategy as well as
the agitational strategy operate characteristically in relation to
the central leadership of the Congress party and Congress government in New Delhi, either directly through meetings and
discussions with it or indirectly, and more importantly, through
convincing it of the powerful public support behind the Akali
Dal.

The methods under the constitutional strategy cover a wide
range in order to obtain decisions favorable to the Akali Dal.
At the governmental level, the Akali Dal may submit memoranda and petitions to government officials, including commissions of inquiry, outlining the alleged grievances of the Sikh
community and urging acceptance of Akali demands. As a
further step, Akali leaders may wait in deputation upon the
President of India, the Prime Minister, the Home Minister, or
the president of the Congress party, to convince them of the
necessity and justness of Akali demands. Since the real power
to make decisions concerning the kinds of demands the Akali
Dal makes is located in the leadership at the center, the Akali
Dal bypasses the Congress leadership in the Punjab. Further,
there is the element of deliberate contempt aimed at the Punjab Congress leaders by showing that Akali leaders deal with
leaders at a higher level. Also, since the political leaders of both
parties at the Punjab level are often involved in a bitter conflict, there is less possibility of communication between them.
On the other hand, despite the vehement criticism made of the
Congress party, there is the unstated feeling that leaders at the

center are genuinely the protectors of minorities and willing to listen, no matter how exaggerated the claims of these minorities.

In regard to the substantive demands of the Akali Dal, the submission of memoranda and petitions and waiting in deputation are usually preparatory to the launching of an agitation. Discussions with Congress leaders take place against the backdrop of a threat of an imminent agitation. Such discussions may continue during the period of the agitation, at times through mediators, such as the Maharaja of Patiala. When an agitation ends, Akali leaders may again submit petitions and hold discussions. They may call in person on important leaders for the release of persons arrested during the agitation. They may also resort to the courts for the release of prisoners.

At the public level, the Akali Dal arranges large meetings and conferences where speeches denunciatory of the government and the Congress leaders and other groups are delivered, and resolutions are passed setting forth the alleged grievances of the Sikhs as well as the demands of the Akali Dal. The Akali leaders are able organizers of large political conferences, which usually have a religious aura about them. The Guru Granth graces the stage on which the leaders are seated, and audiences bow to it as they gather. Speeches begin and end with religious greetings and are interrupted by many war cries. At such conferences it is more the sacrifices and bravery of the Sikhs rather than the principles of Sikhism that are recounted. Apart from speeches, a few poets may recite eulogies of Master Tara Singh or Sant Fateh Singh. At times, with the frustration of its attempts to gain Punjabi Suba, the Akali Dal develops front organizations, where what are considered Sikh demands are under-emphasized but political support is sought around such slogans as "save democracy" or "annihilate corruption." At Akali meetings inside the gurdwaras, however, Akali leaders stress more vigorously and emotionally the glory of the Panth, the alleged injustices done to the Sikhs, the evil intentions of the Hindus and the Congress, and the necessity of a Punjabi Suba for the Sikhs.

The Akali Dal further holds mass rallies and long, disciplined marches of Sikhs stretching over several miles in order to protest against government policies and to convince Congress leaders of the support that the Akali Dal has among the Sikhs. Such rallies and marches often coincide with some Sikh religious holiday. Another form of protest may be the organizing of a "black-out" day among the Sikhs as was done at the time of the inauguration of the Indian constitution.[1] The Akali Dal's political activities extend to New Delhi in addition to the Punjab, for New Delhi is adjacent to the Punjab and includes the largest aggregate of Sikh population in any city in India; besides, it is the capital of India where central government offices, diplomatic missions, and world-wide press bureaus are located.

At the level of the mass media, the Akali appeals are directed through newspapers in Indian languages. The Akali Dal publishes *Jathedar* in Gurmukhi, issued simultaneously from Delhi and Jullundur, and *Prabhat* in Urdu, issued from Jullundur. It does not possess any English newspaper though until recently an English weekly, *The Spokesman,* presented the Akali viewpoint. Though now in disagreement with the leadership of the Akali Dal and its methods, the weekly continues to support Akali demands. The language press serves more to reach Akali supporters than to convince members of non-Sikh communities among whom it is not read. Like the rest of the language press in the Punjab, the Akali newspapers emphasize the virtues of their party and the vices of their opponents rather than provide general news coverage. To put it mildly, as one British official did, "the Punjab vernacular press exceeds in virulence, in obscenity and in deliberate fomentation of communal hatred the press of all other provinces in India."[2] Dur-

[1] Lanka Sundaram, "Implications of Master Tara Singh's Revolt," *Hindusthan Standard,* January 16, 1950.

[2] Statement by H. D. Craik, in *Punjab Legislative Council Debates,* x, No. 16 (July 18, 1927), 814.

ing agitations the government is compelled therefore to impose restrictions on the language press. Akali leaders also seem to be quite sensitive to the world press and are eager to seek out foreign correspondents to present their viewpoint. In addition to the press, the Akali Dal and its supporters publish a large number of pamphlets in Gurmukhi and English, and sometimes in Hindi. In the number of pamphlets published on political affairs in the Punjab, the Akali Dal seems to be second only to the Punjab government itself.

Under the constitutional strategy, the Akali Dal also participates in parliamentary activity, not only to use the legislature as a forum for the propagation of its demands but also, if possible, to gain a share in political power. It endeavors to send to the legislature, in the periodic general elections, as large a bloc of Akali representatives as possible in order to influence the governmental process. Since independence there have been three general elections in the Punjab. In 1952 the Akali Dal fought the elections on the twin issues of Punjabi Suba and the independent political entity of the Sikh Panth. In 1957, under a political compromise, the Akali Dal did not set up candidates on its own ticket, but 26 candidates recommended by it ran on the Congress ticket. In 1962, the major issue in the election was, by general acceptance, that of Punjabi Suba. An examination of the 1962 general elections would therefore provide not only a test of the Akali claim that a majority of the population supports its demand for Punjabi Suba, but also an understanding of Akali election tactics and an insight into the interplay between the requirements of "joint electorates" and the self-imposed isolation of the Akali Dal.

Third General Elections, 1962

When in the first half of 1961, Master Tara Singh threatened a fast-unto-death for Punjabi Suba and then asked for a referendum on the Punjabi Suba issue in the so-called Punjabi-speaking region, Congress leaders proposed that the forthcoming general elections in 1962 be considered a referendum. At first Tara Singh refused but later, when coercing the government failed, he accepted the challenge to fight the elections on the issue of Punjabi Suba. The elections soon became for the Akali Dal a "war" for Punjabi Suba, with their immediate aim the defeat of the Congress party by mobilizing all anti-government forces. The Akali press editorialized on the "impending election battle," [3] and Tara Singh asked the Sikhs to "consider this election as the war for Punjabi Suba," [4] and exhorted: "Sikhs! supporters of Punjabi Suba!! fight." [5] He emphasized that "Khalsa ji! to win this election will prove decisive in favor of the Punjabi Suba," [6] and urged the Sikhs to bury the corpse of the Congress for "the country cannot be saved without finishing the Congress." [7] Even more important than Punjabi Suba for the Akali Dal became "the finishing of the curse of the Congress." [8]

The Akali Dal now started negotiations with the other political parties in the Punjab to break through its own isolation and to confront the Congress party, especially its "big guns," with a joint opposition. The wide ideological differences among these parties precluded an overall electoral alliance, but the Akali Dal was able to arrange in about 40 constituencies electoral adjustments of some sort with these parties ranging from the extreme right (the Swatantra party) to the extreme left (the Communist party) with the Republican party and the Praja Socialist party in between.[9] Some of these electoral ad-

---

[3] "Honewaala Chunao Ghamsaan," [The Impending Election Battle], *Prabhat,* November 13, 1961.

[4] *Ibid.,* January 1, 1962.

[5] *Ibid.,* February 1, 1962.

[6] *Ibid.,* January 1, 1962.

[7] *Ibid.,* February 4, 1962.

[8] *Ibid.,* February 20, 1962.

[9] A recent entrant on the political scene in India and the Punjab, the Swatantra party is for some a conservative party supporting undiluted free enterprise, and for others a reactionary challenge to the policies of the Congress party. On the issue of Punjabi Suba, its membership is split along communal lines though the top leadership has found it advan-

justments, however, had their limitations. If the Communist party and the Republican party associated too closely with the Akali Dal they would lose Hindu and Harijan votes, yet they could not get Sikh votes without doing precisely that. Furthermore, these arrangements provided the Congress party with an effective propaganda point, that the opposition parties had nothing in common ideologically and that the strange alliances and "political marriages" were merely to defeat the Congress.

The Akali Dal did not reach any agreement with the Jan Sangh on electoral adjustments, but Congress leaders and other observers alleged the existence of a secret alliance between the two parties.[10] At any rate, the leaders of the two parties acted as if there were one.[11] If there were an agreement, it would have been disastrous for both parties to proclaim it openly, since in public both of these communal parties bitterly oppose each other. At the same time they evidently need each other's assistance in getting their candidates elected to the legislature. In this case, it is not even necessary to withdraw one or the other party's candidates in order to defeat the Congress party. On the contrary just the opposite is necessary. For example, if in a largely Sikh constituency the contest is between the Akali Dal and the Congress party, the Hindu votes are likely to go to the Congress party; it is thus in the interest of the Akali Dal to have a Jan Sangh candidate to deprive the Congress of Hindu votes. The Akali Dal also finds it advantageous to have some party put up a candidate to divert Harijan votes which would otherwise go to the Congress party.

---

tageous to cooperate with the Akali Dal. The appeal of the Republican party, previously known as the Scheduled Castes Federation, lies among some sections of the Harijans. While its mass base is strongly opposed to the formation of Punjabi Suba, the Republican party is officially uncommitted on the issue, even though the political exigencies of the Punjab often make its office-bearers enter into alliances with the Akali Dal. The Praja Socialist party supports the Punjabi Suba demand, but it is devoid of any mass support in the Punjab.

[10] *The Tribune,* February 20, 1962.
[11] *The Hindustan Times,* February 23, 1962.

Within the framework of electoral adjustments with other opposition parties, the Akali Dal launched its own election campaign. It involved most of the same techniques that the other parties employed—holding public meetings, issuing manifestoes and pamphlets and posters, passing out handbills, arranging processions, canvassing individual voters, approaching traditional and elected leaders in villages. However, apart from the content of its appeal, what distinguished the campaign strategy of the Akali Dal from that of other political parties was the use of gurdwaras, most of which were under its control. One cannot overestimate the importance of Akali control over gurdwaras, especially the historic gurdwaras connected with Sikh religion and history. Since Sikhism originated in the Punjab and has flourished there only, the Akali Dal operates on its home base. Furthermore, the origins of Sikhism do not fade into some hoary past but are intimately connected with recent history, for the last Guru died in the first quarter of the eighteenth century. The fact that there were ten Gurus who traveled extensively in the Punjab has made for innumerable gurdwaras, apart from other regular places of worship, commemorating some event connected with the life and travels of the Gurus. Control of this network of gurdwaras offers a tremendous election advantage to the Akali Dal, especially when it considers religion and politics inseparable.

During the 1962 general elections, gurdwara workers actively helped Akali candidates in election campaigning.[12] The free kitchen and dining facilities of the gurdwaras were always at

[12] Observations on the 1962 general elections are based on a two-month study, involving extensive touring of the Ludhiana district, during January and February 1962. To the many candidates and party workers belonging to both the Congress party and the Akali Dal, the author's grateful thanks for their hospitality and transport facilities. For an intensive study of election campaigning and voting behavior in a single constituency in Ludhiana district, see Baldev Raj Nayar, "Studies in Voting Behaviour: Religion and Caste in the Punjab: Sidhwan Bet Constituency," *The Economic Weekly*, xiv, No. 31 (August 4, 1962), 1267–76.

the disposal of Akali candidates and workers. Akali leaders, including Sant Fateh Singh, addressed religious congregations in gurdwaras, especially on religious holidays, urging Sikhs to vote for the "Panth," that is, the Akali Dal. In speeches, which began and ended with slogans of the Sikh religion, Akali spokesmen urged everyone "who had the grain of Sikhism in him and had drunk of the Guru's nectar" at the baptismal ceremony to vote for the Panth. Professional musicians rendered martial songs on the heroism and sacrifices of the Sikhs to help create an atmosphere of emotional receptivity to the political speeches. Under the auspices of some gurdwaras, processions were organized on religious holidays, but the slogans shouted did not discriminate between religion and Akali politics. In some gurdwaras where protest was expected from the audience about mixing religion and politics, Akali candidates merely talked about Sikh religion and history.

While in gurdwaras Akali leaders appealed in the name of the Panth and talked of the tyranny of the Congress regime under which the Sikhs allegedly lived, in meetings outside gurdwaras they attacked the Congress party for its economic and political policies. When addressing largely Hindu or mixed Hindu-Sikh audiences, among whom the candidate had personal influence cutting across religious ties, Akali leaders played down, and sometimes totally ignored, the demand for Punjabi Suba. One sophisticated Akali candidate in Ludhiana district actually rebuked his workers for having shouted slogans about "long live Punjabi Suba" after he had delivered a speech criticizing the government for corruption, inefficiency and tyranny, which were hurting both Hindus and Sikhs. To Hindu audiences it was even said that there was no difference between Hindus and Sikhs except for the external symbols. On the other hand, Akali candidates were so convinced that Hindu and Harijan voters would oppose the Akali Dal that they were often reluctant even to visit Hindu and Harijan voters in villages and usually passed them by or greeted them only superficially. When canvassing individual Sikh voters, a local village or neighborhood leader merely introduced Akali candidates by saying that "the Panth has chosen Sardar Sahib for this area, vote for the Panth," or that "the symbol of the Panth is the Panja, vote for the Baba [Guru Nanak]." A series of election posters, issued by the Akali Dal headquarters in Amritsar and distributed in all constituencies, reinforced the Akali campaign. Among these were a poster entitled "old souls, new lives" showing Nehru with Aurangzeb in the background, and Partap Singh Kairon with the Nawab of Sirhind [13] in the background—Aurangzeb and Nawab of Sirhind being the two most hated characters in Sikh history.

The Akali press and leaders had pictured the Akali Dal as an invincible force in the Punjabi-speaking region, but the election results repudiated the Akali claim that a majority of the population favored its demand for Punjabi Suba. Of the 89 seats in the so-called Punjabi-speaking region, the Akali Dal was able to win only 19 seats, and secured only 19.8 percent of the total vote polled. In the Punjab as a whole, the Akali Dal obtained only 11.7 percent of the vote, with no seats outside the Punjabi-speaking region. The two other parties on record as supporting Punjabi Suba, at least as they conceived it, were the Communist party and the Praja Socialist party; they received 10 percent and 0.7 percent respectively of the total vote polled in the Punjabi-speaking region. The Jan Sangh, which vigorously opposed the demand for Punjabi Suba, secured 7.7 percent of the vote in the same region, while the Congress party polled 45.8 percent of the vote.[14]

The verdict of the elections in 1962, however, did not deter the Akali Dal from persisting in its demand for Punjabi Suba. In the first place it started a campaign protesting alleged use

[13] The governor of Sirhind who ordered the execution of two of Guru Gobind Singh's sons aged 9 and 10.

[14] For details, see chapter VII.

of unfair election practices by the Congress party in order to divert attention, as it had done in 1952, from its own election defeat. The Akali Dal also claimed that the right type of Sikhs did not vote for the Congress:

> We don't say that Congress candidates did not get Sikh votes. They got and certainly got. But those votes were of such Sikhs as factory-owners, capitalists, or are permit-quota-license holders; or the Congress candidates got the votes of such elements that are undesirable.[15]

Furthermore, although the Akali Dal had contested the elections on the Punjabi Suba issue it made reservations against accepting the election verdict as decisive for the fate of the demand. In several articles Master Tara Singh had said that "the result of this election does not bind us but it binds the Congress party," [16] for he wanted a specific referendum on the issue.

Such reservations aside, the Akali Dal conceives the electoral process as really not a medium for the resolution of conflict but an opportunity to create group solidarity for use in the pursuit of other methods of "struggle." An article written by Master Tara Singh on the eve of the first general elections throws interesting light on this aspect of the Akali conception of elections: "I wish to fight elections and win as many seats as possible, but I do not believe that we shall attain our objective through legislatures. I want to win elections solely to create unity and consequent strength in the Panth which strength will be utilized for the struggle through which we may have to pass. . . . What form our struggle will assume cannot be divined at present; for all depends upon circumstances, upon our determination and strength, and upon the strength of those who might be arrayed against us." [17]

15 *Prabhat,* March 30, 1962.

16 *Ibid.,* January 1, 1962.

17 Tara Singh, "We Will Not Live As Serfs!" *The Spokesman,* Vol. 1, No. 2 (August 29, 1951).

INFILTRATIONAL STRATEGY

Pursued in relation to the state government in the Punjab, this strategy has involved the merger into the Congress party of the well-knit group of Akali members in the legislature in order to work for such objectives as the Akali Dal may direct. On a sheer political basis, the strategy must obviously seem a highly rational one for the Akali Dal. Since representatives from the Akali Dal are not only a minority in the total membership of the Punjab legislature but also in the group of Sikh representatives in the legislature, they cannot form a government themselves to implement Akali goals. The next best alternative would appear to be an alliance with the party in power, but the Congress party proclaims itself to be a secular party and ideally desists from aligning itself with communal parties. In this situation, Akali members have from time to time joined the Congress party as a group in an attempt to, as the record would indicate, gain political concessions or to consolidate concessions otherwise obtained.

Apart from a single, disciplined organization sending these members, the particular ideology of the Akali Dal reinforces the tendency among such members to operate as a cohesive group inside the Congress party. The basic ideological premise here is that Sikhs, or at least Akalis, should not act as individuals in their choice of a political party but that, on the contrary, the Akali Dal as the sole representative body of the Panth "shall decide from time to time whether we are to join the Congress, stay therein or to go out of it and join some other political party." [18] In view of this premise, it is logical to assume that any group of leaders or members that the Akali Dal sends into the Congress party must ideally act on its behalf inside the Congress party. In short, acting as a group, they pursue, to the extent that they abide by the Akali ideology, objectives that are opposed to the Congress ideology even though they

[18] Tara Singh, *Charhdi Kala,* pp. 44–45.

are members of the Congress party. In fact, Akali leaders justify their presence in the Congress party in precisely these terms. When differences arise between the "ins" (the Akali group in the Congress party) and the "outs" (the Akali Dal), the "outs" pointedly ask as to what the "ins" have done for the Panth, whereupon the "ins" list their achievements in the cause of the Panth. For some, even the publicly expressed differences between the two groups are misleading, for both work in collaboration; the "outs" put pressure through agitations, while the "ins" bargain for more concessions as a condition of the support of their cohesive group for one or another faction into which the Congress may be divided.

Although the purpose of the infiltrational strategy has been to achieve political power for the attainment of Akali objectives, this strategy performs certain other functions, which may or may not necessarily be the reasons for any particular merger. Two of these functions seem obvious. One, the strategy has provided for Akali political leaders, who have achieved considerable political eminence but cannot advance any further, more fruitful alternative channels of political power and responsibility in the Congress party. Two, by transferring to the Congress party what may have been potential rivals, this strategy has assured the continued leadership of certain leaders in the Akali Dal. An additional result of the strategy, however, has been to discredit the oft-repeated solemn statement by Akali leaders that religion and politics are inextricably combined in Sikhism. By their willingness to renounce adherence to this notion of politics, at least publicly, in order to join and remain in the Congress party, Akali leaders have given the impression that the emphasis on inseparability of religion and politics is not a matter of conviction or sincere belief, but rather a handy tool to be used to drive a political bargain.

How has the infiltrational strategy worked out in practice? How successful has the Akali Dal been in the achievement of its goals through this strategy? An examination of two instances of the implementation of this strategy by the Akali Dal would shed some light on these questions.

Akali-Congress Merger, 1948

The Akali Dal fought the 1946 general elections to the Punjab legislature on its own ticket, at many places opposing the Congress party. In these elections, the Akali Dal won 23 out of the 33 seats reserved for the Sikhs. The Congress party won a total of 51 seats, including several Sikh seats. After independence these Congress and Akali representatives, plus another group of about half a dozen Hindu and Sikh members, constituted the legislature for that part of the Punjab which fell to India's share. The Congress party assumed power in the state with Dr. Gopichand Bhargava as Chief Minister, or Premier as the office was then known. Bhargava included in his ministry representatives from the Nagoke group of the Akali Dal, which was known for its pro-Congress sympathies in the pre-independence period. However, the Congress legislature party was about equally divided between two factions with a long history—the Satyapal group and the Bhargava group—and Bhargava's position was quite precarious. The Hindus in the party were about equally divided, while the Sikhs in the party were overwhelmingly opposed to him, for they suspected that Bhargava was working in alliance with the Akalis,[19] who had helped his group to power inside the Congress party in 1938. Dr. Bhargava and the Akali leader Baldev Singh, then Defense Minister at New Delhi, "were known to be friends" and "the advice from Delhi was sought for and willingly accepted by the Doctor. On that score he was criticized by his friends and opponents alike."[20]

[19] Feroz Chand, "What Is Happening in East Punjab?" *N.C.*, April 8, 1948. This article is available in the files of newspaper clippings at the Congress party library in New Delhi, and is marked as having been taken from the newspaper "N.C." It is not certain what "N.C." stands for, perhaps *Indian News Chronicle*.

[20] Political Observer, "East Punjab Politics," *The Tribune*, April 10, 1949.

With the opposition to Bhargava growing, the Akali Dal decided on a new course. In February 1948 Master Tara Singh had announced that "we have nothing in common with the Congress," and that he wanted "the right of self-determination for the Panth." [21] A few weeks later, however, Akali leaders met in New Delhi and directed the Akali members of the Punjab legislature to resign from the Akali Dal and join the Congress party.[22] Tara Singh commented that "the Panthic members have joined the Congress with our approval," but that "they will dissociate themselves from the party when called upon to do so." [23] Subsequently, in his position as president of the Akali Dal, Giani Kartar Singh had a resolution passed by his executive committee, stating that the Akali Dal would not engage in political activity henceforth.[24]

The Akali Dal's decision to join the Congress party was interpreted by some as a victory for secular nationalism as the Akali Dal had decided to give up its separate "communal" politics, but in fact the decision was "actuated by the desire to assure continuance of the existing leadership." [25] To some it seemed that "the era of appeasement of Akalis and of open dictation from Sardar Baldev Singh from Delhi commenced" and that "dictation and interference from Delhi became more insistent and persistent." [26] The Akali members inside the Congress party functioned as a separate group under the leadership and direction of Giani Kartar Singh, and Bhargava became increasingly dependent on the support of this group to maintain his position as Chief Minister.[27]

Bhargava's opponents, now led by Bhim Sen Sachar, severely criticized him for a secret deal with the Akali Dal and for succumbing to Akali demands, but they themselves "carried on

[21] *The Statesman*, February 29, 1948.
[22] Harbans Singh, *ibid.*, April 4, 1948.
[23] *The Hindustan Times*, April 10, 1948.
[24] Giani Gurcharan Singh, p. 165.
[25] Feroz Chand, *N.C.*, April 8, 1948.
[26] Political Observer, *The Tribune*, April 10, 1949.
[27] *Loc. cit.*

secret negotiations with the Akali party with a view of wresting power." [28] The Akali group then switched its support to the group led by Sachar, who became Chief Minister in April 1949, amidst rumors that he too had made important political concessions to the Akali Dal. Meanwhile, outside the councils of government, the Akali Dal led by Master Tara Singh vehemently criticized the government for not acceding to Akali claims on behalf of the Sikh community and threatened agitations. The government arrested Tara Singh and several other Akali leaders on account of activities prejudicial to the maintenance of law and order. Observers noted that the pressure through agitations was being applied in order to assist the Akali group within the Congress party in the pursuit of its demands. One newspaper commented:

> Two readings of Sikh politics hold the field: one which believes that with the passage of time differences will be composed and the other which takes the uncharitable view that there is an understanding between those leaders who are within the Congress and those outside that the former should secure from within while the latter exert themselves from outside towards the attainment of other ends. No cause will be advanced by concealing the fact that the latter view has been gaining ground in recent months.[29]

Sachar's ministry lasted for a bare six months, as the Akali group decided to switch its support to Bhargava. Apparently, the Akali members in the Congress had "skillfully used their bargaining power to precipitate crises between rival Hindu leaders in the Congress Party or to reap the maximum advantage out of the crises when they occurred." [30] Bhargava now included Giani Kartar Singh in his ministry. In return for Akali support, Bhargava had to yield "all along the line to im-

---

[28] *Loc. cit.* See also Feroz Chand, *N.C.,* April 8, 1948.
[29] *The Tribune,* August 3, 1950.
[30] *National Herald,* editorial, November 6, 1949.

portunate demands" of the Akali group,[31] while Giani Kartar Singh "had everything his own way in directions which there is not space enough here to recount." [32] The leadership of the Congress party organization strongly criticized the Congress government headed by Bhargava. Partap Singh Kairon attacked the Bhargava ministry for including persons "who are directly responsible for the communal bitterness that existed in the province today." [33] He remarked that "some of them were active and bitter opponents of the Congress. They joined the Congress only when they realized that the only way to get into power was through the Congress." [34] Finally, the "insatiable ambition" [35] of Kartar Singh forced another ministerial crisis, but this time the central Congress leadership in New Delhi reacted by directing Bhargava to resign and then imposed "President's Rule" in the Punjab in June 1951 on the ground that the constitutional machinery had broken down in the state. The legislature was dissolved, and the Governor of the Punjab administered the state until after the first general elections in 1951–52.

The Akali group was thus deprived of the opportunity to influence the government any further, but it could look back with justifiable pride on the many political concessions it had been able to secure through its association with the Congress party —the "services formula"; the "parity formula"; and the "Sachar formula." Under the "services formula," proportions were established in the services of the Punjab government as between the Hindu and Sikh communities, with the Sikh share in excess of their proportion in the population. In spite of repeated questions in the Punjab legislature, ministers refused to divulge the exact proportions allocated to each community. Under the "parity formula," the Punjab ministry is supposed to include

[31] *The Tribune,* editorial, August 3, 1950.
[32] *Ibid.,* editorial, May 16, 1951.
[33] *Ibid.,* April 6, 1951.
[34] *Loc. cit.*
[35] *Ibid.,* editorial, May 16, 1951.

an equal number of Hindus and Sikhs, even though the Sikhs were less than 35 percent of the Punjab population.

The most far-reaching of the formulas was the "Sachar formula," the "Sachar" being a misnomer, for its real author was Giani Kartar Singh. This formula later became the basis for further Akali demands for the division of Punjab and for government concessions in this regard. *The Spokesman* therefore rightly expressed gratitude to Kartar Singh for obtaining this concession which it characterized as the father of the "regional formula" secured in 1956.[36] The importance of the Sachar formula lay in the fact that the government accepted the Akali claim that the Punjab could be demarcated into Hindi-speaking and Punjabi-speaking regions. In its origin, the Sachar formula sought to settle the problem of the medium of instruction in public schools. It provided that Punjabi in Gurmukhi script and Hindi in Devnagari script should be the regional languages of the Punjabi-speaking and Hindi-speaking areas, respectively, which areas were to be demarcated by the government. It also provided that Punjabi would be the medium of instruction in the Punjabi-speaking areas up to the high school stage, with Hindi as a compulsory subject from the fourth grade. The reverse arrangements were to apply in the Hindi-speaking areas. In case, however, ten children in one class or forty children in one school desired to be instructed in a language other than the regional language, provision was to be made for such instruction, but such children were obligated to learn as a compulsory language the regional language from the fourth class. In the secondary stage the medium of instruction might be a language other than the regional language, provided one-third of the students so desired, but the regional language would be taught as a compulsory subject throughout the secondary stage.

It is noteworthy that the Sachar formula is not a resolution passed by the legislature, but is in the nature of a pact, the "Final Draft Proposals of Language Question in East Punjab,"

[36] *The Spokesman*, VII, No. 3 (January 21, 1957), 4.

signed by four leaders—two Hindus and two Sikhs—though all were officially members of the Congress party. Through accident or design, the Punjabi-speaking region turned out to be a Sikh-majority area. On the other hand, the Hindi-speaking region was an overwhelmingly Hindu-majority area and consisted of two blocks of unconnected territory, one located in the north and the other in the southeast of the Punjab, in which dialects are spoken that are no less or no more close to Punjabi than to Hindi. But once the government accepted the principle that there were two linguistic regions in the Punjab, Master Tara Singh quickly demanded that the government should now declare these linguistic regions to be politically autonomous areas. Later, with hindsight, observers noted that Kartar Singh was more interested in the demarcation of linguistic regions than in the provisions concerning the medium of instruction used.[37] However, subsequent events showed that the provisions regarding language instruction too were of immense political advantage to the Akali leadership. Since the study of Punjabi in Gurmukhi script is compulsory in the Hindi region in some form or another and the people in this region, like the Hindus in the Punjabi-speaking region, are hostile to learning it, they must agitate against the compulsion to learn Punjabi. Since the Akali Dal strongly opposes any such revision of the Sachar formula, the people of the Hindi region must, in the alternative, agitate for the separation of their area from the Punjab, which would only complement the demand of the Akali Dal for Punjabi Suba and facilitate its achievement.[38]

[37] See the editorial in *The Tribune,* August 2, 1955, which said, in part: "Indeed the feeling has persisted in our mind that Gyani Kartar Singh was clearer in his mind of the possibilities of regional demarcation of the Punjabi-speaking area than Mr. Sachar was about its implications. With it has been associated the suspicion that Akali interest did not extend beyond implied delimitation of the area of the Punjabi-speaking state secured by renouncement of claim to it."

[38] One political leader notes that "Giani Kartar Singh has been saying publicly that provision for compulsory study of Punjabi in the Hindi region was made deliberately in the Regional Formula, so that the people of that area may feel the pinch and cry for separation." Sher Singh, p. 32.

These political concessions obtained between March 1948 and November 1949 added to a sizable achievement for the small Akali group within the Congress party. On the heels of these accomplishments, however, apparently to put further pressure on the government, the Akali Dal directed its members to leave the Congress party and return to the Akali Dal as the Congress party had allegedly failed to "appreciate the sentiments and ambitions of the Sikh community." [39] Master Tara Singh now divulged that the Akali legislators had been sent to the Congress party on the understanding that "in case they failed to secure certain demands of the Sikhs within six months they would leave the Congress and come back. Of these Sikh demands the chief one related to the creation of the Punjabi-speaking province." [40] Even earlier, in June 1949, an Akali Dal resolution said that Akali leaders who had joined the Congress party "with a view to serve and strengthen the Panth, be called upon to explain how and in what manner they have done so or intend doing so. . . ." [41] However, only two Akali members resigned from the Congress party.

Those Akali members who continued to stay in the Congress party justified their position by maintaining that it was more beneficial to the Panth for them to stay in the Congress party. Narotam Singh noted that "the Sikhs' share in the services according to the latest figures is more than their proportion in the population." [42] In a speech on February 8, 1951, at Amritsar, one Punjab minister, Isher Singh Majhail, said that even if the situation were viewed from a selfish angle the Sikhs should continue in the Congress party, for they now enjoyed 50 percent representation in the cabinet. In another speech Giani Kartar Singh remarked that the Sachar formula and the rights given to Sikh Harijans were achievements of which they could be justly proud. He added that in accordance with

[39] Resolution of the Akali Dal, *National Herald,* July 21, 1950.
[40] Press statement issued on August 5, 1950.
[41] *The Tribune,* June 18, 1949.
[42] *The Tribune,* August 6, 1950.

the demand of the Akali Dal, he secured postponement for three years of the plan to nationalize the transport business, almost wholly owned by the Sikh community. While expressing his support for the demand for a Punjabi-speaking state, he said that the methods employed by Master Tara Singh could not achieve it. He assured the audience that the Akali legislators had served the Panth and that they hoped to serve it better.[43] Kartar Singh continued in the Congress party but resigned later in 1951, when his group was unable to get a sufficient number of tickets for the forthcoming general elections in 1951–52, and then raised demands that were "akin" to those of the Akali Dal.[44] He again joined the Akali Dal and became its general secretary and participated in its activities.

Viewed from any aspect, the infiltrational strategy employed by the Akali Dal from 1948 to 1951 proved eminently successful. Part of the reason for the success of the strategy was the factional strife within the Congress party and the general confusion in the Punjab following the partition, with its mass migration and resettlement problems. Whether such a strategy would achieve similar success in the future would depend on the internal condition of the Congress party and the political situation in the Punjab rather than in the mere fact of infiltration.

Akali-Congress Merger, 1956

In 1955 the Akali Dal launched a massive agitation. Apparently this agitation convinced the government that the Akali Dal was a powerful political force, and the government made a conciliatory gesture to bring the agitation to a close. Subsequent to the end of the agitation, negotiations were held between the central government leaders and several Akali leaders,

[43] Information on speeches of Majhail and Kartar Singh on February 8, 1951 at Amritsar, is from newspaper files at the Congress party library in New Delhi.
[44] "Giani's Demands," *The Spokesman*, 1, No. 10 (October 24, 1951), 9.

including Master Tara Singh, Giani Kartar Singh, Hukam Singh, and Gian Singh Rarewala. Meanwhile, the States Reorganization Commission recommended the merger of Punjab, PEPSU and Himachal Pradesh, but this recommendation was absolutely unacceptable to the Akali Dal. Eventually, a compromise solution—later known as the "regional formula"—was reached, which the Akali Dal formally accepted on March 11, 1956, in a resolution of its general body. An outline of the formula was placed before parliament only after a Hindu leader went on a hunger strike.

Under the regional formula the state of PEPSU was merged in the Punjab in 1956 but Himachal Pradesh—which was overwhelmingly Hindu—was retained as a separate territorial unit.[45] For the reorganized Punjab a single Governor, with a single council of ministers and a single legislature, was provided. However, the new state was divided into two so-called Punjabi-speaking and Hindi-speaking regions, and two regional committees of the legislature were provided, consisting of the members of the legislature belonging to the respective regions. Any proposed legislation on some fourteen subjects, dealing with economic and social development, had to be referred to the regional committees, and the state government and the state legislature were normally expected to accept the advice given by the regional committees; in case of difference of opinion, the decision of the Governor was to be final and binding. The regional committees were further empowered to make proposals, not involving financial commitments, on those fourteen subjects for either legislation or executive policy. The provisions regarding the regional committees meant that any political party with a majority in a regional committee, even if without a majority

[45] In Akali circles there remains the fear nonetheless that at some future date Himachal Pradesh will be merged in the Punjab. On the other hand, there are demands on the part of some political leaders from the hill districts in northern Punjab that their region be merged in Himachal Pradesh, for the Punjab government has neglected the economic development of their region.

in the whole legislature, could still implement its program on the fourteen subjects that were listed in the formula.

The regional formula further provided that the provisions of the Sachar formula concerning the medium of instruction would continue to apply in the areas of the Punjab before the merger, and that in the areas of the former PEPSU state the arrangement already existing therein regarding language instruction would continue. In contrast to the Sachar formula, the PEPSU formula made no provision for students to opt out of the regional language as medium of instruction. It simply stated: "PEPSU is a bilingual State consisting of two zones known as Hindi speaking and Punjabi speaking zones. In the Hindi speaking zone, Hindi is taught from the very first primary class and Punjabi as second compulsory subject from third primary standard and similarly Punjabi from the first primary class and Hindi as second compulsory language from third primary standard in Punjabi speaking area. Hindi is medium of instruction in the Hindi zone and Punjabi in Punjabi speaking area." (From the *Report of the Commissioner for Linguistic Minorities* [*Fourth Report*]). The Punjab as a whole was now to be considered bilingual, but the regional languages of the Punjabi-speaking and Hindi-speaking regions were to be considered the official languages for the respective regions. The demarcation of the state into Punjabi-speaking and Hindi-speaking regions was not included in the regional formula but was left for later determination. However, as in the case of the Sachar formula, the actual demarcation was not made solely on a linguistic basis. Certain overwhelmingly Hindu areas were excluded from the Punjabi-speaking region, even though they were linguistically no different from other areas that were included in the region, with the result that the Punjabi region turned out to be a Sikh-majority region.[46]

[46] Although Akali leaders and some other Sikh leaders may have at one time thought that a Sikh majority in the population of the Punjabi-speaking region was essential to the exercise of effective political control

A political compromise having been reached between the government and the Akali Dal and all Sikh grievances, on the admission of Akali leaders themselves, having been redressed, the important question then was what course the Akali Dal should pursue in the future. The Akali Dal had not yet reached any decision, when Gian Singh Rarewala—a former Chief Minister of PEPSU, who had been called the "Panzer Division" of the Akali Dal [47]—issued a statement in May 1956 urging that, under the changed circumstances, the Akali Dal should leave the political field and confine itself to only social, cultural, religious, and educational activities of the Sikhs. [48] He wanted the Akali Dal to allow its members and supporters "to join the progressive and national forces and take full part in the rebuilding of the country." [49] He later started discussions with Congress leaders in order to facilitate the entry into the Congress party of his group, which was especially strong in the former PEPSU area. An acrimonious debate followed among the Akali

by Sikh legislators in the Punjabi regional committee or in a state legislature if the region was subsequently converted into Punjabi Suba, there now seems to be a decided change in this viewpoint. The nature of the delimitation of electoral constituencies worked out in 1956 and the geographical distribution of the population have seemingly convinced the advocates of Punjabi Suba that Sikhs can control the regional committee or a possible state legislature even with the inclusion in the Punjabi-speaking region or Punjabi Suba of large areas with a Hindu population. Their feeling now is that the exclusion of only a few districts rather than of all Hindu-majority areas would suffice to give Sikhs political control in the legislature of Punjabi Suba. As one former Congress leader notes: "Giani Kartar Singh who was so particular in getting Kangra District included in the Hindi Region now wants this district to become part of Punjabi Suba. He and other so-called nationalist Sikhs now feel that they could safely rule a state where Sikh legislators are in a majority or even equal to the others. They have 65 legislators now in a house of 154. After excluding the three districts of Rohtak, Gurgaon and Mahendragarh, 24 constituencies will be excluded making the number of Sikh legislators just equal to all others, Hindus and Muslims." Sher Singh, p. 31. An examination of Akali pronouncements before and after independence would show that Akali leaders have always been more interested in a majority in the legislature rather than in the population.

[47] *The Spokesman,* III, No. 12 (March 25, 1953), 2.
[48] *The Tribune,* May 25, 1956.
[49] *Loc. cit.*

leaders. Master Tara Singh immediately branded Rarewala's move as a "treachery" and made it clear that the Akali Dal would maintain its independent existence, because of his belief in the independent political entity of the Sikhs.[50] Hukam Singh characterized Rarewala's advice to join the Congress party as "virtually an act of sabotage" and a "betrayal of trust." [51]

Rarewala answered [52] that "the Akali Dal should not try to arrogate to itself the role of the Panth, as it is not representative of all sections of the Sikh community." He urged that since all genuine grievances had been redressed there was "no sense in waging a futile war against the Congress party or the Congress Government," and warned that if the Akali Dal persisted in its old ways "we shall only doom the Sikh community to an unending age of frustration and stagnation." He further regretted that Master Tara Singh should now state that the regional formula offers the Sikhs much less than they wanted in the form of Punjabi Suba and that nothing would prevent the Akali Dal from pursuing that demand in case the regional formula did not work satisfactorily. Rarewala thought this was "against the letter and spirit of the compromise."

Finally, the executive committee of the Akali Dal expelled Rarewala and four of his prominent supporters from the Akali Dal for their endeavor to join the Congress party.[53] Earlier it passed a resolution reiterating its strong belief "in the maintenance of distinct Panthic entity, and in the necessity of the existence of the Dal as a representative organization" and in the combination of religion and politics.[54]

The mutual recriminations among the Akali leaders at the time might give the impression that Master Tara Singh and his associates, including Hukam Singh and Giani Kartar Singh,

[50] *The Times of India,* June 9, 1956, and *The Tribune,* June 12, 1956.
[51] *The Spokesman,* VI, No. 23 (June 18, 1956), 1.
[52] *The Tribune,* June 15, 1956.   [53] *Ibid.,* July 16, 1956.
[54] *The Hindustan Times,* June 18, 1956.

were bitterly opposed to the Akalis joining the Congress party. In fact, they were as desirous of entering the Congress party, but on their own terms, the most important of which was an arrangement that would, in effect, give the Akali Dal the prerogative of directing the activities of the Akalis as a group inside the Congress party. Master Tara Singh seemed to suggest precisely that at the very beginning of the debate with Rarewala.[55] The strong criticism of Rarewala was really not because of his advice to join the Congress party but that, by openly advocating it, he had weakened the bargaining capacity and reduced the "purchasing power" of the Akali Dal and that further, by actually joining the Congress with his large following in the PEPSU area, he had deprived the Akali Dal—either by itself or in alliance with other political groups—of securing a majority in the regional committee of the Punjabi-speaking region.

It was not long after the Rarewala group joined the Congress party that the Akali Dal started negotiations with Congress leaders about political cooperation. The Congress party said that it was unwilling to entertain the demand that Akali members be allowed dual membership both in the Akali Dal and the Congress party. The Congress took this stand reportedly because of the repeated statements by Master Tara Singh on the inseparability of religion and politics for all "true" Sikhs and because of its unhappy experience during 1948–51, when the Akali group inside the Congress party precipitated ministerial crises in the Punjab.[56] It was up to the Akali Dal to change its position. Although in June 1956 the Akali Dal had reiterated that religion and politics were inseparable in Sikhism and that it would maintain its separate political existence, in October 1956 it decided through a resolution that the Akali Dal "would in future concentrate and confine itself to religious, educational, cultural, social, and economic betterment of the

[55] *The Tribune,* June 12, 1956, and *ibid.,* July 6, 1956.
[56] *The Hindustan Times,* September 3, 1956.

Sikhs," and that "in regard to political activities the members and supporters of the Akali Dal will be advised to join" the Congress party.[57]

The Congress party, however, wanted these changes incorporated in the Akali constitution and desired the amendment of three clauses which related to the goal of *desh-kaal* which had been interpreted until then to mean a separate Sikh state, the requirement that a member of the Akali Dal could not become a member of another political party, and the inseparability of religion and politics in Sikhism.[58] After some hesitation, the Akali constitution was amended in accordance with the wishes of the Congress party. In its endeavor to join the Congress party, the Akali Dal thus gave up its political character despite its repeated assertions over the years about the separate political entity of the Sikhs. Most of the prominent Akali leaders and their supporters joined the Congress party, but Tara Singh decided to stay out, saying: "I will consider the question of joining the Congress after the general elections"[59] (which were only a few months ahead). Nonetheless, an era of close and cordial relations between the Congress party and the Akali Dal seemed to have begun, and Tara Singh remarked that "Nehru's honour is our [Sikhs'] honour."[60]

The period of cordiality did not last long. Hardly two months passed after the Akali Dal had so solemnly agreed to give up political activity before it once again asserted itself in the political field. The immediate occasion for the reversal of a policy so recently decided was the allocation of party tickets for the forthcoming second general elections in February 1957. The Congress party had offered to allocate a quota of about 25 tickets for election to the 154-member legislative assembly to former Akalis, in addition to the Rarewala group. The Akali Dal, on the other hand, wanted a quota closer to 40 tickets

[57] *The Spokesman*, vi, No. 40 (October 8, 1956), 2.
[58] *The Tribune*, October 22, 1956.
[59] *The Hindustan Times*, October 5, 1956.
[60] *The Spokesman*, vi, No. 40 (1956), 1.

which would make the Akalis a powerful group in the 89-member regional committee for the Punjabi-speaking region and possibly a majority if collaboration could be worked out with the Rarewala group of former Akalis or other opposition groups. (When the Akali Dal fought the 1962 general elections on its own ticket it was able to win only 19 seats.)

After much bargaining, the Congress party eventually established a quota of 26 seats for the Akali Dal. Master Tara Singh was still not satisfied, but he now undertook a step which completely "amazed and astonished" the Congress leaders, especially after all their endeavors to reach a political settlement with the Akali Dal.[61] Apart from the Akalis running on the Congress ticket, Master Tara Singh set up more than 15 candidates of his own—whom he called Panthic candidates—against Congress but non-Akali quota nominees, thus arousing the suspicion that the Akali Dal had reached agreement with the Congress party not in good faith but that "there is some intrigue and conspiracy between Master Tara Singh and his old associates. And that both have taken apparently divergent routes to converge ultimately at one moment and bag as many seats as possible," [62] with the goal of dominating the Punjabi regional committee. During the election campaign Tara Singh made strong speeches against the Congress party, declaring that it was futile to repose confidence any more in the Congress party as "the Congress has deceived us." [63] Congress leaders, on the other hand, charged Tara Singh with "having committed a breach of faith" [64] and "betrayal of Akali-Congress compromise." [65]

None of the Panthic nominees of Tara Singh succeeded, however, whereas the Congress party won 120 seats in a house of 154. Among the newly elected Congress legislators were 22

[61] Speech by Prime Minister Nehru, *Lok Sabha Debates,* LVII, No. 17 (August 29, 1961), 5689.
[62] Hukam Singh, "What an Unenviable Position They Occupy," *The Spokesman,* VII, No. 7 (February 18, 1957), 1–2.
[63] *The Times of India,* February 16, 1957.
[64] *Ibid.,* February 17, 1957.   [65] *Ibid.,* February 9, 1957.

elected on the Akali quota and about 6 who belonged to the
Rarewala group. Two of these former 28 Akalis—Giani Kartar
Singh and Gian Singh Rarewala—were taken into the ministry
headed by Chief Minister Partap Singh Kairon. Because of the
inclusion of these two powerful Akali leaders the Congress
ministry soon began to be described as a "Panthic" ministry;
the Hindu ministers from the Punjabi-speaking region were
considered rather ineffective and "unrepresentative" upper-
house legislators. The largest group in the Congress legislature
party at this time was that of Kairon, with a following of about
55 members.

After the elections were over Tara Singh accused Congress
leaders of breaking the Akali-Congress agreement and said that
he would now again stand for the independent entity of the
Sikh Panth.[66] In a signed article in *Prabhat,* he charged that
Congress leaders were treating the Sikhs as a "conquered nation" and were favoring those persons who had "betrayed the
Panth." [67] He now maintained that the Akali Dal had, indeed,
never abandoned politics since its fundamental aim was to "retain the separate entity of Sikhs." [68] To this claim came the
retort from a former colleague, Hukam Singh, that "it is not
honesty to assert now that the Akali Dal never intended to
eschew politics." [69] If it were so, he asked, "where was the sense
in the advice tendered to its members and supporters" to join
the Congress party? He also refuted the allegation "that Master
Tara Singh was misled by any of his colleagues or friends,"
and said that Tara Singh himself piloted the amendment of
the Akali constitution after meeting, unaccompanied by anyone, Nehru and the Congress president and being impressed
with the necessity of amending the constitution.

Despite this controversy among the Akali leaders, they all
came together, whether inside the Congress party or outside,

[66] *The Tribune,* March 5, 1957.
[67] *The Times of India,* March 16, 1957.
[68] *The Tribune,* March 25, 1957.
[69] *Ibid.,* March 31, 1957.

when some Hindu communal organizations launched "the
Hindi agitation" in 1957 with the goal of removing any compulsion in the teaching of languages. Akali leaders in the Congress party threatened to revive the demand for Punjabi Suba
if the Hindi agitation continued.[70] While the government was
attempting to handle the agitation on an administrative level,
the Akalis engineered counter-demonstrations against the Hindi
agitation.[71] Some leading members of the Congress party complained that former Akalis in the Congress party "continued to
behave as Akalis and conducted themselves in the same old
communal fashion caring little for Congress discipline, and that
they were unable to adjust themselves to the Congress ideology,
approach and outlook." [72] On the other hand, several Hindu
leaders in the Congress party actively sympathized with the
Hindi agitation, but many of them were subjected to disciplinary action and suspended from the party.

Some 8,000 persons were arrested in the Hindi agitation over
a period of eight months, but the agitation was finally suspended unconditionally. The failure of this agitation demonstrated that no agitation was likely to succeed against a government headed by Partap Singh Kairon, with his special skills
in handling agitations. There also apparently grew the realization in Akali circles that the Akali group in the Congress party
could not be as effective and influential as it had been during
1948–51 so long as Kairon remained firmly in control of the
party. Be that as it may, after the suspension of the Hindi
agitation, Tara Singh attacked not only the Congress party, but
also Kairon personally. As he said on one occasion, "I have
been against Sardar Partap Singh Kairon since long ago. Any
political power in his hands is dangerous." [73] In their desire to
overthrow Kairon from the leadership of the Congress party,
the Akalis found new allies among the Hindu members who

[70] *Hindusthan Standard,* November 19, 1957.
[71] *The Hindustan Times,* October 25, 1957.
[72] *Loc. cit.*
[73] *The Spokesman,* VIII, No. 16 (April 28, 1958), 9.

had been disaffected by Kairon's handling of the Hindi agitation. A motion of no-confidence was brought forward against Kairon in 1958, and Giani Kartar Singh voted against Kairon even though he was a member of his cabinet. Kairon, however, survived the motion of no-confidence and continued to stay in power.

Having voted against his leader in the Congress party, it was incumbent on Kartar Singh to resign from the ministry but now he turned against Tara Singh in an apparent attempt to demonstrate his loyalty to the Congress party and to forestall removal from the ministry. Some observers concluded that he had launched this "cold war" against Tara Singh in order to "hoodwink" the Congress leaders and prevent the expulsion of the Akali group from the Congress party for engaging in anti-party activities.[74] Apart from the immediate loss in political power, expulsion from the Congress party would have deprived the Akali group of any future opportunity to remove Kairon from power.[75]

Following the failure to dislodge Kairon, Tara Singh became even more critical of the Congress party. He charged the Congress now with interfering in the gurdwaras and with attempts to disrupt the Sikhs, though all his former prominent colleagues continued to work in the Congress party. He announced that "the one year old Akali-Congress compromise might be stopped at any minute because the Congress was not acting up to the terms of the compromise."[76] Later he declared that as far as he was concerned there was no Akali-Congress agreement,[77] and that the "Khalsa Panth will either be a ruler or a rebel."[78] He raised again the "Panth in danger" cry,[79] and threatened to "clamour for separate electorates" if the Sikhs were not as-

[74] *The Times of India,* July 31, 1958.
[75] *Loc. cit.*
[76] *The Spokesman,* VIII, No. 23 (June 16, 1958), 1–2.
[77] *The Times of India,* June 25, 1958.
[78] *Hindusthan Standard,* July 4, 1958.
[79] *The Times of India,* August 10, 1958.

sured a square deal in India.[80] He now revived the demand for
Punjabi Suba because of his grievance that the regional formula
had not been implemented, but added that "even if the Regional Formula had been implemented it would not have satisfied fully their demand." [81] However, a Congress leader, Darbara Singh, challenged him to specify what provisions of the
regional formula had not been implemented. After he was defeated in the election to the presidentship of SGPC in 1958,
Tara Singh immediately blamed his defeat to "betrayal" by
Giani Kartar Singh and announced a program to "liberate" the
gurdwaras.[82] He now revealed that he had accepted the regional formula as Kartar Singh and Hukam Singh had assured
him that it was a "stepping stone" to Punjabi Suba and that
they both would be in the forefront in the war for the Suba.[83]

The Akalis in the Congress party were now split into two
groups, one headed by Giani Kartar Singh, and the other directed by Tara Singh even though he himself was not a member of the Congress party. The pro-Master Tara Singh group,
while still in the Congress, increasingly acted in defiance of
Congress discipline and opposed Congress policies as well as
Congress-supported candidates in the gurdwara elections in
1960 and in the elections to the legislative council and Rajya
Sabha. When the Akali Dal secured an overwhelming victory
in the gurdwara elections of 1960, it became even more strident
in its demand for Punjabi Suba and launched a full-fledged
agitation for its achievement. In March 1960 the Akali Dal
finally declared the Congress party an "anti-Panth" organization, and asked Akali legislators to quit the Congress party.
About half a dozen legislators resigned from the Congress party
and formed a Panthic group, while the rest continued to function inside the Congress party. During the fast-unto-death by

80 *The Tribune,* December 20, 1958.
81 *The Spokesman,* VIII, No. 38 (October 6, 1958), 9.
82 *Indian Affairs Record,* IV, No. 11 (December, 1958), 249.
83 *The Tribune,* February 25, 1959.

Tara Singh in 1961 Giani Kartar Singh also thought of resigning from the Congress party and returning to the Akali Dal in a demonstration of loyalty to the Panth, but was restrained by the lack of enthusiasm for such an idea on the part of his other supporters. Many of the former Akalis who continued in the Congress party, however, claimed in private that during the Akali agitation in 1960–61, they were able to secure several concessions for the Sikhs by exerting pressure from within the party. The precise nature of these concessions is not known. But the Akali Dal was not able to repeat its performance of 1948–51 because of the presence in the Congress party of a strong leader in the person of Partap Singh Kairon.

Suggestions for Akali-Congress Settlement in 1961

In October 1961 Master Tara Singh ended his fast-unto-death [84] without securing any substantial concessions from the government except the establishment of a commission to inquire into the alleged grievances of the Sikhs. Soon after ending his fast he mentioned the possibility of a settlement between the Akali Dal and the government at a political level even before the inquiry commission would start functioning. He said, "maybe, things will not reach the commission stage; the tangle may be resolved earlier." [85] If the reference to a possible political settlement was a suggestion for another Akali-Congress merger, it was obvious that the Congress party, for its part, was firmly convinced, in the light of the past record of its relations with the Akali Dal, that no political settlement reached with the Akali Dal would long endure. It was therefore in no mood to entertain any proposals for another merger, especially after the serious challenge to its authority through a fast-unto-death.

[84] On this development, see the section on agitational strategy in this chapter.
[85] *The Hindustan Times,* October 3, 1961.

This is the most dramatic of the strategies employed by the Akali Dal, and involves the launching of a series of agitations or, in the more expressive term used by the Akalis, *morchas.* A morcha literally means an entrenchment, but while the Akalis do entrench themselves firmly inside the gurdwaras, where police normally do not intervene, they also engage the government in a direct confrontation, organized and directed from within the gurdwaras. This confrontation takes the form of sending out quasi-military, though not necessarily violent, formations, known as *jathas,* that deliberately violate the law in an attempt to fill the jails. While violent symbolism has been employed in Akali agitations and threats are made of recourse to violence in case Akali demands are not conceded and the methods being used are frustrated, little organized attempt at violence has so far been made. The purpose of the morchas is to overwhelm the government by inducting into the agitation thousands of volunteers ready to court imprisonment, and creating a situation where all government activity concentrates on coping with the agitation, which contains a high potential for the imminent breakdown of law and order, thus coercing the government into making concessions.

The crucial importance of the gurdwaras in Akali agitations is indicated by the fact that the two massive agitations launched so far came at a time when the SGPC was under Akali control. Characteristically, Akali agitations have been launched soon after the gurdwara elections, in an apparent attempt to capitalize on the spectacular success that the Akali Dal has usually achieved in such elections and on the mass support generated through an election campaign fought on the very issues which provide the occasion for starting agitations.

A successful agitation launched by the Akali Dal is usually followed by a process of bargaining with the government, in the background of which may be an Akali threat to revive the agitation. A political settlement may result from the negotiations, and perhaps even an Akali-Congress coalition may be formed. Many Akali leaders become extraordinarily active during agitations in the expectation that an eventual political settlement reached with the government may open up possibilities of entry into the state cabinet. To the extent that the government seems to make political concessions in response to agitations, it seems equally rational for Akali leaders to pursue the agitational strategy for the achievement of their demands. The nature of concessions accepted by the Akali Dal is interesting in one respect—that while the agitations are launched in the name of a secular principle, the concessions obtained are for the satisfaction of a single religious group. Apart from the fact that the agitations are launched from Sikh gurdwaras and only Sikh volunteers participate in them, they highlight the tension between the linguistic principle professed as underlying the demand for Punjabi Suba, and the insistence on the satisfaction of political claims of the Sikhs as such which is made explicit in the speeches given, appeals issued, and arguments used by Akali leaders.

The inevitable effect of agitations has been to increase communal tension and bitterness between Hindus and Sikhs, but at the end of an agitation the Akali Dal usually launches a drive for Hindu-Sikh unity. The Hindus ignore such unity drives, however, in the belief that their purpose is to stifle criticism of the political concessions obtained by the Akali Dal or, in the event of an unsuccessful agitation, to soften opposition to Akali demands now sought to be achieved through other channels. The Hindus merely express amusement at the notion that the Akalis should talk of unity after having used extremely harsh and hostile language against the Hindu community during the agitation.

While the purpose of the Akali Dal in launching morchas is

to obtain concessions from the government toward its demand for Punjabi Suba, these morchas seem to perform two other functions, which are not necessarily the reasons for starting them. One of these may be referred to as "the boundary-maintenance function" insofar as agitations intensify group consciousness and consequently counteract any tendency toward unorthodoxy among Sikhs. Several Akali workers have often recounted how people who were not strict in observing the external symbols of Sikhism have under the influence of agitations become somewhat more orthodox.[86] On the other hand, of course, the frequent Akali agitations against the government serve to mark the Sikhs for some as a group pursuing anti-government and anti-nationalist policies, even though the agitations themselves are launched only by a section of the Sikh community. As a consequence it has been suggested that Sikh officers in the civil and military services tend to discard the observance of external Sikh symbols in order to dissociate themselves from such Akali policies. The other function which Akali agitations have seemingly performed in the past has been to sustain within the Congress party in the Punjab a leadership which may otherwise not be acceptable to the party, but has made itself seem indispensable by its demonstrated ability to control agitations launched against the government.

What are the different circumstances under which Akali agitations have been launched? What are the various techniques employed in the agitations? What appeals are made to mobilize mass support? What is the response, administrative and political, of the government to these agitations? How does previous experience with agitations influence government response to new threats of agitations? A better understanding of the agitational strategy and the concomitant or subsequent bargaining process can be had by an examination of the two massive agitations thus far launched by the Akali Dal.

[86] From several interviews.

Punjabi Suba Slogan Agitation, 1955

The immediate reason given for starting this agitation was to uphold the right to shout slogans—which incidentally led to communal tension by provoking counter-slogans—about demands for the reorganization of states. The main objective, however, in the light of political developments before and after the agitation, was to intimidate the government through a contest of will and strength into making concessions which the Akali Dal had found difficult to achieve through constitutional methods.

By 1950 the Akali Dal had secured important political concessions from the government by working within the Congress party, but it encountered resistance to the demand of Punjabi Suba. The Akali Dal then decided to break away from the Congress party and participate as an independent political party in the first general elections to be held in 1951–52. The Akali Dal went into these elections with great enthusiasm and rather unjustified optimism, reminiscent more of the days of separate electorates. It fought the elections on the basic issue of Punjabi Suba, but the results were a great disappointment to the Akali leaders. The Akali Dal was able to win only 14 seats in a house of 126. Some Akali leaders were of the opinion that the interests of the Sikhs as conceived by the Akali Dal could best be pursued through sharing political power by either an alliance or merger with the Congress party, especially since even the SGPC was under the control of a group opposed to the Akali Dal. At the same time, it was felt that the Akali Dal should secure political concessions on the demand for Punjabi Suba and favorable terms for entry into the Congress party.

In October 1952, as a result of a new coalition of groups, the Akali Dal once again assumed control of the SGPC after being out of office for a period of four years. Meanwhile, the Akali Dal began to press vigorously the demand for Punjabi Suba, and threats were made about the use of other methods of struggle for its achievement. Master Tara Singh declared that "we are prepared to make any amount of sacrifice for the achievement of our objective." [87] Although the ultimate objective was to achieve Punjabi Suba, for the moment, the Akalis decided to launch a morcha against alleged government discrimination toward the "untouchable" classes in the Sikh community.

Under the Indian constitution Harijans had been given special privileges, including reservation of seats in legislatures. Since the phenomenon of caste and untouchability has been associated with Hinduism, and other religions, including Sikhism, repudiate the caste system, the special privileges and other economic and social measures for the advancement of Harijans were to be provided only for such as were Hindus. The prospect of the special privileges for Hindu Harijans raised the possibility that members of Sikh backward classes might simply declare themselves Hindus, since the Sikhs had so far failed to integrate them into the community. Faced with a likely decrease in the number of Sikhs in this way, which might have important political implications, Sikh leaders persuaded the constitution-makers, despite the clear injunction against caste in Sikhism, to declare as scheduled castes four Sikh castes which constituted the overwhelming majority of the Sikh backward classes— Ramdasi, Kabirpanthi, Mazhabi, and Sikligar. But this concession was achieved in return for an agreement by the Sikh leaders that no further political demands would be made in the future in behalf of the Sikh community.[88]

The four Sikh castes that were recognized as scheduled castes constituted about 85 percent of all backward castes.[89] Even the remaining 15 percent were later given the same privileges as other Harijans in the matter of recruitment to services, educational scholarships and other services; the only privilege that

[87] *The Tribune,* January 19, 1953.

[88] See the speech by Sardar Patel, in India, Constituent Assembly, *Debates: Official Report,* x, No. 7 (October 14, 1949), 249.

[89] See the statement by Giani Kartar Singh, *The Times of India,* November 4, 1953.

they did not have was that, while entitled to vote and run for office from general constituencies, they could not run from constituencies reserved especially for Harijans. The Akali Dal, however, considered this a case of gross discrimination against the Sikh community, and threatened a morcha against the government in 1953. The government's position was that the matter concerned a very small proportion of the Sikh Harijans and was not of such urgency as to call for a morcha, since the next general elections were several years hence in 1957. The Akali Dal persisted in its threat, and was criticized for it by Congress leaders. The most vigorous denunciation of the threatened morcha, however, came from among the Harijan Sikhs themselves.

Representatives of several Harijan organizations, while emphasizing that "we are Sikhs in every sense of the term," asked the Akali Dal to keep its "hands off Sikh Scheduled Castes" and not to "exploit them for your political game." [90] With unusual prescience, looking beyond the immediate issue, they warned:

> Our province is once again passing through a critical stage. The Akali party, under Master Tara Singh's leadership, has decided to launch an all-out offensive for the establishment of a Punjabi speaking state. Their immediate objective is to secure the same rights for Sikh backward classes which our Constitution has given to Hindu Scheduled Castes. In our opinion, both these objectives are interlinked and the present agitation for securing equal rights for Sikh scheduled castes is a part of a bigger game, namely fight for a Punjabi speaking state, which the Akali party intends to launch at a later stage. Their present agitation is the first step towards their final goal.[91]

Pointing out that Akali members in the legislature opposed such tenancy legislation as sought to give protection to the land-

[90] *The Tribune,* October 13, 1953.   [91] *Loc. cit.*

less Harijans, they emphasized that "we are wholly opposed to the creation of a Punjabi-speaking state which, in our opinion, would be a state of big jagirdars and in which members of backward classes will be treated as cattle." [92] They made it clear that they refused "to jeopardise our present safety and future prosperity by strengthening the hands of those who are already oppressing us and terrorising us in villages." [93]

Some of the Harijan Sikhs declared that they would even launch a counter-morcha if the Akali Dal persisted in its plans to start a morcha. On the other hand Master Tara Singh asked Sikhs to be ready for "a grim struggle" for the protection of their rights.[94] Finally, when the government gave assurance that it was not its policy to discriminate between Hindus and Sikhs, the Akali Dal called off the agitation,[95] but proclaimed the government's assurance as a "complete victory" for the organization.[96]

The amicable settlement of the issue of Sikh Harijans, however, did not bring about any improvement in the relations between the Akali Dal and the government. A month later the Akalis arranged what one press correspondent called "an ugly demonstration" against Prime Minister Nehru.[97] As Nehru rose to speak at a Patiala meeting in 1953, Akalis near the platform attempted to shout him down with the slogans, "we shall wrest Punjabi Suba" and "long live Master Tara Singh." [98] Then Tara Singh himself appeared and shouted a few feet away from Nehru that "I will not allow Mr. Nehru to speak." [99] Finally, Nehru left without proceeding any further in his speech. The meeting then broke up in confusion, while brickbats were thrown at the police.[100] The incident occasioned much condemnation by many prominent leaders, and people

---

92 *Loc. cit.*   93 *Loc. cit.*
94 *The Hindustan Times,* November 16, 1953.
95 *Ibid.,* November 19, 1953.
96 *The Times of India,* November 26, 1953.
97 *The Hindustan Times,* December 28, 1953.
98 *Loc. cit.*   99 *Loc. cit.*   100 *Loc. cit.*

asked if this was the shape of things to come under a Punjabi Suba. One Akali member of parliament even resigned from the Akali Dal in protest against the insult shown to Nehru.[101]

In the succeeding year the Akali Dal intensified its campaign for Punjabi Suba, especially since the demand was to be reviewed by the States Reorganization Commission. The Akali Dal fought the gurdwara elections to the SGPC in 1954 on the issue of Punjabi Suba and, having won an overwhelming majority of the seats in those elections, pressed the demand for Punjabi Suba with renewed vigor. Tara Singh also complained now about government interference in the gurdwaras, and went to see Chief Minister Bhim Sen Sachar on this matter. In the interview with Sachar in January 1955, Tara Singh made his famous statement that Punjabi Suba was merely a cover for a Sikh state.

While the Akali Dal campaigned for the demand of Punjabi Suba, the Hindu communal organizations opposed the demand and, in turn, asked for the expansion of Punjab's boundaries. The rival campaigning between the supporters and opponents of the two demands, the shouting of derogatory slogans and counter-slogans,[102] led to a very tense situation in the Punjab, with the ever-present possibility of a violent communal flareup between Hindus and Sikhs. In several towns there were cases of throwing stones and brickbats at processions. Faced with this situation the Punjab government imposed a ban on the shouting of slogans about states reorganization. At this Master Tara Singh issued an ultimatum to the Punjab government to withdraw the ban by a certain date or face an Akali morcha.[103] He was also nominated to be the first "dictator" of the morcha. In consultation with the central government, the Punjab government announced that it was not ready to bow to Akali threats.

[101] *The Tribune,* January 5, 1954.
[102] Some typical slogans: "drive the Hindus across the Yamuna," "when the Sikh sword will rattle, Nehru will flee," and "get ready the scissors."
[103] Jakhmi, p. 26.

The Akali Dal announced that the morcha would start May 10, 1955. Of note is the fact that the Akali Dal made no attempt to challenge the validity of the ban in the courts, but sought instead to challenge the authority of the government.

As scheduled, the morcha was launched on May 10. Master Tara Singh was to be the first one to offer himself for arrest.[104] He addressed a huge congregation inside the Golden Temple at Amritsar and declared that the time had now arrived for members of the community to offer their heads in sacrifice in order to maintain the honor and freedom of the Sikhs.[105] In addition, he sent the following message to Sikh congregations:

> O Singhs! We ask for freedom and they want to ensnare us deeper into slavery. We are not satisfied with the present situation and ask for Punjabi Suba, but they stop us even from propagating the demand of Punjabi Suba. They have imposed a ban on raising slogans for the demand. Khalsa Ji! Understand this that all this is to finish our honor. This is all we have, if this is gone then all is gone. So stake everything to maintain our honor. In the present time we should offer our heads peacefully like Guru Tegh Bahadur. The rivals are haughty rulers, but we have faith in the Guru.[106]

Then, setting the pattern that was to be followed for another two months, the first group of four volunteers, including Tara Singh, marched out of the gurdwara shouting slogans and were arrested by the police stationed outside to arrest violators of the ban.[107] Volunteers came to the Golden Temple at Amritsar

104 Former Akali leaders, who have since left the Akali Dal, remark that Master Tara Singh not only enhances his prestige by being the first volunteer but also safeguards his leadership. For one thing, he does not have to bear the responsibility for the organization of the morcha. If a morcha is successful, then all the credit goes to him as the supreme leader of the Akali Dal; if it ends in failure, then the blame falls on the organizers who are left behind; and if a successful agitation throws up new rivals to challenge his leadership, they are vulnerable to charges by him about the misuse of party funds.

105 Jakhmi, pp. 28–29.   106 *Ibid.*, p. 29.   107 *Loc. cit.*

from different parts of the Punjab to offer themselves for arrest. New "dictators" and leaders of daily *jathas* were nominated as the previous ones got arrested. In order to arouse greater enthusiasm for the agitation among the Sikh masses, Punjabi Suba days were celebrated on significant dates of Sikh history, notably the martyrdom of Guru Tegh Bahadur.[108] Amritsar was the focal point of the morcha, but Akali workers violated the law in other towns and courted arrest. The police also made arrests of Akali workers and leaders who were likely to organize morchas against the government in different towns.

Congress leaders vehemently criticized the Akali morcha. Some Sikh leaders in the Congress charged that the Akalis were violating the sanctity of the gurdwaras by using them for political purposes.[109] Kairon declared that the government could not be intimidated by this "reactionary and anti-social" morcha. He further chided the Akali leaders for their newfound concern for civil liberties since they previously "used to be stooges of the Britishers." [110] Some Congress Sikhs, on the other hand, while they condemned the morcha, also criticized the government on the score that the Sikh community is "rightly or wrongly frustrated." Two Congress Sikh leaders issued an appeal for a round table conference between government leaders and Akali leaders, but the Akali "dictator" Iqbal Singh rejected the appeal.[111]

Despite the various measures adopted by the government, the morcha continued. From the towns it spread to the rural areas. As the morcha lengthened into nearly two months and volunteers kept coming forward for arrest, the government made a rash move one day by having the police enter the premises of the Golden Temple to arrest Akali leaders and volunteers.[112] During this action the police used tear gas and, allegedly on provocation of gunshots and throwing of brick-

---

[108] *Ibid.*, p. 40.   [109] *The Tribune*, June 13, 1955.
[110] *Ibid.*, June 14, 1955, and *ibid.*, July 11, 1955.
[111] Jakhmi, pp. 44–45.   [112] *Ibid.*, pp. 96–107.

bats, engaged in some shooting.[113] This incident created great
resentment among the Sikh community, and the morcha came
to be considered as something beyond a conflict between merely
the Akalis and the government. Participation in the morcha did
not slacken, and as *The Tribune* commented editorially, "What
overshadows the entire situation is that every weapon in the
armoury of the Government has been brought into play. A
great tragedy is being enacted in the Punjab. . . . The Punjab
is facing the greatest crisis in its history." [114] According to Akali
figures, some 12,000 Sikhs were arrested in the morcha. Finally,
in a conciliatory gesture, Chief Minister Bhim Sen Sachar
lifted the ban on slogans in commemoration of Nehru's return
home after an eminently successful visit abroad. Many Congress leaders thought this action of Sachar a mistake tactically,
since the ban was to lapse two days later in any case, but the
Akalis interpreted it as a "surrender" by Sachar [115] and a "victory" for the Akalis.[116]

Soon after the end of the agitation the Akali Dal initiated
moves to take advantage of the "victory" it had won. After a
meeting of the executive committee of the Akali Dal on July
14, 1955, an Akali spokesman announced that Akali leaders
would be willing to meet with Prime Minister Nehru, if invited, in order "to discuss the problems of the Sikh community." [117] Rarewala now spoke of Nehru as "the idol of India
and apostle of peace" and said that the Sikhs had full confidence in him.[118] The Akali Dal's acting president stated in
Amritsar that Akali leaders would accept a decision by Nehru
"regarding Sikh grievances and creation of the Punjabi-speaking State, if our leaders are convinced and satisfied by his

113 *Loc. cit.*   114 *The Tribune,* July 6, 1955.
115 Jakhmi, p. 131.
116 Statement by Gian Singh Rarewala, *The Times of India,* July 13,
1955.
117 *Ibid.,* July 16, 1955.
118 *The Tribune,* July 18, 1955.

arguments and reasoning through mutual consultation and negotiation." [119] Although the agitation had been launched presumably for the protection of civil liberties, the Akali Dal wanted the government to concede Punjabi Suba now to redress Sikh grievances in view of the demonstrated support the Akali Dal commanded in the Sikh community. All the arguments about Punjabi Suba at the time referred more to the claims of the Sikh community than to the linguistic principle.

Meanwhile, in October 1955, the States Reorganization Commission issued its report, in which it rejected the demand for Punjabi Suba on the ground that the problem in the Punjab was not linguistic but communal, and therefore territorial demarcation was no solution for it. On the other hand, the Commission recommended the merger of Punjab, PEPSU and Himachal Pradesh to create a larger territorial unit. Akali leaders immediately denounced the Commission's report. Master Tara Singh called it a "decree of Sikh annihilation." [120] Hukam Singh referred to it as "another deadlier blow to Sikhs," [121] and threatened that the Akalis would launch an agitation if peaceful negotiations failed.[122] When the Punjab legislature discussed the report in November 1955, Akali legislators pressed for the Punjabi Suba demand.

The Akali leaders later entered into negotiations with the Congress leaders at the center, and met with the Prime Minister. Akali announcements indicated that the government was ready to make some political concessions to the Akali Dal. As *The Tribune* observed: "The Akali attitude gives no occasion for surprise, except their willingness to abide by Prime Minister Nehru's final decision and their exhortation to others to acquiesce in the same course, is coloured by a strong tinge of anticipation of what that decision should be. It may be summed

[119] *The Statesman,* July 19, 1955.
[120] *The Spokesman,* v, No. 40 (October 19, 1955), 1.
[121] *Ibid.,* No. 39 (October 12, 1955), p. 1.
[122] *Ibid.,* No. 40 (1955), p. 1.

up as: 'Leave the Prime Minister free to decide in favour of Punjabi Suba.'"[123] What seems to have finally persuaded the Congress party leadership into giving political concessions to the Akali Dal was the impressive procession organized in February 1956 by the Akali Dal at Amritsar where the Congress party was holding its annual session.[124] While Nehru said that the place of swords and sticks was in the museum,[125] the Akali Dal produced a three-mile-long procession of blue-turbanned Sikhs, marching eight abreast, armed with shining swords and axes, with Master Tara Singh seated on an elephant. Hukam Singh emphasized that the procession was proof that the Sikh community "is united behind the demand of Punjabi Suba" and that the Akali Dal was the "only representative body" of the Sikhs, and Tara Singh "the undisputed leader," [126] while *The Spokesman* warned that "the great procession is but a symbol of the surging tide of Sikh feeling for the realization of their objective. Any frustration would be attended with grave consequences." [127]

In the following month the negotiations between the Akali leaders and the Congress government resulted in the regional formula, which the Akali Dal accepted on March 11, 1956.[128] The 1955 agitation thus was a tremendous success in view of the political concessions that flowed from it. The Akali Dal had secured the regional formula despite the strong opposition of many groups in the Punjab, especially the Hindu community, but Akali spokesmen soon began saying that it was only "a first step" toward the final goal of Punjabi Suba.[129]

[123] *The Tribune,* December 2, 1955.
[124] A Nationalist, "The Punjab Tangle," *The Modern Review,* ciii, No. 1 (January 1958), 32.
[125] *The Hindustan Times,* February 12, 1956.
[126] *The Spokesman,* vi, No. 8 (February 27, 1956), 1.
[127] *Ibid.,* No. 7 (1956), p. 3.
[128] *The Hindustan Times,* March 12, 1956.
[129] *The Times of India,* March 12, 1956.

Punjabi Suba Agitation, 1960–61 [130]

Subsequent to its acceptance of the regional formula, the Akali Dal entered into a political settlement under which the Akalis joined the Congress party and the Akali Dal gave a solemn undertaking to refrain from political activity thereafter. However, once the regional formula was firmly established in the political setup of the Punjab, the Akali Dal under Tara Singh's leadership entered the political arena with a vengeance. Despite this political somersault on the part of the Akali Dal, the Congress party abided by its commitment and accepted in its fold all those Akali leaders who desired to stay, and furthermore gave several important political positions in the Congress government to many of the former prominent colleagues of Master Tara Singh. On the other hand, Tara Singh revived the Akali Dal as an opposition party against the government and pressed for the demand of Punjabi Suba in repudiation of the settlement under which most of the Akali leaders functioned within the Congress party and government. Thus, in spite of all the political concessions given to the Akali Dal, the government was faced with precisely the same situation, so far as Punjabi Suba was concerned, as it was before the political settlement. The Akali Dal, for its part, rather than consider the regional formula as a final settlement, now endeavored to use it as the basis for the further division of the Punjab in order to form Punjabi Suba.

Knowing that no agitation would succeed as long as Kairon was in power, the Akali Dal first turned its attention to dislodge him from his position as Chief Minister. In this it was unsuccessful, however. The Akali Dal then pressed even more stridently for Punjabi Suba and also started a campaign against

[130] This section is based on interviews with Akali and Congress leaders; newspaper accounts; parliamentary debates; pamphlets issued by the Punjab government and the Akali Dal; and a series of forty articles entitled "Sikh Siyaasat, Sikh Siyaasatdaan ki qalam se" [Sikh politics, by a Sikh politician] which appeared in *Pratap* in March, April, and May, 1962.

alleged government interference in the gurdwaras. Meanwhile, the gurdwara elections were approaching and the Akali Dal spent much of 1959 in organizing its election campaign. It declared that the gurdwara elections would be considered a plebiscite on the demand for Punjabi Suba. In January 1960 the results were announced, and the Akali Dal secured a tremendous victory. Soon after, the Akali Dal began telling the Sikh masses that a morcha for Punjabi Suba would be launched immediately.[131] However, the Akali Dal was again anxious to remove Kairon from power before starting an agitation,[132] but to no avail. The Akali Dal then directed its attention toward other endeavors.

In April 1960 Master Tara Singh resigned from his position as SGPC president in order to devote himself entirely to the movement for Punjabi Suba. In the same month the Akali Dal decided to call a convention of various political parties that supported its demand for Punjabi Suba.[133] Organized and financed by the Akali Dal, this convention was held in Amritsar in May 1960 and supported the demand for Punjabi Suba. Although emphasizing the linguistic aspect of the demand Akali speakers made the demand a question of life and death for the Sikhs. The non-Sikh speakers at the convention were either from outside the Punjab or of no political consequence in the state.

The Akali Dal now decided to organize a *shahidi jatha* (a group of potential martyrs), which would start from the Akal Takht at Amritsar under Master Tara Singh's leadership and, leisurely moving through the Punjab, reach Delhi in about two weeks to head a massive procession.[134] Meanwhile, the

[131] *The Spokesman,* x, No. 11 (March 21, 1960), 1–2.

[132] *Loc. cit.*

[133] *Punjabi Sube de Morche da Itihas* [History of the Punjabi Suba Morcha] by Sikh scholars (Amritsar: Gurbani Prakashan, 1960), p. 15. This book has a foreword by Professor Satbir Singh, one of the top organizers of the morcha, and another by Harcharan Singh Hudiara, then general secretary of the Akali Dal.

[134] *Ibid.,* p. 18.

Akali Dal issued posters in which Sikhs were warned that Hindus wanted to destroy them, and Tara Singh in his speeches asked the Sikhs to be prepared for a *dharam yudh* (religious crusade) and to come forth "with their heads on their palms." [135] Convinced that the Akalis were about to launch a morcha and, unlike the government under Sachar, eager to retain the initiative in such a contest, the Punjab government under Kairon proceeded to arrest Master Tara Singh under the Preventive Detention Act on account of his "indulging in such activities so as to arouse religious sentiments of the Sikhs against the Hindus." The government deemed such a step necessary in order "to save the state from getting into chaotic conditions and with a view to maintaining peaceful relations between the two communities." Simultaneously, the government made large-scale arrests of other Akali leaders and workers whose activities were likely to adversely affect peace and communal harmony in the state, and also imposed several restrictions on the press.

The Akalis were later to claim that they had not planned to launch a morcha; however, they do maintain that "Masterji before going to jail had appointed Sant Fateh Singh as the dictator of the morcha." [136] Sant Fateh Singh had spent his life in the propagation of Sikhism, but had recently been brought into politics by Tara Singh, and was at the time a vice-president of the Akali Dal. After Tara Singh's arrest, the Akali leaders at the Golden Temple in Amritsar established contact with the field organization for mobilizing volunteers. They sent forth a call to the rural areas that the "Panth is in danger" and that unless Punjabi Suba was secured there would be "no security or protection for the community." [137] Akali workers were able to generate considerable enthusiasm in the rural areas through emphatic declarations that this agitation was the "last struggle," "a fight to the finish," and that until Punjabi Suba was achieved

[135] Iqbal Singh, *et al.*, *Facts About Akali Agitation in Punjab* (Chandigarh: Fairdeal Press, 1960), p. 6.

[136] *Punjabi Sube de Morche da Itihas*, p. 24.

[137] *The Spokesman*, XI, No. 6 (February 13, 1961), 1.

there would be neither compromise nor "talk for a compromise." [138] To emphasize their determination not to settle for anything less than Punjabi Suba, Akali leaders warned mediators against intervening, and declared that they would enter no discussions unless the government accepted the formation of Punjabi Suba beforehand.[139] Given this determination of the Akali leaders, volunteers flocked for arrest in the belief that the Kairon ministry, like the Sachar ministry, would also "surrender" and that it would be best to enlist on the winning side. According to Akali accounts some 57,000 volunteers—the government put the figure around 26,000—courted arrest.[140] Fateh Singh personally blessed these volunteers, asking them to give when arrested the name of Guru Gobind Singh as their father. After taking an oath at the Akal Takht that they would not return home unless Punjabi Suba was achieved, the volunteers filed out of the Akal Takht to deliver speeches to the congregation, comparing Nehru and Kairon to Aurangzeb and threatening recourse to violence if the government did not come to its senses and carve out Punjabi Suba. Later, as they marched out of the Golden Temple shouting slogans, they were arrested by the police.

The Punjab government under Kairon, however, was not unnerved by the agitation and tried to meet it firmly on both the administrative and political levels. Under an ordinance issued by the governor on July 19, 1960, the government assumed greater powers to handle the agitation. It then made large-scale arrests of those who it suspected were engaged in agitational activity and continued to arrest the groups of volunteers that came out of the Golden Temple and other gurdwaras in an apparently unending flow. On the political level, the government vigorously implemented those provisions of the regional formula which it had not been able to effect thus far.

[138] *Ibid.*, No. 2 (January 16, 1961), p. 1.
[139] *Punjabi Sube de Morche da Itihas,* p. 75.
[140] *The Tribune,* February 23, 1961.

Going beyond the regional formula, it established a commission to inquire into the feasibility of starting a Panjab University.[141] Apparently in an effort to divert the attention of the rural masses to local politics, elections to the village councils were ordered.[142]

The determination of the Punjab government to meet the challenge of the agitation finally convinced potential volunteers and those already arrested that the Kairon ministry was not likely to collapse. Not only did the flow of volunteers now slow down, but those already arrested petitioned to be pardoned and released. To demonstrate that the agitation had lost its momentum the government then made large-scale releases of prisoners arrested during the agitation. In spite of their earlier oath not to return home unless Punjabi Suba was achieved, few of those now released offered themselves again for arrest. At this point the flow of volunteers completely slackened and consternation prevailed in the Akali headquarters inside the Golden Temple. All of the resources of the Akali Dal were nearly exhausted, and the agitation seemed headed for complete failure. The Akali leaders found it hard to countenance such a possibility because they had repeatedly proclaimed that Akali morchas never failed, as the Guru's blessings were with them.[143] Some of the younger Akali leaders and workers advocated a policy of violence,[144] but the Akali Dal finally decided to allow Sant Fateh Singh to make a dramatic move by undertaking a fast-unto-death. Fateh Singh's advisers believed that the government would concede Punjabi Suba once it received his ultimatum or at least when he started his fast.

In November 1960 Fateh Singh wrote Nehru informing him of his intention to go on this fast and his determination to remain on fast until he became a martyr or Nehru formed the Punjabi Suba. On December 18 he took an oath at the Akal

[141] *The Hindustan Times,* January 15, 1961.
[142] *Indian Observer,* November 1961, p. 52.
[143] *Punjabi Sube de Morche da Itihas,* p. 25.
[144] *Ibid.,* p. 95.

Takht and started his fast-unto-death. In a number of appeals Nehru asked Sant Fateh Singh to give up his fast, promised to do everything possible for the advancement of the Punjabi language, but left no doubt about his opposition to the demand for Punjabi Suba which he thought would be harmful for the Sikhs, the Punjab, and India. He asked Fateh Singh to meet with him to discuss matters as he did not regard fasts as proper solutions for such problems. Subsequently, on January 4, 1961, in a move to bring about the end of the fast, the government released Master Tara Singh. Tara Singh went to see Nehru, but Nehru refused to alter his earlier declarations concerning Punjabi Suba. Tara Singh then declared that after Fateh Singh's death he would be next on the list and that the series of fasts would continue until Punjabi Suba was obtained.

On January 8 Nehru again repeated his appeal for an end to the fast, adding that the non-formation of Punjabi Suba was not due to any discrimination against the Sikhs, but making clear his conviction that Punjabi Suba would be harmful to all concerned. On the linguistic reorganization of states, Nehru reiterated that "many matters have to be taken into consideration for each area" and that "language is not the sole consideration." [145] All observers were agreed that Nehru had said nothing that he had not repeated at least three times before, except for the statement that no discrimination was implied in the non-formation of Punjabi Suba. Dissidents within the Akali Dal were emphatic that neither Punjabi Suba nor its principle had been accepted. However, on the urging of Tara Singh, Fateh Singh broke his fast on January 9. Later the Akalis circulated rumors that the Prime Minister had given secret assurances to Tara Singh, that the principle of Punjabi Suba had been conceded, and that only the demarcation of boundaries remained to be decided in the forthcoming talks between Nehru and Fateh Singh.[146]

[145] *The Spokesman*, XI, No. 2 (1961), 12.
[146] *Ibid.*, No. 6 (1961), p. 3.

After breaking his fast Fateh Singh held three rounds of talks with Nehru, during which he emphasized the linguistic principle supposed to be underlying the demand. Even during the agitation, when volunteers were mobilized on the basis of an appeal to Sikh religious sentiments, the Akali leaders, in their public utterances, had mainly stressed the need for a demarcation of Punjabi Suba on a linguistic basis. At the same time, this agitation saw a rise in the popularity of Fateh Singh on account of his undertaking the fast, while there was now some resentment against Tara Singh for having brought the fast to an inconclusive end. Fateh Singh's meetings with Nehru also helped to bolster his prestige. Soon after the fast was over, Tara Singh not only began to assert his own leadership but also began to underscore once again the real purpose of the demand for Punjabi Suba. At one press conference, in January 1961, he announced that the Punjabi Suba was being demanded to improve the position of the Sikhs.[147] On Fateh Singh's emphasis on language, he remarked that "the Sant is a religious man. He is not a politician and might have been misled." [148] He also pointed out that Fateh Singh was only a vice-president of the Akali Dal and therefore could not negotiate independently with Nehru. Among the Sikh masses Tara Singh again raised the cry of "Panth is in danger" and said that Punjabi Suba was necessary for the protection of the Panth.[149] In one statement, aimed indirectly at Fateh Singh's negotiations with Nehru, he declared: "Listen Oh Sikhs! listen oh Singhs! listen oh friends, listen oh elders, listen oh well wishers; all listen to me very attentively that the circumstances are such that any one who agrees to accept anything short of Punjabi Suba shall be finished; be that Akali Dal, the Sikh community or any individual; now when the resolve has been taken, the solution lies only in effacement." [150] The Akali Dal then officially passed

[147] *Ibid.*, xi, No. 2 (1961), 2, and *ibid.*, No. 20 (May 29, 1961), p. 1.　　[148] *Ibid.*, and *ibid.*, No. 2 (1961), p. 2.

[149] *Ibid.*, No. 3 (January 23, 1961), p. 1.

[150] *Ibid.*, No. 6 (1961), pp. 1–2.

a resolution saying that "nothing less than Punjabi Suba will be acceptable" with the emphasis that it should consist of the *"pure* Punjabi-speaking areas of the state"; even then within a few minutes after adopting the resolution, Tara Singh declared that the struggle for Punjabi Suba was a *dharam yudh*.[151] Increasingly, Tara Singh linked Punjabi Suba with the Sikh religion,[152] insisted that nothing less than Punjabi Suba would be acceptable to the Akali Dal,[153] and asserted that the demand will have to be conceded "talks or no talks." [154] In the background of these Akali declarations, the talks between Nehru and Fateh Singh ended in failure.[155] One senior Akali leader, Sarup Singh, accused Tara Singh of having gone back on his commitment as to the bases of negotiations, but Sarup Singh was soon expelled from the Akali Dal.

Tara Singh now decided to undertake a fast-unto-death himself in order to coerce the government into conceding Punjabi Suba. He charged that it was out of discrimination against the Sikh community that the Indian government was not willing to form Punjabi Suba. He proclaimed that this was the "last struggle" and would not end until the objective was achieved.[156] Nehru answered that if Tara Singh had any particular grievances on behalf of the Sikh community, the government would be willing to look into them, but he did not understand the Akalis making vague charges.[157] However, Tara Singh declared that he was determined to undertake the fast, and Akali leaders warned that if he died other leaders would follow him until Punjabi Suba was conceded.

[151] *Ibid.,* No. 10 (1961), p. 3. My italics.
[152] *Ibid.,* No. 9 (March 6, 1961), p. 3.
[153] *Ibid.,* No. 7 (February 20, 1961), p. 1.
[154] *Ibid.,* No. 9 (1961), p. 9.
[155] For an Akali version of the talks, see Shiromani Akali Dal, *Synopsis of the Nehru-Fateh Singh Talks on the Issue of the Formation of Punjabi-speaking State* (Amritsar: Secretary, Shiromani Akali Dal, 1961).
[156] *The Spokesman,* xi, No. 21 (June 5, 1961), 9.
[157] *Ibid.,* No. 27 (1961), p. 1.

The government had earlier offered to make Punjabi Suba an issue for the next general elections in 1962, and promised to give sympathetic consideration to the demand in case the Akali Dal won a majority in even the Punjabi-speaking region, which constituted the so-called "pure" Punjabi-speaking area in the estimation of the Akali Dal. The Akalis, however, reckoned that they had little chance of securing a majority in the elections, but the government would give in if a threat to Tara Singh's life was involved. There still prevailed in Akali circles the impression that the government would yield to pressure and that the prospect of violence, following the possible death of the Akali leader, would scare the government into accepting their demand. On the other hand, the government was anxious to establish precisely the opposite point—that it would not yield to pressure of this kind.

On August 15, 1961, Indian independence day, amidst the most spectacular publicity, Tara Singh started his fast-unto-death after taking an oath in the Golden Temple that he would not break his fast until Nehru accepted the demand for Punjabi Suba. Within a week the Akalis began proclaiming that their leader's life was in serious danger, and that the government should give in. This was to have an adverse impact on Akali strategy later, for the danger to Tara Singh's life in a fast which was to last for 48 days soon began to be discounted by the government. Even Nehru said, "so far as one can see, this fast may indefinitely go on and on."

Meanwhile, further talks took place between Nehru and Fateh Singh, but Nehru would not go beyond the promise of a high-level inquiry into any charges of discrimination and the willingness to consider measures for the advancement of the Punjabi language. After the talks ended unsuccessfully Nehru placed copies of his correspondence with Akali leaders before parliament, presumably to discount any Akali rumors that he had given secret undertakings in regard to Punjabi Suba. In parliament, Nehru declared that the demand for Punjabi Suba was a communal one even though presented in linguistic terms.[158] He emphasized that the Punjab was socially, linguistically and economically a single unit, and a further division would do great damage to the state.[159] Despite the government's firm policy in regard to Punjabi Suba, Nehru made some significant concessions to the Akali Dal: (1) to arrange a "high-level inquiry" into charges of discrimination against the Sikh community; (2) to examine ways and means to make the regional committees more effective; and (3) to grant, if necessary, additional powers to the regional committees. Nonetheless, he warned that "their proposal to partition the Punjab again was harmful for the country, for the Punjab and more especially for the Sikhs."[160]

Nehru's statement was followed by a vigorous debate but, as he himself noted, no member of parliament from the Punjab or an adjoining state had supported the demand for Punjabi Suba and that, on the contrary, "they have objected to it strongly for various reasons which they gave."[161] Summing up the discussion, Nehru again emphasized the fundamental unity of the Punjab and the dangerous consequences that would flow from another partition of the state. Finally, he declared that "hunger-strikes will not be recognised as legitimate in the solution of any problem . . . because if that impression grows that the hunger-strike has succeeded in achieving a certain object, then there will be no end to trouble in India."[162] In the debate in the upper house of parliament, Nehru stated that Akali leaders themselves had told him that the Punjabi Suba was demanded for the protection of the Panth, but he was interested in knowing, "protection from what?"

The concessions made by Nehru represented some success for the Akali Dal, but it was not satisfied. Although the Akali

[158] *Lok Sabha Debates*, LVII, No. 16 (August 28, 1961), 5193.
[159] *Ibid.*, p. 5194.
[160] *Ibid.*, p. 5195.
[161] *Ibid.*, No. 17 (August 29, 1961), pp. 5676–77.
[162] *Ibid.*, p. 5697.

Dal at this time did not accept Nehru's offer of a "high-level inquiry," it was evidently willing to climb down from its demand for Punjabi Suba. In an interview with foreign correspondents on September 2, Tara Singh made two proposals in order to break his fast: one, that either Great Britain or some other nation should promise to raise the issue of Punjabi Suba in the United Nations; two, that the British governor of the Punjab at the time of partition (Jenkins) or the one-time British deputy commissioner in Amritsar (P. E. Moon) be made an arbitrator for the issue. These proposals met with strong criticism as being anti-national. Later, Tara Singh again emphasized his determination to "do or die" and "I will get a Punjabi Suba or I will die." [163] In spite of the strain of the fast he continued to issue innumerable statements.

Meanwhile, in the Golden Temple, Akali leaders delivered strong speeches threatening the government with violence in case Tara Singh died.[164] Harcharan Singh Hudiara called Kairon a mad dog and Nehru a cowardly, dishonest, and mischievous person; he warned that the Sikhs would resort to the sword and there would be an upheaval in the country and that neither Nehru nor his agents would be found on earth. Hudiara said that they did not want a Sikh state out of Punjabi Suba because that would be such a small unit; instead, they wanted to make a Sikh state of the whole of India. Other Akali leaders warned that the Sikhs would take to violence and first deal with the Hindus, that they would bring Nehru on a nose-string to the Golden Temple and there have him beaten with shoes by the congregations, that the Sikhs would take to the sword and "devour" Congress leaders, and if Tara Singh died then neither Nehru and Kairon, nor railways and post offices, would survive. They declared that Nehru would not be able to find refuge anywhere and asked him to learn a lesson

---

163 *The Spokesman,* XI-A, No. 4 (September 11, 1961), p. 9.

164 Punjab, Public Relations Department, *Sidelights on Akali Strategy* (Chandigarh: Controller, Printing and Stationery, 1961), pp. 3–24.

from the hanging of Menderes of Turkey. Some of them stressed the importance of bloodshed for the achievement of Punjabi Suba, and urged the Sikhs to besmear their weapons with blood.

Chief Minister Kairon had, however, been able to maintain complete law and order in the state. He had pledged that he would not let a single leaf stir in the Punjab, and he lived up to the reputation he had built for himself as the "iron man" of Punjab. When the Communists decided to participate in the agitation in the belief that they could take advantage of the political situation that would follow the death of the Akali leader, Kairon arrested their chief leaders before they had a chance to go underground. The Akalis did not offer volunteers for mass arrests for fear apparently that not many would be forthcoming. Kairon further established the principle that the gurdwaras could no longer remain "privileged sanctuaries" if they gave refuge to people for whom the police had issued warrants. He organized several raids on gurdwaras to arrest proclaimed offenders of the law and to confiscate arms and ammunition. It was let out that the government would even have the police enter the Golden Temple when politically expedient. Apart from the government machinery, Kairon's personal network of intelligence sources kept him informed of the various activities within the Akali headquarters.

On the political level, the Indian government stuck to its position that it would not go beyond the earlier concessions because, as Nehru had explained in parliament, "the policy which the Government is pursuing is not only a firm policy but a right policy, and any marked deviation from it would be very injurious to the country." [165] However, as the fast lengthened into the second month, the Akali Dal began to step down from its earlier demands. Before the fast, the Akalis wanted a declaration about the formation of Punjabi Suba. After the commencement of the fast, they said they would be

[165] *Lok Sabha Debates,* LVII, No. 17 (August 29, 1961), 5698.

satisfied with government acceptance merely of the "principle" of Punjabi Suba with actual formation postponed until circumstances were appropriate. Later they desired the conversion of the regional committees into sub-legislatures. Still later they wanted the appointment of arbitrators of their own choice, foreign or Indian. Finally, when they indicated agreement to the government offer of the appointment of a commission to inquire into grievances of the Sikh community, they wanted the government to accept their terms in regard to the scope and personnel of the inquiry commission: one, that the inquiry commission should confine itself merely to the question of Punjabi Suba; and, two, that the personnel or at least one member of the commission should be chosen from a panel suggested by the Akali Dal.

On the question of the inquiry commission considering the issue of Punjabi Suba, Prime Minister Nehru declared, after his return from the Belgrade conference of the non-aligned nations, that "Punjabi Suba is not a subject which can be referred to any commission," [166] since it was a "political question." He remarked, however, that it was difficult for him to say how far it may incidentally "creep in" and that it would be for the commission to decide whether it was within its frame of reference.[167] On the question of personnel of the commission, the government's position was that it was the privilege of the government to appoint members of the commission though it might consider any suggestions the Akali Dal would have to make.

The firm policy of the central government in regard to the inquiry commission, and Kairon's effective maintenance of law and order, convinced the Akalis that they were fighting "a losing battle." [168] Once they called off their talks with the government, but finally agreed to the appointment of an inquiry commission on the government's terms, and Master Tara Singh

---

[166] *The Hindustan Times,* September 18, 1961.
[167] *Loc. cit.*
[168] *The Tribune,* September 18, 1961.

ended his 48-day fast on October 1, 1961. The same day, the government issued a statement about its decision to appoint a commission which "may go into the general question of discrimination and examine any charges of alleged differential treatment or grievances of the Sikhs." [169]

Just before Tara Singh broke his fast, the "extremist" wing of the Akali Dal voiced great objection against such a step, as nothing by way of Punjabi Suba had been achieved. On the other hand, Tara Singh sought to intimate that he had assurances concerning the scope and personnel of the commission from the eminent Sikhs who had acted as mediators, including the Maharaja of Patiala and Ambassador Malik.[170] Soon after breaking the fast, Tara Singh mentioned the possibility of a political settlement with the government even before the inquiry commission would start functioning.[171] As pressure grew from within the Akali Dal that he had violated his oath, he declared in a lengthy statement in Punjabi that he stood by his oath to achieve Punjabi Suba.[172] He said that he had given up the fast as the Sikh mediators had told him that his life was important for Sikh unity, for if he died "the Panth will disintegrate and with it will finish Punjabi Suba." [173] Tara Singh declared that "they have ended my fast but not my pledge to sacrifice my life for Punjabi Suba. Now either I shall die or see my pledge to achieve Punjabi Suba honoured." [174]

As a result of the efforts of one of the mediators, Tara Singh later met with Prime Minister Nehru and expressed satisfaction with this meeting. However, when the government announced the personnel of the inquiry commission, Tara Singh declared that the Akali Dal would not be bound by the commission's findings and would boycott the commission as the

[169] *The Spokesman*, XI-A, No. 8 (October 9, 1961), 9.
[170] *The Hindustan Times*, October 2, 1961.
[171] *Ibid.*, October 3, 1961.
[172] *The Tribune*, October 28, 1961.
[173] *Loc. cit.*   [174] *Loc. cit.*

names earlier conveyed to him had not been appointed.[175] Nehru immediately denied that the government had "discussed" any names for the commission with either Tara Singh or anyone else on behalf of the Akali Dal.[176] Referring to the constant references that the government had given them secret assurances, Nehru asserted: "One thing I wish to make clear. Repeatedly hints are thrown out either by Master Tara Singh or someone on his behalf about some assurances having been given to him. Whatever has been given has been said in our statements in public. No assurances of any kind have been given except what I have said in Parliament to which I am giving effect." [177] On the various turns and shifts in Akali commitments, Nehru commented: "I regret to find some confirmation in these developments of my feeling that it is very difficult to deal with the Akali Dal or its representatives." [178] Nehru later announced that even the mediators had written him, confirming that no promises had been made by the government in regard to the personnel of the commission.[179] Observers concluded that the Akali decision to boycott the inquiry commission was an attempt on the part of the Akali Dal to extricate itself from a predicament into which it had landed. As one former Akali leader, who was expelled from the Akali Dal in 1961, stated, "since Masterji feels that he will be fully exposed before the Sikh masses and the country with the appointment of the Commission as Masterji cannot prove the allegation of discrimination against the Sikhs, he is trying to go back out of his commitments." [180] Incidentally, it should be noted that as early as 1956 the government had agreed to form a commission of this type, provided only that the Akali Dal submit a list of cases of discrimination against Sikhs, but the commission

[175] *The Hindustan Times,* November 3, 1961.
[176] *The Tribune,* November 4, 1961.
[177] *Loc. cit.*   [178] *Ibid.,* December 25, 1961.
[179] *Ibid.,* January 24, 1962.
[180] Statement by Nirbhai Singh Dhillon, in *The Hindustan Times,* November 10, 1961.

was never formed because the Akali Dal furnished no such list.[181]

In the aftermath of his breaking the fast, Tara Singh faced a revolt within the Akali Dal. Taking the initiative, he suspended four members of his executive committee who had sought to prevent his re-election as president of the SGPC and Akali Dal, because of his failure to honor the pledge taken at the Akal Takht.[182] When one of the dissidents went on a hunger strike, Tara Singh reluctantly agreed to the appointment of a five-member *ad hoc* Sikh body to inquire into Tara Singh's conduct during the agitation. Finding him guilty of violation of the oath taken before the fast, this five-member body stated that Tara Singh had repeatedly said that "either a Punjabi Suba will be formed or I shall die," but broke his fast by merely accepting an inquiry commission.[183] This body further prescribed for Tara Singh a few measures by way of punishment and expiation.[184] However, a day later he was elected president of the SGPC. The revolt within the Akali Dal continued, and in 1962 Fateh Singh established a rival Akali Dal.

In contrast to the 1955 agitation, the end result of the 1960–61 agitation was not only a complete failure of the agitation, but also a disarray in the Akali ranks and an irreparable blow to the leadership of Master Tara Singh.

SUMMARY AND CONCLUSIONS

Agitations and morchas have been its most spectacular instruments, but the Akali Dal has actually employed a variety of strategies in the pursuit of its goal of *desh-kaal* (country and era). While the clause incorporating this goal was eliminated with great reluctance from the Akali constitution in 1956, the demand for Punjabi Suba—implementing that clause, if only

[181] *The Spokesman,* XI-A, No. 10 (October 23, 1961), 1.
[182] *The Hindustan Times,* November 17, 1961.
[183] *The Tribune,* November 30, 1961.
[184] *Loc. cit.*

in part—continues to be pressed. Undoubtedly, the Akali Dal has met with considerable success so far as the agitational and infiltrational strategies are concerned, but results of the general elections have demonstrated its complete failure to secure even 25 percent support not only in the Punjab as a whole but even in what it considers the "pure" Punjabi-speaking areas. In the third general elections in 1962 it obtained less than 20 percent of the total vote polled in the so-called Punjabi-speaking region. Assuming that the Sikhs constitute half the population of the Punjabi-speaking region—estimates put it at 55 percent—and that the same proportion of Sikhs take part in the elections as do members of other communities, then the results show that the Akali Dal has been able to secure the support of not more than 40 percent of even the Sikh community, since support for the Akali Dal is confined solely to the Sikhs. It may be argued that the Sikh population is rural-based with possibly a lower voter participation, but it is even more true that the Harijan sections, who vehemently oppose the Akali Dal, are likely to have a far lower voter participation than higher caste Hindus or Sikhs, for not only are they rural-based but also educationally backward and economically and socially underprivileged. At any rate, in the face of its performance in the elections, the Akali Dal cannot claim, as it seeks to do, that a majority of the population supports its demand for Punjabi Suba.

Despite this lack of support for the Akali demand among the population in the Punjabi-speaking region, it speaks well of the resources of the Akali leadership and organization that the Akali Dal has been able to secure substantial political concessions toward its demand for Punjabi Suba through the agitational and infiltrational strategies. Some observers have summarily concluded that the Akali Dal is not really interested in Punjabi Suba but launches agitations merely to maintain some leaders in power in the Akali Dal organization and to provide an outlet for other leaders in the Congress party and government. The fact that the Akalis have settled for less in ending their agitations, and have expressed willingness at times for an arrangement which would allow them to join the Congress, is offered in support of the view that the Akali Dal is not really concerned about Punjabi Suba but merely engaged in bargaining for government positions. Such a conclusion may seem plausible if each agitation is examined by itself, but when looking at the history of demand-making and bargaining by the Akali Dal over the period since independence one can unmistakably discern an *escalation pattern* pointing toward its goal of Punjabi Suba.

If one holds Punjabi Suba to be a constant objective, he can see that each political concession obtained by the Akali Dal has been a step further toward the formation of Punjabi Suba. The Akali Dal first obtained the "parity formula," which put Hindus and Sikhs on an equal basis in terms of sharing cabinet positions, even though the Sikhs constituted about 35 percent of the population, in order to emphasize that the Sikhs have special claims. The "Sachar formula" was secured ostensibly to facilitate language instruction, but the actual division of the Punjab into language zones took place so as to remove almost all Hindu-majority areas from the Punjabi-speaking region, which was then to serve as the basis for further demands for Punjabi Suba. Once Hindu-majority areas were excluded through political bargaining, the very fact that the government had agreed to their exclusion was adduced as proof that they were not Punjabi-speaking. Later, building on this demarcation between so-called Hindi-speaking and Punjabi-speaking regions, regional committees with certain legislative powers were established through the "regional formula" for the two regions. Even the agitation during 1960–61, at which time the government seemed extraordinarily firm, led the government to offer concessions in respect to strengthening the regional committees and, if necessary, granting them additional powers. At this time the Akali Dal pressed for the conversion of regional committees into at least sub-legislatures, undoubtedly to raise later the question of their conversion into full and separate legislatures. Thus, every time the Akali Dal has arrived at a political settlement with the government—a settlement which the government has presumed to be final—the Akali Dal has immediately moved on to the next step after consolidating the earlier concessions. As *The Spokesman,* which favors the Punjabi Suba demand, has observed: "Masterji has been a fighter throughout his life. Very rarely he descends down to make a compromise; and even if one is made, it is used as a hopping ground for another assault under the cover of something else." [185] One should not be misled by the imputation to Master Tara Singh personally of what is built into the very nature of the Akali Dal. In all that Master Tara Singh has done, he has had eminent and ardent supporters, some of them later entering the Congress party, however. The Akali Dal has seemed to act on the principle that what it has obtained is its by right, but what it wants further is certainly negotiable though all of it may not necessarily be conceded to the Akali Dal in one round. The most dramatic illustration of this phenomenon came in 1957 when Tara Singh reactivated the Akali Dal in politics, revived the demand for Punjabi Suba and put up Panthic candidates against the Congress, soon after the organization under his leadership had accepted the regional formula in settlement of the demand for Punjabi Suba and had undertaken to refrain from politics as part of the political compromise under which the Akalis joined the Congress party en masse.

It seems that at this point the Indian government and the Congress party became aware that the Akali Dal was playing for higher stakes, and that the settlements negotiated by the Akali Dal were only intermediate points toward its ultimate goal, an integral part of its constitution until 1956, of "creation of an environment in which the Sikh national expression finds its full satisfaction." The government had sought to satisfy Akali claims—though it too did so in the name of language—in

[185] *The Spokesman,* x, No. 48 (December 19, 1960), 3.

the belief that they were based on some genuine grievances. However, the *volte face* by the Akali Dal within three months of a political settlement brought the realization to the government that, in the words of Ambedkar in another context, "there is a difference between safeguards to allay apprehensions of the weak and contrivances to satisfy the ambition for power of the strong: that there is a difference between providing safeguards and handing over the country" and that "what may be conceded with safety to the weak to be used by it as a weapon of defense may not be conceded to the strong who may use it as a weapon of attack." [186] It is precisely this realization that explains why the Indian government in 1960–61, after giving concessions in one form or another up to that time, finally adopted a firm policy toward the Akali Dal. But it still remains to be seen how lasting this policy of firmness on the part of the government will be in the future.

Despite the repeated attempts to present the demand of Punjabi Suba in the name of language—and that too in recent years —Master Tara Singh and other Akali leaders have even then been quite outspoken in their speeches and statements of the underlying purpose and motive of such a demand. At the same time the Akalis allege that it is out of lack of trust in the Sikhs that the government does not concede Punjabi Suba because the Sikhs will be in a majority in that state. The government's answer has been that such a charge is baseless since the Sikhs occupy important and powerful positions in the economic, political and social fields. The government has repeatedly denied that it has distrust of the Sikhs, but that it may have developed doubts about the political objectives of the Akalis is quite possible. As *The Spokesman* has pointed out: "The Congress leaders must have serious doubts about Master Ji's consistency and faithfulness to implement an agreement even if at any time, it

186 B. R. Ambedkar, *Pakistan or The Partition of India* (3d ed.; Bombay: Thacker and Co. Ltd., 1946), p. 195.

may be entered into by his Dal under his own leadership. This is the lesson of the past experiences. . . ." [187]

In recent years some former Akali leaders, either in the Congress party or outside, and their journals, have argued that it is distressing that Tara Singh has given a communal color to the Punjabi Suba demand, but that the government should concede it on a language basis. Opponents of the Punjabi Suba comment that what this attitude means is this: give the Akali Dal what it wants but do so in the name of language, notwithstanding the Akali Dal's past record pointing out why it wants it. The questions that arise if such an argument is accepted are many. How will the actual demarcation be decided? What can prevent the Akali Dal from making the demarcation itself an occasion for more agitations? Given the ideological framework of the Akali Dal, what assurance is there that the Akali Dal won't agitate for further political claims, with Punjabi Suba as the territorial base? The point is that Punjabi Suba is not an objective in itself, but an instrument for other goals made explicit by Akali leaders from time to time. The Akali leaders are already on record as not satisfied with the present distribution of powers, and want the center to have control over only foreign affairs, defense and communications.[188] Another question of some importance is: How have these leaders who now emphasize the linguistic basis been able in the past to restrain the Akali Dal from revoking agreements? Moreover, whatever their present fascination with the linguistic argument, these leaders themselves achieved prominence not only under the aegis of Master Tara Singh, whom they now criticize for mixing religion and politics in relation to Punjabi Suba, but also through the religious appeal of the Akali Dal and its communal demands. In one sense, Master Tara Singh, in his presentation

---

[187] *The Spokesman,* xi, No. 7 (February 20, 1961), 1.

[188] See, for example, the resolution of the Akali Dal, *The Tribune,* January 1, 1953.

of the Punjabi Suba demand, has been more conformant to the origins of the demand than these leaders who now emphasize the linguistic basis; some observers cynically suggest that the linguistic argument suits their earlier objective and at the same time enables these leaders to maintain their positions of power in the Congress. The earlier career of these leaders, their speeches and statements and the resolutions passed with their approval does not, a review of their own journals would indicate, support their present contention that language has been the only basis of the demand. It is this configuration of unanswered questions that explains the firmness of the government in 1960–61. As Lord Birdwood had said on one occasion in relation to the demand for Punjabi Suba, "Mr. Nehru had not taken office to preside over the liquidation of the Indian Union." [189]

Despite the firm opposition which it encountered in 1960–61, the Akali Dal had over the years, through the employment of various political strategies, secured substantial political concessions toward its goal of Punjabi Suba. Interestingly, though, the Akali Dal seems not to have been equally successful with the same strategy twice, for apparently the Congress party, too, learns from past experience. Thus, the merger in 1948 brought significant concessions, but the merger in 1956 did not. The agitation in 1955 led to substantial concessions, but not so that of 1960–61. Has the Akali Dal exhausted the various strategies that it is capable of employing? Perhaps a policy of violence may seem an alternative but, while some Akalis may aspire for "country and era," there may be some difficulty in mobilizing substantial support for a policy of violence, precisely because the Sikhs do not suffer, relative to other segments of society, from any social and political disability and have too much at stake in the existing social and political order to risk giving support to such a policy. Moreover, unless the Congress leadership loses its nerve, the powers of the government are so great that no

[189] Lord Birdwood, *The Hindustan Times,* December 26, 1954.

policy of violence can possibly succeed under normal circumstances. On the other hand, it is obvious that the Akali leadership is too committed to the demand for Punjabi Suba to give it up, as the threats of self-immolation on the part of several Akali leaders, most notably Sant Fateh Singh in the latter half of 1965, so vividly testify. At the same time, the government may well come to feel that, in order for it to confront more adequately the Akali challenge specifically in relation to secular nationalism, it would be desirable to mute, through some change in policy concerning the so-called Punjabi-speaking region, the linguistic aspect of the demand. Obviously, in doing so the government would have to reckon with strong opposition from the Hindus and Harijans of that region.

CHAPTER VII

Support for the Political System

IN THE particular political configuration of the Punjab the Congress party sees itself as the only guardian of the existing political system. Insofar as the Akali Dal and other opposition parties have attempted to challenge the authority of the state in terms of law and order—and all of them have at one time or another been engaged in massive agitations—the Congress party being the party in power has not hesitated to use the coercive machinery of the state. But the ability to handle the law and order problem posed by opposition parties presupposes that the Congress party holds power in the government. Continued control of the government by the Congress party is therefore of crucial importance to the maintenance of the political system. Moreover, apart from the aspiration to political power on the part of political parties generally, the Congress party needs the resources of the government for the creation of a new social and economic order in India to which its leadership has been committed. Since the Congress party is at the same time committed to a democratic framework, it must seek political legitimacy for its rule by a reference to the popular will through regular elections. Toward this end the Congress party has participated in a series of general elections held since independence. How successful has the Congress party been in securing political support? What is the extent of popular support that the Congress party has received in the Punjab? How does its popular strength compare with that of other political parties?

CONGRESS PARTY STRENGTH IN PUNJAB POLITICS

One should note that, whatever the strength of the Congress party before the partition in other states of India, in the Punjab it did not by any means command overwhelming support among either the Hindus or the Sikhs. Not until the 1946 general elections, when the Muslim community united behind the Muslim League, did the Hindu community and a large part, but not a majority, of the Sikh community vote for the Congress party. Before then, the Unionist party had monopolized the support of the Muslim community. Among the Hindus the Congress party had considerable support, but even here in the urban areas the Hindu communal parties cut deeply into its strength and in the rural areas, especially in the Hariana region, the Unionist party proved a formidable and unbeatable competitor. A large portion of the Sikh community supported the Congress party, but the major political force among the Sikhs was the Akali Dal. Although the prospect of independence and partition brought increased support to the Congress party, the actual event of partition not only made it vulnerable to the charge, especially among the millions of refugees, of being responsible for the vivisection of the Punjab and the holocaust that followed it, but also disrupted the party organization. Against this background it would seem that the Congress party has made significant progress in mobilizing political support in the Punjab during the period since 1947.

There have been three general elections in the Punjab, as in the rest of India, since the partition—in 1952, 1957, and 1962. The results of the third general elections in 1962 were interpreted by many observers as signifying a great depletion in the strength of the Congress party. Typical of such interpretations is a comment by one political scientist that the "Congress party was severely mauled, dropping 3.2% of votes polled and 28 seats compared with the previous election." [1] Such observations made on the basis of a comparison between the 1957 and 1962 general elections ignore the fact that these two elections, in fact, are not strictly comparable. Prior to the second general elections in 1957, the Akali Dal had merged with the Congress

[1] Surinder Suri, *1962 Elections: A Political Analysis* (New Delhi: Sudha Publications Pvt. Ltd., 1962), p. 139.

party, and 26 of its nominees ran on the Congress ticket. The
Akali Dal did not officially contest the 1957 elections, whereas
in 1962 it entered the third general elections as an independent
political party and declared the campaign a "war" over the
issue of Punjabi Suba. Thus the party configuration for these
two general elections was entirely different; in one case the
Akali Dal was politically an integral part of the Congress party
whereas in the other it was its most formidable opponent.

A more appropriate comparison for the evaluation of the
strength of the different political parties would be that between
the first general elections in 1952 and the third general elections
in 1962. Such a comparison would not only refer to the same
party configuration insofar as the main political parties are concerned, but would also provide some perspective over a longer
period of time. To be sure, the 1952 general elections were for
two separate legislatures corresponding to the two states into
which Punjab was split at the time. However, the two general
elections covered the same territory and population, and were
fought over the same political issues. Therefore, if the number
and percentage of votes actually secured by the different political parties, rather than the number of seats won or lost, are
taken into account a better measure of the changes in political
support over the decade from 1952 to 1962 can be obtained.

What conclusions emerge, then, from a comparison of the
1952 and 1962 general elections? What does such a comparison
indicate more specifically about political support for the Congress party? Rather than the conclusion that the Congress party
has been losing support, one finds that the party has over a
ten-year period not only consolidated the support it had won
in the first general elections, but has actually made tremendous
strides in getting a larger share of the total vote polled (see
Table 2). Its share of the vote in the third general elections
was 43.8 percent as against only 34.8 percent in the first general elections. The increase in the Congress party vote of 9
percent represents the largest increase of any political party in

TABLE 2

Results of Three General Elections in the Punjab [a]

Political Group	1952			1957			1962		
	Number	Per cent	Seats	Number	Per cent	Seats	Number	Per cent	Seats
1. Congress party	2,206,898	34.8	122[b]	3,612,709	47.5	120[b]	2,943,839	43.8	90
2. Akali Dal	927,916	14.7	33				789,925	11.7	19
3. Communist party	337,904	5.3	6	1,030,898	13.6	6	493,910	7.3	9
4. Jan Sangh	315,110	5.0	2	654,395	8.6	9	639,565	9.5	8
5. Republican party (SCF)	145,484	2.3	1	410,364	5.4	5	145,040	2.2	..
6. Swatantra party							261,276	3.9	3
7. Praja Socialist party	257,701	4.1	1	94,564	1.2	1	60,390	0.9	..
8. Independents	1,602,133	25.3	21[b]	1,800,960	23.7	13	1,294,896	19.2	25
9. Others	539,921	8.5		..	..	..	98,128	1.5	..
Total	6,333,067	100.0	186	7,603,890	100.0	154	6,726,969	100.0	154
Electorate	11,265,725			13,105,735			10,738,443		
Vote participation		56.3	..		58.0	..		62.6	..

[a] Statistics for the 1952 elections were obtained from India, Election Commission, *Report on the First General Elections in India 1951–52* (New Delhi: Election Commission India, 1955); the figures here given for the 1952 elections are based on combining the statistics for the then states of Punjab and PEPSU. Statistics for the 1957 elections are from India, Election Commission, *Report on the Second General Elections 1957* (New Delhi: Election Commission, 1959), while those for the 1962 elections have been calculated from information furnished by the Elections office in Chandigarh in March, 1962. (For a later, more accurate tabulation of the 1962 general election results, based on final official figures, see Appendix I.) The decrease in the electorate evident in 1962 compared to 1957 is a result of the abolition of double-member constituencies in 1962. Before 1962, in over thirty double-member constituencies each voter had two votes, and as a result the total number of votes was much larger than the total number of voters. With the abolition of the double-member constituencies now, the number of votes and voters is the same.

[b] Including one member elected unopposed.

the Punjab. The Congress vote in the third general elections dropped by 3.7 percent compared to its vote in the second general elections in 1957, but in 1957 the Akali Dal was nonexistent as a political party. In general, organized political parties increased their vote at the expense of "independents" and "other" smaller political groups.

In contrast to the position of the Congress party is that of the Akali Dal which lost considerable political support between 1952 and 1962. The vote for the Akali Dal in the third general elections was 11.7 percent compared to its record of 14.7 percent in the first general elections, a decrease of about one-fifth in Akali strength over a decade. Thus, in the context of the contest between the Congress party and the Akali Dal, the Congress party has emerged much stronger and has improved its political position substantially over the three general elections, whereas the Akali Dal has suffered a considerable reduction in its vote.

What has been the record of the other two major opposition parties—the Communist party and the Jan Sangh? The strength of the Communist party increased by only 2 percent, from 5.3 percent in 1952 to 7.3 percent in 1962, whereas the Jan Sangh almost doubled its share of the vote polled, from 5 percent to 9.5 percent. An interesting point is that the Communist vote dropped from 13.6 percent in the second general elections to almost half (7.3 percent) in the third general elections. The decrease occurred in almost the same proportion in both the Hindi-speaking and Punjabi-speaking regions (see Tables 3 and 4). One tentative hypothesis for the decrease in the Communist vote is that there is present in the electorate a hard core opposition vote of almost half a million which, under all circumstances, remains opposed to the Congress party or government whether or not there is an Akali Dal in the Punjabi-speaking region or some strong opposition group in the Hindi-speaking region. In 1957 the merger of the Akali Dal, the Zamindara League, and other groups into the Congress party

TABLE 3

1957 ELECTION RESULTS BY REGIONS IN THE PUNJAB

Political Group	Punjabi-speaking Region			Hindi-speaking Region		
	Number	Per-cent	Seats	Number	Per-cent	Seats
1. Congress party	2,242,165	48.4	73	1,370,544	46.1	47
2. Akali Dal	..	..	..	..	..	..
3. Communist party	835,279	18.0	4	195,619	6.6	2
4. Jan Sangh	331,817	7.2	5	322,578	10.9	4
5. Republican party (SCF)	279,551	6.0	1	130,813	4.4	4
6. Praja Socialist party	40,596	0.9	..	53,968	1.8	1
7. Independents	903,942	19.5	6	897,018	30.2	7
Total	4,633,350	100.0	89	2,970,540	100.0	65

TABLE 4

1962 ELECTION RESULTS BY REGIONS IN THE PUNJAB

Political Group	Punjabi-speaking Region			Hindi-speaking Region		
	Number	Per-cent	Seats	Number	Per-cent	Seats
1. Congress party	1,807,427	45.8	51	1,136,412	40.9	39
2. Akali Dal	780,105	19.8	19	9,820	0.4	..
3. Communist party	396,080	10.0	9	97,830	3.5	..
4. Jan Sangh	302,130	7.7	4	337,435	12.1	4
5. Republican party (SCF)	111,441	2.8	..	33,599	1.2	..
6. Swatantra party	93,484	2.4	..	167,792	6.0	3
7. Praja Socialist party	28,231	0.7	..	32,159	1.1	..
8. Independents	425,556	10.8	6	869,340	31.3	19
9. Others	1,835	..	..	96,293	3.5	..
Total	3,946,289	100.0	89	2,780,680	100.0	65

served to swell the vote for the Communist party but apparently without implying any deep ideological commitment to the Communist party. The revival of the Akali Dal in 1962 as an independent political contestant in the Punjabi-speaking region and the setting up of several independent opposition groups in the Hindi-speaking region brought about a heavy reduction in the Communist vote. It would appear that there is resistance on the part of the hard core opposition voter to an abrupt change in favor of the Congress party when the opposition group to which he belongs chooses to merge with the Congress. At the same time it cannot be denied that the mergers of different political parties into the Congress party just prior to the 1957 elections did help the Congress party to get a larger vote in 1957—and, to some extent, maybe even in 1962; the reason for this perhaps could be that the floating and uncommitted vote, though somewhat sympathetic to the opposition—and not the hard core opposition vote—changed in favor of the Congress party as a result of the mergers.

The ability of the Jan Sangh to double its vote over a period of ten years (from 5 percent in 1952 to 9.5 percent in 1962) and, more significantly, to improve, however slightly, upon its 1957 record (8.6 percent) seems to represent the emergence of a potentially powerful opponent to the Congress party in the Punjab (see Table 2). The performance of the Jan Sangh in the 1957 elections supposedly constituted the high water mark of Hindu support for the Jan Sangh, for the second general elections followed first the major political concession in the form of the regional formula to the Akali Dal from the Congress party and then the merger of the Akali Dal into the Congress party. Both the regional formula and the merger had made for great resentment in the Hindu community on the ground that the concessions were being given to the Akali Dal at the expense of the Hindu community and that the Congress party in the Punjab was coming under the control of Akali influence. The third general elections in 1962, on the other hand, had followed an extremely firm stand taken by the Indian government against the Akali demand of Punjabi Suba and the Akali agitation during 1960 and 1961. However, there was no diminution in the strength of the Jan Sangh; on the contrary, there was a slight increase.

A likely explanation for the persistence of the Jan Sangh strength is that it is based on setting up candidates indiscriminately to mobilize the largest possible vote, not with the intent necessarily to win, but in order to obtain recognition as a national party in India. One factor, however, runs counter to this explanation: it is the vote in parliamentary constituencies that is relevant in relation to recognition as a national party, and not the vote in constituencies for the state legislature, though there is likely to be some interaction between the vote for the two. Some observers feel that the growing strength of the Jan Sangh represents a reaction on the part of the Hindu community, especially the refugee elements, to the activities of the Akali Dal and a growing Hindu alienation from the Congress party because of the feeling that the Congress party in the Punjab is allegedly not only under the domination of Sikhs but also acts, overtly and covertly, to favor the Sikh community at the cost of the Hindu community. It should be recognized that the Hindu refugee from West Pakistan, like his Sikh counterpart, no longer means a destitute person, but one who has done well economically and, in most cases, improved upon his economic status before the partition. It is interesting to note also that while, in the share of the popular vote, the Jan Sangh (9.5 percent in 1962) approaches closely the record of the Akali Dal (11.7 percent in 1962), in its ability to engage in agitational activity and extract political concessions from the government it is far surpassed by the Akali Dal—apparently because the following of the Jan Sangh is not concentrated in a compact region and the resources that the Akali Dal commands are far superior.

An overview of the three general elections held since 1952 (see Table 2) shows that the Congress party has increased its strength considerably during this decade. That the Congress party still does not command an absolute majority in the electorate is obvious, but no other organized political party has even one-third the size of its vote. Moreover, the lack of an absolute majority in the electorate has not prevented the Congress party from assuring a stable government in the Punjab, for the frag-

mented nature of the opposition, and especially the presence
of a large number of independents, has meant that the Congress
party has been able to win thus far an absolute majority of
seats in the legislature in these elections. Thus, for instance,
the larger number of independent candidates in the Hindi-
speaking region in 1962 (Table 4) enabled the Congress with
only 40.9 percent of the vote to win 60 percent of the seats
(39 out of 65), whereas in the Punjabi-speaking region, where
there was a smaller number of independent candidates, the
Congress won 57 percent of the seats with 45.8 percent of the
vote.

The argument can be made that the Congress party represents only a minority vote, but there is some evidence that if
the issues are sharply drawn and there is a straight contest
with the opposition, the Congress party is capable of a better
performance. In the Punjabi-speaking region, where there was
an electoral agreement among all major opposition parties except the Jan Sangh—that is, the Akali Dal, the Communist
party, the Republican party, the Swatantra party, and the Praja
Socialist party (who altogether received 35.7 percent of the
1962 vote)—the Congress party secured 45.8 percent of the
vote, whereas in the Hindi-speaking region, where the opposition was divided and the number of independents was much
larger, the Congress party won only 40.9 percent of the vote
(see Table 4).

A closer look at a breakdown of the results for the third general elections by Punjabi-speaking region and Hindi-speaking
region (Table 4) reveals some interesting information. Among
the four parties that are of some political significance in the
Punjab—the Congress party, the Akali Dal, the Jan Sangh, and
the Communist party—only two are in fact all-Punjab parties,
the Congress party and the Jan Sangh. The Akali Dal has virtually no support in the Hindi region (a mere 0.4 percent) and
the Communist party was able to secure in the Hindi region
only about a third (3.5 percent) of the vote it polled in the

Punjabi region (10 percent). The vote polled by the Congress party in the Punjabi-speaking region and the Hindi-speaking region was 45.8 percent and 40.9 percent, respectively; that of the Jan Sangh, 7.7 percent and 12.1 percent.

In the Hindi-speaking region, except for the Jan Sangh, there seems to be really no organized opposition to the Congress party. The Congress party could indeed have done even better in the 1962 elections but for its failure to accommodate Congress leaders of that region, and especially from the Hariana area, who had either been squeezed out from the party or had bolted it. Loyalties in Hariana tend to be more candidate-oriented than issue-oriented or party-oriented, and the Congress party suffered for the tactical mistakes of the incumbent leadership. The opposition to Congress candidates, who were mostly newcomers to the party, came from former stalwarts of the Congress party like Sri Ram Sharma, Ch. Devi Lal, Professor Sher Singh, and their lieutenants and followers. Ch. Devi Lal and his group, in fact, bolted the Congress not many weeks before the 1962 general elections over dissatisfaction with the allocation of party tickets, which had been so allocated as to keep in check a prospective rival to the existing leadership of the Congress party in the Punjab.

In the Punjabi-speaking region, the Congress party has been faced with a tri-pronged opposition—the Akali Dal, the Jan Sangh, and the Communist party. Here, in 1962, the Congress party was able to win 45.8 percent of the total vote polled. It is surprising indeed that the Congress party vote in 1962 decreased only by 2.6 percent from the 1957 vote (see Tables 3 and 4) even when in 1962 the Akali Dal contested as an independent political party. On the other hand, the performance of the Akali Dal (19.8 percent) served to point up the fact that it did not command the support of a majority of even the Sikh community for whom it has insistently claimed to be the sole spokesman. How wrong then is the commonplace assumption that every Sikh is an Akali supporter! Next to the Akali

Dal, the Communist party polled 10 percent of the vote in the Punjabi-speaking region; much of this vote is presumed to have come from small-scale landholders in the Sikh community. The Jan Sangh vote of 7.7 percent in the Punjabi-speaking region is less than the 12.1 percent it polled in the Hindi-speaking region.

In summary, then, despite the highly organized—though far from united—opposition in the Punjab, especially in the Punjabi-speaking region, the Congress party has done reasonably well in mobilizing political support for itself and, in turn, for all levels of the political system—the government, the regime, and the political community.

FACTORS IN CONGRESS PARTY SUPPORT

What policies of the Congress party have enabled the party to secure this political support? What factors in the political situation have helped the Congress party in mobilizing support? From an observation of the political scene in the Punjab, four factors seem especially important: (1) the nature and status of the Congress party; (2) Congress control of the state government; (3) economic development and planning; and (4) the strategy of coalition-building among various groups.

Nature and Status of the Congress Party

The Indian National Congress, including its state branches, is a secular, broad-based, all-India political party, which is committed to parliamentary democracy and planned economic development for the welfare of the Indian people. It is a coalition of diverse political and social groups and, in its historical growth, has developed the machinery and skills to aggregate a variety of groups and viewpoints. The party rejects identification with any particular religion or caste; its membership is open to all, regardless of their religious, caste, or linguistic affiliation. It includes people covering a wide variety of political views across the right-left spectrum, but the party's political gravity lies somewhere in the center.

Before independence the Congress party had become the strongest political force, the embodiment of nationalism, and an all-India political organization unlike other political parties which were regional or sectional in character. As a result, it succeeded to the government after the end of British rule in India. Since independence the Congress party has remained in unchallenged control of the government at the center, because the opposing parties represent local or regional pockets of strength, whereas the strength and organization of the Congress party are spread all over India. The control of the Congress party at the center enables it further, formally and informally, to assist its state branches to remain in power in the states, which in turn helps to maintain the party in power at the center. If the voters in a state want the center's cooperation and assistance, without which no state government in India can function for long, they must avoid a deadlock with the center by electing a government for the state which is not opposed to the principles and policies of the Congress party. Whether or not the voter really thinks and acts in such terms is not demonstrable, but Congress leaders running for election do make the appeal that voters should elect a party which can get things done for them and that this is possible only for a political party that has the cooperation of the center.

Of great significance is the aura of sacrifice and struggle that is woven into the history of the Congress party. It is the Congress party which is identified with the struggle for freedom. Whatever its faults, it still evokes sympathetic memories at least among the older generation. Congress leaders and workers underwent great hardships for the freedom movement. No other party has such a long history of persistent struggle in the cause of freedom, and no other party's name is as well known across the land as that of the Congress. All the major political heroes of the century are associated with the Congress party. It is the party of Gandhi and Nehru. The admiration and adoration for Gandhi and Nehru are skillfully used by Congress leaders to gain support for the Congress party. In the past the prestigious position of India in world affairs and Nehru's role as "the angel of peace" have been counted on to win support.

The Congress party also seeks support on the basis of the claim that it alone is the guarantor of the political system, that it alone can assure the continuance of parliamentary democracy, the secular state and economic planning in India. Its leaders remind the voter that it is the Congress party that provided him with the vote and civil liberties, and continues to protect his rights and privileges. They also inform the voter of the amount of power that has been given him through the development of local democratic institutions. They further warn him that the other political parties are all feudal, communal, foreign-inspired and totalitarian, pursuing their own vested interests, and would put an end to all the rights and power the voter now commands once they came into power.

An indication of the sense of power that the citizen feels as a result of having the right to vote is the way in which he at times attempts, illiterate and poor though he may be, to humiliate candidates through his very embarrassing questions and comments during election campaigns.

Even the advocacy of a secular political order is helpful to the Congress party to some extent, for there is some sentiment against communalism. No party wants to be labeled communal. This indicates that the Congress party has been successful to some extent in instilling doubts among opposition parties about communalism. Despite the claims of other political parties to being non-communal, they are not taken at their face value, for they are held inconsistent with the deeds of party leaders and workers. Voters ask why it is that the same political party preaches communal harmony one day and launches agitations the next to coerce other communities. On the other hand, the

Congress party's commitment to a secular state reaches far back into its history, and is especially noteworthy in the background of the party's determination to remain loyal to it even at the height of the crisis that followed the partition of India.

Apart from the ideological commitment on the part of the Congress party to the policy of a secular state, there is something to be said for the political value of such a policy in a society which is divided into numerous groups, many of them in conflict with each other. As a secular, broad-based party the Congress party is able to benefit from the bias built into the nature of social diversity in the Punjab for such a party.[2] There is no single religious or caste group that can form the government by itself. Even if one religious or caste group *qua* group were to establish itself in power, there could be no peace in the state because of the intense opposition it would provoke from other hostile groups. Nor would such a situation be tolerable to the Congress party at the center. Since the various groups inhabit the same territory it becomes essential for them to cooperate for the sake of political stability. The Congress party, with its doors open to members of all communities, provides precisely the platform where the moderate sections of all communities can meet. Furthermore, the Congress party is not credited with any designs to suppress minority groups. On the contrary, minority groups look up to the Congress party as their sole protector. Even if some group is disaffected with the Congress party at the state level it feels that it has a chance to be heard by the Congress party at the center and to have its grievances redressed.

The fact that the other political parties have appeals limited to sectional groups is used by the Congress party to secure political support for itself. During election campaigns Congress leaders emphasize that no political party other than the Congress party can form a government by itself even if all its candidates were to win, simply because none of them has enough

[2] See chapter II.

candidates in the field compared to the number of seats in the legislature. Nor can such a political party form a government in an alliance with other political parties because they are all irreconcilably opposed to each other. Congress leaders therefore urge voters not to waste their votes in supporting opposition parties, but instead to vote for the Congress party and thus be on the winning side. They attempt to convince voters that the Congress party alone can form the government because it is able to set up candidates in every constituency. They advise voters to vote for a party which will assuredly come into power and therefore will be able to get things done for them in the political and economic fields. The Congress party thus appeals on the basis of the certainty of its victory.

However, the Congress party is not without its weaknesses. Congressmen themselves are perhaps their own severest critics. The newspapers of the region are filled daily with exhortations by Congress leaders to get rid of such weaknesses. One point of criticism is the entry into the party's ranks and leadership of such elements as are not sympathetic to the party's ideology or program, but merely aim to obtain the privileges and benefits that influence in the party brings. In June 1962, the then Chief Minister reportedly lashed out at people who had become Congressmen in order to obtain such privileges, and urged them to leave the party so as to save it from "further annihilation." He remarked that such "opportunists" took advantage of benefits from the party for five years and then betrayed it at election time.[3] The general public, however, is not impressed with such criticisms for it believes that the top Congress leaders themselves are responsible for the encouragement of "opportunist" elements and for the demoralization of the services, and further that the leaders are not personally free from blame in the specific practices they so vehemently condemn in public. During his tenure as Chief Minister, Partap Singh Kairon was subjected to severe and vociferous criticism both by his own party

[3] *The Tribune,* June 17, 18, 1962.

men and opposition groups for corruption and nepotism and also for allegedly foisting a personal despotism on the state under the facade of constitutional government. Several were the charge sheets that his own party men frequently carried to the central Congress party. Eventually Kairon had to resign when an inquiry commission found him guilty of certain charges of corruption and nepotism.

Furthermore, the Congress party has been a house divided against itself. Factionalism has been rife within the party. Most of the factions have a basis in personal loyalty to a leader; some have an ideological basis, like the Giani Kartar Singh group which consisted of some of the former Akalis; others are organized around regional interests, like the groups of members from Hariana and PEPSU areas; and still others are organized around caste, such as those of the Harijans. There are factions within factions. Factionalism based on personal loyalty is the most common, yet there is nothing constant about these loyalties. Members switch from one faction to another, and even bolt the party, as best serves their interests.

The fact that the Congress party in a strategically important state such as the Punjab is divided into many factions makes possible frequent intervention on the part of the central Congress party in the affairs of the Punjab Congress. The closeness of New Delhi to Chandigarh serves to increase the opportunities for such intervention. Thus, the central Congress party becomes an influential element in the final disposition of the claims of various factions. In the last analysis, it is not sufficient for a factional leader to establish control solely over a majority in the Punjab Congress legislature party; he must also have the support of the central Congress party. The outcome of any struggle for power within the Punjab Congress may often depend on the wishes of New Delhi.

Between 1947 and 1956, the Congress party in the Punjab was torn by factional struggles within the ministerial wing and by conflict between the ministerial wing and the organizational wing.[4] In 1956, with the ouster of Bhim Sen Sachar from the office of Chief Minister, both the ministerial wing and the organizational wing came under the control of Partap Singh Kairon. However, dissident factions within the Congress party agitated for Kairon's removal, as did the opposition parties. Though compelled by political events to resign in 1964, Kairon nevertheless provided a stable and effective—but for some, harsh and corrupt—government in the state for a period of over eight years.

The Congress party is also criticized for not being free from elements of communalism. As one member of parliament explained, "you cannot see communalism in the Congress party but you can smell it." [5] Communalism in the party may take subtle forms like giving favors to members of one's own community. On certain issues members belonging to the Hindu and Sikh communities may split along communal lines in party discussions. Some factions in the Congress party may even be organized on a communal basis. However, the Congress party continuously strives to maintain the image of itself as a party of secular nationalism.

The various weaknesses and shortcomings of the Congress party in the Punjab have made for dissatisfaction among many groups in the population. Many are the statements that the Congress party is highly unpopular in the state. The electoral strength of the Congress party is held to be not a true reflection of the feelings and sentiments of the population, for the choice of the Congress party on the part of the voter is alleged to be governed more by the fear of other parties and groups than any positive affection for the Congress party. Be that as it may, the Congress party does manage to pre-empt the area of the widest possible political consensus among conflicting groups in the state.

[4] For a discussion of factions within the Congress party in the Punjab, see Baldev Raj Nayar, "Political Development in the Punjab," in Myron Weiner (ed.), *State Politics in India* (forthcoming).

[5] From an interview.

Congress Control of State Government

Except for a brief period of President's Rule in 1951–52, the Congress party has been in control of the state government since independence. This adds to the ability of the government to secure political support. The oriental respect for authority is often remarked upon as making for political support for the Congress as the party in power, and there may be some element of truth to such a statement. However, there is need for a great deal of skepticism in accepting this statement, for more than 50 percent of the electorate chooses to vote against the Congress party. The significance of Congress control of the state government, in fact, lies in another direction. Since independence there has occurred a revolutionary change—the groundwork for which was laid during the nationalist movement—in the conception of the functions of government. Government now is not merely an instrument to maintain political stability, but has become an active agent for economic development and social change. The wide intervention of the government in the economic and social fields means not only a change in the nature of governmental functions, but also in the magnitude of governmental resources compared to other economic and social groups in the society. No longer is the government simply a broker between other groups in Indian society; compared to them, the government is an economic colossus. This change in the nature of the functions of government, and in the scope of government efforts in the economic and social spheres, involves far-reaching implications in terms of obtaining political support for the Congress party. These can be discussed in several categories.

1. *Ability to provide goods and services.* Government activity now includes the provision of a wide variety of goods and services to the people. Under several five-year plans, the government has opened new schools and colleges, as well as hospitals and dispensaries, established community development pro-

288   *Support for the Political System*

grams for the rural areas, dug wells and canals to provide better irrigation, built huge TVA-type dams to make electricity available for home and industry, constructed new roads, provided free education up to high school, and given seeds and fertilizers and agricultural loans to farmers, and generous financial assistance to cooperatives.

Over the years expenditures by government on the provision of goods and services have progressively increased. Expenditures on developmental and social services formed about 60 percent of the government budget of 647 million rupees for 1961–62.[6] Although a breakdown of the figures is not available for later years, government expenditures in general have increased substantially. The revenue expenditure budget for 1964–65 amounted to 1,129,000,000 rupees, and the capital expenditure budget for the same period amounted to another 197 million rupees.[7]

The increasing ability to provide goods and services gives the government greater means of securing political support. The allocation of such goods and services can be made a condition for political support. The vast resources of the government in this respect may also mean that the new village and district councils with economic development functions, under the program of "democratic decentralization," will come under the dominance of the Congress party. Voters are likely to elect those leaders who can secure the most economic advantages for their areas. Even when non-Congressmen are elected, they are likely to move closer to the government in an effort to get goods and services allocated to their areas. In a survey of the leaders elected to panchayats (village councils) in the Punjab, it was found that while 61 percent of the leaders interviewed declared that they had no party affiliation, another 31 percent belonged to the Congress party, and only 8 percent belonged to the

[6] Punjab, *Punjab Budget at a Glance 1961–62* (Chandigarh: Government of Punjab, 1961), p. 1.

[7] *The Tribune*, February 26, 1964, and *Facts About Punjab*, pp. 57–58.

Communist party, Akali Dal, and Jan Sangh, or refused to name their party.[8] The development of a new leadership from the village up will most likely strengthen the Congress party rather than other political parties.

2. *Control of the economy.* A planned program of development in an economy of scarcity has meant the introduction of various types of monetary and physical controls. In the allocation of scarce but essential commodities to several developing sectors of the economy, the government has imposed controls over the distribution of several commodities, such as steel, iron, and coal. The government has further assumed powers of control over other economic sectors, such as the trucking business. These various controls not only enable the government to plan for economic development but also provide it with new sources of influence to attract political support. In the presence of these controls, it becomes impossible for an individual to engage in any significant economic activity without the specific permission of the government. Permission on the part of the government has to be specific and personal, not general. One cannot run a truck or a passenger bus unless he secures a "permit" from the government; he cannot start a coal business or an industrial concern without a "quota" for coal and steel; he cannot construct or operate a movie house or a cold storage plant without a "license" from the government. In the face of the tremendous demand for these permits, quotas and licenses, political considerations enter the final decision, and the recipients of the privileges provide great financial and political support to the Congress party or to certain Congress leaders. One veteran leader has consequently characterized the government in India as "Permit, License, Quota Raj." An excellent example of the skillful use made in granting quotas and permits to secure political support is the allocation of bus and truck routes to transport operators in the Punjab who proved a source of great

[8] Indian Institute of Public Opinion, *Monthly Public Opinion Surveys*, VI, Nos. 8–9 (May-June, 1961), 65.

strength to Partap Singh Kairon. In addition to quotas and permits, control by the Congress party over cooperatives, local banks, and other quasi-government developmental bodies can be of immense importance in securing political support.

3. *Patronage in jobs.* The change in the nature and size of governmental activity has meant a tremendous increase in the official bureaucracy that now spreads out from the executive secretariat in Chandigarh to the remotest village with its village level worker. Many of these positions are subject to selection on a competitive basis through the Public Service Commission but a large number of them are not. The government has entrusted the recruitment of positions with salaries less than Rs. 159 to a Subordinate Services Selection Board, whose membership and very existence have been the subject of searching criticism both in the Punjab legislature [9] and by the Public Service Commission itself.[10] The Public Service Commission has repeatedly objected, without effect, to the steady attempts of the government to remove many positions from the purview of the Commission and to make direct appointments.[11] Whole new categories of positions with political possibilities have been created by the government. For example, in 1963 the Punjab government ordered the appointment of 2,000 zaildars and safaidposhes (village officials) over the next four years to help in the collection of government revenue.[12] Other methods of direct control over the vast patronage are alleged to be the substitution of merit for seniority in promotions to a large number of positions in the government,[13] and the assumption of powers to bring about the compulsory retirement of any government

[9] *The Tribune,* May 4, 5, 1962.

[10] Punjab, *Annual Report on the Working of the Punjab Public Service Commission from 1st April, 1959 to 31st March, 1960* (Chandigarh: Controller, Printing and Stationery, 1961), pp. 5–6.

[11] *Ibid.,* p. 12.

[12] *The Tribune,* November 12, 1963. This plan was later dropped after a new ministry took over in 1964.

[13] *Ibid.,* January 31, 1962.

servant with ten or fifteen years of service, if it is found that "his general reputation is bad even though specific charges of inefficiency and corruption may or may not be proved." [14] In addition, the Congress party possesses tremendous patronage power in quasi-government development bodies.

4. *Assumption of party functions.* While governments deem it necessary to have an effective liaison with the press, the work of the public relations department in the Punjab approaches more nearly the functions of a political party in mobilizing public support for government policies. This department has branches in every district, with their retinue of public relations officers, supervisors (men and women), organizers, rural publicity workers, folk musicians, singers and poets. Most of the positions in the public relations department are outside the purview of the Public Service Commission and the Subordinate Services Selection Board [15] since, as was argued in the case of one category of positions, "candidates for these posts have necessarily to be prominent public speakers who are able to speak fluently, have suffered for the cause of the country, and who can control rural publicity." [16] Apart from issuing press notes and arranging press conferences, the public relations department distributes newsreels and film documentaries, organizes every year thousands of public meetings where audiences are collected through recitation of poetry and singing of songs, arranges programs of cultural entertainment, publishes a vast amount of literature on political issues, maintains several hundred reading rooms, and installs and repairs thousands of radio sets. Appointments in the department are said to be directly controlled by the Chief Minister and, when Kairon was Chief Minister, public relations workers are said to have acted as if they were his "personal minstrels."

[14] *Ibid.*, May 15, 1958.   [15] *Ibid.*, June 9, 1962.
[16] Punjab, *Annual Report on the Working of the Punjab Public Service Commission from 1st April, 1958 to 31st March, 1959* (Chandigarh: Controller, Printing and Stationery, 1960), p. 4.

Economic Development and Planning

Apart from the material resources that programs of economic development place directly at the disposal of the party in power for mobilizing political support, economic development by bringing about better and higher standards of living can potentially make for greater political support for the party sponsoring economic development. However, one cannot take for granted that increased economic prosperity need automatically lead to such political support; the contrary is as likely. In the process of economic growth some classes may gain but others may be adversely affected, movements of people from rural to urban areas and from one region to another may lead to social tensions, and the costs of economic development may be painful for many. Furthermore, even economic prosperity may only give rise to new expectations and aspirations which, if not met immediately, may lead to withdrawal of support, regardless of the satisfaction given earlier. A British civil servant, with many years of experience in the Punjab, once stated that "it has often struck me in listening to the prosperous canal colonists in the Punjab that, with the peasant who has enough to eat and to wear, contentment is almost in inverse ratio to material progress." [17]

On the other hand, the awareness that economic growth does not necessarily make for greater political support cannot, in the case of India, subserve a policy arguing against economic development, for here the revolution of rising expectations was built into the nationalist movement led by the Congress party. In the struggle for independence the Congress party became an effective mass organization and mass movement only when it was able to mobilize the peasantry and the laboring classes in the nationalist movement through voicing and vigorously supporting their economic demands and felt urges. Through its leader-

[17] Malcolm Lyall Darling, *At Freedom's Door* (London: Oxford University Press [1949]), p. 323.

ship of agrarian and labor movements the Congress party brought political awakening among farmers and workers, made them aware of a possible better life, and demonstrated to them the power of organized political action on a mass basis. Having given the Indian masses this political consciousness and this political training, the Congress party has perforce to fulfill their aspirations, for to do otherwise would be to commit political suicide.

Even if economic development were successful and resulted in higher standards of living, however, the conversion of economic prosperity into political support would ultimately depend on the political skills of the Congress party leadership. Nonetheless, given the present level of aspirations and expectations, efforts at economic development seem a necessary condition for the mobilization of political support for the Congress party. What has been the record of economic growth in the Punjab? How successful have been the various government plans? What has economic growth meant for the standards of living of the individual citizen?

The Punjab has 4.0 percent of the area of India and, in 1961, had 4.6 percent of the population of India and a population density of 430 persons per square mile compared to the average for India of 373.[18] The partition in 1947 dealt a severe blow to the economy of the state. Only 34 percent of the area and 20 percent of the irrigated area, but 47 percent of the population, of the parent province came to the share of the Punjab on the Indian side.[19] Much of the agriculturally productive area and industrial potential remained in Pakistan. Several million destitute and homeless refugees came from Pakistan, putting added strain on the economy of the fledgling state, while an equivalent number of the local population left for Pakistan, further

[18] India (Republic), *Census of India: Paper No. 1 of 1962* (Delhi: Manager of Publications, 1962), pp. XI, 5.
[19] National Council of Applied Economic Research, *Techno-Economic Survey of Punjab* (New Delhi: 1962), p. 105. (This study is hereafter referred to as *Techno-Economic Survey.*)

disrupting the economy. With a breakdown of the state's administrative machinery in the aftermath of the partition, the whole economy lay in ruins.

In a few short years the Punjab made a remarkable recovery, and its economy has since developed rapidly despite the state's many political problems. With significant assistance from the government but largely through their own efforts, the refugees were quickly rehabilitated and soon became a catalyst for economic progress rather than a burden on the economy. Economic planning within a democratic framework, which started with the first Five-Year Plan in 1951, gave further impetus to the economy. Government assistance in the form of grants and loans to farmers and industrialists has certainly been important, but of greater significance for economic growth has been "the provision of economic and social overheads." [20] The government has assumed an increasingly important role in the economy. According to one estimate, published in 1960, the government's share in capital formation in the state had increased from half to nearly two-thirds over the preceding ten years.[21]

The Punjab has achieved progress in several directions but "the rate of growth of agriculture since 1951 has, indeed, been striking." [22] In a comparative study of different states in India one economist rated the growth of agriculture in the Punjab as "phenomenally high." [23] In general, the growth rate in agriculture in the Punjab has been much higher than the rate for India as a whole.[24] The per capita net output in agriculture has been higher in the Punjab (Rs. 260) than the all-India average (Rs. 195).[25] The Punjab not only provides for its own needs

[20] Panjab University, *The Growth of Punjab Economy* (Chandigarh: Department of Economics, 1960), p. vi.7.

[21] *Ibid.*, p. vi.1.

[22] *Techno-Economic Survey*, p. 5.

[23] K. N. Raj, "Some Features of the Economic Growth of the Last Decade in India," *The Economic Weekly*, xiii, Nos. 4, 5, 6 (February 1961), 259.

[24] *Techno-Economic Survey*, pp. 15–16.

[25] *Ibid.*, p. 5.

of foodgrains, but also exports to other states in India. Over the first two five-year plans, production of foodgrains, sugarcane and cotton almost doubled.[26] The presence of a flourishing agricultural sector in the Punjab has provided an important stimulus for over-all economic growth.

Remarkable as the growth in agriculture has been, progress in the field of industry has been equally striking. Paucity of natural resources by way of raw materials for industry and the absence of great disparities in wealth and income among the people of the Punjab have inhibited much advance in the sphere of large-scale industry. However, in small-scale industry the growth has been quite rapid, even though based on the importation of raw materials. The number of registered factories in the Punjab increased from 600 in 1947 to over 4700 in 1964.[27] One source points to an increase of 225 percent over the period from 1950 to 1958 in the net value added by factories in several major industries covered by the Census of Manufacturing Industries.[28] Cement, paper, bicycles, and sewing machines all show tremendous increases. Thus, the case of the Punjab effectively demonstrates the possibilities of economic growth within a democratic framework.

The significant economic growth in the Punjab since independence may also perhaps have made for some increase in the incomes of the people though increases in price levels render this assumption doubtful. On a comparative basis, the per capita income in the state in 1960–61, according to a recent estimate, was Rs. 451 compared with the average of Rs. 333 for India as a whole.[29] The Punjab stands third among the states with the highest per capita income in India, with Ma-

[26] See the table in Rai, p. 52.

[27] Comrade Ram Kishan, Chief Minister, Punjab, "Punjab Forging Ahead," press release, January 26, 1965.

[28] J. Krishnamurty, "Some Regional Contrasts," *Seminar* (May 1964), p. 32.

[29] *The Hindu Weekly Review,* February 15, 1965, p. 5. The news report is based on a survey by the National Council of Applied Economic Research.

harashtra and West Bengal leading with Rs. 468 and Rs. 464, respectively.[30]

Two facts relating to the per capita income in the Punjab need to be noted: one, that it is higher than the all-India average despite the greater density of population in the Punjab; and, two, prosperity in the state is diffused among the people in general, unlike the big concentrations of income in the industrial areas of some other states. In both urban and rural areas unemployment as well as under-employment "is a less serious problem in Punjab than in many other States." [31] The backlog of unemployment, including frictional unemployment, amounted to 3 percent of the labor force in 1961 in the urban areas. It is believed that there is not much under-employment in the rural areas of the Punjab because of the relatively larger farms, the prevalence of better and more intensive agricultural practices, the larger area under irrigation, and the greater role of animal husbandry in the rural economy of the state.[32] In short, the Punjab occupies a privileged economic position among the states in India.

No systematic study is available on the impact, if any, of economic growth in the Punjab on the state's politics, or on the question of whether economic progress has meant increased political support for the Congress party. It may be that economic development has had no appreciable effect on the state's politics, or that it may have even alienated certain classes from the Congress party. Whatever the long-term effects of economic development, the period since independence, which has seen perhaps the fastest economic growth in the history of the Punjab, has also witnessed a series of massive political agitations of progressively increasing gravity. In addition, there is growing dissatisfaction among the economically backward classes—a result not so much of any absolute decline in their economic posi-

[30] *Loc. cit.*   [31] *Techno-Economic Survey,* p. 120.
[32] *Loc. cit.*

tion as of the greater political consciousness of their situation relative to other groups. Nor has it been established that the groups that have benefited economically, especially the land-owning castes, have provided greater political support to the Congress party. One of the best nursed constituencies in the Punjab was that of the former Chief Minister Kairon, yet in the 1962 general elections Kairon was re-elected by the bare and doubtful margin of 34 votes. Again, higher incomes and higher education may not mean the automatic erosion of com-munal loyalties. The Sikh voters of the modern city of Chandi-garh elected in 1960 an Akali representative to the Shiromani Gurdwara Parbandhak Committee (SGPC), and the Jan Sangh derives its support from the educated Hindu middle classes in the cities of Punjab.

Such considerations may militate against the notion that the Congress party necessarily gains from economic development, but there is another facet to the question of the impact of eco-nomic development on Punjab politics. Given the revolution of rising expectations among the population, the pursuit of a policy of economic stagnation must spell political disaster for the Congress party. Furthermore, the immediate effects of eco-nomic development may be undesirable from the viewpoint of some social groups, but they may also be beneficial for other groups. On the other hand, the Congress party, by vigorously pressing for a program of economic development, can sustain the belief among the disaffected groups that economic benefits for them would also be forthcoming shortly. This is especially significant in view of the fact that none of the other political parties in the Punjab, apart from the Communist party, has any economic program, or even an economic policy. Both the Akali Dal and the Jan Sangh are known for their lack of con-cern with economic questions. Under the circumstances, the fact that the Congress party can demonstrate its dedication and its ability to push forward an economic program, and also show some measure of actual economic progress, marks it out as the only party around which all who favor economic progress must rally.

At any rate, the Congress party itself appeals for popular support by proclaiming that it has been responsible for the economic progress made in the Punjab since independence. During election campaigns Congress leaders declare that the masses have more to gain through a party which is dedicated to an economic program assuring higher standards of living than from other parties whose sole concern is to arouse religious emotion and channel it in wrong and destructive directions. For example, Giani Kartar Singh reminded his audiences during the third general elections that the choice was between prosperity and Punjabi Suba and that, whereas 90 percent of the Sikhs will benefit by the prosperity which will result from economic development undertaken by the Congress party, Punjabi Suba will be detrimental to Sikh interests.[33] Also, economic development in general, and the glamor of some of the more spectacular economic projects in particular, is used to foster new loyalties cutting across religious ties. Such projects as the TVA-type Bhakra–Nangal Dam, and the picturesque and modernistic new capital of the Punjab, are presented as the "new temples," the product of economic planning under secular democracy. Nonetheless, it must be realized that economic growth by itself is no substitute for political policy. An active political strategy is imperative in converting higher incomes into political support for the party in power. For instance, higher incomes for Hindu and Sikh supporters of the Jan Sangh and Akali Dal may not necessarily mean the erosion of communal loyalties among them if such supporters believe, as a result of political vacillation and appeasement on the part of the Congress party, that their respective parties are invincible historical forces. On the other hand, the Congress party can take political advantage of having been responsible for the provision of higher incomes if

[33] *The Tribune,* February 2, 1962.

it can at the same time convince the people that the communal parties are fighting for a lost cause.

Strategy of Coalition-Building Among Various Groups

Intensive attachment to religious, linguistic, and caste ties has been deep-rooted in the history and tradition of the Indian subcontinent. In some respects, the Western impact sharpened conflicts based on loyalties to religion, language and caste. The demand for a sovereign state of Pakistan represented the apotheosis of loyalty to a single religion, and the tragic holocaust that followed the formation of Pakistan resulted in the killing of several hundred thousand persons and the uprooting of many millions. Despite the experience of the partition, loyalties to religion, language and caste have remained strong, and political claims based on such loyalties have continued to be pressed in independent India.

The Congress party, on the other hand, throughout its history has been committed to the political ideology of secular nationalism. The long-term aim of the Congress leadership is the creation of a social order in which such ties as that of religion and caste would cease to be material in politics. However, the Congress party functions within a democratic framework— a framework of its own creation—and in its endeavors to marshall political support it has had to contend with religious and caste loyalties. There may be a small core of citizens who genuinely believe in secular nationalism, but in a system that provides for adult franchise the Congress party has to secure the support of the Indian masses, a majority of them illiterate, who may feel strongly about traditional loyalties. Under such circumstances the Congress party has to take into account these loyalties in a variety of situations, such as the composition of ministries, the distribution of party tickets for elections, and in election strategy generally, notwithstanding its violent denunciations in public of the evils of communalism, casteism and provincialism.

In the final analysis, it is not merely upon the political ideology of secular nationalism that the Congress party places its reliance in securing political support but also on an adroit political strategy that seeks to construct coalitions of various groups. The important instruments that the Congress party has employed in the construction of such coalitions have been (1) political concessions; (2) co-aptation of leaders and members of other groups; (3) assurance of protection to groups; (4) economic benefits; and (5) patronage. The fact that the Congress party has been in control of the government since independence has enabled it to use these instruments effectively. Both patronage power and the ability to bestow economic benefits play an important part in the Congress party's effort to attract support from among various communal groups and to weaken communal loyalties. Important as these elements are, one must not overlook the political framework which makes their use effective. It is the secular and broad-based nature of the Congress party that enables it to use these instruments to secure support from different communal groups. For instance, with the same amount of patronage the Congress party can secure a level of political support from the Sikh community that the Jan Sangh, standing for Hindu interests, could never hope to match. It is important, therefore, to remember that political patronage and economic benefits are not self-sufficient instruments, but that their effectiveness depends on the broader political framework.

The political coalitions that the Congress party constructs, however, may not endure permanently. The reason for this is that a group, after temporarily extending support, further steps up its demands, or that the Congress party feels it necessary to accommodate another group for fear of entirely alienating it because of accommodation afforded to some other groups. Being a secular political organization, the Congress party attempts not to be too closely identified with any one single group, nor to block completely other avenues of support. It therefore has to delicately balance and aggregate the claims and aspirations of various groups. As a result, one may see over a period of time several changing coalitions, though there may be at the same time a hard core of continuing support for the Congress party. For example, during the 1952 general elections the Congress party firmly opposed the demand for Punjabi Suba and was able to win considerable Hindu and Harijan support. Prior to the 1957 general elections, the Congress party conceded the regional formula to the Akali Dal and allowed the Dal to merge politically into the Congress party; in this manner it was able to secure larger support from that part of the Sikh community which was under the influence of the Akali Dal, but in the process it also lost a large part of the Hindu vote. Before the 1962 general elections the Congress party firmly opposed the Akali demand for Punjabi Suba and refused to be intimidated by Akali agitations, and consequently was able to count on Hindu and Harijan votes to a greater extent than would have been possible if it had made further concessions to the Akali Dal.

What has been the application of this strategy to specific groups in the Punjab? How has the Congress party tried to secure the support of different groups with conflicting political claims? The politics of the Punjab since independence have been dominated either by Akali agitations or threats to launch such agitations for the achievement of political claims the Akali Dal makes on behalf of the Sikh community. The Congress party has had to undertake measures not only to secure the political support of members of the Sikh community, but also to deal with the Akali Dal politically in order to prevent the state from being thrown into constant political turmoil by Akali agitations.

As far as the major demand of the Akali Dal for Punjabi Suba is concerned, the Congress party has been quite determined in its rejection of the demand and the basis on which it has been made. However, short of conceding Punjabi Suba, the Congress party has attempted to meet the political claims of the Akali Dal. The actual concessions made have generally been couched in linguistic terms, just as the demand for Punjabi Suba itself has been. The concessions that the Congress party has extended to the Sikh community, either on its own or under pressure from the Akali Dal, have covered a wide range—parity formula, services formula, Sachar formula, regional formula, and several others. It is characteristic of the concessions made that nearly all of them were given under the pressure of a current Akali agitation, in the aftermath of an agitation, or following the threat to launch one. This fact had enhanced the value of the agitational technique for the Akali Dal, since it yielded significant results. Significantly, the major political concessions were either preceded or followed by political support to the Congress party on the part of the Akali Dal, but such support has always been temporary.

Although the concessions made by the Congress party brought only temporary support, they made for a more sustained support for the Akali Dal among the Sikhs, insofar as they enabled the Akali Dal to establish for itself an image of an inexorable historical force moving toward the inevitable accomplishment of its political aims. It is in this context that the Akali agitation during 1960 and 1961, or rather the government's response to it, may constitute a watershed in the relations between the Akali Dal and the Congress party. The failure of that agitation, it is believed, is likely to lead to erosion of support for the Akali Dal among the Sikh masses, including the intelligentsia, as the illusion of the organization's invincibility was damaged in the process. It may be premature to say, but one may raise the question of whether the loss of one-fifth of the vote in 1962, compared to the Akali vote in 1952, is conclusive evidence for the foregoing belief. Despite the fact that the Congress party was finally moved to taking a determined stand on the Akali demand, it did over the years make several substantial concessions to the Akali Dal, over the vigorous opposition of the Hindus and Harijan Sikhs.

The policy of co-aptation adopted by the Congress party in relation to the Akali Dal to secure its political support has complemented the Akali Dal's own infiltrational strategy. In 1948, and again in 1956, the Congress party co-opted Akali leadership on a large scale and even provided positions in the state ministry to former Akali leaders who had been agitating against it. However, the Congress policy of co-aptation did not deter the Akali Dal from reviving the demand for Punjabi Suba and launching more agitations in support of it. It is apparently the conviction of Congress leaders that co-aptation had only served to import into a secular nationalist organization, like the Congress party, large numbers of leaders who had achieved prominence on a communal appeal, without a corresponding reduction in Akali activities for Punjabi Suba, that seems to have brought the policy of massive co-aptation in relation to the Akali Dal to something of a halt. Although the policy of co-aptation emphasized for some that opposition—rather than support—to the government was a rapid pathway to positions of power, and even led to some demoralization among Congress Sikhs with a long record of service in the Congress party, there is little doubt that it also weakened the subsequent political activities of the Akali Dal, as former party stalwarts, with their areas of local support, continued to function in the Congress party and support its program.

In addition to the political concessions made to the Akali Dal, which directly or indirectly served to secure some support from the Sikh community, the Congress party has pursued a liberal and generous policy, insofar as positions of opportunity and political power are concerned, toward Sikhs in general as well as those in the Congress party. In fact, Congress Sikh leaders emphasize, when appealing for political support from

Sikhs, that the Sikhs have and can get more through the Congress party than otherwise. One such statement led *The Tribune* to comment editorially:

> In order to fight the communalist demand for this, that and the other, it has become necessary to adopt the communal tactic and to say that the alternative policy advocated will bring far greater and exclusive benefits to the community than the communal policy would. . . . The Punjab has not solved the communal problem; it has subjected it to a kind of super-strategy in which the people at the top are allowing a certain latitude which they believe to be temporary and a prophylactic against communalism, to persons who, in their turn, believe that what is intended to be temporary is in fact the thin end of the wedge and can be made permanent. It remains to be seen whose is the superior strategy. S. Partap Singh too has had to resort to the same argument when he offered, through the Congress, a prestige for the Sikhs far superior to anything that communalism could tempt them with. "Join the Congress in large numbers," he said.[34]

During election campaigns Congress Sikh leaders stress the need for communal harmony and Hindu-Sikh unity but they also emphasize, when addressing Sikh audiences, that the interests of the Sikhs as a community can be better served through the Congress party than through the Akali Dal. In fact, some of them even say that they are Akalis. Chief Minister Kairon himself remarked at one election meeting that he was still an Akali at heart and that he had left Master Tara Singh, but not the Akali Dal.[35] Another Congress Sikh leader, running for parliament, told an election meeting: "Wahe Guru ji ka Khalsa, Wahe Guru ji ki Fateh! The Congress is bound to win in the elections, for other parties have not even set up candidates for

[34] *The Tribune,* November 22, 1950.
[35] Speech at village Dholan in Jagraon assembly constituency, Ludhiana district, on February 13, 1962.

all the constituencies. The Congress will have control of the treasury, and it alone can give you benefit. Send somebody to the legislature who can get your work done from Partap Singh Kairon, not one who disrespects him. . . . The Congress is making a Punjabi Suba which is larger, more prosperous than the one Master Tara Singh has in mind. Punjabi language will flourish more this way, more people will speak the Punjabi language. Panjab University is being established. These are the ways to make Punjabi Suba. What has the Akali Dal done for Punjabi? They have no program except shouting slogans for Punjabi Suba. I also am an Akali. I also went to jail in the Akali movement. Let us take the country forward. Agitations only waste resources. If there is no Hindu-Sikh unity, Punjab will be destroyed." [36]

The Congress party thus makes political appeals on the basis of adopting various measures favorable to the Sikh community and, if election statistics are sufficient evidence, it has been able to maintain for itself a significant level of support from the community or, at least, to deprive the Akali Dal of majority support among the Sikhs. At the same time, the cumulative effect of these measures has been to generate strong resentment against the party among the Hindus, who constitute the majority community in the Punjab. Such resentment against the Congress party for grievances, imagined or real, has been mounting over the years as the Hindus have watched the Akali Dal obtain one concesion after another from the Congress party —concessions which the Hindus believe to have been made to the complete detriment of their interests and in utter contempt for their sentiments. The appointment of the Das commission by the Indian government in 1961 to inquire into charges of discrimination against the Sikhs in the Punjab made for a curious spectacle—whereas the Akali Dal, which for years had been vociferous about such charges, refused to provide evidence before the commission, Hindu leaders now vigorously de-

[36] From field notes; speech delivered in Punjabi.

manded that the terms of reference of the commission be widened to include an inquiry into discrimination against the Hindu community in the Punjab. The government did not agree to the proposals to widen the commission's terms of reference, but Hindu organizations and leaders presented memoranda to the commission just the same.

The grievances that Hindu organizations, such as the Jan Sangh, Arya Samaj, and Hindi Raksha Samiti, and their spokesmen articulate make an extensive list. In the first place, there are charges of government discrimination against the geographical area which is overwhelmingly Hindu, the Hindi-speaking region. The debates of the Punjab legislature and the Punjab newspapers are filled with speeches by leaders from the Hindi-speaking region about the discriminatory treatment given to the region in the matter of representation in the political councils and in the public services of the state, and in the economic development of the area and allocation of funds and patronage.

Though the Hindi region contains over 43 percent of the state's population and covers nearly 60 percent of the state's territory, it is complained, it has never received adequate representation in the cabinet and the ministers usually included are weak leaders with unimportant portfolios. The basic cause for this complaint lies in the fact that the Sikhs, with about 35 percent of the population and Hindus with over 60 percent of the population, are given equal representation in the cabinet. Even stronger is the case for the inadequacy of the Hindi region's representation in the public services. Among the gazetted officers of the Punjab government the Hindi region, with 43 percent of the population, has a share of only "about 5 percent, it may be a little more." [37]

The backward state of the economy in the Hindi-speaking

[37] Sher Singh, *The Case of Haryana and Hindi Region of the Punjab* (Rohtak: Haryana Lok Smiti, 1962), p. 23. A comparative statement of lists of officers in the various departments of the Punjab government appears on pp. 35–38 of his pamphlet.

region, compared to the Punjabi-speaking region, provides further material for grievances against the government, for government policies are held responsible for the backwardness. It is alleged that in the Hindi region less than one-third of the net sown area is under irrigation compared with more than two-thirds in the Punjabi region.[38] The number of electrified villages in the Hindi region is said to be only one-fourth of those in the Punjabi region.[39] Similar facts and figures are cited for factories established, loans granted for starting industries, the assets of cooperative banks, the number of truck permits issued, the number of institutions of higher learning and of students admitted to engineering colleges, and so forth.[40] The Punjab government maintains, with some validity, that it is now spending more in the Hindi region in proportion to the region's population.[41] However, the disparities in economic development and in representation in the public services between the two regions are so wide that any charges of discrimination carry immediate conviction with the people of the Hindi region. The Hindi-speaking region is likely to become an area of serious concern for the Congress party in the future in its attempt to mobilize political support. "They do not want any reward, they only want a fair share and equal treatment," pointed out one Hariana leader, and warned that "nobody could be expected to tolerate a differential treatment for long." [42]

Beyond the complaints about government discrimination against the Hindu-majority region, there are several other grievances that Hindu leaders voice in relation to the policies pursued by the Congress party and government vis-à-vis the Hindu community. The language policy of the government seems to evoke the most resentment. While maintaining that they have nothing against the Punjabi language as such, they hold compulsion in the study of Punjabi as intolerable and be-

[38] *Ibid.*, p. 15.   [39] *Ibid.*, p. 19.   [40] *Ibid.*, pp. 19–23.
[41] Punjab, *Stronger Punjab Through Unity, Not Turmoil* (Chandigarh: Public Relations Department, 1960), pp. 11–12.
[42] Sher Singh, p. 4.

lieve that "this ugly situation has been created because the Government wanted somehow to placate the Sikhs." [43] When, in 1962, Punjabi was made the official language for district administration in the Punjabi-speaking region, as was Hindi in the Hindi-speaking region, the Hindus charged that this was a discriminatory policy as they, who constituted 45 percent of the region's population, "still claim Hindi as their language." [44] The Hindus especially object to being "forced under the compulsion of law to accept a script, which is primarily a religious script." [45] In 1957 several Hindu organizations launched an agitation against the government's language policy. Some 30,000 volunteers participated in the agitation and about 8,000 were arrested, but without any material results. In 1960 the regional committee for the Hindi-speaking region passed a unanimous resolution for the removal of compulsion in the study of Punjabi, but with no response from the government.[46]

There is also resentment over the fact that "the Government of India generally ignores them whenever it has to settle any Punjab problem." [47] It is alleged that the Sachar formula was a secret compromise and that it "has no legislative sanction even today, but it is being implemented much against the will of the majority of the people living in the Punjab." [48] Resentment among the Hindus ran especially deep in relation to the regional formula, wherein they saw a "clear and unashamed attempt at appeasing the communal intransigence of the Akalis at the cost of the wider interests of Punjab and the country as a whole." The Jan Sangh wanted the political problem of the Punjab settled through a round table conference rather than a bilateral settlement between the government and the Akali Dal.[49] Referring to the government's concern for the opinion

---

[43] "Memorandum by Punjab Hindi Raksha Samiti," p. 6. (typescript.) This memorandum was submitted to the Das commission in January 1962; (hereafter referred to as HRS Memorandum).

[44] *Ibid.*, p. 9.   [45] *Ibid.*, p. 7.   [46] Sher Singh, pp. 7–9.

[47] HRS Memorandum, p. 14.   [48] Sher Singh, pp. 33–34.

[49] *The Times of India*, May 28, 1956.

of other political groups, one Jan Sangh leader asked in behalf of the Hindus, "What about our sentiments? Are we dumb-driven cattle?" [50] The government, however, ignored such demands and pleas. A former Congress leader has charged that "the So-called Regional Formula was the result of a Secret Compromise of the Government with the Akalis. Even the five man Committee appointed by the Punjab Pradesh Congress Committee (of which I was a member) was not taken into Confidence." [51]

The Hindi Raksha Samiti's memorandum to the Das commission also extensively documented the unequal share given to Hindus in the public services and in political offices in the government and the Congress party in the Punjab. It complained that "the fact is that the Government and the Congress have given all the political power and patronage to the Sikhs in the Punjab. Though the Hindu population of the State is 70% yet they are nowhere in the picture." [52] With a substantial amount of statistics on the senior cadres in the major departments of the Punjab government, the memorandum concluded that "the Sikhs have much more representation in the services than their population." [53] In relation to the central government it made special note of the fact that "since independence, no Hindu from the Punjab has been given any position in the Central Cabinet." [54] Proceeding to the Congress party organization, the Hindi Raksha Samiti in its memorandum complained that the Sikhs have, in proportion to their population, a much larger representation on the working committee of the Punjab Congress, and that "no Hindu has been taken on the Congress Working Committee [of the Indian National Congress] since independence. Punjab has always been represented by a Sikh in the Working Committee." [55] Representation for the Punjab on any committee appointed by the central government or Con-

[50] Statement by Krishan Lal, *The Tribune,* June 13, 1956.
[51] Sher Singh, p. 8.
[52] HRS Memorandum, appendix, p. 1.   [53] *Ibid.,* p. 10.
[54] *Ibid.,* appendix, p. 1.   [55] *Ibid.,* appendix, p. 2.

gress party, it noted, "generally goes to a Sikh." [56] The Samiti
stated that "it sometimes looks as if there has been a planned
endeavour to boost up the Sikhs and reduce the political importance of the Hindus." [57] The complaint by the Samiti that
"no Hindu has been elected President of the Punjab Pradesh
Congress Committee since independence" is, however, no
longer valid since a Hindu was appointed to the position in
1963. While maintaining that "the Hindus of the Punjab are
not against giving a fair treatment to the Sikh community,"
the Samiti felt that "no community should be ignored, as it is
being done in the case of Hindus. Though they are in majority
of 70%, yet they have been reduced to worse than a minority." [58]

The predominance of Sikhs in positions of political power
in the government and Congress party organization up to 1964
led to criticism that this predominance was used to further the
interests of the Sikh community at the expense of those of the
Hindu community. It was charged that the ministries are so
constituted as to include powerful Sikh representatives but only
weak and unrepresentative Hindu leaders and that a larger
number of ministerial portfolios and the more important portfolios were given to Sikh leaders. It has further been alleged
that important decisions, such as the postponement of nationalization of the transport business, have been made to favor Sikh
interests. Complaints have also been made that Hindu schools
have been discriminated against in the allocation of grants-in-
aid by the government to various schools. [59]

Hindu leaders find evidence of discrimination against their
community especially in the representation in the legislature
and in the allocation of party tickets, as these can be conveniently demonstrated with statistics. The Hindi Raksha Samiti's memorandum commented that "while Sikhs' population
in the Punjabi Region is 55%, they got 70% seats, on the other

[56] *Ibid.,* p. 10.   [57] *Ibid.,* p. 12.
[58] *Ibid.,* p. 14.   [59] *Ibid.,* p. 13.

hand, though the population of the Hindus is 45%, their representation in the Punjabi Region was reduced to 30%." [60] The issue of representation for the Hindu community in the Punjab legislature took a dramatic turn on the eve of the third general elections in 1962, when the Congress party's own vice-president protested against discrimination toward Hindus in the distribution of party nominations. He argued that, on the basis of population in the Punjabi region, Sikhs should be allotted 49 seats and Hindus 40 seats, but that in fact Hindus had been given only 25 seats. He further pointed out that by giving to Sikh leaders 11 out of 13 seats for the parliament from the Punjabi-speaking region, Hindus had been denied their rightful share. [61] When he eventually resigned from the Congress party in February 1962, the former vice-president reiterated his charges of discrimination against Hindus but stated that "if anybody protests against it he is immediately dubbed as a communalist by the rank communalist leaders of Punjab." [62] Congress leaders justified, in private, that they are primarily interested in winning the maximum number of seats, and that the religious composition of the constituencies dictated the final allocation of tickets. On the other hand, Hindu leaders pointed out—as indeed the vice-president of the Congress himself did—that there were several constituencies where Hindus were in a majority and were in the past represented by Hindu legislators, but had now been allocated for Sikh candidates. Moreover, Hindu leaders have alleged that "constituencies were formed in such a way that the Sikhs could get much more than their population justify." [63]

Some Hindu critics do not stop at merely criticizing the nationalist Sikh leaders in the Congress party for what they consider favoritism toward the Sikh community, but further allege

[60] *Ibid.*, p. 12.
[61] *The Tribune,* November 14, 1961.
[62] *Ibid.*, February 7, 1962.
[63] *Ibid.* See also Alakh Dhari, "The Punjab Elections Tangle" (mimeographed, n.d.), p. 2.

that these Congress Sikh leaders and the Akali leaders are in some sort of conspiracy to work secretly for the same goals. The fact that most of the prominent Sikh leaders now in the Congress party had at one time or another been active in the Akali Dal serves to lend plausibility to such charges among Hindu audiences. One Hindu leader who has spent most of his political life in the Congress party and at one time occupied important offices in the party and the government, wrote:

> These so-called nationalist Sikh friends are playing a very clever game. They are one with Akalis and all that the Akalis do is according to a pre-meditated plan. The morchas that they launch are the result of a plan decided upon by the Akalis and the Ex-Akalis who now call themselves Nationalists. A very prominent Ex-Akali and now a nationalist Sikh told me in June, 1960 that Sikhs are ruling over Punjab and leading an honourable life because of these morchas which they have to start after every five years, about a year and a half before the general elections, otherwise he said these Communal Congress leaders called the High Command would have finished them. The stunt of the Punjabi Suba serves a dual purpose. It is used for getting more favours for the Sikhs in all spheres.[64]

Again, he said:

> I have no doubt in my mind that Akalis and other Sikhs (who call themselves nationalists) are one and are playing a very clever game, everything is pre-planned. One raises the stunt of Punjabi Suba and the other unnerves the Prime Minister for getting more and more from him and compelling him to proceed one step further every time this slogan is raised.[65]

In support of their allegations that the Congress Sikh leaders

[64] Sher Singh, pp. 2–3.   [65] *Ibid.*, p. 30.

are no better than their Akali counterparts, Hindu newspapers remind their readers of the statement Chief Minister Kairon is supposed to have made before a group of friends, including Baldev Singh, that he had destroyed Hindu leadership in the Punjab for the next twenty years.[66] Even some of the Congress leaders recount the way Kairon squeezed out of the Congress party able Hindu leaders such as Sri Ram Sharma, Lala Jagat Narain, Professor Sher Singh, Ch. Devi Lal, Lala Kedar Nath Sehgal, Lala Bhim Sen Sachar, and prevented the rise of strong Hindu leaders in the Congress party. Some Hindu leaders have pointed out how they were brought under disciplinary action when they raised questions on behalf of their community whereas Sikh leaders have in the past, while in the Congress party, openly acted solely for the Sikh community. More specifically, they have mentioned that Kairon and other Congress Sikh leaders, at a time when Kairon was a minister in the Sachar cabinet, organized a convention of Sikhs only and passed resolutions complaining that justice was not being done to the Sikhs under the Sachar ministry.[67]

Many Hindu leaders believe that Congress Sikhs, even though in the Congress party, support and work for the goal of Punjabi Suba. They refer to the support of Congress Sikhs for the demand of Punjabi Suba at the time of the discussions over the States Reorganization Commission's report, when even the usually sedate newspaper, *The Tribune,* remarked that the contribution of Congress Sikhs to the discussion "reveals their inclination to go the whole hog with the Akali demand or expectation." [68] Some interviewees referred to the remarks Kairon made at the time of the parleys over the regional formula of 1956 when, in response to Giani Kartar Singh's suggestion that the office of Chief Minister in the Punjab should alternate be-

[66] *Pratap* (Jullundur), editorial, May 9, 1962; *Hind Samachar* (Jullundur), editorial, May 26, 1962.

[67] *Loc. cit.* See also statement of Lala Jagat Narain in *The Tribune,* August 4, 1956.

[68] *Ibid.,* editorial, December 2, 1955.

tween a Hindu and a Sikh, he reportedly said: "Gianiji, think it over seriously if it is to our benefit." [69]

Some Hindu newspapers charge that Kairon was, during his term as Chief Minister, endeavoring to establish a Punjabi Suba but that his Suba covered the entire Punjab rather than half the Punjab which the Akalis want.[70] One editorial said: "The Congress government is making the Punjab a Sikh Suba, but it is not willing to make it an Akali Suba." [71] On the other hand, some Hindu leaders maintained that Kairon was trying to lay the basis for Punjabi Suba precisely in accordance with the desires of the Akali Dal. Among other things, they pointed to the language policy of the Punjab government and the plans to reapportion administrative districts as intended to facilitate the establishment of Punjabi Suba. One Jan Sangh leader stated:

> If suppose the government creates two regions and in one region there will be absolutely one language and in another region there will be another language, then linguistically the province has been definitely divided into two regions. And if Master Tara Singh says there is linguistically a complete division then government has nothing to say against it.
>
> Therefore such steps that Partap Singh Kairon takes are definitely against the interests of the Punjab. He and other nationalist Sikhs may not consciously want Punjabi Suba but they unconsciously are working for it by advancing to meet the demands of the opposition.[72]

The delicate political position of Sikh leaders in the Congress party is obvious from the fact that, while some Hindu leaders charge them with working in league with the Akali Dal, the

[69] From interviews with two important leaders; one of the interviewees was in on these negotiations.

[70] *Pratap,* editorial, May 11, 1962; *Hind Samachar,* editorial, May 26, 1962.

[71] *Pratap,* editorial, December 7, 1961.

[72] From an interview with a Jan Sangh MLA.

Akali leaders accuse them of having sold themselves and Sikh interests to the Congress party. It is noteworthy at the same time that after a Hindu, Ram Kishan, assumed the office of Chief Minister in 1964, Akali and other Sikh leaders, and their newspapers and journals, once again began levelling charges of discrimination, by a government allegedly dominated by Arya Samaj elements, against the Sikh community in the area of language policy, patronage, appointments and promotions in the government and so forth.

In the presence of the various charges and allegations of discrimination against the Hindus, why then do Hindus in the Punjab continue to support the Congress party? Why is the Jan Sangh able to secure no more than 10 percent of the polled vote in the Punjab? Insofar as the Hindus in the Punjabi-speaking region are concerned, it seems that, despite the concessions given to the Akali Dal and the privileges extended to the Sikh community, the Congress party still remains for the Hindus the major bulwark against the formation of Punjabi Suba. As one Sikh leader explained, it is only when there is peace in the Punjab that the Hindus call Congress Sikh leaders like Partap Singh Kairon communal and complain about discrimination, but the moment there is an Akali agitation, the Hindus consider them nationalists and rally around them.[73] Not positive satisfaction with the current policies of the Congress party then, but rather its ability to resist the Akali demand for Punjabi Suba is what accounts for Hindu support of the Congress party, at least in the Punjabi-speaking region. During elections the fear of an Akali victory binds the Hindu voter to the Congress party. To vote against the Congress party would mean dividing the Hindu vote and assuring the Akalis of a majority in the Punjabi-speaking region. As one Hindu voter remarked, "for five years we curse the Congress party, but then on election day we feel we should vote for it." Moreover, the Hindus believe that with the Congress party, which

[73] From an interview.

is an all-India secular political organization, there may be hope eventually of some redress of their grievances. As one Hindu newspaper wrote: "They don't like either Kairon's policy or the policy of the Akalis but under the Congress they may be able to get some hearing; under the Akalis they will be finished." [74]

The same newspaper, while bitterly critical of Congress policies, was at the same time concerned over the tendency of strong Hindu leaders to quit the Congress party, for that, in its view, only made them politically ineffective and served to further strengthen Sikh control over the Congress party. Despite its hostility to the Congress party at the time, the newspaper advised Hindu leaders to remain in the Congress and said: "Hindus should get their things done within the Congress party. After all that's what the Akalis have done. If we keep fighting with the Congress, our political existence will be finished." [75]

For some it is unfortunate that the Jan Sangh, as an extremist spokesman of Hindu claims, has emerged as a political force of some importance in the Punjab, as it only divides the Hindus while it has no prospects of forming an alternative government either at the center or in the state. They point to strong Hindu leaders in the Congress party being defeated by Jan Sangh leaders at elections and consequently unable later to exert influence on behalf of the Hindu community in either the party organization or the government. On the other hand, others argue that only the strengthening of the anti-Congress forces will make the Congress party realize the importance of the Hindu community. However, the presence of the Akali Dal imposes limits to this anti-Congress protest on behalf of the Hindu community in the Punjabi-speaking region. In the larger cities, where they are concentrated, Hindus may success-

[74] *Pratap,* editorial, January 14, 1962.
[75] *Ibid.,* editorial, January 19, 1962. See also *ibid.,* editorial, February 3, 1962.

fully support a Hindu communal party, but in more than two-thirds of the constituencies the Sikhs are in a preponderant position, including some one-third in which they are in an absolute majority; here the Hindus can reject the Congress party only at the price of Akali victory. Therefore, the compulsions of the composition of the constituencies and the configuration of political forces dictates support of the Congress party, regardless of Hindu dissatisfaction with that party.

In the Punjabi region the Akali Dal thus looms large in leading the Hindu community to support the Congress party, but it is not a factor of any importance in the Hindi-speaking region where the Hindus are in an overwhelming majority and have no fear of the Akali Dal. Dissatisfaction with the Congress party here is not apt to be moderated by the considerations that influence the Hindu voter in the Punjabi-speaking region. In fact, if the people here were sure that their territory would not be splintered among several states, they might be happy to be severed from a state which is constantly in political turmoil and where they are denied their proper share in the administration and political councils. It is here that the more critical challenge to the Congress party may emerge, for the Hindi region, if sufficiently aroused, can weaken the ability of the Congress party to secure a majority in the legislature. In reality, the polls have already witnessed the dissatisfaction on the part of the Hindi region. The Congress party's vote fell from 46.1 percent in 1957 to 40.9 percent in 1962, whereas in the Punjabi region it fell from 48.4 percent in 1957 to only 45.8 percent in 1962. The decrease in the Congress party vote in the Hindi region is especially noteworthy since, in contrast to this region, in the Punjabi region the Akali Dal had by 1962 once again emerged as a political force whereas in 1957 it was a part of the Congress party as far as votes were concerned.

Strangely enough, the Congress party has been strongest in the area which it has most feared. It would be ironical indeed if, in the forging of policies to deal with the Akali problem in one region, disaster ensued by alienating the other region. Here, the Congress party cannot count on support, merely because of its opposition to Punjabi Suba, as it can in the Punjabi-speaking region. To be sure, in 1962, the Congress party was able to secure a larger percentage of seats relative to the percentage of votes in the Hindi region than in the Punjabi region, but it cannot rely permanently on construction of caste coalitions and a splintered opposition, though the scheduled castes or Harijans may continue to be the hard core of its political strength here as in the Punjabi region. Eventually, the Congress party will have to re-examine its policies toward the Hindi-speaking region if it expects broad-based support.

The Harijans—whether Hindu or Sikh—form a group similar to the Hindus in the Punjabi region in that their support of the Congress party is based on the protection the party gives them from more powerful groups—primarily the Sikh Jats in the Punjabi-speaking region and the Hindu Jats in the Hariana region. The Harijans support the Congress party not only because it is a secular party, taking in a multiplicity of groups, but also because of its opposition to the division of the Punjab, for they fear that the result of such a division would be to place them under the domination of the very groups they so distrust. They prefer the present boundaries of the Punjab, which contain a number of different and competing groups that have to be aggregated and accommodated in politics, rather than a single group dominant over others as they fear would be the case in Punjabi Suba or Hariana state.

Harijan support of the Congress party also stems from the specially favorable policies pursued by the party toward the Harijans not only in the Punjab but in India as a whole. Since the Harijans had been suppressed economically, politically, and socially for hundreds of years, they are genuinely grateful for such Congress policies. The Indian constitution abolished untouchability and prohibited discrimination against any citizen on grounds of caste whether in public employment or access to shops and public places. After guaranteeing equal rights to the Harijans, the constitution further laid down that "the State shall promote with special care the educational and economic interests of the weaker sections of the people." To ensure adequate political representation for the Harijans, the constitution provided for the reservation for them of legislative seats and of positions in the public services. Of the 22 seats for the Punjab in the national parliament, five are reserved for Harijans.[76] Of the 154 seats in the Punjab legislature, 33 are similarly reserved for them.[77] In the Punjab state administration, 21 percent of the positions are reserved for Harijans and other backward classes.[78]

The Congress party has been equally concerned to raise Harijan levels in the economic and social spheres. A separate department in the Punjab government is responsible for implementation of welfare programs for Harijans and other backward classes. The second Five-Year Plan provided a total sum of 26 million rupees, and the third Five-Year Plan another 34 million rupees, for welfare purposes for these classes.[79] Included among the welfare programs are: exemption from all tuition fees; monetary grants to students from the 9th grade to M.A.; free training in vocational schools and factories; grant of interest-free loans for setting up business or industry; subsidies for housing; legal assistance; subsidies for purchase of land, livestock and agricultural equipment.[80] The provision for tuition fees and scholarships accounts for half the total amount allocated, and benefits more than 200,000 students.

While there is genuine appreciation for all that the Congress party has attempted to do for them in the political, economic and social spheres—which by any definition amounts to a revolution in the Indian context—there is also a tremendous increase in new-found aspirations and unfulfilled expectations

[76] Punjab, Public Relations Department, *Harijan Welfare in Punjab* (Chandigarh: Controller, Printing and Stationery, 1961), p. 4.
[77] *Loc. cit.*   [78] *Loc. cit.*
[79] *Ibid.*, p. 14.   [80] *Ibid.*, pp. 4–13.

among the Harijans, which have occasioned a feeling of dissatisfaction with the Congress party. A special grievance relates to the Congress party's failure to provide them with land in order to cope with the problem of unemployment among their landless agricultural workers. Some Harijan leaders complain that all the privileges given by the Congress party are meaningless until Harijans receive agricultural land. In the Punjab they attribute the Congress party's failure to solve the land problem to the domination of the party by a leadership from the landowning Sikh and Hindu Jats, who are naturally unsympathetic to their needs.

The alienation of Congress Harijan leaders, especially those who get elected to legislative office, from fellow Harijans in their constituencies is partly responsible for the current dissatisfaction among the mass of the Harijans. These Harijan leaders begin to behave like higher caste persons, an action quite natural in itself, yet one that could have harmful results for the Congress party in terms of political support. Many such legislators move out of villages, set up house in town, and rarely visit their constituencies or, when they do visit a village, stay with higher caste persons rather than with their fellow Harijans. Their friendships tend to be more among the higher caste people, and they are more apt to get things done from the government for their friends than for the Harijans in the constituency.

Whatever their grievances against the Congress party, there is evidence indicating that Harijans vote overwhelmingly for the Congress party, for the Akali Dal in the Punjabi region and front organizations for the high-caste landowning classes in the Hindi region are not feasible alternatives. The Communist party in the Punjab is also identified with Sikh Jats. The Harijans appear to have solidly supported the Congress party in the 1962 general elections, and it was evidently in appreciation of their support that the Congress party shortly after the elections enacted special legislation to levy a tax in the Punjab, amounting to about 40 million rupees, in order to provide housing specifically for Harijans. If properly nursed in the future, Harijan support for the Congress party seems assured, given the configuration of political and social forces in the Punjab.

SUMMARY AND CONCLUSIONS

The Congress party has attempted to mobilize political support not merely to form the government but also to preserve the political community and maintain the constitutional order. In the present configuration of political forces, the Congress party has been the great bulwark of the new political system. Despite the serious challenge from communal parties, the Congress party has been preeminently successful in mobilizing support. In its efforts to obtain popular backing, the Congress party has combined the appeals of secular nationalism and economic progress with a political strategy of accommodating communal demands and leadership. In so doing, the Congress party has been accused of being unfaithful to its ideals but, given the political environment and the party's commitment to democracy, to act otherwise would, at least perhaps in the short run, imperil the very existence of the Congress party. To be sure, concessions to one communal group have generated resentment among others, but the newly established democratic framework and the desire of the Congress party not to be identified with any single group provide some safeguard against the long-run alienation of any group with substantial voting power. At the same time, a discussion of the patterns of political support in the Punjab points up once again that one cannot just assume social and political homogeneity for linguistic regions. Sub-regional divisions, such as those of religion and caste, in the so-called Punjabi-speaking and Hindi-speaking regions of the Punjab seem to be of greater importance in the state's politics than a common loyalty to the linguistic region.

CHAPTER VIII
Summary

As IN many other newly independent nations, the nationalist leadership in India has been faced with a variety of centrifugal political pressures. The Congress party leadership, which took over power from the British in 1947, is committed to the ideals of national unity, parliamentary democracy and the secular state. In the period since independence, however, the Congress party has had to contend with various territorial claims based on race, religion, or language. The Dravida Munnetra Kazhagam movement in south India demands the secession of territories inhabited by the "Dravidian" people, or at least of those inhabited by the Tamil-speaking people. In northeast India several of the tribes have been engaged in armed hostilities for some years now in the pursuit of a separate and sovereign Nagaland. For some writers, the different linguistic regions in India, most of them now reorganized as states within the Indian Union, are all likely to press for secession from India in the decades ahead.

One of the territorial demands which has been of major significance in Indian politics in the post-independence period is that made by the Shiromani Akali Dal in behalf of the Sikh community for the creation of Punjabi Suba, or Punjabi-speaking state, by the exclusion of certain areas from the existing state of Punjab. The demand has been made in the name of the Punjabi language, but the real purpose is believed to be the formation of a state which would be under the political control of the Sikhs. In view of the Akali goal of creating *desh-kaal* (country and era) for the Sikhs—a goal that was part of the Akali constitution until recently—and in view of the history of the Akali Dal and the explicit pronouncements of Akali leaders regarding Punjabi Suba, the linguistic argument is considered to be merely a camouflage for the eventual creation of a Sikh theocratic state. The ideal of the secular state, to which the nationalist leadership of the Congress party has been committed, thus seems threatened. There is further the unstated fear that since Punjabi Suba would border on Pakistan there may be possibilities for future secessionist claims, especially in view of past Akali demands for a sovereign Sikh state. These considerations, and the further fact that large groups—perhaps a majority of the population—in the area of the proposed Punjabi Suba oppose the demand, have persuaded the Congress party not to concede the formation of such a state.

As far as the Akali Dal is concerned, the demand for Punjabi Suba has important historical and social roots. The Sikhs were the sovereign rulers of the Punjab before it was annexed by the British in the mid-nineteenth century. Although there is dispute over the fact whether the founders of Sikhism really intended to create another religion or merely to reform Hinduism and provide it with a militant wing to confront the Muslim rulers, important segments of the Sikh community have endeavored, since the last quarter of the nineteenth century, for the separation of the Sikhs, religiously and politically, from the Hindu community. Recent reform movements in Sikhism have emphasized that the Sikhs are a separate political entity, not just a religious community, that their religion and politics are combined, and that they must have political power as a group. In the perspective of history, the demand for Punjabi Suba would seem to be yet another step in the promotion of the earlier goal of creating a separate political entity of the Sikhs apart from the Hindus. However, the Akali leadership deems Punjabi Suba especially important today because of the alleged modern tendency among Sikhs toward unorthodoxy in the observance of the prescribed external symbols, most prominently the wearing of unshorn hair on the body. It is feared that religious unorthodoxy among Sikhs would mean their assimilation into Hinduism, because the two religions are said to have the same philosophical foundation and the two religious groups have close social and cultural relations. Political power in the hands of the Sikh community in the proposed Punjabi Suba, it is believed, would help stem such religious unorthodoxy through coercion or otherwise.

Notwithstanding the refusal of the nationalist leadership to concede the demand for Punjabi Suba, the Akali leadership has persisted in pressing for it with great vigor. In the pursuit of its demand, the Akali leadership has had the use of substantial manpower and organizational and financial resources. As a political party, the Akali Dal considers itself to be the sole representative of the Panth, and even equates itself with the Panth. To the extent that it can maintain its claim to be the sole agent of the Panth, the Akali Dal becomes heir to a great tradition of political and military organization, for the Panth is considered to have been originally founded as a Leninist-type organization of "the elite, the chosen, the pure." The overthrow of Muslim rule and the establishment of Sikh sovereignty in the Punjab in the mid-eighteenth century is a testimony to the organization and militancy of the Sikhs, who did not constitute a very large group at the time. The high level of organization among the Sikhs today is apparent in the existence, apart from the thousands of local associations, of a central committee (SGPC) to manage all Sikh historic shrines in the Punjab.

The SGPC, elected by the Sikh adult population, manages an annual budget of some 6 million rupees. Because of its contribution to the movement for the reform of Sikh shrines in the 1920s, and its extremist claims in behalf of the Sikh community, the Akali Dal has invariably been voted to power in the SGPC and has consequently controlled the resources of the SGPC over a period of forty years. Control over the SGPC provides the Akali Dal with vast powers of patronage. In addition to the appointment of staff in an extensive network of shrines spread all over the Punjab, the power to spend funds for any non-political purpose enables the Akali Dal to secure political support from strategic groups. The SGPC further provides the Akali Dal with the opportunity to combine the dissemination of the Akali ideology with the propagation of Sikhism. The shrines also serve as the privileged sanctuaries from which anti-government agitations can be launched.

The Akali Dal has made quite effective use of its considerable resources for the accomplishment of its political demands. Though public attention has usually focused on the more spectacular methods employed by it, the Akali Dal has, in fact, pursued the goal of Punjabi Suba at several levels of political activity. Three major strategies seem to have been used by the Akali Dal for extracting political concessions from the government: One, the constitutional strategy, under which Akali leaders make use of the political institutions established by the Indian constitution. They submit memoranda and petitions, wait in deputation on important officials and ministers, resort to courts, arrange public meetings and mass rallies, organize long marches, publicize their views through the mass media, and participate in the parliamentary and electoral processes. Two, the infiltrational strategy, under which Akali leaders and members join the Congress party on a large scale to exploit factional divisions within the Congress party and to secure significant political concessions from within while other Akali leaders put pressure from without through agitations. Three, the agitational strategy, under which Akali leaders launch massive agitations from the privileged sanctuaries of Sikh shrines and attempt to overwhelm the government by sending out endlessly quasi-military formations that deliberately violate the law in an endeavor to pack the jails and paralyze the government machinery. The objective here is to intimidate the government by creating an imminent threat to peace and stability, and coerce it into making concessions.

Although Akali leaders have been able to secure significant political concessions toward their demand for Punjabi Suba through these strategies, yet they have met with stubborn opposition insofar as the substance of the demand is concerned.

In the first place, opposition to Punjabi Suba is rooted in the nature of social diversity in the Punjab state and in the area which the Akali Dal wants constituted into Punjabi Suba. Though Punjabi Suba would have a Sikh majority, the area is not exclusively Sikh; the Sikhs would form only about 55 percent of the population. The Hindus who would form about 42 percent of the population of this Suba are opposed to its formation because of their belief that a Sikh majority state would, in view of the Akali ideology, mean theocratic rule of the Sikhs. Understandably, it is not easy to form Punjabi Suba in the face of strong opposition from such a substantial part of the population.

Important as the opposition of the Hindus is, there are other elements in the political and social situation of the Sikh community itself that militate against the formation of Punjabi Suba. Though the claim is made that Sikhism requires its members to act as a single united group, wherein individuals *qua* individuals have no right to join another political group, the evidence of history is that the Sikh community has always been divided into more than one group, at times violently in conflict with each other. Such divisions in the past, as today, have been based on differing economic and political interests, and on differing doctrinal interpretations, but the major social division is that of caste which divides the Sikhs into Harijan Sikhs and non-Harijan Sikhs. This division in the Sikh community serves to repudiate the doctrine of the Sikhs being a single political entity and the Akali Dal's claim of being the sole representative of the Sikh community. The Harijan Sikhs oppose the demand for Punjabi Suba because of their fear that, as an economically and socially underprivileged group, they would come under even greater political domination by the non-Harijan Sikhs. The Harijans of today are socially and politically mobilized, and have to be reckoned with. By opposing the claims of the Akali Dal, they destroy the right of that organization to speak in the name of the total Sikh community.

Caste divisions thus seem to assume great importance where the question of political power and political domination emerges as between different caste groups. This is apparent in another area of the Punjab also. There have been demands for the formation of a state consisting of the overwhelmingly Hindu-majority area of Hariana in the Punjab. But here too the Harijans have opposed the demand for Hariana state because of their fear of being dominated by the Jat Hindus. The Harijans of Hariana area, like the Harijans in the Sikh-majority area, prefer to live in the larger state of Punjab where there is a larger number of groups whose demands and aspirations have to be accommodated and aggregated. Political interests of a caste group thus override here any loyalty to a religious group or a linguistic region.

In the final analysis, the Akali Dal in the pursuit of any communal demand, to which other important groups like the Hindus and Harijans are opposed, must contend with the government. The Congress party as a secular, broad-based party has since independence been in power in the Punjab as well as at the center and in other states of India. However, even if the Congress party were not in power in the Punjab, the Akali Dal would still have to face opposition from the government. An important political implication of the social diversity in the Punjab is that, given a democratic framework, only a political party or coalition, which is secular and broad-based, can remain in power in the government of the state. On the one hand, no single religious, caste, or sectional group constitutes a solid enough majority to form the government by itself. As a religious category, the Hindus do form a majority of over 60 percent in the Punjab as a whole, but the community is cut across by caste and economic divisions which would make it impossible for it to act as a single political unit. On the other hand, the religious and sectional minorities in the Punjab are not small and insignificant, but substantial minorities. There could be no peace in the state if the government were under the control of a communal party that worked for the interests of a single caste or religious group. The bias for a secular, broad-based political party, rather than a communal party, is thus built into the nature of social diversity in the Punjab. Therefore, any party that makes communal demands would have to reckon with resistance on the part of the government in addition to the other opposing groups.

The resources of the government in the Punjab in meeting the Akali challenge are enormous and far-reaching. Apart from the coercive instruments at the disposal of the state, political power and patronage can be obtained only through the Congress party, which is in control of the government. Outside the Congress party there is no political salvation. This is a vital factor, indeed, in the periodic shifts of political leaders from the Akali Dal to the Congress party. The Akali Dal may have a strong political appeal among a significant segment of the Sikh community, but since it restricts itself to the Sikh community it must remain a permanent political minority. As a consequence, it is unable to hold its leaders and members permanently in a political environment which provides adequate opportunities to share in political power through a secular, broad-based party like the Congress party. The Akali appeal may be a useful instrument for recruitment to leadership, but does not seem to be adequate in ensuring a sustained commitment to the organization. The period since independence has seen two large-scale migrations of Akali leaders to the Congress party. It is quite likely that there may be some tension between a continuing loyalty to the Akali ideology and the pursuit of personal goals among those Akali leaders who join the Congress party, but most of those who joined the Congress party have not left it even when the two organizations have been in bitter conflict.

Apart from the attraction of political power, the government has developed other important resources, which are the result of a remarkable change in the conception of the functions of government in India. In contrast to the earlier notion of government as merely an instrument for political order and stability, the government in India today is an active agent for economic development and social change. As a result of vigorous government intervention in the economy, the magnitude of government resources has increased tremendously. The government is a veritable economic leviathan compared to the other economic groups in society. The resulting increased resources of the government have important implications for its role in meeting the Akali challenge. The ability of the government to provide goods, services, and patronage is enhanced and with it the ability to secure greater political support. Expenditures on developmental and social services have increased progressively and tremendously over the years; they formed over 60 percent of the state's budget for 1961–62. The revenue expenditure budget for 1964–65 amounted to more than 1,120,000,000 rupees; the annual budget of the SGPC seems in contrast rather insignificant. Further, the government's active role in economic development and planning has provided it with important levers of control over the entire economy. These levers of control give the government tremendous power to secure support from important sections of the population. A comparative study of the resources of the Congress party and the Akali Dal would indicate that the former is more than adequately equipped at all levels to meet the challenge of the Akali Dal.

In order to utilize the various resources that go with the state government, however, the Congress party must secure a popular mandate since it functions within a democratic framework. Through three successive elections the Congress party has made significant progress in mobilizing political support for itself. The Congress party has further been able to demonstrate effectively that the Akali Dal does not command the support of a majority of even the Sikh community. In the 1962 general elections, the Akali Dal was able to secure no more than 40 percent of the Sikh vote.

Several factors account for the popular support given to the Congress party. (1) First is the very nature and status of the Congress party. Being a secular, broad-based party of an all-India character amidst various communal and sectional parties, the Congress party is in a better position to take advantage of the bias for such a party resulting from the nature of social diversity in the Punjab. The assured control of the center by the Congress party further enables it to exercise decisive influence in favor of its state branches. Moreover, the Congress party has the strongest political machine in India, backed by several decades of political experience. Again, there is some regard for the many sacrifices its leaders underwent during the struggle for freedom. (2) The control over the state government by the Congress party provides it with an opportunity to utilize government resources to enhance its political position. (3) Then there is the Congress party's dedication to economic development and planning. Among the different parties in the Punjab, the Congress party alone has an economic program assuring higher standards of living for the people. (4) The strategy of coalition-building among various social groups is crucial in mobilizing political support for the Congress party. Although the Congress party is committed to a secular polity, it has to function within a democratic system and among a population in which loyalties to religion, language and caste are strong. As a consequence, the Congress party is obliged to take these loyalties into account. Apart from the appeal of the political ideology of secular nationalism then, the Congress party attempts to construct coalitions of various groups in its efforts to mobilize political support. It has employed several important instruments in the building of such coalitions: (a) political concessions; (b) co-aptation of leaders and members of other groups; (c) assurance of protection to some groups; (d) economic benefits; and (e) patronage. The party's control over the state government since independence has helped it to make effective use of these instruments, especially since their use has been accompanied by an ideological commitment and a political policy assuring protection to all minority groups.

By demonstrating through the electoral process that the Akali Dal does not command popular support, the Congress leadership has weakened the Akali case to some extent. On the other hand, by making significant political concessions it has demonstrated its own capacity for generosity and fairness. But under Nehru's leadership, the Congress party refused to concede the demand for Punjabi Suba; in its view, to do so would have been to undermine both the secular state and national unity. During the 1960–61 Akali agitation, when some 26,000 Akalis went to jail and two top Akali leaders went on a fast-unto-death, the government did not yield and remained firm in its refusal to concede Punjabi Suba. Insofar as the demand for Punjabi Suba is concerned, the Akali Dal seemed then to have reached somewhat of an impasse. It is interesting to note that, despite its many political skills, the Akali leadership has found it difficult to employ the same political strategy successfully more than once, for the Congress party also learns from experience. By 1962, at any rate, the Akali Dal seemed to have used all the strategies that it was apparently capable of. Its unsuccessful attempt to coerce the government plus the resulting dissensions within the Akali ranks appeared to adversely affect its attempts to secure electoral support. Compared to the 1952 elections, the Akali Dal lost one-fifth of its popular vote in the 1962 elections. A recourse to violence, while an attractive alternative for some, is not likely to get much support because the Sikh community has too much at stake in the present regime. Moreover, given the powers of the existing government, no policy of violence is likely to succeed under the present circumstances. Nonetheless, by 1965, the Akali Dal was again pressing with great vigor for its demand of Punjabi Suba.

Whatever the disposition of the demand for Punjabi Suba—

and the government has tremendous resources to successfully confront and overwhelm, if it is so minded, any Akali challenge—the Congress party will have to live with the "irritant" of a continuous conflict in one form or another. Eventually the Congress party may be able to weaken the Akali Dal by attracting, through the proper use of its resources, even greater political support for itself from among the Sikhs. Given the religious underpinnings of the demand for Punjabi Suba, however, it would be idle to expect that the Akali challenge would swiftly vanish. Indeed, it is the potency of the Akali appeal that is the basis of the challenge to the Congress party. Were it not so, the various large-scale shifts of Akali leaders to the Congress party would have incapacitated it from future political activity. Furthermore, though the resources of the Akali Dal seem comparatively small they are sizable enough for the creation of political instability in the Punjab. Of greater significance is the fact that the Akali resources cannot be taken away, since any attempt to do so would be bitterly opposed not only by the Akali Dal but also by the Sikh community, as the resources are connected with religious shrines. The path of wisdom for the Congress party would thus seem to lie in the realization of its own tremendous strength and simultaneously the necessity of patience in the years ahead. The record of its ability to meet the Akali challenge in the past should also at the same time serve to sustain its faith in its ability to handle similar problems in other areas of India, for few groups in India compare with the Akali Dal in militancy, organizational skills, and manpower and financial resources.

What lessons can one draw for the larger question of national unity in India from this study of the Punjab? The general literature on Indian politics usually lists and describes—in the study of prospects for political stability and national unity —the various social cleavages in Indian society and discusses the disintegrative effects of each cleavage for Indian unity, but does not examine the dynamic relationships between the cleavages themselves.[1] Thus the linguistic regions are held to be potential bases for secessionist movements, and at the same time caste is considered disintegrative of Indian society. The political pressures resulting from loyalty to both language and caste, it is suggested, tend to the inevitable balkanization of India. Underlying this viewpoint is the conception that all social cleavages by themselves, without any consideration of their mutual relationships, are inherently detrimental to national unity, and that social conflict as such is bad. Since language divides society, and so does caste, it is assumed that the two together present a graver danger to national unity than each by itself would. The danger more heavily emphasized is the splitting up of India into as many independent states as there are linguistic regions.

For any student of the social sciences, however, the important undertaking in the study of social and political conflict must be not merely the recounting of different cleavages in society, but an examination of the relationships between them. One should ask, after Dahrendorf,[2] whether there is a "superimposition," "congruence," or "dissociation" among different conflict groups. Where conflict groups are dissociated, or they cross-cut each other, the intensity of conflict will be less than where they are superimposed on each other.[3] Indeed, where there is dissociation or cross-cutting among conflict groups, a greater number of conflict groups is likely to reduce the intensity of social conflict by preventing the investment of energy into a few major conflicts.[4] It is in this context that one must examine the various cleavages in Indian society in relation to the question of the viability of the Indian nation, and it is here that our study of the Punjab is instructive.

[1] For an excellent illustration of this approach, see Selig S. Harrison, *India: The Most Dangerous Decades* (Princeton: Princeton University Press, 1960). See also Naresh Chandra Ray, *Federalism and Linguistic States* (Calcutta: Firma K. L. Mukhopadhyay, 1962).

[2] Ralf Dahrendorf, *Class and Class Conflict in Industrial Society* (Stanford: Stanford University Press, 1959), pp. 213–39.

[3] *Ibid.*, p. 239.

[4] *Ibid.*, p. 215.

In inquiring into the demand for a Punjabi-speaking state, we found that the population which supposedly spoke Punjabi split along religious lines over the reorganization of the state on a linguistic basis. It may be argued that the Punjab is an exceptional case, with the presence of two substantial religious groups. But even more significant than the split along religious lines is the division within the Sikh community between Harijan and non-Harijan Sikhs, with the Harijan Sikhs opposing the demand for Punjabi Suba because of their fear of complete domination by the non-Harijan Sikhs in a smaller state. The non-Harijan Sikhs are further divided into Jats and non-Jats, which division also is of some importance in the politics of the Punjab. Again, the Hindus in the Hariana region are split between Jats and Harijans, and the Harijans oppose the demand for a separate Hariana state for precisely the same reasons that Harijan Sikhs oppose the demand for Punjabi Suba.

In other words, one does not find in the Punjab any over-all loyalty to the region as against the center. Instead, there are divisions within the region and, while some may desire greater autonomy or even separation, others resist such demands and look to the center for support. Although the split along religious lines may be peculiar to the Punjab, the cleavage along caste lines is of universal significance in India. Indeed, it could be argued that it is the very weakness of caste in the Punjab that has made for a substantial polarization along religious lines. At any rate, loyalty to a linguistic region is cut across by religion and caste as well as by class. The linguistic region therefore does not present a united front against the center but, on the contrary, constantly seeks the latter's intervention in order to moderate the conflict between the various groups within the region.

Another study of politics in Andhra state provides evidence in support of the foregoing analysis.[5] Here, the two potent caste groups of the Kammas and Reddis bitterly oppose each

[5] Harrison, pp. 204–45.

other. As in the case of the Punjab, while such sub-regional groups may compete or cooperate within a linguistic region, which is part of the larger Indian political system, one group or another is not likely to countenance, for fear of domination, any proposal or project for secession, but will instead depend on the center for protection. And one should not underestimate the power of substantial sub-regional groups and the leverage they provide the center in maintaining a viable political system. The suspension of the Communist ministry in Kerala in 1959 provided ample testimony of how sub-regional groups, whether based on caste, class, or religion, strengthen the hands of the center, not so much because they are in any sense in collaboration with the center, but because the center stands above the intra-regional conflicts. Here was a case where one section of a regional linguistic group appealed to the center against another section of the same linguistic group. One finds thus that there is no simple correlation between cleavages on the one hand and disintegration on the other, but rather a complex relationship which may often serve to sustain a strong and viable center. One can make this point over and over again for most of the linguistic regions in India.

The fundamental difference between the analysis (1) that solely concerns itself with loyalty to a linguistic region and, though mentioning sub-regional cleavages, fails to evaluate their impact on such loyalty, which then is assumed to be pushing the region toward secession, and the analysis here presented (2) which examines the inter-relationships between loyalties to regional and sub-regional groups, can be seen in the following diagram.

The question may be raised that to emphasize the role of caste divisions in this manner may only indicate the direction for balkanization on an even larger scale than would be the case if linguistic regions alone were the objects of loyalty. However, the noteworthy aspect of caste divisions is that any caste group is dispersed over a large territory and does not constitute,

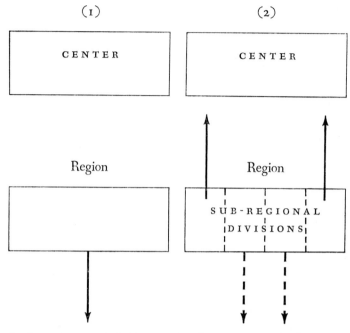

in the main, a majority in any significant portion of a linguistic region. Caste divides not merely the region, but every town and village in it. As a consequence, it does not present a territorially-based threat of its own. We find therefore that though caste divides society it does so at the regional level. By weakening loyalty to a linguistic region it becomes, in turn, a significant factor in promoting national unity. The fact that structural factors like caste, and not simply the exhortations of political leaders, should serve to strengthen national unity may not necessarily appeal to the modern-day Indian intellectual; however, one must realize that political goals in actual life are often achieved in unintended ways, and that the role of traditional institutions in a modern setting calls not for a visceral reaction but for unemotional analysis.

The fact that different social and economic groups within the various linguistic regions can and do look to the center for protection has been possible precisely because the center is not under the domination of any single group. The center has been able to play, in large measure, the role of an umpire or impartial judge, though in this case the role is backed by instruments of tremendous power. Was such a situation in the past a result of the personality and appeal of Jawaharlal Nehru? To some extent, perhaps yes. But to a large extent, this role for the center is built into the nature of Indian society and polity. Here, again, diversity is the key, with diversity understood not only from the social and economic viewpoint but also from the viewpoint of India's sheer geographical size.

The great diversity within India assures a center that is not identified with any state or set of states, apart from any intra-state group, because no state or coalition of states can wield a permanent majority at the center. Such would not be the case if a single cleavage, for example, divided society into a majority group and a minority group. To be sure, charges are made from time to time about the domination of the center by one state or another, but without substantial evidence. Any tenacious attempt to demonstrate such a domination by one state can only lead to *non-sequiturs* like the statement by one author: "but the fact remains that the sons of U.P. do, in fact, guide the country's destiny; seventy-one percent of the Council of Ministers, according to a 1956 study, were native to the Gangetic watershed and the Bombay region." [6] A similar outcome awaits the attempt to reduce the great diversity of India into a north-south cleavage, a concept which some students of Indian politics have borrowed, without critical examination, from the pronouncements of some politicians.

In India there are some 16 states with substantial diversity within and between each, not a north and a south. In what sense can one classify Maharashtra, Madhya Pradesh, Orissa, and Gujarat as either north or south? In what sense can Assam and West Bengal, West Bengal and Bihar, Bihar and Uttar

[6] Harrison, p. 307.

Pradesh, Uttar Pradesh and Punjab, Punjab and Rajasthan, with their mutual differences, be said to constitute a compact northern region? In what respect are Andhra Pradesh, Madras, Mysore and Kerala united in a southern region? Within any possible division on a north-south basis there are existing and potential inter-state conflicts, preventing states in one division from acting in concert against another division. For instance, the states of the Dravidian "south" have been unwilling to merge into a single state, the proponents of a separate "Dravidistan" have been the very ones to oppose such a merger,[7] and Andhra Pradesh itself was formed not as a protest against the "north" but against fellow "southerners" in Madras state.

It is thus the wide diversity between and within regions that provides an assurance against the domination of the center by any single group or permanent coalition of groups and, in turn, enables different social and economic groups to look to the center for protection. No one can dispute the role of Nehru in having maintained a government at the center which rested on the widest possible social base in India, but one must see that role in the context of the social and political situation in India which prescribes and makes possible such a role. It should be recognized at the same time that to emphasize the importance of "the uses of diversity" in the Indian political system is not to uphold any equilibrium theory of politics, but merely to point out that diversity is not pulling the linguistic regions in a single direction away from the center, that there are countervailing tendencies existent within this diversity, and that Indian leadership is not faced with some form of linguistic determinism.

Apart from the important bearing that the great diversity in India, stemming from both its peculiar social structure and the large size of the political unit, has on the question of national unity, one should recognize that this diversity further contains

[7] Joan V. Bondurant, *Regionalism versus Provincialism: A Study in Problems of Indian National Unity* (Berkeley: University of California Press, 1958), pp. 69–70, 138–39.

a favorable potential for the success of the kinds of values that the nationalist leadership in India today holds and desires to disseminate throughout the entire social and political order—the values of political democracy, protection of minorities, safeguarding of liberties, egalitarianism, and social change. Nearly two hundred years ago, one of the fathers of the American Constitution pointed out the importance of size and diversity for the protection of different groups from oppression in society. In the *Federalist* Number 10, Madison wrote: "The smaller the society, the fewer probably will be the distinct parties and interests composing it; the fewer the distinct parties and interests, the more frequently will a majority be found of the same party; and the smaller the number of individuals composing a majority, and the smaller the compass within which they are placed, the more easily will they concert and execute their plans of oppression. Extend the sphere, and you take in a greater variety of parties and interests; you make it less probable that a majority of the whole will have a common motive to invade the rights of other citizens; or if such a common motive exists, it will be more difficult for all who feel it to discover their own strength, and to act in unison with each other." [8]

The presence of a great variety of interests in a society of diversity means, as Madison pointed out, that it is difficult for any single group or coalition to achieve a permanent majority. The large number of interests assures that the threat of domination by any single group or coalition would call into play other interests to check such a threat. If a society were divided merely into two unequal groups, the minority is likely to be dominated by the majority. On the other hand, in a society of greater diversity, a minority would have the opportunity to combine with other groups to restrain the ambitions of any group aspiring to domination. The Negroes of the South, for instance, would be in a hopeless position if the South were not

[8] Jacob E. Cooke (ed.), *The Federalist* (Cleveland: The World Publishing Company, 1961), pp. 63–64.

a part of the United States but a separate sovereign state. Functioning within the larger political system of the United States, the Negroes can look for protection beyond the South. It would thus run against the interests of the Negroes to have the South secede from the United States, as that would throw them completely at the mercy of the local dominant white majority. Similarly, the Harijans of the Punjab instinctively react against any division of the state's territories that would place them under the domination of a local group.

Moreover, in a society where a few groups are more advanced than others and are politically dominant, diversity favors political and social change. The existence of a greater diversity of interests militates against unequal distribution of political power; it prevents the exploitation of one group by another by making difficult the formation of a permanent majority. Greater diversity further provides some protection against extremist movements. In a society of greater diversity members are apt to belong to many different groups. The very multiplicity of membership in groups would prevent the expenditure of energy in a single mass movement—unless the cleavages are cumulative and not divergent. Moreover, groups in conflict may have overlapping memberships which would serve to reduce the intensity of group conflict. Diversity in society would seem to encourage the politics of bargaining and compromise.

The fact that India encompasses great diversity within itself should therefore, far from being made into a cause for grave concern, be recognized as a condition necessary for the functioning of the kind of political system the Indians have set out to establish for themselves. One may leave aside here the question of whether such a system is the most appropriate or not for India's present stage of economic and political development, but merely note that that is the kind of system they prefer at the time. Though democracy is essential, in the first instance, to stimulate the interplay of interests in a society of diversity, one should realize that diversity, in turn, may favor democratic values. One must refrain from assigning deterministic values to any one among several variables involved in a given political situation. But there may be something to the great diversity that has made for a more successful functioning of democratic institutions until now in India than in any of the other newly independent nations. Should democracy face darker days in the future in India, one should give some consideration then to the notion that this may be due not so much to the presence of diversity, as has often been argued, but perhaps despite it.

The diversity in India would seem then to favor democratic values as it at the same time provides some assurance that the center, since it is not dominated by any one group or coalition, can be counted on for support by different groups that are threatened at the local level. The center can, in one way, enhance its position of being above inter-regional and intra-regional conflicts by refusing to intervene too frequently in such conflicts and directly entering into agreements embodying political concessions with one group over the heads of another group. The center should undoubtedly let its presence be felt and should see to it that the rules of the game are observed and that the institutions for the regulation of conflict, primarily the parliamentary processes, remain secure, but the actual conduct of conflict should be left to the parties within a state. The center must exercise its authority when the need arises, especially when the parties to a conflict are unequally balanced. However, a more effective way for the regulation of conflict seems to be the organization of interest groups.[9] The absence of a high level of organization of interest groups only provides an opportunity for some powerful group to dominate over others, which may then give rise to an episodic response on the part of those dominated. Insofar as interests that are likely to look to the center for protection and support are con-

[9] See in this connection, Dahrendorf, p. 226, and Myron Weiner, *The Politics of Scarcity* (Chicago: University of Chicago Press, 1962), p. 72.

cerned, their organization would seem further to help the cause of national unity. The center should therefore view with favor the organization of interest groups.

Above all, the inevitability of conflict among groups in politics should be genuinely accepted. Conflict is an inevitable and omnipresent, and perhaps even an essential, aspect of human life.[10] To be sure, there must be a larger political consensus within which political conflict can be carried on, but the acceptance and institutionalization of conflict is an essential precondition for such a consensus.[11] The question of whether India constitutes a nation is intimately connected with the notion of political consensus. This subject has been debated interminably since independence, but one should realize that there is no test yet devised to prove the existence of a nation except the one that calls into question the very existence of that nation. When the nation is not faced with a crisis threatening its integrity, then internal differences must inevitably come to the fore. As has been said in another context:

> Men differ, their situations differ, and so do their interests. Loyalty is always proportionate to the threat. An "American" is a nearly meaningless abstraction unless the country is at war; a "union" man is most identifiable when the plant is on strike; a Catholic, a Protestant, a Jew is most recognizable at the critical moments of birth, marriage, and death. During the long interludes in which the questions do not involve ultimate loyalties, the interior differences within the membership are numerous and real.[12]

In 1962, India did face a crisis that threatened its national integrity, and the response to it brought out the underlying

[10] Dahrendorf, p. 208.

[11] Lloyd H. Fisher and Grant McConnell, "Internal Conflict and Labor-Union Solidarity," in Arthur Kornhauser, Robert Dubin, and Arthur M. Ross (eds.), *Industrial Conflict* (New York: McGraw-Hill Book Company, Inc., 1954), p. 143.

[12] *Ibid.*, p. 141.

fundamental unity of the Indian nation. Referring to those that had predicted that the south would take advantage of the troubles on India's northern borders, a British observer noted that "far from stimulating separatism in the South, the patriotic upsurge was as strong there as in the rest of the country. . . . However vague and undirected, a quite new climate of opinion had come into existence, confounding pessimists and optimists alike." [13] He commented that earlier analysts had been "too rationalistic" and had ignored "the imponderables of patriotic emotion" as well as "the elements that bridge the linguistic divisions of India." [14] At the time of this crisis, the committee which had been set up by the National Integration Council to inquire into the phenomenon of communalism wound up its affairs, stating that the crisis had accomplished what fifteen years of talk could not.

Be that as it may, one cannot expect a perpetual upsurge of patriotic emotion in the absence of a crisis. What the experience of 1962 demonstrated is that conflict in normal times does not run counter to an ultimate loyalty to the nation. Furthermore, what an apparent consensus in periods between crises signifies is not the absence of conflict but its suppression, achieved either through a belief-system like the one that upheld the caste system, or through the exercise of total power. One should recognize that what the democratic parliamentary system does is not to eliminate group conflict, but only to institutionalize and regulate it. The utopian prescriptions by the advocates of Marxism and Sarvodaya for a society without conflict provide only the rationale for a totalitarian solution which does not so much end conflict as suppress it and sanctify the domination of one group over another.

One should expect to find serious problems arising out of conflict among groups in India in the years ahead, even at times

[13] John Mander, "Indian Autumn: Letter from New Delhi," *Encounter*, xx, No. 2 (February, 1963), 21.
[14] *Ibid.*, pp. 21–22.

perhaps the breakdown of the constitutional processes, but one should at the same time recognize that progress does not pursue a linear course. Even the most powerful democratic nation in the world today went through the bloodiest civil war in history. In the Indian case, the widespread diversity to some extent assures that most conflicts may remain localized and not assume an all-India character. Moreover, one cannot hold conflict to be necessarily detrimental to economic development. The case of the Punjab, where economic progress has gone forward simultaneously with serious conflict, supplies an excellent illustration. Perhaps economic progress would have been greater in this state if the conflict had been less intense, but one cannot dismiss the stimulus provided to economic growth by rival groups in a bid to outpace each other politically as well as economically.

However, even granted the presence of such countervailing forces in the Indian political situation, as have been indicated above, the role of leadership is still paramount in the maintenance of national unity and the democratic political framework. The leadership must have, and display, a confidence in itself to manage the political concerns of India. Its public behavior should also be such as to inspire faith on the part of the citizenry in the country's political framework.

Here, the Congress party in the Punjab has not been exactly a model of behavior. The factional splits and the interminable disputes among Congressmen have given the party, notwithstanding its ability to win in elections, a somewhat ugly image in the state. Factionalism within a one-party-dominant system may be functional in some respects for the political system, but the spectacle of constant bickering among Congressmen, the public display of inner-party controversies, and the open defiance of party discipline make not only for denigration of the Congress party but also lead to contempt for the political system and politics itself. Cases of corruption and nepotism in the party also further diminish faith in democratic politics.

APPENDIX I

RESULTS OF THE THIRD GENERAL ELECTIONS IN THE PUNJAB, 1962

	Hindi-speaking Region			Punjabi-speaking Region			Total		
	Number	Per-cent	Seats	Number	Per-cent	Seats	Number	Per-cent	Seats
1. Congress Party	1,136,792	40.9	39	1,809,417	45.7	51	2,946,209	43.7	90
2. Akali Dal	9,820	0.4	—	790,105	20.0	19	799,925	11.9	19
3. Communist Party	82,253	2.9	—	396,080	10.0	9	478,333	7.1	9
4. Jan Sangh	353,030	12.7	4	302,130	7.6	4	655,160	9.7	8
5. Republican Party (SCF)	33,599	1.2	—	111,441	2.8	—	145,040	2.2	—
6. Swatantra Party	167,792	6.0	3	93,484	2.4	—	261,276	3.9	3
7. Praja Socialist Party	32,159	1.2	—	28,231	0.7	—	60,390	0.9	—
8. Independents	731,867	26.3	12	425,246	10.7	6	1,157,113	17.1	18
9. Others	233,942	8.4	7	1,835	0.1	—	235,777	3.5	7
Total	2,781,254	100.0	65	3,957,969	100.0	89	6,739,223	100.0	154
Electorate	4,584,779			6,160,873			10,745,652		
Voting Participation (Valid Votes only)		60.7			64.2			62.7	

Source: India, Election Commission, *Report on the Third General Elections in India, 1962* (New Delhi: Election Commission, 1963), II (Statistical), 326–46.

APPENDIX

BIBLIOGRAPHY AND INDEX

The phenomena of factionalism, party indiscipline, and some corruption and nepotism, may be rooted in a society in transition from tradition to modernity, especially within a democratic political framework, though even the more modern political systems are not immune from these aspects of politics. However, the maintenance of the democratic framework itself requires the image—if not the perfect reality—of integrity, discipline and determination on the part of the leadership. As for the Congress leadership at the center, the goals of national unity and democracy both require it additionally to continue to do effectively what it has sought to do in the past: to be ready to redress genuine grievances of the various groups in the society while at the same time to be firm and determined when attempts are made to undermine the basic political framework.

BIBLIOGRAPHY

GOVERNMENT PUBLICATIONS

Great Britain. Indian Statutory Commission. *Report of the Indian Statutory Commission.* 17 vols. London: H. M. Stationery Office, 1930.

India (Dominion). Constituent Assembly. *Debates: Official Report.* Vol. VII (1948) and Vol. X (1949).

————. *Report of the Linguistic Provinces Commission 1948.* New Delhi: Government of India Press, 1948.

India (Republic). Census Commissioner. *Census of India 1951.* Vol. VIII. Simla: The Army Press, 1953.

————. *Report on the First General Elections in India 1951–52.* New Delhi: Election Commission, 1955.

————. Election Commission. *Report on the Second General Elections 1957.* New Delhi: Election Commission, 1959.

————. *Lok Sabha Debates.* Vol. LVII (1961).

————. Ministry of Home Affairs. *Census of India 1961: Population of Punjab (Provisional Figures).* Chandigarh: Controller, Printing and Stationery, 1962.

————. *Report of the States Reorganization Commission.* Delhi: Manager of Publications, 1955.

Punjab. Language Department. *Grierson on Panjabi.* Patiala: Language Department, 1961.

————. *The Sikh Gurdwaras Act, 1925.* Chandigarh: Controller, Printing and Stationery, 1959.

————. *Vidhan Sabha Debates.* Vol. 1 (1956).

————. Vidhan Sabha. *Who's Who 1960.* Chandigarh: Controller, Printing and Stationery, 1960.

BOOKS

Ahmed, Syed Nur. *Mian Fazl-i-Husain: A Review of His Life and Work.* Lahore: Punjab Educational Press [1936].

All Parties Conference, 1928. *Report of the Committee Ap-*

pointed by the Conference to Determine the Principles of the Constitution for India. Allahabad: General Secretary, All India Congress Committee, 1929.

Almond, Gabriel A., and Coleman, James S. (eds.). *The Politics of the Developing Areas.* Princeton: Princeton University Press, 1960.

Ambedkar, B. R. *Pakistan or The Partition of India.* Third Edition. Bombay: Thacker and Co., Ltd., 1946.

Anderson, James Drummond. *The Peoples of India.* Cambridge: Cambridge University Press, 1913.

Archer, John Clark. *The Sikhs in Relation to Hindus, Moslems, Christians, and Ahmadiyyas.* Princeton: Princeton University Press, 1946.

Arnold, Edwin. *The Marquis of Dalhousie's Administration of British India.* 2 vols. London: Saunders, Otley and Co., 1862–65.

Beg, Mirza Mohammad Syed. *Hyat-i-Sikandar.* Lahore: Taj Company Ltd., n.d.

Bondurant, Joan V. *Regionalism versus Provincialism: A Study in Problems of Indian National Unity.* Berkeley: University of California Press, 1958.

Calvert, Hubert. *The Wealth and Welfare of the Punjab.* Lahore: Civil and Military Gazette Ltd. [1936].

Campbell-Johnson, Alan. *Mission with Mountbatten.* London: Robert Hale Ltd., 1951.

Chand, Duni. *The Ulster of India, or An Analysis of the Punjab Problems.* Lahore: n.p., 1936.

Chirol, Valentine. *Indian Unrest.* London: The Macmillan Co., Ltd., 1919.

Cooke, Jacob E. (ed.). *The Federalist.* Cleveland: The World Publishing Co., 1961.

Coupland, Reginald. *The Indian Problem: Report on the Constitutional Problem in India.* New York: Oxford University Press, 1944.

Dahrendorf, Ralf. *Class and Class Conflict in Industrial Society*. Stanford: Stanford University Press, 1959.

Darling, Malcolm Lyall. *At Freedom's Door*. London: Oxford University Press [1949].

———. *The Punjab Peasant in Prosperity and Debt*. London: Oxford University Press, 1925.

Davis, Kingsley. *The Population of India and Pakistan*. Princeton: Princeton University Press, 1951.

Deutsch, Karl W., and Foltz, William J. (eds.). *Nation-Building*. New York: Atherton Press, 1963.

——— et al. *The Integration of Political Communities*. Philadelphia: J. B. Lippincott Company, 1964.

Eliot, Charles. *Hinduism and Buddhism: An Historical Sketch*. 2 vols. London: Routledge and Kegan Paul Ltd., 1921.

Geertz, Clifford (ed.). *Old Societies and New States*. New York: The Free Press of Glencoe, 1963.

Gledhill, Alan. *The Republic of India*. London: Stevens and Sons, Ltd., 1951.

Gopal, Ram. *Indian Muslims: A Political History*. London: Asia Publishing House, 1959.

Griffin, Lepel H. *Chiefs and Families of Note in the Punjab*. Lahore: Superintendent, Government Printing Office, Punjab, 1940.

Gupta, Hari Ram. *History of the Sikhs*. 3 vols. Lahore: Minerva Book Shop, 1944.

Gwyer, Maurice, and Appadorai, A. *Speeches and Documents on the Indian Constitution 1921–47*. 2 vols. Bombay: Oxford University Press, 1957.

Harrison, Selig S. *India: The Most Dangerous Decades*. Princeton: Princeton University Press, 1960.

Husain, Azim. *Fazl-i-Husain: A Political Biography*. Bombay: Longmans, Green and Co., Ltd., 1946.

Jakhmi, Karam Singh. *64 Roza Akali Morche da Ithas* [History of the 64-day Akali Morcha]. Amritsar: Panthic Tract Society, 1955.

Jennings, Ivor. *Some Characteristics of the Indian Constitution*. Madras: Oxford University Press [1953].

Khilnani, N. M. *The Punjab under the Lawrences*. Simla: Punjab Government Record Office, 1951.

Khosla, Gopal Das. *Stern Reckoning: A Survey of the Events Leading up to and Following the Partition of India*. New Delhi: Bhawnani and Sons [1949].

Kornhauser, Arthur, *et al. Industrial Conflict*. New York: McGraw-Hill Book Co., Inc., 1954.

Maftoon, Diwan Singh. *Naqable Framosh* [Unforgettable]. Delhi: Diwan Singh Maftoon, 1957.

Mehta, Harbans Rai. *A History of the Growth and Development of Western Education in the Punjab 1846–1884*. Lahore: Punjab Government Record Office Publications, 1929.

Menon, V. P. *The Transfer of Power in India*. Princeton: Princeton University Press, 1957.

Moon, Penderel. *Divide and Quit*. Berkeley: University of California Press, 1962.

Narang, Gokul Chand. *Transformation of Sikhism*. Fifth Edition. New Delhi: New Book Society of India, 1960.

National Council of Applied Economic Research. *Techno-Economic Survey of Punjab*. New Delhi: 1962.

Nehru, Jawaharlal. *The Discovery of India*. New York: The John Day Company, 1946.

———. *Eighteen Months in India 1937–38*. Allahabad: Kitabistan, 1938.

———. *The Unity of India: Collected Writings 1937–40*. London: Lindsay Drummond, 1941.

Noman, Mohammad. *Muslim India*. Allahabad: Kitabistan, 1942.

Non-Party Political Conference, Non-Party Conciliation Committee. *Constitutional Proposals of the Sapru Committee*. Bombay: Padma Publications Ltd., 1945.

O'Malley, L. S. S. *Modern India and the West*. London: Oxford University Press, 1941.

Panikkar, K. M. *Hindu Society at Cross Roads*. Bombay: Asia Publishing House [1955].

Prasad, Rajendra. *India Divided*. Third Edition Revised. Bombay: Hind Kitabs Ltd., 1947.

Prior, L. F. Loveday. *Punjab Prelude*. London: John Murray, 1952.

Punjabi Sube de Morche da Itihas [History of the Punjabi Suba Morcha], by Sikh scholars. Amritsar: Gurbani Prakashan, 1960.

Pylee, M. V. *Constitutional Government in India*. London: Asia Publishing House, 1960.

Rai, Lajpat. *The Arya Samaj: An Account of Its Origin, Doctrines, and Activities, with a Biographical Sketch of the Founder*. London: Longmans, Green and Co., 1915.

Randhawa, M. S. *Punjab*. Patiala: Language Department, Punjab, 1960.

Ray, Naresh Chandra. *Federalism and Linguistic States*. Calcutta: Firma K. L. Mukhopadhyay, 1962.

Sen, N. B. (ed.). *Punjab's Eminent Hindus*. Lahore: New Book Society, 1943.

Sharma, Sri Ram. *Mahatma Hansraj: Maker of the Modern Punjab*. Lahore: Arya Pradeshik Pratanadhi Sabha, 1941.

Singh, Chanda. *The Hair and Health*. Kot Kapura: Human Hair Research Institute, 1956.

Singh, Durlab. *Sikh Leadership*. Delhi: Sikh Literature Distributors, 1950.

———. *The Valiant Fighter: A Biographical Study of Master Tara Singh*. Lahore: Hero Publications, 1942.

Singh, Ganda. *The British Occupation of the Punjab*. Patiala: Sikh History Society, 1955.

——— (ed.). *Bhai Jodh Singh Abhinandan Granth: Punjab (A.D. 1849–1960)* Patiala: Khalsa College, 1962.

Singh, Giani Gurcharan. *Ankhi Soorma: Jiwan Master Tara Singh Ji* (Life of Master Tara Singh). Delhi: Sikh Literature Distributors, 1950.

Singh, Gurcharan. *Sikh Kya Chahtey Hain?* [What Do the Sikhs Want?] Delhi: New India Publications [1950].

Singh, Gyani Sher. *Thoughts on Forms and Symbols in Sikhism.* Lahore: Mercantile Press, 1927.

Singh, Iqbal, and Rao, Raja (eds.). *Whither India?* Baroda: Padmaja Publications, 1948.

Singh, Kapur. *Parasharprasna.* Jullundur: Hind Publishers Ltd., 1959.

Singh, Kartar. *Rekindling of the Sikh Heart.* Lahore: Lahore Book Shop, 1945.

Singh, Khushwant. *A History of the Sikhs.* Vol. 1. Princeton: Princeton University Press, 1963.

————. *The Sikhs.* London: George Allen and Unwin Ltd., 1953.

Singh, Mohinder. *Sardar-i-Azam: Jiwan Master Tara Singh Ji* [Life of Master Tara Singh]. Amritsar: Panthic Tract Society, 1950.

Singh, Ratan. *The Revolt of the Sikh Youth.* Lahore: Modern Publications, 1943.

Singh, Sarup. *The Forgotten Panth.* Amritsar: Sikh Religious Book Society, 1945.

Singh, Master Tara. *Meri Yaad* (My Memory). Amritsar: Sikh Religious Book Society, 1945.

Singh, Teja. *Essays in Sikhism.* Lahore: Sikh University Press, 1944.

————. *Sikhism: Its Ideals and Institutions.* Lahore: Lahore Book Shop, 1938.

———— and Singh, Ganda. *A Short History of the Sikhs.* Bombay: Orient Longmans Ltd., 1950.

Smith, Donald E. *India as a Secular State.* Princeton: Princeton University Press, 1963.

Smith, Vincent A. *The Oxford History of India.* Third Edition. Oxford: At the Clarendon Press, 1958.

Suri, Surinder. *1962 Elections: A Political Analysis.* New Delhi: Sudha Publications Pvt. Ltd., 1962.

Toynbee, Arnold J. *A Study of History.* Abridged. 2 vols. New York: Oxford University Press, 1957.

Trevaskis, Hugh Kennedy. *The Land of the Five Rivers.* London: Oxford University Press, 1928.

UNESCO. *Selections from the Sacred Writings of the Sikhs.* London: George Allen and Unwin, Ltd., 1960.

United Nations. *Demographic Yearbook 1956.* New York: United Nations, 1956.

Weiner, Myron. *The Politics of Scarcity.* Chicago: University of Chicago Press, 1962.

PAMPHLETS

Chand, Duni. *Congress Service Series: Events of 1937 to 1946.* Indore: Bhargava Fine Art Printing Works, 1946.

Chand, Tara. *Billa Shuba Naveen Sikh Hindu Nahin* [Undoubtedly the New Sikhs Are Not Hindus]. Kotarkhana: Sat Sangh Kutiya, n.d.

———. *Sikh Mat ke Dharam Pustak* [The Religious Scriptures of Sikhism]. Delhi: Punjab National Press, n.d.

Chopra, Giani Raghubans Singh. *Punjabi Sube ka Masla* [The Problem of Punjabi Suba]. Amritsar: Risala "Panch Bhoomi," n.d.

Dard, Hira Singh. *Panth: Dharam te Rajniti* [Panth: Religion and Politics]. Jullundur: Phulwari Office, 1949.

Dhari, Alakh. *Case for United Punjab.* Ambala Cantt: Abha Printing Press, 1956.

———. *States Re-organisation Commission: Maha Punjab: Memorandum Stressing the Need for Re-integration of Punjab, Pepsu and Himachal Pradesh into One Administrative Unit.* n.p., n.d.

356   *Bibliography*

Indian National Congress. *Report of the Linguistic Provinces Committee.* New Delhi: n.p., 1949.

Macauliffe, M. *A Lecture on How the Sikhs Became a Militant Race.* Simla: Government Central Printing Office, n.d.

———. *A Lecture on the Sikh Religion and Its Advantages to the State.* Simla: Government Central Printing Office, 1903.

———. *The Sikh Religion: A Lecture Delivered Before the Quest Society, at Kensington Town Hall, May 12, 1910.* n.p. [1910].

Panikkar, K. M. *The Ideals of Sikhism.* Amritsar: Sikh Tract Society, 1924.

Panjab University. *The Growth of Punjab Economy.* Chandigarh: Department of Economics, 1960.

Punjab Jan Sangh. *Maha Punjab Kyoon?* [Why Maha Punjab?]. Ambala Cantt: The Utthan Publications, 1954.

———. *Why Maha Punjab: Memorandum Submitted by Punjab Jan Sangh.* Ambala Cantt: The Utthan Publications, 1954.

Shiromani Akali Dal. *Punjabi Suba.* Amritsar: Panthic Tract Society, n.d.

———. *Shiromani Akali Dal Di Bantar De Niyam* [Constitution of the Shiromani Akali Dal]. Amritsar: Secretary, Shiromani Akali Dal, 1961.

———. *Synopsis of the Nehru-Fateh Singh Talks on the Issue of the Formation of Punjabi-Speaking State.* Amritsar: Secretary, Shiromani Akali Dal, 1961.

The Sikh Youth Federation. *The Demand for the Punjabi Suba: A Most Crucial Challenge to Indian Secularism.* Calcutta: The Sikh Youth Federation, n.d.

Singh, Bhan. *All India Sikh Students Federation da Aaeen* [Constitution of the All India Sikh Students Federation]. Amritsar: General Secretary, AISSF, 1950.

Singh, Gurbachan, and Gyani, Lal Singh. *The Idea of the Sikh State.* Lahore: Lahore Book Shop, 1946.

Singh, Gurnam. *A Unilingual Punjabi State and the Sikh Unrest.* New Delhi: Super Press, 1960.

Singh, Harbans. *Sikh Political Parties.* New Delhi: Sikh Publishing House Ltd., n.d.

Singh, Hukam. *40th Sikh Educational Conference: Presidential Address.* Delhi: General Printing Company, 1957.

———. *A Plea for the Punjabi-Speaking State: Memorandum by Hukam Singh, Member Parliament.* Amritsar: Shiromani Akali Dal, n.d.

———. *The Punjab Problem: An Elucidation.* Amritsar: Shiromani Akali Dal, n.d.

———. *The States Reorganisation in the North.* Delhi: East Punjab Printing Works, 1955.

———. *The Tenth All India Akali Conference: Inaugural Address.* Amritsar: Reception Committee, 10th All India Akali Conference, 1956.

Singh, Iqbal. *Facts About Akali Agitation in Punjab.* Chandigarh: Fairdeal Press, 1960.

Singh, Jaswant. *Facts Without Rhetoric: The Demand for Punjabi Suba.* New Delhi: Super Press, 1960.

———. *A Plea for a Punjabi State.* Amritsar: Shiromani Akali Dal, 1960.

Singh, Lal. *Punjabi Suba Convention of Sikh Intelligentsia: Presidential Address.* Delhi: Gurdwara Parbandhak Committee, 1961.

Singh, Sadhu Swarup. *The Sikhs Demand Their Homeland.* Lahore: Lahore Book Shop, 1946.

Singh, Sher. *The Case of Haryana and Hindi Region of the Punjab.* Rohtak: Haryana Lok Smiti, 1962.

Singh, Master Tara. *Charhdi Kala: Present Sikh Politics No. 2.* Amritsar: Panthic Tract Society, n.d.

———. *Pradhaangi Address* [Presidential Address]. Amritsar: Secretary, Shiromani Akali Dal, 1961.

———. *Save Hindi Agitation and Sikh View Point.* Delhi: Indian Union Press, n.d.

Singh, Master Tara. *Why This Silent Procession of Protest?* Amritsar: Secretary, Shiromani Akali Dal, n.d.

Surjeet, Harkishen Singh. *Master Tara Singh di Siyaasat te Akali Party di Sankat* [The Politics of Master Tara Singh and the Misfortune of the Akali Party]. Jullundur: Punjabi Suba Committee, 1958.

Tangh, Bhagat Singh. *Azad Punjab ke Mutalaq Pothohari Nukta-nigah* [Pothohari Viewpoint Concerning Azad Punjab]. Amritsar: Dyal Singh, Assistant Secretary, Shiromani Akali Dal, 1943.

ARTICLES AND PERIODICALS

Ambalvi, Amar Singh. "Presidential Address," *The Sikh Students' Bulletin,* Vol. v, Nos. 10–11 (January-February 1958).

Birdwood, Lord. "India and the Sikh Community," *The Hindustan Times,* December 26, 1954.

"Gurdwaras Act—Ultra Vires of the Constitution," *The Tribune,* August 11, 1957.

Hind Samachar. 1961–62.

Hoselitz, Bert F., and Weiner, Myron. "Economic Development and Political Stability in India," *Dissent,* Vol. viii, No. 2 (Spring 1961).

The Indian Annual Register. 1942–46.

Indian Institute of Public Opinion. *Monthly Public Opinion Surveys,* Vol. vi, Nos. 8–9 (May-June 1961).

Khosla, G. D. "The Punjabi Character," *Advance,* Vol. v, No. 1 (January-March 1958).

Mander, John. "Indian Autumn: Letter from New Delhi," *Encounter,* Vol. xx, No. 2 (February 1963).

A Nationalist. "The Punjab Tangle," *The Modern Review,* Vol. ciii, No. 1 (January 1958).

Nayar, Baldev Raj. "Studies in Voting Behaviour: Religion and Caste in the Punjab: Sidhwan Bet Constituency," *The Economic Weekly,* Vol. xiv, No. 31 (August 1961).

Political Observer. "East Punjab Politics," *The Tribune,* April 10, 1949.

Prabhat. 1961–62.

Pratap. 1961–62.

Prem, Prem Singh. "Sanctity of Gurdwaras," *The Tribune,* July 22, 1955.

Raj, K. N. "Some Features of the Economic Growth of the Last Decade in India," *The Economic Weekly,* Vol. xiii, Nos. 4, 5, and 6 (February 1961).

Saroj, S. S. "Battle for Food," *Advance,* Vol. v, No. 4 (October-December 1958).

Sharma, Hans Raj. "S. Partap Singh Kairon and Punjab Congress," *The Tribune,* June 3, 1958.

"Sikh Siyaasat, Sikh Siyaasatdaan ki Qalam Se" [Sikh Politics, by a Sikh Politician], *Pratap,* March-May 1962.

The Sikh Students' Bulletin. 1958–60.

Singh, Bhagat. "Gurdwaras and Politics," *The Spokesman,* Vol. ix, No. 28 (August 3, 1959).

Singh, Harbans. "The Future of the Sikh Community," *The Spokesman,* Vol. x, Nos. 41–42 (Guru Nanak Number, 1960).

———. "Future of Sikhs' Central Political Organization," *The Statesman,* April 4, 1948.

Singh, Hukam. "Sikh Character and the SGPC Election," *The Spokesman,* Vol. ix, No. 30 (Annual Number, 1959).

Singh, Khushwant. "Future of the Sikhs," *The Spokesman,* Vol. ii, No. 1 (January 3, 1952).

———. "Struggle for the Gurdwaras," *The Statesman,* June 18, 1959.

Singh, Lal. "Separation of Religion from Politics," *The Hindustan Times,* August 20, 1956.

Singh, Mangal. "Hindus and Sikhs Are One," *The Tribune,* April 1, 1951.

Singh, Master Tara. "We Will Not Live As Serfs!" *The Spokesman,* Vol. i, No. 2 (August 29, 1951).

Singh, Teja Principal. "Religion and Politics," *The Spokesman,*
     Vol. VI, No. 25 (June 25, 1956).
Singh, Teja. "Solution in the Hands of Sikh Intelligentsia," *The
     Tribune,* February 22, 1959.
The Spokesman. 1951–62.
S.S. "Kairon—The Man and the Crusader," *The Indian Ex-
     press* (Punjab Industries Supplement), February 27, 1962.
Sundaram, Lanka. "Implications of Master Tara Singh's Re-
     volt," *Hindusthan Standard,* January 16, 1950.
The Tribune. 1961–62.
Verma, Vasdev. "Hindu Sikh Ekta" [Hindu Sikh Unity],
     Pratap, December 31, 1961.
Virendra. "Punjabi Suba or A Sikh State," *The Spokesman,*
     Vol. XI, No. 27 (July 17, 1961).
———. "Punjabi Suba or A Sikh State: A Rejoinder," *The
     Spokesman,* Vol. XI, No. 29 (July 31, 1961).

UNPUBLISHED MATERIAL

Dhari, Alakh. "The Punjab Elections Tangle." (Mimeo-
     graphed, n.d.)
Mehta, Satya. "Partition of the Punjab." Ph.D. dissertation,
     University of Delhi, 1959.
"Memorandum by Punjab Hindi Raksha Samiti" submitted to
     the Das Commission. (Typewritten, 1962.)
"The Sikh Case: Presented by Nationalist Sikhs to the Das
     Commission." (Mimeographed, 1962.)

INDEX

Ad-dharmi, 51n
Aggarwal, Dina Nath, 166n
agitations, 29, 30, 73, 269, 296.
  See also Akali agitational strategy
agriculture, *see* economy
Akali agitational strategy, 151–52,
  221, 230, 232–33, 234–64, 269,
  296, 301–303, 312, 325, 331;
  Akali demonstrations against
  Nehru, 240; functions of, 235–
  36, 302; Hindu chief ministers
  and, 151–52; impact on Hindu-
  Sikh relations of, 73, 235; Punjabi Suba agitation of 1960–61,
  247–62, 264, 268, 302, 331;
  Punjabi Suba slogan agitation
  of 1955, 237–46, 268; purpose
  of, 234, 312; role of gurdwaras
  in, 234; view of, as anti-nationalist, 236. *See also* Partap Singh
  Kairon
Akali-Congress relationships,
  before independence: Akali
  attitude to Congress party and
  movements, 76, 79, 80–81, 86–
  88, 145–46; Akali collaboration
  with Muslim League against
  Congress party, 91–92; alleged
  Congress promises to Akali Dal,
  116–17; Congress feeling on
  Akali-British cooperation, 81,
  82, 243;
  post-independence: Akali attitude to Congress party and
  leadership, 135, 202–203, 232,
  244, 250, 257, 258; Akali challenge to Congress party, 27, 30,
  31, 52, 56, 199–200, 332;
  Akali-Congress mergers, *see*
  Akali infiltrational strategy;
  Akali reservations on settlements
  with Congress party, 220, 225,
  232, 246, 265; Akali retractions

on settlements with Congress
party, 220, 228–29, 232, 238,
247, 265; Congress concessions
to Akali Dal, 217–19, 220–21,
233, 238, 247, 256, 258, 264–
65, 268, 302, 303, 312, 325,
331; Congress image of Akali
Dal, 241, 261, 266–67; repercussions of Congress concessions
to Akali Dal, 276, 305–18
Akali constitutional strategy, 202–
11, 263, 325
Akali Dal, attitude toward Hindus
of, 36, 85, 89, 190, 204, 209,
235, 249, 257; the British and,
80–81, 90–93, 257; charges
against government by, 112,
115, 117, 238–40, 241, 254,
261, 305, 315; demands of, 9,
31, 32–41, 49, 75–97, 98–102,
223n, 264–65, 322; effectiveness of appeal of, 142, 175, 208,
332; electoral support for, 210,
228, 263, 271ff, 289, 329, 331,
Appendix I; establishment of
parallel organization to, 194,
262; factions and groups in, 81,
131, 193–95, 198–99, 232, 260,
262, 331; Muslims, Muslim
League and, 77, 79, 81, 91–92,
93–94; nature and status of, 27,
31, 40, 67, 169–76, 178–80,
196n.77, 212, 227, 229, 262–
63, 265, 297, 322; organization
of, 27, 142, 146–49, 175–76,
203, 213
  Panth and, 169–75, 191–99:
Akali claim to be sole representative of Panth, 169–71,
175, 212, 225–26, 229, 324;
identification of Akali Dal with
Panth, 170, 209, 210; limitations on Akali claim in relation to Panth, 200, 279, 326;